A
PRISON
IN THE
WOODS

A VOLUME IN THE SERIES

Environmental History of the Northeast

Edited by
Anthony N. Penna and Richard W. Judd

Environment and Incarceration
in New York's North Country

A
PRISON
IN THE
WOODS

CLARENCE JEFFERSON HALL JR.

UNIVERSITY OF MASSACHUSETTS PRESS
Amherst and Boston

Copyright © 2020 by University of Massachusetts Press
All rights reserved
Printed in the United States of America
ISBN 978-1-62534-536-3 (paper); 535-6 (hardcover)

Designed by Sally Nichols
Set in Adode Garamond Pro and D-Day Stencil
Printed and bound by Books International, Inc.
Cover design by Notch Design
Cover art: (front and back) *Collection of Pine Forests* by Grop; detail from *Silhouette of Watch Tower* by Champ 008; (bottom front) *Barbed Wire* by Baur; (background) *Old Paper Canvas Texture Grunge* by Abstractor. All art used under license from Shutterstock.com.

Library of Congress Cataloging-in-Publication Data

Names: Hall, Clarence Jefferson, Jr., author.
Title: A prison in the woods : environment and incarceration in New York's north country / Clarence Jefferson Hall Jr.
Description: Amherst : University of Massachusetts Press, 2020. | Series: Environmental history of the Northeast | Includes bibliographical references and index. |
Identifiers: LCCN 2020019219 | ISBN 9781625345356 (hardcover) | ISBN 9781625345363 (paperback) | ISBN 9781613767856 (ebook) | ISBN 9781613767863 (ebook)
Subjects: LCSH: Prisons—New York (State—History. | Environmental degradation—New York (State—History. | Environmental protection—New York (State—History. | Adirondack Mountains (N.Y.)—Economic conditions.
Classification: LCC HV9475.N7 H27 2020 | DDC 365/.97475—dc23
LC record available at https://lccn.loc.gov/2020019219

British Library Cataloguing-in-Publication Data
A catalog record for this book is available from the British Library.

FOR CLARENCE JEFFERSON HALL

CONTENTS

PREFACE AND ACKNOWLEDGMENTS

My connection to New York's prison system began before I was born. My father worked for the state's department of correctional services from 1973 to 1998, the majority of that time based at the maximum-security Clinton Correctional Facility in Dannemora. In April 1979, corrections officers across New York State engaged in a three-week-long strike protesting a variety of workplace issues, including salary increases and sick leave provisions. Five days after the strike ended in May, my twin sister, Kerry, and I were born. With my mother on unpaid maternity leave and my father facing stiff financial penalties for violating New York's ban on public employee work stoppages, my dad took odd jobs to make ends meet. Meanwhile, Kerry and I cried, screamed, and smiled, oblivious to the political earthquake that had ruptured our short time in New York's North Country.

My father's job opened a window onto the world of mass incarceration in late twentieth-century New York. Through experiences ranging from the mundane to the surreal, my family became enmeshed in the environment of corrections in the North Country. We regularly passed the penitentiary on car rides through Dannemora, rarely pausing to consider either the institution or its unfree occupants. We overheard Dad's often-bitter complaints about his sergeant, a man he angrily referred to as "Baldy," along with cryptic references to violent clashes between officers and incarcerated men. We consumed food cooked by imprisoned men in a kitchen Dad supervised. We decorated our home at Christmas with ceramic figures painted by incarcerated art students. We witnessed Dad's grief when colleagues died, including one felled by a heart attack while at work. Once, we observed incarcerated African American men sitting in our driveway, shackled inside a prison van. And we experienced Dad's constant frustration with a job he neither wanted nor enjoyed. In these ways and many others, the rhythms of the prison system became natural to our family, just as they did for many other families in towns and villages across the Adirondacks.

Growing up, I had only a vague notion that northern New York hosted correctional facilities besides Clinton. My family's interactions with those institutions were few and far between. I attended wintertime sled dog races held in Gabriels and learned in passing that a minimum-security prison operated nearby. Occasionally I participated in conversations about relatives who worked in correctional facilities in Malone, Altona, and Lyon Mountain. On family outings to Lake Placid, we must have driven hundreds of times past the tiny wooden signs on State Route 86 indicating the locations of the state and federal prisons in Ray Brook. And once, when I was in high school, we passed through a state police roadblock that had been set up after an incarcerated man from Ray Brook had escaped into the surrounding wilderness. That none of these brushes with the area's penitentiaries left any lasting impression on a local resident is a testament to the correctional planners, environmental regulators, residents, and visitors who worked to ensure the facilities would blend seamlessly into the existing landscape.

Built in 1845, decades before the enactment of New York's first environmental laws, Clinton Correctional Facility's cellblocks, guard towers, chain-link fences, and stone wall cast a long shadow over Dannemora. The prison's dominance of the landscape is so complete that residents and visitors routinely refer to the penitentiary as "Dannemora." While Clinton's highly visible structures are a stark reminder of the once-unregulated circumstances in which they were built, the region's other correctional facilities, opened between the 1970s and 1990s, also bear the hallmarks of their historical moment. Constructed during an era of heightened environmental awareness and regulation, the region's younger penitentiaries have operated behind vegetative screens designed to minimize their visual impact. Their nondescript buildings literally hiding in plain sight, the prisons' near-invisibility in the North Country landscape closely parallels the heretofore obscure connections that have inextricably linked the area's penitentiaries to their environment.

In this book, I aim to show how the environment played a central role in the planning, construction, and operation of penitentiaries in New York's North Country. Viewing them as both a remedy for overcrowding

FIGURE 1. Clinton Correctional Facility, Dannemora, New York. Courtesy of the author.

in existing prisons and a panacea for the Adirondacks' chronic economic woes, beginning in the 1840s and accelerating again in the 1970s, lawmakers planned and opened penal institutions in communities across northern New York. In each case, the environment proved a pivotal factor. In the 1840s, correctional planners chose the area that would become Dannemora as part of a scheme to use incarcerated labor to transform the North Country from a rural backwater into an industrial powerhouse. Unburdened by the strictures of modern environmental law, imprisoned workers helped turn an unbroken wilderness into a beehive of economic activity anchored by Clinton State Prison. When again plagued by overcrowding in the 1970s, 1980s, and 1990s, lawmakers in need of prison cells looked to the North Country's struggling towns and villages. One may be tempted to believe that the environmental regulations, organized environmentalists, and affluent visitors absent in the 1840s might have posed insurmountable barriers to penitentiary construction in the late twentieth century. However, in nearly every case, laws, bureaucrats, and agencies that many assumed to be guardians of environmental and public health often came up short, leaving open the threat of prison-induced damage to woods, waters, and wildlife.

Penitentiaries' environmental impacts, however, were not always destructive. Incarcerated men left the most invisible, yet indelible, environmental legacy of the Adirondacks' long carceral history. Without their participation in vital conservation, public works, and infrastructure projects across the region, living and playing in the Adirondacks would be difficult at best, and, at worst, next to impossible. While many North Country prisons may be hidden and difficult to see, residents and visitors alike cannot avoid the countless—albeit unmarked—imprints their unfree charges have created across the landscape of northern New York. Imprisoned men have built roads, blazed hiking trails, constructed ski runs, fought forest fires, controlled flooding, and renovated a panoply of public spaces including churches, libraries, schools, and government offices. Thus, my personal connection to New York's prison system has not been confined solely to family experiences. Incarcerated men literally built and rebuilt much of the world around me. As such, I aim to show the Adirondack environment is as much a product of its penitentiaries as it is of careful environmental planning. The carceral hand, like the prisons, is hiding in plain sight.

This book is the product of good friends, thoughtful colleagues, caring institutions, and loving family members, without whose support and encouragement it would not be resting in your hands. I offer thanks first to Brian Halley of the University of Massachusetts Press. Brian was the first person to identify my project's potential as a book. I owe Brian a huge debt of gratitude for his patience, understanding, and care serving as the best editor any writer could hope for. I also wish to thank the anonymous reviewers, and the series editors, Anthony N. Penna and Richard W. Judd, whose feedback helped make this a stronger piece of scholarship, along with Rachael DeShano, Courtney Andree, Sally Nichols, and Julie Shilling, who happily answered each and every one of my long and meandering emails as this project reached its conclusion.

I will be forever grateful for the wisdom, guidance, and friendship I have received from my fellow historians. At Stony Brook University, I continue to benefit from the mentorship and sage advice of Chris Sellers, Nancy Tomes, Donna Rilling, April Masten, and Robert Chase. Though we see each other only rarely, Connie Y. Chiang of Bowdoin College remains a steady presence in my intellectual and professional development. Finally, I offer thanks to colleagues and friends at Queensborough Community College—past and present—whose kindness and support have proven pivotal to my growth as a scholar and teacher, including Peter Bales, Aithne Bialo-Padin, Edmund Clingan, Sarah K. Danielsson, Belinda Delgado, Ed Doherty, Anna Edick, Cameron R. Hawkins, Susan Jacobowitz, Simran Kaur, Tim Keogh, Courtnay Konshuh, Helmut Loeffler, Nicole Lopez-Jantzen, Denise Martinez, Hayes Peter Mauro, Pedro Meza, James Nichols, Peter Novick, Jo Pantaleo, Ken Pearl, Joan Petersen, Stephanie Rost, Dugwon Seo, Danny Sexton, Emily Tai, Amy Traver, Agnieszka Tuszynska, Ron Van Cleef, Mark Van Ells, Gil Visoni, Shiang-Kwei Wang, and Leslie Ward.

The raw materials out of which this project ultimately took shape came from a variety of archives, libraries, and government agencies. I offer profound thanks to the very helpful and patient staff managing historical records at the following institutions: Adirondack Park Agency, Lake Placid Olympic Museum, New York Public Library, New York State Archives, New York State Department of Environmental Conservation, New York State Library, Northern New York Library Network, Paul Smith's College, State University of New York at Potsdam, and St. Lawrence University. Without their kind assistance, this project simply would not have been possible.

I would be remiss if I did not acknowledge the significant contributions made by two individuals I am proud to know as colleagues and friends. For nearly two decades, Jonathan Anzalone has been the brother I never had. We moved through graduate school together, enjoying coffees, dinners, movies, and conversations that yielded a strong friendship that has withstood both time and distance. Jon's wisdom and good-natured advice greatly improved my writing and analytical skills. This book is as much his as it is mine. Second, I want to recognize Martha Swan and her pathbreaking civil rights and freedom education nonprofit, John Brown Lives! Martha and I met in 2013, when this project was in its infancy and her organization was building relationships with individuals implicated in the North Country prison industry. Working with Martha has allowed me to share my work with a wider audience and expanded my understanding of the penitentiaries' multilayered impacts, both within and outside the Adirondacks. I am humbled to have Martha as a friend and comrade in the ongoing fight for freedom and equality.

Whether they know it or not, my students continue to provide me an unequaled source of strength and encouragement. Their good humor, humility, kindness, and eagerness to learn inspire me to do my best as a person, professor, and scholar. Though by now I have taught thousands of students in different departments spread across several different institutions, I want to acknowledge the following individuals I have had the privilege of teaching and knowing at Queensborough: Andres Frischeisen, Santiago Gonzalez, Sydney Lee, Anca Nicu, Teresa Sierra, Supitcha Tanomwong, and Krystal Williams. It has been a joy working with these highly motivated, mature, and forward-thinking young men and women. It has also been my pleasure getting to know them, providing mentoring, and witnessing their personal and professional development. Their future is bright, and my life is richer for having known them.

Last but not least, my family. Without their unconditional love, care, and support, this project would not have reached completion. I thank my mother, Carol Hall, my sisters, Kim Hall-Stone and Kerry Hall Forgette, my brothers-in-law, Chris Stone and Josh Forgette, my nieces, Courtney Stone, Haley Stone, and Hannah Forgette, my nephew and godson, Noah Forgette, and Supasit Sunko. I end by thanking my late father, Clarence Jefferson Hall. Though our relationship was not always smooth, Dad imparted lessons—and an unusual sense of humor—that help me navigate life's many challenges. While he did not live to see this project reach the finish line, his constant encouragement and pride in my accomplishments remain an everlasting source of comfort. I dedicate this book to his memory.

ABBREVIATIONS

ACF   Adirondack Correctional Facility
APA   Adirondack Park Agency
BOP   Bureau of Prisons
COIC   Chateaugay Ore and Iron Company
CAMPA   Citizens Against More Prisons in the Adirondacks
CCRB   Concerned Citizens of Ray Brook
D&H   Delaware and Hudson Railroad
DOCS   Department of Correctional Services
DEC   Department of Environmental Conservation
HUD   Department of Housing and Urban Development
EDA   Economic Development Administration
EPA   Environmental Protection Agency
FCI   Federal Correctional Institution (Ray Brook)
IOC   International Olympic Committee
IP   International Paper
LPOOC   Lake Placid Olympic Organizing Committee
NACS   Northern Adirondack Central School District
PSC   Paul Smith's College
PASNY   Power Authority of the State of New York
SEQRA   State Environmental Quality Review Act
STOP   Stop the Olympic Prison
TLCC   Tupper Lake Concerned Citizens
USOC   United States Olympic Committee

A
PRISON
IN THE
WOODS

INTRODUCTION

Revitalizing northern New York's anemic economy topped the agenda as the commissioners of the Adirondack Park Agency (APA) met in the spring of 1986. New York lawmakers had empowered the agency, created in 1971, to regulate building projects on public and private lands inside the six-million-acre state park. The agency's commissioners, including the secretary of state, commissioners of economic development and environmental conservation, and eight citizen members appointed by the governor, worked to ensure developments that respected the needs of the park's 130,000 year-round residents, its visitors, seasonal homeowners, and businesspeople, and a natural environment that for many embodied the essence of the Adirondacks. During that 1986 meeting at APA headquarters in the Essex County hamlet of Ray Brook, commissioners debated introducing toxic waste storage as a potential source of jobs for park residents. At the time, the Adirondack Park was in the throes of a prison-building boom begun a decade earlier. The agency had found itself embroiled in protracted and often-bitter disputes over penitentiary construction in several park communities. Leading the discussion that day was Herman "Woody" Cole, who as an administrator at the Lake Placid Olympic Organizing Committee (LPOOC) had witnessed the opening of two correctional facilities in Ray Brook in the run-up to the 1980 Winter Olympic Games. Now serving as chair of the APA, Cole suggested hazardous waste storage could not possibly endanger the Adirondack environment since, as he sardonically observed, "We already live in prisonland."[1]

The question of how best to punish individuals convicted of unlawful activity vexed policymakers long before the first prisons rose in the Adirondacks. To avoid the high costs of imprisonment, residents of colonial America had adopted a hodgepodge system of unevenly applied civil and criminal sanctions including fines, public humiliation, torture, short-term jail sentences, banishment, and execution. A post-Revolutionary surge of nationalism inspired lawmakers to abandon the violence and unpredictability of European colonial legal codes in favor of a supposedly more humane system centered on incarceration. Unfortunately, the promise of America's early prisons quickly met the grim realities of chronic overcrowding and insufficient public funding.[2] The following pages explore how one state—New York—sought to meet this significant challenge. During the nineteenth and twentieth centuries, the Empire State relied on imprisonment to discipline its growing population of convicted men. Whenever crowding plagued one penitentiary, lawmakers built another. To ensure public support for its carceral projects, legislators planned correctional facilities designed both to confine convicted men and spur economic growth in the remote locales targeted for prison construction. Beginning in the 1840s and accelerating again in the 1970s, New York deployed its penal system as a development program for the isolated and depressed communities of the Adirondack Mountains. Though seemingly beneficial for both state and region, long-standing disputes over the use and meaning of Adirondack nature complicated the planning, building, and operation of penitentiaries opened in New York's North Country. To an extent rarely seen elsewhere, the non-human world proved central to the growth and day-to-day functioning of prisons in New York's Adirondack Park.

It may seem counterintuitive to investigate the environmental history of incarceration. The artifice, control, and discipline characteristic of prison life would appear the antithesis of what many perceive as nature. Moreover, in contrast to developments whose environmental impacts are impossible to miss, these geographically remote, socially isolated, and architecturally unremarkable penitentiaries may seem ecologically benign. Perhaps unsurprisingly, then, until very recently scholars have paid little heed to the complex relations tying prisons to their surrounding environments.[3] Construction and operation of the U.S. penal system—a network of jails, penitentiaries, and detention centers confining millions and employing hundreds of thousands at an annual cost of more than $180 billion—has entailed significant environmental transformations. Correctional facilities require food, clean water, electricity, sewage disposal, and other services essential to the functioning of similarly large-scale public works. Further, their construction and long-term use have contributed to deforestation, pollution, and habitat decline, among other harmful effects. Finally, the opening of penitentiaries in the Adirondack Park—a place long considered synonymous with wilderness—unearthed long-running conflicts over the use and meaning of nature. For these reasons and others, we must consider incarceration a historically significant environmental phenomenon.

Much as the first Earth Day in 1970 spurred renewed curiosity about environmental history, scholarly studies of the U.S. carceral state have grown in response to the crises of law enforcement that beleaguered American society in the late twentieth and early twenty-first centuries. This interdisciplinary endeavor explores the historical underpinnings of problems ranging from police violence to the War on Drugs and the rise of mass incarceration. Scholars have shown that anti-crime and anti-narcotics initiatives enacted after World War II fueled the growth of a carceral state that pacified anxious whites by condemning primarily poor people of color to long and debilitating terms of imprisonment. However, while studies of the carceral state have uncovered how legal and political forces nurtured a new form of Jim Crow, this emergent scholarship has generally sidestepped the circumstances under which mass incarceration has unfolded in prisons' host communities. Indeed, scholars' generally narrow focus on the individuals, organizations, and institutions directly tied to the justice system may leave the impression that questions related to law enforcement apply only to specific sectors of U.S. society. Filtered through the lens of environmental history, studies of the carceral state shine a light on a boundaryless prisonland whose reach extends beyond the precinct houses, courtrooms, and jails of U.S. cities to include correctional facilities built—and unbuilt—amidst protected forests, fragile wetlands, abandoned industrial sites, the country estates of the elite, and the modest homes of the rural poor. In this sense, "prisonland" perfectly captures mass incarceration as an all-encompassing historical transformation.

The land upon which the state and federal governments built prisons in the Adirondacks has long been contested terrain. The fortunes of the region's year-round inhabitants, stymied by geographic isolation, short growing seasons, difficult terrain, and limited public infrastructure, witnessed only scant improvement in the 131 years separating the opening of the area's first two penitentiaries: Clinton State Prison at Dannemora in 1845, followed by Camp Adirondack at Ray Brook in 1976. Beginning in the mid-nineteenth century, unrestricted logging, mining, and farming provided employment for locals, enriched an array of corporate executives, and degraded large swaths of the landscape. Simultaneously, scores of wealthy industrialists began erecting second homes in the region's unspoiled wilderness as a refuge from the nation's increasingly overcrowded and unsanitary cities. Driven to safeguard the area's business prospects, its rustic aesthetic, as well as environmental and public health, urban elites began in the 1880s to pressure lawmakers to adopt a program of state-directed conservation. The creation of the Forest Preserve in 1885, Adirondack Park in 1892, and enactment of Article XIV of the New York State Constitution in 1894—the "Forever Wild" provision—placed unprecedented limits on natural resource consumption and took the first steps toward healing a ravaged environment. A bitter conflict, however, promptly ensued between permanent residents accustomed to using nature without restriction and a growing cohort of seasonal visitors for whom leisure and recreation in an aesthetically pleasing environment superseded basic human survival.

Growing interest from business owners and visitors posed increasingly grave threats to the Adirondack environment as the twentieth century wore on. Improved rail and road access accelerated both industrial activity and the construction of second homes on private land, while the park's undeveloped public properties provided recreation for the masses. Aided by higher incomes and the 1967 opening of Interstate 87, the region's popularity as a tourist destination skyrocketed in the decades after World War II, but the area's discovery by a new generation of outdoor enthusiasts reignited nineteenth-century debates over the use and meaning of nature in New York's North Country. Hordes of middle-class visitors tramping through the mountains threatened irreversible harm to environmental and public health. To forestall disaster, lawmakers created the Adirondack Park Agency in 1971 to ensure that human needs did not overwhelm the non-human resources that for many embodied the park's very essence. The near-simultaneous contraction of the region's once-dominant logging, mining, and health care industries forced many Adirondackers to choose between irregular, low-paid work in the burgeoning tourist trade or migration to the Sunbelt. By the mid-1970s, many longtime park dwellers grappled with high unemployment, poverty, and dependence on public assistance programs. For many permanent residents, the collapse of the traditional economy and intensification of state environmental controls reaffirmed the continued dominance of wealthy "outsiders" for whom nature was only an object of enjoyment. Many feared, much like their forebears a century before, a grim and uncertain future.[4]

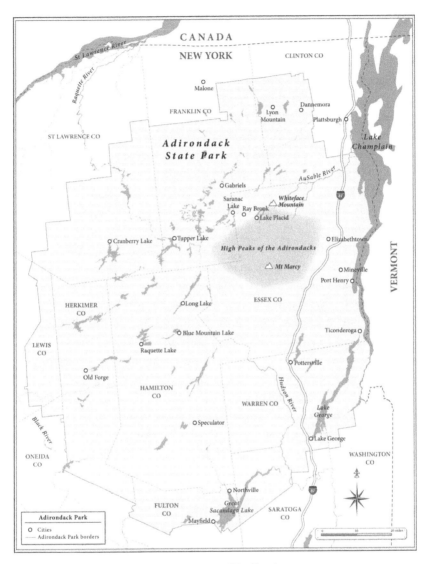

FIGURE 2. Adirondack Park. Courtesy of Gerry Krieg, Krieg Mapping.

Political and economic shocks in the 1970s had profound consequences for the Adirondack Park. Signed into law by Republican Governor Nelson Rockefeller in 1973, revisions to the Narcotics Control Act of 1966—popularly known as the Rockefeller drug laws—imposed harsh criminal penalties for most narcotics offenses. Under the act, individuals convicted either of selling two ounces or possessing four ounces of banned narcotics received a mandatory minimum fifteen-year sentence. Moreover, the Second Felony Offender Act of 1973 mandated lengthy imprisonment for individuals convicted of any two felonies committed within a ten-year period. Within two years, New York's thirty-two correctional facilities were full. As the population of convicted men surged, the worst economic crisis since the 1930s forced lawmakers to manage jam-packed penitentiaries with increasingly scarce resources. While the state's draconian approach to "law and order" proved broadly popular, most affluent New Yorkers did not want penitentiaries built in their backyards. Correctional planners thus hoped the depressed communities of the Adirondack Park would prove amenable to becoming New York's next prison towns. As in the mid-nineteenth century, penal bureaucrats in the 1970s viewed building correctional facilities in the Adirondacks as a potential silver bullet. The region's remoteness and sparse population, they argued, would mitigate against escapes and NIMBYism from area communities. Further, the area's numerous shuttered hospitals, public schools, and mining facilities might be cheaply and easily converted for penal use, providing both much-needed cell space and employment for jobless locals. If successful, penitentiaries would simultaneously reduce overcrowding, satisfy anxious white voters, and stimulate northern New York's struggling economy.

Within these circumstances, two of the most significant historical phenomena of the late twentieth century, mass incarceration and the modern environmental movement, emerged almost simultaneously in the early 1970s. Their coincidental arrival in the Adirondack Park, a time-tested battlefield of environmental politics, complicated the work of correctional planners. Battle lines were quickly drawn. Concerns about environmental and public health drove most local environmental organizations, the Park Agency, seasonal homeowners, and tourists into the ranks of the opposition. Struggling permanent residents, meanwhile, aggressively pursued the high wages, generous benefits, and job security attached to penal employment. The experience of planning, building, and operating prisons, however, often ruptured these seemingly ironclad alliances. With rare exceptions, new penitentiaries endangered environmental and public health in their host communities. Such harm could turn fervent prison advocates into unexpectedly strong opponents. By the same token, political loyalties and practical realities sometimes pushed environmentalists and the APA to endorse correctional facilities that posed grave ecological risks. Finally, the myriad benefits accrued to local communities from the low-paid work of incarcerated men on conservation, public works, and infrastructure projects could make supporters out of prisonland's bitterest foes. Thus, each penitentiary proposed for an Adirondack town or village from the 1840s through the 1990s forced interested stakeholders to enter age-old debates over the use and meaning of nature in New York's North Country. From the beginning, then, prison politics and environmental politics in the Adirondacks were indistinguishable.

Studying mass incarceration in the Adirondacks also offers new ways of exploring the racial and class disparities that remain a defining feature of the American carceral state. By the early twenty-first century, the United States incarcerated 2.3 million people in penal institutions scattered across the country. Over three-quarters of the population under confinement were people of color from primarily low-income African American and Latino urban communities.[5] Convicted men exiled to the Adirondacks arrived in a remote, conservative, low-income, and predominantly white region. While penitentiaries provided the area's working-class homeowners much-needed job security, their sharp racial disparities—mainly white men confining an incarcerated population composed primarily of men of color—aggravated already-strained relations between officers and imprisoned men. Though tensions in Adirondack prisons almost never exploded into full-blown rebellion, incarcerated men of color often served as convenient scapegoats for facility employees confronted with work-induced stress and anxiety. At the same time many local homeowners fostered a climate of inclusivity by engaging with imprisoned men in penitentiary-sponsored volunteer programs, outreach initiatives, and public events. Thus, divisions that might have conditioned relations inside correctional facilities were not easily mappable onto peoples and places just beyond the razor wire. Though racial animus surely figured in the day-to-day functioning of many North Country prisons, studying their host environments permits a more nuanced view of relationships that were sometimes less fraught than anticipated.

While year-round residents understood the park as a home and workplace, affluent homeowners and visitors valued the region for health, leisure, and recreation. Wealthy locals thus deemed penitentiaries incompatible with the park's history as an enclave for outdoor play. The concerns of well-to-do residents and tourists also extended beyond potential impacts on the non-human world. Many rich homeowners understood racial and class privilege to be components of the Adirondack environment as natural as its woods, waters, and wildlife. As such, they resisted sharing their wilderness retreats with low-income, incarcerated men of color. For elites, harm to environmental and public health often proved less worrisome than sharing their communities with people whose residence, even if confined behind bars, seemed unnatural. As threatening as any chainsaw or earth-moving machine, imprisoned men became embedded in the North Country's nature. After all, most of the area's cash-strapped towns and villages could not have otherwise afforded the numerous conservation, public works, and infrastructure projects that were undertaken by poorly paid incarcerated men. Occupying a servile role that seemed to reaffirm the supposed dominance of well-to-do whites, imprisoned men helped maintain facilities and structures necessary to visitors' continued enjoyment of the park. By literally reinforcing the park's status as a wilderness resort dedicated to health, leisure, and recreation, incarcerated men over time gained the grudging acceptance of a North Country elite once firmly opposed to their presence. Examining the history of mass incarceration through an environmental lens shows that, unlike the isolated institutions often depicted in popular culture, penitentiaries did not operate in a vacuum. So long as they buttressed elite interpretations of the park's mission, seemingly unnatural correctional facilities and their unfree occupants might be considered part of Adirondack nature.

In the chapters that follow, I use case studies of five Adirondack Park communities—Dannemora, Ray Brook, Gabriels, Lyon Mountain, and Tupper Lake—whose involvement in New York's carceral state underscores the centrality of local communities to the history of mass incarceration. Though sometimes separated by only a few miles, no two Adirondack prison towns were ever the same. Circumstances including past industrial activities, demographics, economic conditions, and residents' uses of nature shaped a penitentiary's position within its host community. Thus, *A Prison in the Woods* shows that while mass incarceration became a nationwide phenomenon, local context is critical to understanding how the carceral state functioned on a daily basis, and town- and village-level analysis illuminates how non-human nature figured in the planning, construction, and operation of correctional facilities. Though existing law granted penal

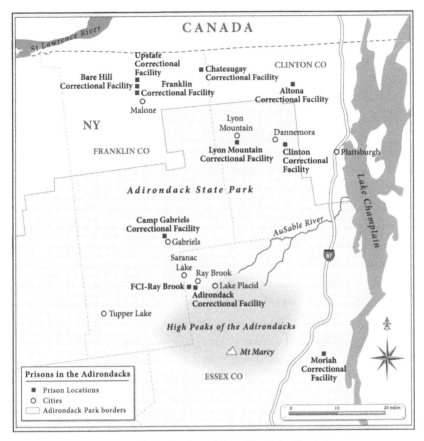

FIGURE 3. Prisons in the Adirondacks. Courtesy of Gerry Krieg, Krieg Mapping.

planners almost unfettered authority to build wherever and whenever they pleased, opening penitentiaries in the park involved both formal regulation from the Adirondack Park Agency and informal oversight from residents and environmental organizations. While public hearings and environmental impact statements highlighted prisons' potential ecological risks, environmental laws often proved a weak barrier to prison-induced degradation. Citizens, however, often achieved results that environmental regulators and activists could not, forcing either ecologically minded design modifications or project cancellations. *A Prison in the Woods* therefore demonstrates that while the simultaneous emergence of mass incarceration and environmentalism was purely coincidental, the growth of prisons in the Adirondack Park made these seemingly disparate phenomena historically inseparable.

Exhibiting a force similar to that of the Erie Canal and interstate highways, mass incarceration drew together city and countryside in new and unusual ways. Rural and urban whites each reaped significant benefits from a carceral state whose relentless expansion had no historical precedent. While urban whites cheered the removal of individuals convicted of unlawful activity from their neighborhoods and park residents welcomed the investments necessary to plan, build, and operate penitentiaries, the growth of mass incarceration posed harm to New York's rural and urban poor. In the Adirondack Park, correctional facilities were not always the silver bullet their planners anticipated. New corrections employees often endured long and expensive commutes to facilities far from home. Many North Country residents working outside the penal system still struggled with the high unemployment and poverty that penitentiaries were supposed to have fixed. The park's remote locale, sparse population, limited transportation, development restrictions, and prisons proved significant barriers to the new, private-sector developments that correctional planners predicted their facilities would generate. Beyond failing to become the panacea many had hoped for, the steady growth of the correctional system inflicted incalculable harm on New York's communities of color. African American and Latino communities fractured as narcotics and sentencing laws exiled male breadwinners, marital partners, and fathers to North Country prisons. Family members who were left behind struggled to survive in neighborhoods where high unemployment and poverty—as in the Adirondacks—had been constants long before the birth of mass incarceration. Rural and urban. Black, white, and Brown. Incarcerated and free. Rich, middle-class, and poor. None could resist the ever-expanding footprint of New York's late twentieth-century carceral state. Sadly—and predictably—the system's weight fell most heavily on those least able to bear it.

The challenge of untangling the complex web of relations that constituted New York's Adirondack prisonland, in part, helps explain scholarly reticence toward the subject. In the case of the Adirondacks, exploring how nineteenth-century penal innovations shaped the twentieth- and twenty-first-century carceral state provides a smooth entryway. Two centuries ago, New York lawmakers contending with overpacked penitentiaries established a framework for incarceration predicated on environmental transformations and dedicated to achieving both carceral and fiscal objectives. Correctional planners targeted locales where prisons could be constructed with minimal delay and whose environments could be manipulated to benefit prison and region alike. In the mid-1840s, neither convenience nor ease drove state leaders to build New York's third correctional facility in the isolated and undeveloped Adirondack Mountains. To the contrary, officials undertook the difficult, expensive, and time-consuming construction of Clinton State Prison in Dannemora with the goal of using the poorly paid labor of incarcerated men on a variety of industrial and infrastructure projects designed to spur regional economic growth. Vividly described in legislative documents, local periodicals, and the annual reports of the Prison Association of New York, the first two decades of operations at Clinton remind us that the economic impulses and ecological changes characteristic of the modern carceral state have deep and familiar historical roots. Consciously or not, this framework found a new lease on life when New York's prisons once again burst at the seams in the 1970s.[6]

Scholars' hesitation to conceptualize the carceral state as environmental history may also stem from a slew of preconceived notions rooted in contemporary political debates. Some might fear that exploring mass incarceration as a historically expansive and boundaryless phenomenon might distract attention from the racial and social injustices endemic to policing, prosecutions, sentencing, and other elements of the justice system. Others might interpret the growth of the carceral state itself as evidence of tacit public approval of the narcotics and sentencing laws that made mass incarceration possible in the first place. Finally, the relative paucity of headline-grabbing environmental calamities linked to penitentiaries might suggest, as correctional planners long claimed, that imprisonment constituted a sustainable form of punishment and economic development. The evidence, however, suggests a different story on all three fronts.

First, locating correctional facilities in the Adirondacks exacerbated the unfairness endemic to the broader justice system. Though both the state and federal prison systems mandated new institutions be opened near the home-towns of incarcerated men, overcrowding combined with NIMBYism among affluent New Yorkers drove planners to build in the distant and remote Adirondack Park. With few relatives of incarcerated men able to afford the expensive journey to visit their loved ones, the state's forced separation of families risked creating a revolving door of recidivists and a perpetually expanding carceral state. Chronic overcrowding in North Country penitentiaries, meanwhile, yielded warehouse-style facilities where providing educational and vocational opportunities became increasingly expensive, and the prospect of disturbances a constant source of concern. Correctional bureaucrats' promises to operate disciplined and orderly prisons—featured prominently in planning documents, correspondence, and APA hearing records—became impossible to achieve amid the nonstop influx of new incarcerated men. From the 1970s to the early 2000s, local press reports chronicled how less-than-ideal conditions inside cramped North Country penitentiaries led more than a few incarcerated men to rebel against state authority. While some destroyed prison property, others used physical violence against both staff members and other imprisoned men, escaped into the surrounding wilderness, and, on occasion, died by suicide. Thus, the opening of correctional facilities in the Adirondack Park, contrary to planners' hopes and dreams, only exacerbated the injustices that drove the creation of the carceral state in the first place.

By promising to revitalize the North Country's bleak, postindustrial economy, correctional planners forced residents into a devil's bargain from which there was no escape. With seemingly limitless resources, state officials dangled correctional facilities as a source of economic salvation for communities abandoned by the private sector. Beginning in the 1980s, government documents and local press accounts described how the state's insatiable demand for cell space sparked aggressive competition among park communities desperate to become New York's next prison town. Residents formed bid committees, crafted proposals, and awaited lawmakers' decisions. However, winning a penitentiary often proved a hollow victory. First, seniority rules meant not all local homeowners would be eligible for correctional employment, let alone offered a position. Even for those living near a new prison, working in one's hometown was never guaranteed. Second, correctional facilities entailed heightened threats to public safety from escaped incarcerated men and unrest on penitentiary grounds. Though officials promised safe and orderly facilities, security risks both behind and beyond the razor wire were often impossible to predict. Third, the stigma associated with being a prison town likely drove potential private investors to seek opportunities elsewhere. Caught up in the throes of correctional expansion, few could have predicted that the mammoth carceral state might someday contract, forcing postindustrial prison towns to contemplate a post-penal future. Finally, overcrowding and underfunding bred tension inside penitentiaries that endangered the well-being of anyone connected to the correctional system. Though research studies have confirmed these links, the physical and psychological toll of incarceration for both free and unfree is as old as prisonland itself.

Second, the rapid and enormous growth of the carceral state could appear an uncontested transformation. Mounting effective challenges to a nationwide phenomenon transpiring at disparate speeds, under different circumstances, and in far-flung locales would have taxed the resources of even the best-funded activist groups. Thus resistance happened one penitentiary and one community at a time. Between the 1970s and 1990s, large and influential anti-prison organizations—Stop the Olympic Prison (STOP), Concerned Citizens of Ray Brook (CCRB), Citizens Against More Prisons in the Adirondacks (CAMPA), and Tupper Lake Concerned Citizens (TLCC)—worked to prevent correctional expansion across the North Country. With memberships composed primarily of middle- and upper-middle-class seasonal homeowners, permanent residents, and visitors, these organizations played an important role in highlighting facilities' potential harm to environmental and public health. With few exceptions, the state's heavy reliance on imprisonment and the penal system's glaring injustices were of little consequence to the local resistance. Prison opponents forged alliances with powerful politicians and government agencies, launched petition drives, held protest marches, and utilized other tools of grassroots organizing to keep penitentiaries out of the park. Under often-difficult circumstances, they achieved impressive results. In Ray Brook, critics forced the abandonment of a potentially damaging sewage treatment system, the cleanup of prison-induced water pollution, and the cancellation of plans to build additional penitentiaries. In Gabriels, strong opposition compelled construction of a smaller correctional facility than originally planned, and inclusion of its unused land in the Forest Preserve. Finally, over a decade of sustained resistance ultimately killed Tupper Lake's hopes of becoming a prison town. The resulting physical shape of the Adirondack prisonland was the product of both careful state planning and a groundswell of grassroots opposition.

Third, it would have been impossible for a concrete-and-steel phenomenon as pervasive as the carceral state not to affect the environmental and public health of communities targeted for penal expansion. In the Adirondacks, the worst prison-induced impacts occurred in remote, lightly populated areas. Small when compared to oil spills and toxic waste dumping, these relatively contained calamities garnered little attention beyond the state and region. While their relative invisibility to the broader public may have contributed to a sense that penitentiaries were sustainable developments, the historical record shows otherwise. From the 1970s through the late 1990s, correctional planners labored to circumvent environmental regulations in the interest of building prisons. Little-known limitations built into existing environmental laws often facilitated efforts to erect penitentiaries quickly and cheaply. Political and practical considerations sometimes drove the Adirondack Park Agency and local environmental groups to shepherd potentially damaging penal developments. Local periodicals and opposition groups described how an unsustainable approach to prison construction endangered environmental and public health. Penitentiaries destroyed forests and wetlands, polluted waterways, killed wildlife, restricted access to recreational sites, and threatened fresh water supplies, among other harmful transformations. In fact, memories of particularly egregious environmental tragedies at Ray Brook in the late 1970s galvanized anti-prison activists in the North Country for the next two decades. Nevertheless, correctional planners' disregard for environmental and public health only extended the inherent injustice of the justice system to the nonhuman world and those who depended on it.

While mass incarceration unfolded at the local level, examining the broad historical forces that gave rise to the carceral state offers a deeper understanding of the ties that bind prisons and their environments. Viewed as a reaction to the achievements of the civil rights movement, the use of narcotics and sentencing laws to imprison millions of low-income people of color was central to state and federal policy agendas in the postwar era. Though commonly associated with the New Right, the legislative machinery that produced mass incarceration reflected conservative ideologies ascendant in both the Republican and Democratic parties. Operating in the militarized climate of the Cold War and Vietnam, policymakers treated the nation's increasingly chaotic urban centers as war zones whose lawbreaking residents required pacification. Wars on drugs and crime waged from the 1960s through the 1990s enjoyed widespread support from voters across racial, class, and political spectra. Promises to restore "law and order" by being "tough on crime" fueled the ascent of self-identified conservatives and liberals including Richard Nixon, Nelson Rockefeller, Ronald Reagan, Hugh Carey, Mario Cuomo, Bill Clinton, and George Pataki, among others. The bipartisan flavor of New York's carceral project had little impact on politics in the historically conservative towns and villages of the Adirondack Park. In communities targeted for prison construction, it was the rare local leader who dared resist the jobs, investment, and heightened political influence—New York legislative districts counted incarcerated men as residents of the areas in which they were confined—penitentiaries brought. North Country homeowners whose survival relied on the largesse of Albany lawmakers looked past the aversion to state dependency that formed the bedrock of modern conservatism with ease. Many park residents likely theorized that as participants in a war to restore law and order—not unlike the Cold War or Vietnam—no expense was too great.

The political consensus that coalesced around mass incarceration closely mirrored the widespread support offered for environmentalism at its inception. Repairing degraded environments and mitigating threats to public health proved broadly popular in the early 1970s. The North Country's brief honeymoon with the environmental movement ended abruptly in 1971 with the creation of the Adirondack Park Agency and the implementation of its development rules. Tarred as little more than a tool of wealthy visitors, the APA quickly became a popular punching bag for low-income residents and local politicians. It was the arrival of correctional facilities in the park that finally forced area homeowners to reckon with their own preconceived notions of both environmentalism and the APA. Far from being a radical environmental organization in disguise, the APA consisted of professional scientists and political leaders who possessed only nonbinding authority over state projects undertaken in the park. With many of its administrators serving at the pleasure of the governor, partisanship figured prominently in APA oversight of Adirondack prisons. Location and timing thus proved critical in determining whether penitentiaries would pass Park Agency muster. Organized environmentalists in the park often proved as open to prison-building as their APA counterparts, a factor that dispelled the caricatures of liberal tree huggers that were shared widely among North Country residents. Most importantly, the construction of correctional facilities in the Adirondacks helped expose significant limitations in New York's environmental laws. While APA rules limited private developments in the interest of environmental and public health, public projects could be built almost without restriction, potentially damaging environments many assumed were subject to strict protection. Thus, the growth of the carceral state forced North Country homeowners reared in anti-statism and anti-environmentalism to reconsider their once-black-and-white view of environmental politics.

One of those realities concerned deindustrialization, another late twentieth-century historical phenomenon whose emergence overlapped with the growth of environmentalism and mass incarceration. The consequences of postwar trade and labor policies made themselves felt beginning in the late 1960s and early 1970s. As foreign imports, rising inflation, and high labor costs drove private firms to relocate either to "right to work" states or overseas, unemployment and poverty afflicted the residents of a growing northern Rust Belt. The collapse of the American industrial sector hit people of color the hardest, driving many into a world of narcotics, unlawful activity, and incarceration from which there would be little chance of escape. While deindustrialization in urban areas helped fuel the rise of mass incarceration, the decline of rural industry played an equally important role in the growth of Adirondack penitentiaries. The closure of North Country iron mines, logging camps, tuberculosis hospitals, and public schools from the 1960s to the 1980s imposed new financial strain on residents at the same time that it provided the infrastructure for much of New York's Adirondack prisonland. Correctional planners anticipated a rapid reindustrialization that would give unused properties a new lease on life and reinvigorate stagnant local economies. Thus, deindustrialization in both the cities and countryside paved the way for the carceral state that emerged in its wake.

Let us now turn our attention to the peoples and communities whose lives, experiences, and environments help tell the story of New York's Adirondack prisonland. We begin in the Clinton County village of Dannemora, which was an as-yet unnamed, nonexistent community when Clinton State Prison, New York's third penitentiary, opened in 1845. Choosing the site for its proximity to a cornucopia of unharvested natural resources, planners hoped the industrial-style prison would both relieve overcrowding in the state's two other correctional facilities and jumpstart the nascent North Country economy. While jam-packed cells and sometimes-violent unrest repeatedly stymied state leaders' best efforts, using incarceration to effect environmental change, rehabilitate imprisoned men, and promote economic growth provided an unexpectedly durable roadmap for future correctional planners. It was 131 years later when the fortunes of Olympic organizers and penal bureaucrats converged in Ray Brook, home to a shuttered tuberculosis hospital seemingly tailor-made for housing either athletes or incarcerated men. Fierce competition for control of the facility left Ray Brook with two penitentiaries: Camp Adirondack, a state minimum-security prison opened inside the former hospital in 1976, and the Federal Correctional Institution-Ray Brook (FCI), a medium-security facility built on undeveloped public land that opened in 1980 after it first housed athletes participating in the 1980 Winter Olympics in Lake Placid. Interestingly, the two penitentiaries' sharply different environmental impacts helped shape equally disparate public responses to their presence long after opening. In particular, destruction unleashed during the construction of FCI inspired resistance to a correctional facility planned for an abandoned tuberculosis hospital in the Franklin County hamlet of Gabriels in 1981. Unlike Ray Brook, Gabriels' largely affluent homeowners and visitors identified incarcerated men of color as the primary threat to environmental and public health. Forging an alliance with the APA, Gabriels opponents waged a long campaign that, while ultimately unsuccessful, yielded significant environmental concessions from a Corrections Department eager not to repeat the tragedies of Ray Brook.

With Gabriels in its rearview mirror, corrections planners contending with record-breaking overcrowding sought North Country communities they hoped might prove amenable to welcoming convicted men. Environmental factors figured heavily in their choices. Sixteen years after its iron mines shut down, the Clinton County hamlet of Lyon Mountain still bore the scars from nearly two centuries of unrestricted industrial activity. With its built and unbuilt environments in a shambles, residents hoped the minimum-security penitentiary planned to open inside their shuttered public school in 1983 would entail repairs to a landscape still reeling from decades of corporate exploitation. Unfortunately for Lyon Mountain homeowners, Corrections Department interest in their community extended only as far as the penitentiary gates, leaving the struggling hamlet to contend with lingering environmental and public health concerns on their own. We end our journey in the Franklin County village of Tupper Lake, where an alliance of local politicians and residents struggled for nearly two decades to attract a correctional facility to their forlorn, postindustrial community. Long a central player in the Adirondack logging industry, by the 1970s

Tupper Lake had fallen on hard times. However, as in Gabriels, working-class residents shared Tupper Lake with a cohort of well-to-do homeowners and visitors resistant to the presence of incarcerated men. Though they repeatedly denied the town's requests for a prison throughout the 1980s and early 1990s, lawmakers in 1997 finally awarded Tupper Lake its long-sought penitentiary. Unfortunately for supporters, legally dubious activities attributed to the Corrections Department and Adirondack Park Agency while building the facility attracted the attention of environmentalists, whose pressure ultimately killed the project and, unbeknownst to many at the time, spelled the beginning of the end of New York's long experiment with incarceration in the Adirondack Park.

CHAPTER ONE

"THIS GREAT AND IMPORTANT EXPERIMENT"

Nature, Business, and the Quest for Reform at Clinton State Prison

Introduction

On a cool night in June 1845, two convicted men from the recently opened Clinton State Prison in Dannemora lay in a swamp eight hundred feet from the penitentiary grounds, contemplating their next move. Earlier that day, the duo had scaled the wall—finished only weeks earlier using local timber cut and shaped by Clinton's imprisoned men—and spent hours in hopeless pursuit of freedom a few miles north in Québec. To their dismay, the men discovered the unfamiliar rugged environment surrounding the prison in the northeast corner of the Adirondack Mountains was an insurmountable barrier that put the penitentiary's wall to shame. Disoriented by thick underbrush, dense forests, biting insects, and mountains as far as the eye could see, the pair ascended and then unwittingly descended nearby Dannemora Mountain, completing a circular route that landed them back within sight of the roughhewn wooden stockade by nightfall.[1]

Determined to remain free, the men embarked the next morning on a hardscrabble road bearing east toward Plattsburgh. Having concealed their identities long enough to enjoy breakfast at the cabin of an unsuspecting local widow, they continued their journey, only to be interrupted by "groups of men with guns and sticks." As they dashed into the woods, a search party officer disabled one with a skillfully aimed rock throw and then apprehended him. The remaining fugitive's "hunger was so intolerable that he came out and surrendered himself to the men who were still watching along the road" the following morning. After two days on the run, Clinton's first escapees were back behind bars. In light of their weakened physical condition, the warden imposed a suspended sentence to be meted out only in the event of future misbehavior. The gambit worked. Penal officials noted the men "conducted themselves with such perfect propriety as not to have deserved even a reproof" in the months following their unplanned adventure in the Adirondack wilderness.[2]

The drama of Clinton's first escape underscores the tensions that conditioned life in New York's third penal institution and the surrounding region during the penitentiary's first two decades. The state's inability to reconcile the prison's profitmaking priorities with its carceral purpose created challenges that were both predictable and intractable. In particular, the penitentiary's isolated and undeveloped environment stymied state leaders' lofty expectations that Clinton simultaneously fulfill its penal obligations, modernize an unbroken wilderness, enrich corporate investors, and stimulate the local economy. Planners' indifference to the perils of using correctional facilities for non-carceral purposes both fostered and continually aggravated fraught relations among incarcerated men, administrators, residents, entrepreneurs, and the natural world, sometimes with destructive consequences. Some valuable lessons regarding the dangers of deploying correctional facilities as agents of environmental change and economic development gathered dust well into the twentieth century, when New York once again pursued the construction of prisons in the Adirondacks whose objectives would extend far beyond mere incarceration.

The Adirondacks before Clinton

The Adirondack Mountains stretch from the Québec border to the outskirts of Albany, and west from Lake Champlain to the hinterlands of Lake Ontario. For centuries before geologist Ebenezer Emmons affixed the name "Adirondack" to the region in the 1830s, Indigenous peoples traversed and occasionally inhabited the region. The French navigator Jacques Cartier, standing atop Montreal's Mount Royal on a clear day in 1535, recorded viewing the northern reaches of what would one day become New York, describing "the country toward the south" and its "rivers, 'seas,' lakes," and other scenic wonders. Subsequent travelers encountered the area's soaring mountains, rushing waterways, abundant wildlife, bountiful vegetation, dense forests, and vast stores of minerals. By the late eighteenth century, increasing anecdotal knowledge of the North Country's plethora of unharvested resources prompted a slow trickle of white migrants to establish a tenuous foothold in the as-yet unnamed region.[3]

The obscurity and remoteness of the area's scattered farmsteads left the northern mountains unknown to most Revolutionary-era Americans. The majority of state residents living outside New York City were concentrated in the Mohawk and Hudson River Valleys and along the Great Lakes. While post-revolutionary migrations and high birthrates helped swell those regions' populations, the Adirondacks' geographic isolation, rocky soil, inhospitable climate, short growing seasons, and primitive roads deterred many potential settlers. However, in the early nineteenth century popular beliefs regarding the fertility of tree-covered soil helped draw a slew of mainly low-income newcomers from British Canada, New England, and other parts of New York to the woodsy north, where the challenge of transforming old growth forest into productive farmland shattered many a settler's Jeffersonian dream. Mere survival in the North Country required most residents to find alternative, seasonal employment in the region's other emergent trades: mining, logging, and tourism.[4]

Expanding settlements and improved understanding of this heretofore blank spot on New York's map attracted the attention of state leaders. In 1827, Governor DeWitt Clinton warned that future generations would regret squandering the Adirondacks' rich resources. Accordingly, the legislature funded a comprehensive scientific investigation, the Natural History Survey, to inventory and catalogue the raw materials New York had to offer. A group of scientists began the five-year project in 1836, their work informed by an ambivalent view of non-human nature as simultaneously a source of wealth and prosperity, an obstruction to the progress of civilization, an "antidote to the evils of modernity," and a "source of spiritual power." Thus did they extol the supposedly healthful qualities they believed inherent in northern New York's environment, describe how its landscape might be transformed for human use and commercial gain, and map the area to promote continued settlement and economic growth. The surveyors established county and township boundaries; named prominent features such as mountains, lakes, and streams; and, in keeping with white Americans' increasingly sentimental attitudes toward Indigenous peoples, imprinted a supposedly Iroquoian word, "Adirondack," over the entire region.[5]

Publication of the survey's laudatory reports attracted a new and wealthier wave of visitors and migrants. Unsanitary conditions and overcrowding in the nation's congested cities drove growing numbers of affluent urbanites—including artists, business leaders, and people diagnosed with respiratory illnesses—to make the difficult journey to breathe the region's unpolluted air, stalk its fish and wildlife, and seek spiritual rejuvenation through exposure to its natural beauty. Joining them were logging, mining, and recreational tourism entrepreneurs eager to transform the Adirondacks into a center of commercial activity. The region's mineral deposits proved particularly tempting. Local legend tells of an 1826 meeting in Essex County between a Jersey City lawyer interested in entering the mining trade and an Indigenous man who guided him toward an area containing "various and immense amounts of ore, equal almost to the demands of the world for ages," as well as "boundless forests of hard wood and an abundant water power."[6] Though unknown at the time of this fabled encounter, fewer than two decades later the Adirondacks' minerals, waters, and woods would prove instrumental in establishing correctional services as a distinct sector of the North Country economy.

Crime, Punishment, and Prisons in Early National New York

New York witnessed a revolution in criminal justice policy in the decades following U.S. independence. Historically, law enforcement had preferred public corporal punishments and executions as efficient and inexpensive forms of deterrence. Depending on circumstances, convicted offenders might also be forced to sit in the stocks, participate in public works projects, or perform other tasks to pay for their offenses. European workhouses, where poor people labored under close supervision for room and board, provided inspiration for New York City's first such institution, which opened in 1735. Chronic labor shortages, however, made such facilities impractical in a growing economy. With an eye toward maintaining an adequately sized free workforce, judges in many cases either imposed fines or dismissed charges altogether. Such instances of relative leniency generated popular fears of both recidivism and the creation of a permanent and potentially unmanageable class of lawbreakers. Accordingly, many Revolutionary-era New Yorkers favored the construction of prisons dedicated to achieving both punitive and preventative objectives.[7] Punishment and rehabilitation via incarceration and hard labor thus provided the foundation for New York's post-colonial correctional system.

The state's first penal institution, Newgate, opened in Manhattan in 1796. Warden Thomas Eddy fed incarcerated men a steady diet of Christian teachings and formal education, and he forbade physical punishments. Poorly paid imprisoned men spent most of their time producing shoes, barrels, linen, woolen cloth, and woodenwares inside prison factories. If successful, revenue generated from the sale of prison-made goods in domestic markets would ensure Newgate's financial solvency and incarcerated men who recommitted to thrift and hard work might never return. Within two decades, however, Newgate was in trouble. Sadly, the ingredients for failure had been present from day one. First, a staffing system based on political patronage all but guaranteed the misuse of monies allocated for educational and spiritual programming, effectively thwarting the facility's mission. Second, the notion that hard labor would transform imprisoned men into productive citizens ignored the external factors that fueled much lawbreaking. Many incarcerated men held jobs prior to their arrests, and the actions leading to their convictions were often rooted in financial strain. Population increase, social inequality, racism, and xenophobia—each of which figured prominently in the competition for jobs and housing among a growing, poor, urban populace—were problems a penitentiary could not fix. The likelihood of recidivism thus remained high, and by the early nineteenth century Newgate had become an overcrowded unsanitary warehouse plagued by disease, corruption, and violence.[8]

Unfortunately, few who occupied positions of authority in early America understood or bothered to analyze the root causes of either poverty or lawbreaking. In New York, lawmakers responded to overcrowding at Newgate not by overhauling patronage rules or investigating the reasons for unlawful activity. Lacking empathy for constituents susceptible to lawbreaking, officials looked instead to move Newgate's problems out of sight and mind. Legislators entertained ideas ranging from the establishment of penal colonies upstate to the deployment of imprisoned workers on rural road construction before deciding to erect a new prison in the Finger Lakes village of Auburn in 1817. Auburn, though, would be no Newgate. People incarcerated there lived and worked in silence; occupied tiny, poorly ventilated and unlit cells; consumed substandard food; labored under constant surveillance; and faced savage beatings for minor infractions. Once released, formerly incarcerated men contending with prison-induced psychiatric and physical trauma often reoffended and found themselves back behind bars. Overcrowding thus exacerbated Auburn's already brutal conditions, thereby disproving the supposed deterrent value of violent punishments but prompting no evaluation of existing penal policy. Instead, insufficient cell space spurred correctional leaders simply to transfer what had become known as the Auburn system to another new penitentiary. Opened in 1825 near marble mines along the Hudson River north of New York City, Sing Sing quickly became a cruel replica of Auburn. Abhorrent work and living conditions drove many despondent incarcerated men to end their lives in a river treasured by artists and urban elites for its natural splendor. The phrase "going up the river" soon came to represent a culture of fear and anxiety that pervaded the homes and communities of New York's poorest and most vulnerable residents.[9]

The question remains as to why New York's penal system, originally dedicated to the notion that steady work habits, religious instruction, and formal education could reduce unlawful activity, became characterized by violence so extreme that it attracted international condemnation. The answer lay in the state's decision to turn its prisons into profit-making enterprises. Seeking to minimize penitentiaries' budgetary impacts, in 1817 lawmakers authorized the leasing of incarcerated men to private firms producing a variety of consumer goods—shoes, barrels, carpets, combs, furniture, clothing, and marble, among others—for the domestic market. Gone was even the false pretense that hard labor might curtail recidivism. Instead, officers guarding prison factories enforced production quotas and wielded threats of violence against imprisoned workers in a bid to maximize profits. While low paid, poorly fed, and violently abused incarcerated men toiled in factories, on farms, and deep inside quarries, corporate executives, private investors, correctional administrators, and politicians reaped handsome dividends.[10] Thus did New York's penitentiaries become businesses dependent on a steady flow of raw materials, convicted men, and cash. As the line between public institution and private enterprise disappeared, any impulse to help incarcerated men—vital cogs in New York's prison-industrial machine—earn a second chance at life evaporated.

At the same time, some wealthy urbanites began to investigate the law-breaking that had become a prominent feature of city life in the early nineteenth century. In particular, a small number of middle- and upper-class

Manhattanites linked New York City's increasingly unsafe living and work-ing conditions to those faced by imprisoned men. They feared that if left unreformed, the penitentiaries would continue churning out damaged individuals who would reoffend—potentially ensnaring others in their unlawful endeavors—and return to prison, trapping them in a vicious cycle. Though creating a society free of lawbreaking remained a dubious prospect—especially in densely populated, poor neighborhoods—many elites did believe establishing peace in the cities required ending terror and exploita-tion in the state's rural penal institutions.[11] Thus did the Prison Association of New York, founded by a cohort of concerned elite men and women in 1844, seek the creation of a properly funded, politically independent, and morally oriented correctional system. Coincidentally, the association's inau-gural meeting in Manhattan occurred just as the proposed solution to overcrowding in Sing Sing—another penitentiary—was taking shape in the Adirondacks.

An Adirondack Prison

By the early 1840s, the Auburn system—characterized by silence, violence, surveillance, and corruption—had long been the governing framework of New York's penitentiaries. The system's seemingly intentional exacerbation of overcrowding, and the horrendous consequences resulting therefrom, greatly worried reformers. The state's skilled craftsmen, wary of the rise of unskilled, factory-based production, staunchly opposed further use of prison labor in private-sector industrial work. Nevertheless, the existing penal system did have supporters. Politicians in the Adirondacks who were attuned to the investments that would be needed to plan, build, and operate a penitentiary in a remote, unbroken wilderness welcomed the prospect of a new prison as a potential vehicle for development.[12] Many envisioned a large, bustling correctional facility employing hundreds of area residents, the mere presence of which might generate significant ripple effects, includ-ing the creation of new small businesses, expanded logging and mining, construction of new towns and villages, and the development of a modern transportation network linking the North Country to the rest of the state and nation. For residents of the Adirondacks, then, any new prison—whether violent and corrupt or humanely inspired—would be more than just a prison.

Every proposal to build a penal institution in the Adirondacks therefore fixated on how the facility might help unlock the riches of the North Country environment. Most focused on applying the existing penal labor system to the extraction and processing of iron ore. While private mining firms had staked many North Country claims by the early nineteenth century, politicians and businessmen alike salivated at the fortunes to be made—via the poorly paid labor of imprisoned men—from the region's numerous untapped veins. The Natural History Survey's 1840 report suggested using incarcerated men to build roads, operate sawmills, and mine ore, an idea that resurfaced a year later in a supportive letter sent from a local resident to Governor William Seward. In 1842, the New York State Assembly's Committee on Prisons endorsed a North Country penitentiary—ostensibly to relieve overcrowding in Sing Sing—only after reviewing data indicating vast ore deposits and enlisting Saratoga County inventor Ransom Cook to find a site suitable for both mining and incarceration.[13] Just as planners had chosen Auburn for its proximity to the Erie Canal and Sing Sing for its marble and closeness to the Hudson, the natural bounty of the Adirondacks—and the potential revenues to be derived therefrom—figured prominently in the decision to build New York's next penitentiary in the state's most remote and undeveloped region.[14]

Cook's investigation brought him to the mining districts of Clinton County, and his 1843 report revealed an area primed for extractive industry. He described the region's magnetic ore as "very valuable," its mines as "the best located . . . in regard to an abundant supply of fuel," meaning both timber and water, and noted that "the soil of the adjacent country . . . [is] good, furnishing an abundant supply of provisions at a cheap rate." Thus, Cook could confidently inform lawmakers "that for the manufacture of wrought iron, this is the best locality for such an establishment [prison]." Cook's findings, focused squarely on the area's moneymaking potential, reinforced the prevailing view that incarceration was, at its core, an economic development program. Seeking to minimize the anxieties of both private mine operators—for whom poorly compensated imprisoned men represented unwanted competition—and skilled craft workers, Cook pledged that iron cheaply produced at Dannemora would only "be put in competition with the manufacturers of iron in Europe," and not with domestic producers.[15] Strangely, he left unexplained how this promise would be kept in a nation whose private mining sector expected to meet the demand for its products exclusive of wage- and price-depressing competition from incarcerated workers.

In spite of Cook's pledge, fear that the inexpensive prison laborers at Dannemora might further harm the already imperiled livelihoods of free workers prompted 4,500 New York City craftsmen to urge suspension of the penal-industrial work program at the proposed North Country penitentiary. Their March 1844 petition to the legislature read, in part:

> The . . . Mechanics of the City of New-York . . . respectfully pray your Honorable Body to consider favorably the Bill providing for the building of a new Prison, in the Northern section of this State . . . We are earnest and anxious for the passage of this bill, under the full belief and assurance that it will eventually divert the labor of our State convicts from all interference with the labor of any and all of our citizens, it being our sincere conviction that the labor of the convicts . . . will interfere only with . . . imported goods consisting mostly of the best iron from Russia and Sweden, made by the convicts chiefly of those countries.

Like politicians, skilled professionals questioned neither the transformation of New York's correctional institutions into industrial workplaces nor the penal system's rapid and unsustainable growth. However, mounting income losses from the prisons' inexorable expansion frightened mechanics statewide. Though the governor's May 1844 request for $75,000 to build an Adirondack penitentiary—stipulating that its incarcerated men would work in iron production—seemed designed to assuage skilled laborers, the bill left unaddressed the future of the prison labor lease program. Believing that legislators had heeded their demands, craftsmen cheered the bill's quick legislative approval with an unprecedented spasm of parades, speeches, toasts, fireworks, and artillery salutes in Albany, New York City, and "most of the villages in the State."[16] The only people not celebrating, it seems, were the convicted men whose futures lay in an unbuilt prison located in a nonexistent community in a region that remained, for most New Yorkers, a mystery.

Building Clinton State Prison

Once the festivities ended, the building of New York's next prison began. Handsomely rewarded for his hard work, Ransom Cook, an inventor with no experience in corrections, received the plum appointment as Clinton's first warden. Returning to northern New York, Cook laid claim to land containing mines "of magnetic oxide of iron . . . about fourteen miles west of Plattsburgh, and about fourteen hundred feet above Lake Champlain." The chosen forested tract had, since 1836, hosted a total of two inhabitants squatting in a log cabin. Faced with an overcrowding emergency at Auburn and Sing Sing, lawmakers oblivious to the harsh realities of the North Country climate called for construction to begin in the winter of 1844–1845. Cook's description of the work underscored the challenges of transforming an undeveloped remote alpine environment:

> About the first of February [1845], the stockading of the yard for this prison was commenced and prosecuted through the winter, notwithstanding the snow here was more than five feet deep on an average . . . On the 21st of April, the erection of temporary buildings for . . . officers, guards, workmen, and convicts, was commenced amid a heavy growth of timber, and with nearly three feet of snow still remaining on the ground . . . The cold late spring, the want of roads, and other inconveniences incident to the location, combined to retard the completion of these buildings until June.

As the penitentiary rose from the forest floor, Cook traveled south to collect Clinton's first cohort of incarcerated men from Auburn and Sing Sing. He told the men where they were being taken and described the work, treatment, and discipline they could expect. Cook reported the men at Sing Sing—having resided up to that point in a brutal penal environment and likely fearful of what awaited them up north—spent "a restless night" aboard a boat on the Hudson River before embarking for the new institution at Dannemora, the fledgling North Country settlement recently named for the renowned iron mining district in Sweden.[17]

As the prison took shape in the spring of 1845, state lawmakers set in motion a series of environmental transformations designed to ensure Clinton would fulfill both its carceral and non-carceral objectives. Building a penitentiary in an area lacking even basic infrastructure, officials quickly learned, entailed costs unrelated to the work of incarceration. In April, legislators withdrew from sale all uncultivated state lands, "or which may hereafter become the property of said state," within a twenty mile radius of Clinton, creating a twenty-thousand-acre domain replete with timber for heating, cooking, construction, and industrial production at the prison. They also established state control over water resources located on public lands as exclusively for penal use; solicited bids from area contractors to begin building roads connecting Clinton to surrounding communities; and mandated that the penitentiary—planned as a cash-generating enterprise—and local taxpayers share equal responsibility for funding future road repairs.[18] Area politicians and businessmen likely looked on with glee as groups of incarcerated men, three to four dozen at a time, began arriving through the spring and summer of 1845 to help build the growing facility.[19] Their vision of state-financed, prison-based economic development in the Adirondacks—encouraged by the actions of elected leaders in Albany—seemed to be coming to fruition.

That August, journalists from the Plattsburgh *Republican* offered readers an eyewitness account of what had transpired at Dannemora in the previous half-year. They described the creation of a new community that from its inception began perpetuating the inequalities and cruelties of the existing social, economic, and penal order. Reporters noted that Dannemora, only nine weeks old, already boasted "several comfortable dwellings standing among the recently blackened stumps," presumably homes for officers and administrators; featured "block-houses, log-houses, and shanties," primitive structures reserved for private contractors and imprisoned men; and, from behind "the tall palisades enclosing the prison yards," came forth the din of "stone-chisels, stone-hammers, trowels, picks, saws, planes, and blacksmiths hammering, with the occasional booming of the blasts." Amid the cacophony of industrial tools, the journalists heard not a single human voice, a reminder of the durability of the Auburn system in a state where the pursuit of financial gain directed correctional policy.[20]

The building of Clinton State Prison—begun by two hundred incarcerated men and a cadre of skilled contractors supervised by twelve armed officers—remained a work in progress for years.[21] In 1846 alone, imprisoned workers added more spruce pickets to the ever-expanding wall; used stone cut from prison quarries to construct cell blocks and a building containing a kitchen, mess hall, toilets, showers, chapel, hospital, and store rooms; installed a sawmill; began building foundries, kilns, crushing mills, separating machines, and other iron production facilities; and crafted a pipe one-third of a mile in length to connect Clinton's stone-and-cement reservoir to a nearby natural spring. Once the clean water reached the prison, a network of pipes carried it to each of the complex's buildings, affording incarcerated men and staff members a rare luxury. Imprisoned men also enjoyed the benefit of attending literacy and math classes in the penitentiary's school and could read one of the nearly seven hundred books found in its library. Though Cook claimed in his 1847 report that the prison was half finished, costs remained high as its revenue-generating enterprises—the apparent ticket to achieving financial solvency—took years to complete.[22]

To make matters worse, the years-long construction meant that structures finished early in the process—especially those crafted from wood—risked succumbing to the elements long before building was complete. During Clinton's first two decades, state prison inspectors reported on the troubles associated with maintaining roads, stairways, doors, roofs, and other wooden structures in a climatically harsh and isolated environment. The penitentiary wall was a perennial source of concern. Though the Dannemora area contained an ample supply of trees, inspectors lamented the infrastructural barriers—especially the poor roads—preventing their quick and easy removal. As early as 1849, state inspectors noted the wall was "becoming decayed, and will soon require to be replaced, either by new picketing, or the erection of a permanent stone wall." Clinton's warden concurred, pointing out that imprisoned workers had installed wooden braces to hold up portions of the wall at risk of collapse. Security was the top priority, as the warden reported the wall was "open in many places, leaving cracks sufficiently large to insert the hand or drive in sticks and make a temporary ladder sufficient for making a successful effort to scale them." More than fifteen years after the prison opened, in 1861, Clinton's warden feared the stockade was "liable to fall with the first heavy wind." Thus, while Clinton remained an active construction site throughout its first two decades, restrictions related to climate, environment, and infrastructure made using the area's abundant natural resources difficult at best. State prison inspectors noted this phenomenon in their 1859 report to lawmakers, writing that for all the changes that had occurred in the previous decade and a half, Clinton remained "a prison in the woods."[23]

For all its troubles, each new incarcerated man, paid employee, and built structure at Clinton represented potentially lucrative public investments in a correctional system where the creation of private profit determined the rhythms of everyday life.[24] Thus, the delayed launch of Clinton's mining operation frustrated politicians, businessmen, and residents eager to reap its promised financial rewards. Holdups also helped fuel opposition among once-supportive area residents. For their part, state leaders and prison

officials blamed the endless wait on both inadequate funding and the
exhausting work of transforming untouched wilderness into an industrial
workplace. The time, money, and energy required to move heavy mining
equipment to Clinton's remote locale was a constant source of frustration.
These explanations, however, proved unsatisfactory to locals—some possibly intoxicated by Cook's glowing appraisals—who may have unrealistically
anticipated an effortless construction process. Some argued the ceaseless
building proved the site lacked ore, musing that officials hoping to skirt
public scrutiny had deliberately slowed construction. Other residents,
meanwhile, griped that North Country communities with proven and
accessible mineral deposits had somehow escaped lawmakers' attention. A
few even held out hope that officials might eventually abandon the incomplete penitentiary at Dannemora in favor of a presumably more profitable
location elsewhere in the region.[25] Regardless, critics' narrow focus on
Clinton's business operations—and not its disciplinary regime or working
conditions—must have pleased officials anxious to erase the already-blurred
line between the prison's carceral purpose and its profitmaking objectives.

For their part, opponents likely felt vindicated when Clinton administrators reported in early 1854 that the result of nearly ten years of construction
was an inoperable iron mine and production facility. Finishing quickly was
of the utmost importance as Jacob Kingsland, a businessman from the nearby
hamlet of Keeseville, had contracted to employ 150 incarcerated men for five
years in the production of nails—crafted from Clinton iron—for the domestic consumer market.[26] Officials were finally able to announce the beginning
of iron work at Clinton in September 1854, thus proving the skeptics wrong,
but a nighttime fire in 1856 caused over $15,000 in damage to newly com-
pleted buildings and recently installed machinery vital to the nascent trade.
The facility had no firefighting equipment, and its sophisticated waterworks
were no match for an uncontrolled blaze that in just a few minutes' time
consumed a decade's worth of work.[27] As delays once again plagued production, necessitating even more state spending on repairs, Kingsland still had
neither his workers nor his nails. The exasperated entrepreneur swiftly sued
the state for breach of contract, and in 1859 won $59,000 in damages.[28]

The Kingsland affair highlighted one of the many risks involved in operating public prisons like private businesses. Though accidents, bad weather,
and budgetary constraints were hard to predict, the state's ambitious, non-
carceral plans for Clinton guaranteed a time-consuming and expensive

ordeal made worse by the facility's remote, unbuilt environment. Each year that passed without a marketable commodity or consumer good both burdened taxpayers, including those who had welcomed Clinton's construction, and alienated potential partners uneager to become the next Jacob Kingsland. Without private investment, Clinton's existence as a mere prison would be impossible to justify. The wanton seizure and destruction of previously untouched and unregulated natural resources had reconfigured residents' relationships with the natural world. The creation of a prison-centered, restricted public domain—construed as an evil necessary to fulfill Clinton's economic promise—threatened to harm the livelihoods of locals accustomed to exercising free use of nature's bounty. It is likely that at least some Adirondackers viewed with suspicion the transfer of valuable natural wealth away from the poor, toward the prison, and, eventually, into the hands of private businessmen. Accordingly, achieving Clinton's financial objective, while still an end in itself, also became crucial to ensuring long-term public support for the struggling penitentiary.

Clinton and the North Country Economy

The arrival of the facility's predicted economic ripple effects relieved politicians and penal administrators worried over the slow pace and high cost of construction. Clinton's undeveloped and isolated setting, the source of so much difficulty, proved a boon to entrepreneurs eager to fill the gap of previously unneeded small businesses and modern infrastructure. Within weeks of the prison's opening, advertisements in the Plattsburgh *Republican* told of new hotels, each highlighting their proximity to Dannemora, welcoming guests to the region. With more travelers and goods circulating in the area, a new stage line opened between Plattsburgh and Dannemora, and the state announced plans to build new roads—crafted from wooden planks cut and shaped in Clinton's sawmill by prison labor—connecting Clinton to neighboring communities, mining districts, and rail hubs. An array of shops that peddled locally made shoes, matches, lime, and nails— each boasting links to the penitentiary—joined the North Country's growing commercial index. Finally, private real estate transactions became a regular feature of life in the Dannemora area, illustrating the hamlet's steady growth and the new values placed on land that until recently had been covered with trees and populated by wild animals.[29]

In addition to stirring the North Country's capitalist spirit, Clinton became one of the region's largest purchasers of locally made goods. Seeking both fiscal solvency and dividends, prison officials had to ensure their incarcerated workers were properly clothed, fed, and housed. To those ends, facility administrators contracted with area farmers for the delivery of meat, vegetables, dairy products, and woolen cloth, and they purchased wood cut and split by local loggers and stone carved from nearby quarries. In a bid to minimize costs, they sold used meat barrels and prison-made soap to consumers across the region, along with enlisting imprisoned men to grow potatoes and vegetables—for both prison use and the consumer market—on a farm adjacent to the penitentiary.[30] Clinton's steady growth guaranteed local purveyors of agricultural produce and building materials a reliable market seemingly shielded from the vagaries of the capitalist world.

As a stimulant to private investment in the North Country, Clinton seemed to be fulfilling its boosters' ambitions. However, the deepening ties that bound local entrepreneurs to the penitentiary carried considerable risk. Harsh weather conditions, a certainty in the Adirondacks, could deprive the prison of necessary supplies and local businessmen of much-needed income. Uncontrollable market forces might compel farmers, loggers, and stone-cutters to demand higher prices, once again exposing each side to significant loss. The building of modern roads—viewed by most as a sign of progress—could backfire, opening a conduit to outside traders and creating harmful competition for locals expecting priority in prison contracting. As both Clinton administrators and entrepreneurs navigated an increasingly fraught relationship, the expanding population of incarcerated men—the factor upon which the entire project rested—remained a steady and reliable constant. State prison inspectors underscored this reality in their 1859 report to Albany, noting that all of New York's prisons—including Clinton—were dangerously overcrowded. Lawmakers responded not by choosing to erect a new prison, but, rather, by expanding their unfinished penitentiary in Dannemora.[31]

The lives and labor of incarcerated men were central to Clinton's construction, operation, and prominent position in the local economy. Imprisoned men worked a variety of jobs both inside and outside the prison. In addition to construction, road building, farming, and iron production, incarcerated men labored as attendants in the prison hospital, mess hall, washrooms, and tailor shop, among other sites. Imprisoned workers also devoted considerable attention to enhancing the penitentiary's aesthetic qualities, removing stumps, building walkways, and re-seeding lands cleared of vegetative cover. State prison inspectors reported in 1859 that these efforts had rendered "the grounds about the prison beautiful and attractive."[32] Incarcerated men also toiled as leased employees under contract to private entrepreneurs. Skilled craftsmen who in 1844 had celebrated the apparent demise of the Auburn system must have watched in horror as Clinton administrators in 1851 solicited their first bids for the use of prison labor. Seven years in, Clinton's buildings and iron production facilities were incomplete and bleeding red ink. Selling old barrels and soap made from the ash of charred trees would never ensure the penitentiary's financial solvency, to say nothing of recouping the hundreds of thousands already spent. Lawmakers' 1844 pledge to employ Dannemora's incarcerated men in iron production did not, as mechanics sadly discovered, preclude their working in other industrial fields. Thus, while groups of imprisoned men put the finishing touches on Clinton's mining infrastructure, others found themselves producing goods that would one day fill the shelves of local retailers and the homes of North Country consumers, further intensifying the already fraught dependency between the region and its prison.

Area businessmen took advantage of Clinton's cheap labor force by using the Auburn system's standardized bidding process. As at Auburn and Sing Sing, administrators at Clinton accepted proposals for the use of incarcerated workers, and winning contractors paid fees for the use of prison factories and laborers to convert raw materials into sellable goods. Over the two to five years of an average contract, entrepreneurs would control anywhere from one hundred to two hundred incarcerated men paid wages of less than forty cents per day drawn from state coffers. Imprisoned men toiling under the supervision of correction officers in Clinton-based factories manufactured agricultural implements, home construction materials, accessories for horses, carriages, files, nails, barrels, and leather for domestic consumption. While many businesses appear to have concealed their use of penal labor from consumers, one Plattsburgh retailer, the Clinton Prison Boot and Shoe Company, took obvious pride in their Dannemora connection.[33] By the mid-1850s, the various pieces of the Clinton Prison economic puzzle, both inside and outside the penitentiary, had started to coalesce.

The public outbursts heralding Clinton's legislative approval back in

1844 had revealed a popular belief, however misguided, that the new penitentiary would roll back the Auburn system. Yet, a decade later, store shelves stocked with the cheaply made fruits of Dannemora prison labor competed for customers alongside the wares of free craftsmen. What had happened? First, state officials never intended for Clinton to differ from its sibling institutions. If anything, politicians' expectation that the prison fulfill a wide range of non-carceral goals represented an intensification of New York's system of penal governance. Second, the high costs incurred from building Clinton in a remote, unbroken wilderness, especially before its mining operation opened, all but guaranteed the impressment of incarcerated men into the ranks of Auburn-system labor. Achieving solvency and turning profits, as always, remained paramount. Third, the rise of machine-based factories in the United States in the mid-nineteenth century eroded the power of skilled mechanics, paving the way for a race to the bottom among industrialists exploiting cheap labor both in and outside of prison. With no politically or socially influential group standing in their way, state leaders could operate Clinton, like Auburn and Sing Sing before it, with impunity. To the public, the penitentiary would seem a beehive of industrial activity. To its employees and incarcerated men, the prison would come to resemble the horrific institutions some had hoped Clinton might help to reform.

The Struggle for Reform at Dannemora

Upon becoming warden in 1845, Ransom Cook established himself as an innovator in corrections. Having absorbed the lessons of the Auburn system, Cook believed penitentiaries should serve the needs of incarcerated men, not the balance sheets of businessmen or greedy pockets of politicians and prison administrators. Cook's lenient treatment of Clinton's first two escapees demonstrated his belief that since incarceration by itself was a severe form of punishment, only the worst offenses warranted additional sanctions. By Cook's reckoning, breaking out of the penitentiary did not require further correction. In part, the warden did not fear future escapes or disturbances because, in his view, "the woods rather protect the prison." He surmised that at minimum the prospect of getting lost would deter future runaways. Cook further argued that under a humane penal regime, Clinton's wooden wall, which "stood alongside the mountains," might someday be unnecessary.[34]

Inspired by Cook's spirit of optimism and despite the fact that incarcerated men had run off almost as soon as Clinton opened, local journalists labeled the young prison "this great and important experiment."[35]

Just a few months earlier on a chilly night in December 1844, a group of affluent merchants, lawyers, physicians, and educators had gathered in a Manhattan ballroom to form the Prison Association of New York. The association counted among its supporters luminaries such as Dorothea Dix, Alexis de Tocqueville, future Massachusetts Senator Charles Sumner, and King Oscar I of Sweden and Norway.[36] The organization's members, many of whom lived and worked in the overcrowded and chaotic neighborhoods of New York City, connected their community's relatively unsafe living conditions to the failures of the penal system. The group thus strongly objected to the inhumane treatment of incarcerated men forced to toil under brutal conditions to satisfy the greed of correctional employees, politicians, and businessmen. Viewing imprisoned men as victims of circumstances beyond their control, the association believed each possessed "the germ from which, with proper cultivation, the green tree shall spring." In the spirit of Ransom Cook, the reformers called for a penal system dedicated less to generating revenue and more to fostering the well-being of incarcerated men.[37] For many association members, Clinton Prison, which was presumably to be less beholden to market imperatives and guided by a reform-minded warden, offered hope of establishing a more peaceful paradigm for New York's correctional regime.

Empowered by a charter from the legislature, in 1845 the Prison Association began performing annual inspections of the state's correctional facilities and submitting the resulting reports to lawmakers in Albany. Inspectors focused on incarcerated men's physical health and educational opportunities, factors deemed crucial to reducing recidivism. Their 1845 report on New York City jails, for instance, lamented a prohibition on physical exercise and warned that lack of exposure to clean air was as dangerous to health "as the indigestion of bad food." This led reformers to call for a ban on smoking—a behavior "as little conducive to health as it is to cleanliness"—in penal facilities, and to implore legislators to furnish education and vocational training to imprisoned men, many of whom lacked basic literacy and work skills.[38] Unfortunately, reformers' only hope of effecting change lay in convincing lawmakers to improve the lives of incarcerated men through legislative action. Without a groundswell of popular support, and in a state where empathy did not figure in penal policy, reform would remain an uphill battle.

In spite of these seemingly insurmountable challenges, Dr. John Griscom and John Edmonds conducted the association's first inspection of Clinton in 1846. After leaving New York City by boat, the pair spent forty-six hours traveling overland from Albany to Dannemora along "a road distinguished for its roughness . . . an almost uninterrupted ascent, through deep sand, broken rocks, and water-worn gullies." On arrival, they marveled at Clinton's architectural design, radical by contemporary standards, featuring large cells, wide hallways, high ceilings, and a climate control apparatus furnishing "a regulated supply of air, from without, into the prison, warmed in winter." Interviews with the facility's 159 incarcerated men, most below the age of thirty, showed them to be in good health, such as "might be expected in persons at regular labor, with good and wholesome diet," and exhibiting "cheerfulness" and "an elasticity and vigor of mind and body." The environment surrounding the prison provided an added bonus. A "general atmosphere of the greatest purity" and the "pure air of its mountainous altitude"— features believed to possess special restorative qualities—might, the inspectors contended, render Clinton "unrivaled" in the quest to reduce unlawful activity. A combination of thoughtful design, humane treatment, and, despite its numerous challenges, intelligent site selection, made Clinton Prison a place where "cruelty is unknown, and disobedience infrequent."[39]

The association's glowing first review was matched only by its 1848 report. The inspectors, James Titus and Richard Reed, praised Clinton's mess hall, where unlimited servings of nutritional food supplied incarcerated men energy for long days at work. Titus and Reed also commended the unspoiled nature of the Adirondacks, which they claimed produced "evidence of comfort and an aspect of cheerfulness well calculated to alleviate the sadness of spirit which must ever lay heavy upon the minds of the unfortunate inmates." Conversations with Clinton's 143 imprisoned men reinforced this positive view. Most displayed excellent health, and many claimed officers and administrators were kind and attentive, compelling some to state, "they could not reasonably complain." Incarcerated men's desire never to return to prison, even one as progressive as Clinton, impelled some to declare "their intention to call at the office of the Association [in New York] if they should have an opportunity." The inspectors also reported that one incarcerated person, "a colored man, contributed a dollar to our funds," while "another declared that a part of his earnings, after the expiration of his sentence, should be given to the prison."[40] One would have been hard-pressed to hear similar sentiments expressed by men imprisoned at either Auburn or Sing Sing.

However, the inspectors' 1848 visit came at a moment of significant upheaval for New York's newest penitentiary.[41] With prison employment still tied to political patronage, the state's newly installed Whig government had in January 1848 dismissed Democratic Party appointees working at Clinton, including Cook and a large number of his administrators and officers. In February, a group of soon-to-be-terminated staff gathered at the penitentiary to protest their firing. Resolutions adopted at the meeting affirmed their commitment to humane incarceration—corroborated by association inspectors—along with fear of what lay ahead:

> The recent parting which we have all passed through with the convicts of Clinton Prison, together with the leave we are about to take of each other, awaken emotions of pity for the prisoners and regard for each other, which will endure while memory remains . . . We deeply regret the removal of Ransom Cook . . . from the superintendence of this prison as unjustifiable, unprovoked, and vindictive; a proceeding which sacrifices the appropriations from the Treasury, the interests of the Mechanics, and the claims of humanity, to base and groveling party malice.

The same day, Cook addressed the men incarcerated at Dannemora one final time. His remarks revealed the reform impulses that had guided his three-year tenure:

> And now, prisoners, I have to part with you . . . Although my authority here is cheerfully surrendered, I cannot resign or relinquish the solicitude I feel for your welfare. It is at all times a sad spectacle to see our fellow beings, although strangers, in your helpless, and with some, almost hopeless situation. To part with and forget them if we can is often a relief to the mind. But I cannot forget you if I would. . . . You are of my acquaintance—Many of you have been under my care for nearly three years, during which, the anguish of some have commanded my sympathies; the noble efforts of others at reformation and improvement, my admiration. For your industry and good behavior as a body, you have my warmest thanks; and for the few who have occasionally departed from the path of rectitude, I entertain no ill feeling, but indulge the hope that they will hereafter do better. I beseech you all to persevere in a course of good behavior, till a virtuous life becomes habitual. You will find peace, prosperity, and happiness your reward.[42]

Cook and his fired counterparts likely understood that in a state whose leaders both lacked empathy for incarcerated men and fixated exclusively on prisons' cash flow, efforts to achieve reform were now in severe jeopardy.

While the reformers' ouster did not necessarily foretell the establishment of a harsher regime, the association's 1848 report did show Clinton moving in a less humane direction. Interviews with incarcerated men revealed an increase in harsh discipline, and inspectors were alarmed to discover a shower bath, a device designed to simulate the effects of drowning, had recently been installed. Used to punish disobedience, officers would blindfold and restrain imprisoned men in a wooden chair and then pour water over their heads to the point of near death. There was probably little shock, then, when the inspectors subsequently discovered an incarcerated man laid up in the prison hospital recovering from a gunshot wound sustained during an escape attempt. Horrified at what seemed a concerted effort to cleanse the facility of Cook's spirit of generosity, Titus and Reed pleaded with Clinton's leadership to abolish torture and instead adopt solitary confinement—by their reckoning, a more humane punishment—in a below-ground dungeon.[43]

From 1848 to 1852, Clinton operated without Prison Association oversight, allowing administrators a free hand to institutionalize policies that governed Auburn and Sing Sing. Absent the inspectors' prying eyes, it seems likely that the excessive force uncovered in 1848 intensified once Clinton's industrial machinery—the facility's raison d'être—roared to life. Contrary to Cook's predictions, the Adirondacks were no barrier to incarcerated men escaping the penitentiary's new and aggressive system of authority. The rotting and chronically unstable prison wall provided an easy conduit to freedom. While officials recorded only three runaways in 1847, twelve imprisoned men absconded in April 1848 alone. The following month, the Plattsburgh *Republican* reported the escape of "Two convicts, named Lincoln and Nixon," and in August, an incarcerated man who had been shot and wounded while attempting to break out exclaimed, "I may as well die this way as to suffer and starve as we do in prison." Correctional leaders' faith in the value of violent discipline cracked as more incarcerated men risked their lives for a chance at freedom. Unable to maintain control, prison officials asked Albany for help. Instead of remedying the conditions driving men to escape, however, lawmakers sought merely to minimize the risks. Accordingly, Clinton administrators received funds to reward any local residents who assisted in apprehending fugitives; to acquire more powerful firearms for officers; and to preempt future escapes by removing troublesome men from the facility.[44] By the early 1850s, Dannemora was rapidly becoming an ungovernable armed camp.

Though the uptick in escapes coincided with a shift in leadership, breakouts from Clinton did not become an everyday occurrence, and most incarcerated men never attempted to run off. Nevertheless, it is likely that the Auburn system's harsh discipline played a key role in driving men to flee. The new administrators' practice of keeping "the management of this institution as secret as possible from the public" left most outsiders oblivious to the conditions fueling the unrest, but because the August 1848 arrest and trial of Clinton Sergeant George Sanborn for the assault of an incarcerated man named John Thurston could not be concealed, the unknowing public received a brief glimpse of the Auburn system in action. For speaking to another incarcerated man—a charge Thurston denied—Sanborn physically assaulted Thurston while officers held him to the floor. To maximize Thurston's embarrassment, Sanborn then confined Thurston, unclothed, in the shower bath in the presence of other incarcerated men and staff members before applying the water torture. Convicted in Clinton County Court, the judge ordered Sanborn to pay only a $25 fine. Journalists covering the trial could barely contain their rage at Clinton's rapid deterioration:

> We leave others to say, which deserve the prison uniform, the convict or his tormentors? The disgusting practice which these officers have adopted of exhibiting convicts in the stocks in a state of nudity, would excite the indignation of a barbarian, and forcibly exhibits the gross depravity which now controls this institution. Let us pause a while before we make another boast of our superior civilization and refinement.

While the following year brought news of a forced march of putatively subversive incarcerated men from Clinton to Sing Sing—along a circuitous route chosen to expose the men to residents' scorn and ridicule—the story of the assault on Thurston would be the last report of abuse inflicted on incarcerated men to appear in the local press for the next two decades.[45] A lack of coverage, of course, did not mean the problem of violence against incarcerated men—and their attempts to resist—had disappeared.

Unsurprisingly, the association's 1853 report on Clinton revealed an institution that had repudiated its reformist roots. While inspectors John Stanton Gould and James Titus remarked on the high-quality food offered to incarcerated men who worked unsupervised outside the prison wall, they noted this leniency grew less from humane impulses than from the need for strong and healthy workers. The heightened frequency of escapes appears not to have dissuaded administrators of nature's value as a deterrent to would-be runaways. Gould and Titus also lamented the persistence of patronage-based employment, where officers beholden to politicians—and, by extension, to businessmen—did not "enter heart and soul into the duties required of them," thus exacerbating the likelihood of recidivism. Clinton's adoption of an Auburn-style regime eroded the association's confidence in its abilities to effect change. Gould and Titus threw in the towel, arguing "the seed of evil should be destroyed whilst it is young and vigorous; nay, the poisonous blossoms should not be suffered to drop its seed," adding that only unspecified preemptive action would prevent unlawful activity from taking "root on the highways as well as the by-ways, on the most sterile soil and the richest virgin lands." Prisons' inability to subvert lawbreaking, along with their imperviousness to reform, made further inspections an exercise in futility.[46]

Dwindling Prison Association funds combined with a pervasive defeatism led to fewer visits to Clinton by the mid-1850s. Amid a nationwide financial crisis, association members focused attention on penal facilities nearer their New York City homes. Though the organization continued offering proposals to improve conditions, the disappointments of the past decade had drained its spirit. In 1857, for instance, the association made only modest suggestions—allowing incarcerated men to perform salaried work upon completion of their mandatory tasks and granting reduced sentences for good conduct—that would have left intact the profit-making and violence-inducing structures of existing penal policy. The onset of the Civil War four years later led to a suspension of the group's activities, "at a time when the safety of the nation, the perpetuity of democratic government, the preservation of our Federal Union and the defence of our liberties, occupy . . . the minds of all patriots."[47] Strangely, not a single association member seemed to view New York's nearly seven-decade-old penal crisis in similar terms.

The association's extended absence from Clinton coincided with the long-awaited stabilization of the prison's business enterprises. By the mid-1850s, iron production was underway, and the discovery of new mines in 1859 necessitated creation of a larger workforce. Lawmakers promptly funded construction of an additional two hundred cells, and by 1861 a population of incarcerated men that stood at 125 a decade earlier had soared past five hundred. Men imprisoned at Clinton toiled in workshops producing iron, nails, and profits for Jacob Kingsland, along with boots and shoes for a consortium from Troy, among other industrial activities.[48] The fulfillment of its boosters' dream of building a profitable penitentiary in the Adirondacks sadly obscured the repression without which the endeavor might have failed. One reporter gleefully predicted in 1858 that Clinton seemed "destined at any early day to take rank with those [prisons] at Auburn and Sing Sing, not only in regard to numbers but in productive returns."[49] Just ten years earlier, few would have openly hoped that Clinton would resemble penitentiaries internationally synonymous with terror, but, having adopted the horrific system that governed those facilities within the larger context of a society in which abuse of incarcerated men was either tolerated or totally invisible, the final jewel in Clinton's crown would be surpassing Auburn and Sing Sing in the race for profits. The violence that helped smooth Clinton's path to financial glory—and provoked incarcerated men's attempts to resist—continued unabated.

The ten separate escape episodes involving two dozen incarcerated men that occurred between the association's 1853 inspection and the end of the Civil War in 1865 disproved any notion that Clinton had become an orderly penal environment. While some ran off without planning, including two who jumped from a Clinton-bound train into the waters of Lake Champlain, time and experience taught others the value of advance preparations. Officials investigating an 1854 escape in which an officer shot and killed a would-be fugitive discovered extra clothing and bread in the men's possession; this pair had some understanding of the challenge of running away into a mountainous wilderness. In addition, Clinton's porous perimeter proved tempting for would-be fugitives like Abraham Kingsbury, who, sporting a false nose and civilian clothing thanks to the aid of a corrupt officer, walked out the front gate on a clear day in 1860 without arousing suspicion. Improvements to the region's famously unreliable transportation infrastructure facilitated by the construction of Clinton also made absconding a less arduous ordeal. In October 1864, Michael Casey escaped from Dannemora to New York City, where he hid until police officers involved in the manhunt captured him after a gunfight in Manhattan's Fulton Market the following spring.[50] Contrary to Ransom Cook's assertion twenty years earlier, the woods could not protect Clinton, and its walls, both artificial and natural, proved to be little more than flimsy barriers that seemingly anyone could move past.

Yet without independent oversight, administrators were able to draw the veil of secrecy ever tighter over Clinton's internal workings. Glimpses afforded by local press reports had already revealed an institution where violence was fast becoming the norm. Officers assaulting, torturing, shooting, and killing incarcerated men for disobeying rules, running away, or resisting transfer starkly illustrated the mutual animosity that had taken root since 1848. Sadly, this adversarial relationship opened the door to other forms of abuse. An 1856 news story revealed administrators had been forcing Clinton's Black incarcerated men—numbering a total of three out of hundreds—to serve as involuntary, unpaid laborers, running unsupervised errands for officials outside the prison, and "on one or more occasions" accompanying white officers "on fishing and pleasure excursions in the wilderness, acting in the capacity of servant and waiter."[51] The flagrant enslavement of African American incarcerated men demonstrated the power Clinton officials wielded in the area. Abuses previously confined behind prison walls moved outdoors as officers and administrators, unafraid of legal or social sanctions in an isolated region increasingly dominated by correctional staff, treated imprisoned men as their personal property.

Under such conditions, running away was often the only way to resist the tyranny of life at Clinton. However, even well-planned escapes often did not achieve their objectives. Incarcerated men's deep well of contempt thus led some to organize larger and more violent acts of rebellion. Shortly after midnight on July 12, 1861, James Sewell, an incarcerated man working in Clinton's mining facilities, struck an iron bar over the head of Officer Augustus Wright, killing him instantly. While a trusty incarcerated man was able to stop Sewell's counterparts from murdering a second officer, seven imprisoned men—one armed with Wright's revolver—escaped into the night. Within a week all had been recaptured, and in October found themselves indicted in Clinton County Court for murder. After a one-day trial and thirty minutes of deliberations, a Plattsburgh jury convicted and sentenced Sewell to death for striking the fatal blow.[52] In February 1862, the remaining six defendants faced justice. Among them, Marion Hall was found guilty and condemned to hang. Addressing the court, Hall explained his participation in the conspiracy:

My only design was to gain my lost liberty, and the society of those loved ones whom I shall never see again. It was to free myself from that living tomb in Dannemora, and the galling yoke of those stern oppressors and the cruel torture of their inquisition; that place where a man is not allowed to speak, where he is not allowed to smile, and where he is deprived of nearly all the senses that God has given him for his comfort and happiness on this earth.[53]

Just three months earlier, an obituary had noted the death of Captain Hosea Chamberlin, a former officer at Clinton who, in failing health, had retired after three years on the job.[54] One can only wonder what role, if any, the stresses of prison employment played in Chamberlin's short career and untimely passing. By the mid-1860s, a penitentiary once lauded as a "great and important experiment" was now described as a "living tomb" where violence and death stalked residents, incarcerated men, officers, and retirees alike. Something had gone terribly wrong at Dannemora. Or had it?

Reform never had a chance at Clinton. While Prison Association oversight during Cook's tenure had offered glimmers of hope, reformers' reports and news accounts revealed an institution that from day one operated according to the same principles that governed Auburn and Sing Sing. That Clinton became a similarly brutal charnel house should have surprised no one. For all the hullabaloo surrounding the selection of the northeastern Adirondacks for New York's newest prison back in 1844, lawmakers had aimed only toward garnering the political support of skilled workers and never intended either to renovate or replace the Auburn system. Thus, it was possible to appoint a reformer as warden and still require incarcerated men to perform poorly paid, backbreaking work in complete silence; to permit inspections from affluent urbanites while allowing officers to waterboard incarcerated men; and to invite reporters to observe and write about the facility's disturbing inner workings without fear of public scrutiny. Absent widespread outrage over penal conditions, the association's mild recommendations and journalists' harrowing tales would meet an indifferent response from legislators in Albany. For many people, stories of atrocities and unrest at Clinton would come to be seen, like at Auburn and Sing Sing, as simply the cost of doing business. Nearly three-quarters of a century after the opening of Newgate, financial imperatives still trumped empathy in New York's prisons, guaranteeing those unlucky enough to be ensnared in the system a difficult time finding their way out.

Preserve, Park, and Prison(s)

On a cool morning in October 1865, Nicholas Stokes and Henry McCotter began their sixth day on the run after escaping from Clinton. Law enforcement discovered the pair later that same day, hidden on a farm one-and-a-half miles from the Québec border. Hungry, exhausted, and lost, the duo told investigators they would not have "turned into the barn for rest had they known they were so near the free dominions of Her Majesty," Queen Victoria.[55] Though luck had landed them within striking distance of freedom, incomplete knowledge of local terrain had again stymied a successful escape. The men's impressive thirty-mile trek toward Québec shows how two decades of prison-induced environmental change, viewed by many as progress, could backfire. Though forced to contend with the same dense vegetation, dangerous wildlife, bad weather, and dizzying mountains as past runaways, Stokes and McCotter had successfully traversed a landscape where relentless digging, cutting, burning, excavating, and building had created both new opportunities and risks. In their zeal to wring dollars from Clinton, lawmakers and correctional planners had not foreseen the possibility that incarcerated men might exploit for their own nefarious schemes the very infrastructure without which prison-based profits would not have been made. By the same token, roads, businesses, communities, and sight lines not present in 1845 could also now upend the plans of even the best-prepared escapee. As officers hauled Stokes and McCotter back to Dannemora along roads built using prison labor, newcomers seeking leisure and recreation began arriving in the Adirondacks. To the dismay of state leaders, Clinton became a stop on many a visitor's summertime itinerary. In their 1866 report to lawmakers, state prison inspectors took note of this troubling development:

> Particularly during the summer season, there are large numbers who visit the prisons . . . An admission fee of twenty-five cents each is demanded, which creates a fund which is divided among the convicts as their terms of sentence expire . . . We are still of the opinion that general visiting of the prisons is productive of much evil. While the convicts are in the main from the lower strata of society, they nevertheless keenly feel the degradation of their position, a position still more difficult to bear from their being made the subjects of idle curiosity, stared at and commented upon by those who have no interest whatsoever in their welfare.[56]

These concerns notwithstanding, there was little risk of Clinton becoming a must-see destination for the increasing numbers of tourists visiting the Adirondacks. The same could not be said for the area's more unspoiled and aesthetically pleasing locales.

Following in the footsteps of early nineteenth-century urbanites seeking relief from overcrowded and unsanitary cities, Adirondack visitors after the Civil War—titans of big business, artists, and people diagnosed with tuber- culosis among them—flocked primarily to areas where extractive industry and the prison system had yet to arrive. The superrich sought in the central Adirondacks the sort of primeval landscape depicted in paintings of the Hudson River School, largely bypassing any modernized locales like the mining village of Lyon Mountain, the logging camps in Tupper Lake, and the state prison at Dannemora. Ironically, enjoying the visual splendors of Adirondack nature required transforming the very areas elites hoped to preserve. Thus did poorly compensated locals build lakeside hotels, rail lines, game preserves, and seasonal homes for the richest of the nouveau riche. As the wealthy laid claim to estates laden with precious natural resources, the region's low-income residents, many now scraping by in a slew of tourism-related jobs, found themselves cut off from woods, waters, and wildlife they once consumed without restriction. In short order, class tensions revolving around the control and use of nature—likely first expe- rienced by North Country dwellers living near Dannemora decades earlier—became central to everyday life across the Adirondacks.[57]

The Adirondack environment discovered by new generations of visitors was far from pristine. Since the late eighteenth century, farmers, loggers, miners, and incarcerated men had reshaped the sprawling region. A century later, waves of tourists were followed by business executives eager to exploit its timber and minerals. Buoyed by high demand from soaring urban pop- ulations and a growing industrial sector, area men found work in the expanding logging and mining trades. These exploits denuded vast swaths of forest through reckless clear-cutting that heightened the risk of destruc- tive fires and floods. Carried along by floodwaters, the detritus from years of out-of-control logging—dirt, ash, branches, and twigs—destroyed aquatic habitats and threatened to disrupt river commerce across New York State. On land, piles of wood unwanted by loggers furnished kindling for fires that destroyed valuable resources, polluted the air, exacerbated flood- ing, and marred an already compromised landscape. Visitors oblivious to their own hand in modernizing the Adirondack environment looked on in horror as the chaos that had driven them to the North Country in the first place arrived at the doorsteps of their country homes.[58]

By the 1870s and 1880s, calls appeared statewide for the enactment of environmental regulations in the rapidly industrializing Adirondacks. Wealthy elites and politicians, many of whom vacationed in the area, joined a growing chorus of individuals concerned that without limitations on timbering, New York would face crippling wood shortages, unnavigable waterways, and a diminished tourist trade. Unwilling to prohibit logging outright, legislators in 1885 approved the creation of a Forest Preserve comprised of numerous noncontiguous, wooded tracts closed to development. In response, loggers simply moved and continued cutting outside the public domain, exacerbating the risks the preserve was designed to contain. To help resolve this dilemma, the legislature in 1892 drew a boundary around the disconnected Forest Preserve tracts, simultaneously encompassing both private and public lands, and created the Adirondack Park. Officials' long-term plan was to forge—through state purchase of cutover tracts—a single, contiguous preserve bordered by the privately owned lands of residents, visitors, and businessmen. In the meantime, both to protect the Forest Preserve from loggers and to satisfy visitors' demands for outdoor recreation, voters in 1894 enshrined its "forever wild" status in the state constitution, safeguarding those areas from the whims of future politicians. For decades to come, New York expanded its Forest Preserve one parcel at a time, slowly restoring the region's scenic beauty, solidifying its status as a tourist destination, and, by limiting the use of previously unregulated resources, guaranteeing continued conflict between residents and tourists.[59]

Men imprisoned in Dannemora, meanwhile, were likely unaware that their prison, along with the new infrastructure surrounding it, were now situated within the nation's largest state park. When visitors and elected leaders began advocating for conservation in the Adirondacks, however, protecting a place like Dannemora was not a high priority. Though the aesthetic qualities of central Clinton County must have been breathtaking before 1845, decades of penal developments had yielded a thoroughly modernized and unsafe environment unattractive to most tourists. Nevertheless, Clinton Prison's proximity to several forested tracts as well as its own vast public domain guaranteed Dannemora's inclusion, penitentiary and all, inside the new state park.

Its new status as a park community did little to alter the village's character as a prison town. This was true both in the decades immediately before and after the park's creation. Shortly after the Civil War, the state correctional system ended its half-century-old prison-industrial contract labor system. Not long thereafter, Clinton's iron mining business—its raison d'être—collapsed in the depression of the 1870s. As New York redirected its imprisoned laborers away from profits and toward public service, incarcerated men spent their days tending animals and crops on the prison farm, operating machines in its textile factories, and serving as cooks, custodians, and in a variety of other low-paid occupations inside the penitentiary. This shift in governance did not herald the establishment of a more humane regime. Instead, harsh discipline and surveillance increased as the prison population grew. In 1887, more durable stone walls and guard towers—six stories high—replaced the facility's old, unreliable wooden stockade. Five years later, Dannemora became home to New York's death row, and intermittent blackouts induced by high-voltage electrocutions soon became a regular feature of village life. By the turn of the twentieth century, massive new stone-and-brick facilities to confine incarcerated men diagnosed with psychiatric ailments and tuberculosis grew alongside the original penitentiary, further cementing Dannemora's status as a prison town.[60]

Outside Dannemora, tourism and recreation became the lifeblood of the North Country economy by the beginning of the twentieth century. Before World War II, the prohibitive expense of an Adirondack vacation helped the region remain an exclusive, elite enclave. By midcentury, however, higher incomes, increased leisure time, and improved transportation aided in democratizing tourism in the North Country. Middle-class families driving north found new motels, restaurants, shopping centers, amusement parks, and second homes to meet their every need. While many permanent residents found jobs in the expanded tourism sector, the area's wealthy old guard—disdainful of their new middle-class counterparts and the commercial developments their visits helped generate—organized to protect the region from the very people on whose spending the local economy had grown to depend.[61]

In short order, lawmakers in the late 1960s and early 1970s found themselves attempting to balance the interests of low-income year-round residents, middle-class tourists, rich second homeowners, and businessmen against the imperative to safeguard the aesthetic qualities that originally drew visitors. Though protected from commercial development, recreational access to the Forest Preserve had generated mountains of trash and destroyed vegetation, soil, and other precious resources. Unregulated building on private property led to the erection of structures that many deemed inconsistent with the Adirondacks' wilderness character. To resolve these dilemmas, the legislature created a new body—the Adirondack Park Agency (APA)—that was empowered to regulate building on private and public properties inside the park. The APA sharpened divisions between well-off visitors who generally approved of its measures, and poorer year-round homeowners for whom the agency seemed to represent yet another intervention at their expense on behalf of the rich. In Dannemora, where inclusion in the park had always been little more than a legal technicality, the creation of the Park Agency heralded a new era for property owners previously unburdened by the whims of tourists.[62]

||||||||

As the prison population at Clinton—renamed Clinton Correctional Facility in 1970—grew in the early 1970s, an overcrowding crisis in New York not dissimilar to those of the nineteenth century required alternative sites to house a growing population of convicted men. With even the massive complex at Dannemora unable to satisfy demand, correctional planners seeking cheap and accessible cell space looked to Adirondack towns and villages that, unlike in 1845, were established communities where residents and "outsiders" had long clashed over uses and meanings of nature. With the newly constituted APA added to the mix, the stage was set for a conflict among prison leaders selling economic growth, year-round homeowners seeking stable employment, and tourists and seasonal residents defending an environment threatened with a new and potentially pernicious form of development. In addition to furnishing fresh fuel for long-simmering local disputes, the opening of new prisons across the Adirondacks in the last quarter of the twentieth century also disrupted the very social and political divisions that had come to define life in the region since the Civil War. As the prison system reappeared at the North Country's doorstep in the mid-1970s, all eyes turned—with either hope or despair—to the Adirondack community defined exclusively by its penitentiary: Dannemora.

CHAPTER TWO

"ATTICA OF THE ADIRONDACKS"

Environmental Politics and Mass Incarceration in Ray Brook

Introduction

A bus bound for the Essex County hamlet of Ray Brook pulled out of New York City early one morning in August 1978. Its passengers, activists affiliated with Stop the Olympic Prison (STOP), a recently formed anti-prison group, crossed the same terrain traversed by generations of convicted men moving to and from the penitentiary in Dannemora. Renowned for its once-bustling but now-shuttered medical center—the New York State Hospital for the Treatment of Incipient Pulmonary Tuberculosis—Ray Brook had witnessed a frenzy of prison building in the previous two years. STOP members arrived to survey what would soon become the enclave's second penitentiary, and the third in the Adirondacks since 1845. One visitor described the partially completed cellblocks as "depressing," noting they were "tiny concrete cubicles" with "limited natural light flowing in" whereas "outside, a glance in any direction reveals the beauty of the Adirondack mountains and reminds you of the acres of trees felled and land leveled to build this monstrosity."[1]

While STOP's visit highlighted shifting public attitudes toward incarceration and environmental protection, the story of Ray Brook's state and federal prisons illustrates the striking resilience of New York's nineteenth-century approach to crime and punishment. For government officials, the conditions necessary for correctional expansion in the 1970s closely mirrored those of the 1840s: spiraling convictions, insufficient cell space, and a stubbornly held belief in the power of increased capacity to solve overcrowding and to spur development in prison communities. However, correctional planners in the 1970s operated within environmental constraints unknown in the 1840s. Transforming unbuilt environments for penal expansion without restriction—as had happened at Clinton—would no longer be acceptable. Or would it?

The recession of the 1970s exacerbated the high costs of state-run residential institutions. Accordingly, officials in need of space eschewed new construction in favor of recycling surplus properties. Ray Brook's 540-acre, multi-structure hospital campus proved attractive to state and federal correctional planners contending with packed penitentiaries as well as to Olympic organizers in nearby Lake Placid who were struggling to accommodate participants in the 1980 Winter Olympics.[2] New York State's ultimate repurposing of the complex as a prison did not diminish interest in Ray Brook as a site for additional penal growth. After all, the housing dilemmas of the Lake Placid Olympic Organizing Committee (LPOOC) and federal Bureau of Prisons (BOP) had not been solved. Striking an accord shortly after the state prison opened, the LPOOC and BOP opted to build a new facility on 155 acres of undeveloped land that would serve first as Olympic housing and later as a federal prison. This federal seizure of the property would negate protections enshrined in decades' old state environmental rules and threaten prison-induced destruction on a scale unseen since the mid-nineteenth century. At the same time, more recent environmental regulations had permitted lawmakers to repurpose Ray Brook's hospital as a penitentiary with only minimal review. Laws designed to prevent degradation were thus no match for the growing behemoth of incarceration.

With environmental regulators effectively sidelined, the public played an important oversight role in the planning, construction, and operation of Ray Brook's prisons. Unlike at Dannemora in the 1840s, correctional planners in the 1970s were not transforming an unbuilt wilderness. The Ray Brook area was home to thousands of year-round residents, second home-owners, and seasonal tourists for whom social class and length of residency helped mediate relationships with nature: though visitors valued the area for leisure and recreation, decades of economic misfortune had left many permanent dwellers struggling to survive. The ecological and economic questions raised by the prisons' arrival set the stage for renewed warfare over the use and meaning of Adirondack nature. Further, Ray Brook's close proximity to Lake Placid guaranteed that Olympic projects would attract attention beyond the park, transforming what began as local conflicts into a global controversy.

Though both were byproducts of Olympic planning, Ray Brook's penitentiaries elicited divergent reactions from interested stakeholders. The facilities' environmental impacts played a particularly decisive role in shaping public opinion. As a familiar community fixture, the medical center's conversion from hospital to narcotics rehabilitation center to minimum-security prison, all within the space of five years, attracted little more than a shrug from most local homeowners. Across the road, construction of the Olympic Village—planned without local input, built without environmental oversight, tainted by its future as a penitentiary, and harmful to environmental and public health—generated a chorus of criticism whose echoes traveled around the world. Remarkably, views forged in the 1970s only hardened after Ray Brook became a two-prison town in 1980. While many residents remained untroubled by the apparently eco-friendly state penitentiary in their midst, its ecologically destructive federal neighbor would always be an unwelcome intruder.

Prisons Come to Ray Brook

The economic slump of the 1970s pushed Ray Brook away from its health care roots and toward a correctional future. Across the country, rising rates of unlawful activity and public clamor for imprisonment spurred heightened demand for increasingly unaffordable cell space. In the North Country, elected leaders and Olympic organizers hoped the Winter Games might jumpstart a struggling local economy. The contemporaneous space dilemmas of cash-strapped correctional planners and Olympic organizers converged at Ray Brook, home to a mothballed complex that each side viewed as a cheap and simple remedy to their respective housing needs. Under different circumstances, the old hospital's rapid, state-directed penal conversion might have driven rival bureaucracies to seek space elsewhere. Instead, the economic downturn that had attracted BOP and LPOOC leaders to Ray Brook in the first place provided convenient cover for building a new, dual-purpose campus designed to accommodate both Olympic athletes and convicted men.

Ray Brook had flourished as a center for tuberculosis treatment and research since the hospital's opening in 1904.[3] Decreasing demand for tubercular isolation due to the development of antibiotics drove steady declines in patient populations and scientific work, leading to the facility's closure in 1971. The complex quickly reopened later that year as a state rehabilitation center for women addicted to narcotics. Nevertheless, the declining fortunes of one of the Adirondacks' legacy industries—institutional health care—struck a hard blow in the depressed region.[4] As young people fled Essex County in search of better jobs, residents unable to move contended with the low pay and irregular employment of the tourist trade. While the 1970 census recorded a 2 percent drop in the county's population, of those left behind, 9 percent survived on less than $3,000 per year; in Lake Placid, over 8 percent of families lived in poverty; and, in 1973, the year before Lake Placid won its Olympic bid, county unemployment stood at 17 percent, among the highest in the state.[5] Olympic organizers hoped that public investments in the Winter Games—along with the glare of the international spotlight—might reverse these ominous trends.

Equally susceptible to the pressures of recession, Congress, the primary funder of Lake Placid's Olympics, required new facilities to have a viable, post-1980 after-use.[6] Olympic organizers struggled to find housing for approximately two thousand Olympic participants in an isolated community of only three thousand year-round residents while complying with Congress's mandate. To make matters worse, International Olympic Committee (IOC) rules required host cities to accommodate all participants in a single location. After considering several proposals, including lodging athletes at a community college, in 1975 the LPOOC settled on a plan whose components fulfilled its various mandates and acknowledged pressing state needs: Olympic organizers raised the possibility of housing Olympians in Ray Brook's underused narcotics rehabilitation center. Recognizing New York's growing need for prison cells, the LPOOC proposed the facility reopen as a state penitentiary after the Winter Games.[7]

In the mid-1970s, state leaders in Albany struggled to manage overcrowded penitentiaries and underutilized medical institutions with dwindling resources. At its peak, the Ray Brook narcotics rehabilitation center treated 150 women and employed 200 workers. However, passage of the Rockefeller drug laws and Second Felony Offender Act in 1973 meant that growing numbers of individuals convicted of narcotics-related offenses found themselves confined inside penitentiaries instead of treatment facilities. Consequently, Ray Brook's patient population took a nosedive. By September 1975, the facility held only sixty patients and provided work to 135 locals. To make matters worse, state investigators uncovered a facility riven by allegations of abusive staff, alcohol consumption, and illicit sexual relations. Amid a swelling budget deficit and with a dire need for new cells, Democratic Governor Hugh Carey closed the troubled Ray Brook center in December 1975 and proposed its conversion to a penitentiary.[8] In Washington, D.C., fear that Olympic organizers might lose the complex to New York State prompted Congress to appropriate $16 million to fund the LPOOC's housing plan. Governor Carey, equally desperate not to lose the facility to Olympic organizers, unilaterally converted the state-owned compound to a minimum-security prison in August 1976.[9] With time running short, the LPOOC was back at square one.

In its seventy-third year, the Ray Brook complex embarked on its third phase of life as a state-run residential institution. The average age of the new prison's first 148 incarcerated men was twenty-five, and all satisfied the criteria of low security risk and within two years of release for minimum-security classification. The men arrived in Ray Brook from the maximum-security Clinton Correctional Facility in Dannemora, home to a minimum-security annex whose incarcerated men resided in a camp-style facility and partici-pated in a labor program jointly operated by the state Departments of Correctional Services (DOCS) and Environmental Conservation (DEC). Incarcerated workers earned as little as $1.00 per day to labor on conservation and public works projects, including fire and flood control, trail and campsite maintenance, forest management, and soil conservation. Overcrowding at Clinton prompted Governor Carey to close the annex—known as Camp Adirondack—and relocate its operations and name to Ray Brook. Residents once anxious over the former hospital's future greeted the prospect of one hundred well-paying state jobs at the new Camp Adirondack. Local politi-cians contending with dwindling tax revenues welcomed continuing employ-ment in the facility and the free use of prison labor crews by area communities. In addition to saving towns and villages much-needed cash, men imprisoned in Ray Brook would complete projects vital to facilitating tourism and out-door recreation, fusing one of the region's oldest industries with one of its newest. As a peace offering, DOCS offered the LPOOC use of its incarcer-ated workers on Olympic projects and floated the possibility of lodging Olympians inside the new penitentiary during the Winter Games.[10]

The first new correctional facility in the Adirondacks since 1845 welcomed its inaugural cohort of incarcerated men in September 1976. Reviving the nineteenth-century practice of imprisoned men building their own penitentiaries, men incarcerated in Ray Brook renovated the former hospital for penal use. The editors of the Saranac Lake–based *Adirondack Daily Enterprise* trumpeted both the correctional facility and the overcrowding crisis that had made Ray Brook's turn in the correctional spotlight possible:

> The prison population in New York State is rising by leaps and bounds . . . Therefore, it is logical to assume that with the passage of time Camp Adirondack could grow to a size where the local employment will be . . . higher than it was when the drug rehabilitation center was here. Aside from the new employment for the area . . . the community itself may be able to make use of the residents at the camp for some needed community projects—at great savings to the taxpayers. So far the acceptance of Camp Adirondack by the overwhelming majority of the people in the area, and their elected representatives, has been most encouraging.

Several incarcerated men offered their own glowing assessments, calling the area "beautiful," describing the penitentiary as "far superior" to other state facilities, and declaring Ray Brook would be "as pleasant a spot as any to spend" one's last months behind bars.[11] Though disappointing for the LPOOC, the smooth opening of Camp Adirondack—and the overcrowding at its root—convinced Olympic authorities that Ray Brook might still solve their housing dilemma.

The LPOOC's pursuit of Olympic housing paralleled the BOP's equally fruitless quest for new cell space. In the early 1970s, residents of the New York City and Philadelphia suburbs concerned about public safety and property values had hobbled bureau efforts to build federal prisons in their communities. Hoping to settle problems vexing both the BOP and LPOOC, in June 1976 local Republican Congressman Robert McEwen met with BOP Director Norman Carlson and proposed using the shuttered Ray Brook center first as Olympic housing and later as a federal penitentiary. Addressing possible environmental impacts, McEwen promised a modern penitentiary without "high walls like Dannemora" that would blend seamlessly with the landscape and create two hundred well-paying jobs.[12] Though the subsequent opening of Camp Adirondack shattered

McEwen's plan, area residents' apparent acceptance of the new state prison amplified BOP and LPOOC interest in Ray Brook. With McEwen serving as broker, the BOP and LPOOC in November 1976 announced construction of a new, multi-structure complex in Ray Brook that would first house Olympic athletes and later incarcerate five hundred federal medium-security convicted men. Bureau planners promised a facility with deep foundations, extra insulation, roofs designed to hold heavy snow, and enclosed walkways between buildings to withstand the rigors of North Country winters.[13] With the federal prison system operating at 118 percent of capacity, Congress approved the plan in February 1977. McEwen heralded both of Ray Brook's penitentiaries as the first step toward what he envisioned as "the establishment of a new industry in the region."[14]

The local elected officials, former athletes, business leaders, and clergy who comprised the LPOOC never anticipated becoming prison builders. However, the factors that drove Olympic organizers to Ray Brook—a quiet, sparsely populated community home to an empty residential institution that could be easily and cheaply converted—were equally attractive to state and federal correctional planners. Though the creation of Ray Brook's prisons reflected the resilience of penal theories that had driven the construction of Clinton over a century earlier, the idea of introducing penitentiaries to Ray Brook originated neither with lawmakers nor correctional bureaucrats. By proposing the Olympic Village-turned-prison scheme, the LPOOC—like the scientists participating in New York's Natural History Survey in the 1830s—was first to foresee silver linings in the growing cloud of mass incarceration. Strong interest from state and federal prison planners thus quickly transformed the organizers' original goal of using the Winter Olympics to stimulate increased tourism. With two new correctional facilities on the horizon, the 1980 Olympics would revitalize one of the Adirondacks' legacy industries while simultaneously breathing life into its newest. Unfortunately, such intense interest in Ray Brook blinded organizers to the hazards of building on undeveloped land inside the Adirondack Park. The resulting harm to environmental and public health might threaten the very tourist trade the Olympics were intended to promote.

Building Ray Brook's Federal Prison

Pre-existing land use patterns played a central role in shaping public responses to Ray Brook's prisons. Whether it was people diagnosed with tuberculosis, women contending with addiction, or convicted men who occupied the state facility mattered little to nearby residents long accustomed to its sprawling, woodsy campus. Across the road, meanwhile, Olympic and BOP planners' rush to transform an undeveloped tract of forestland, along with a laser-like focus on the facility's predicted economic impacts, blinded them to the bonds linking homeowners and visitors to that environment. The parcel that was targeted for construction had for decades sheltered, nourished, and rejuvenated plants, animals, and humans alike. The complexity of the environment mirrored residents' equally intricate understanding of the interdependence of bodily and environmental health. By damaging the local environment, the construction of Ray Brook's second prison unwittingly validated locals' environmental logic and alienated individuals whose support was needed to ensure the project's success.

Though Ray Brook's prisons fell within New York's public domain, each facility would leave distinct ecological footprints. At the site of the former hospital, environmental manipulations and construction undertaken decades earlier had yielded a large complex whose use was subject only to the whims of Albany politicians. Tuberculosis hospital, narcotics rehabilitation center, minimum-security prison—state ownership meant state control. As an added bonus, the Adirondack Park Agency could exercise only non-binding advisory review over state projects planned for public lands inside the park. Under Section 814 of the APA Act, the Park Agency could analyze a project's potential impacts on the park's natural, scenic, aesthetic, or historic features. Permitted to accept or reject the agency's findings, the state could repurpose existing state-owned facilities located in fragile ecosystems almost without restriction.[15] As a residential facility requiring only minimal renovations for its penal conversion, Camp Adirondack had avoided even the least burdensome forms of state environmental oversight, though as it was a property defined almost entirely by its human-built structures, even the binding APA review process reserved for private developments might have proven only a minor inconvenience. For politicians committed to advancing both environmental protection and incarceration, Camp Adirondack seemed perfect.

The development of the new facility was quite different. Questions surrounding the legal and environmental implications of building a federal prison inside the state-managed Adirondack Park became planners' first major headache. Inexplicably, the original idea of using the former hospital first for Olympic housing and later as a penitentiary reappeared even after the BOP and LPOOC's housing dilemmas had been resolved. The allure of the old complex, it seemed, was simply irresistible. APA memoranda from late 1976 and early 1977 highlighted apparent BOP plans to remove unused structures at Camp Adirondack and redevelop the cleared property as a federal prison. One memorandum even suggested the entire federal facility would be built on the grounds of Camp Adirondack, jeopardizing state control while leaving the tract across the road untouched. The fog finally lifted in late January 1977 when state, federal, and Olympic officials confirmed the unoccupied parcel south of Camp Adirondack as the site of the new complex.[16]

Clarifying the penitentiary's location shed no light on the property's legal classification. The systematic categorization of lands in the Adirondacks, first undertaken with the creation of the Forest Preserve in the 1880s, intensified as the region's popularity grew in the late nineteenth and twentieth centuries. By the mid-1970s, the Adirondack Park was a patchwork of private and publicly owned properties that was subject—depending on the tract—to either DEC or APA regulation. When plans to build a federal prison in Ray Brook became public, the targeted parcel's legal classification required clarification. In early 1977 the DEC, the state agency responsible for managing public lands inside the park, claimed not to know whether the tract was Forest Preserve, and thus protected as "forever wild." APA maps, in contrast, showed the property labeled as private, which opened the possibility of future developments to stringent Park Agency oversight. Recognizing the BOP's intent to build, the APA recategorized the site as public land, eliminating the possibility of legally binding Park Agency review though opening the door to DEC oversight. To scuttle potential DEC review, the APA suggested the bureau acquire the property from its new state owners through eminent domain. The gears of New York's environmental bureaucracy hit a snag, however, when in May 1977, the federal government condemned 155 acres of land—for $1.00—at Camp Adirondack. Though lawyers promptly corrected the error, the significance of this reclassification process cannot be understated.[17] Only six years since its creation, the Park Agency remained unpopular among many permanent residents convinced its oversight served only the interests of the wealthy. The redrawing of Ray Brook's maps, however, showed the agency promoting development at the potential expense of environmental protection.

The parcel's transfer from private to state to federal ownership removed any possibility of New York oversight on the project. APA power that might have compelled legally binding review now was limited to mitigating potential damage through non-binding recommendations. Moreover, the reclassification drama underscored the Park Agency's complex bureaucratic structure. Contrary to much popular opinion, the agency was neither a monolithic entity nor an environmental organization disguised as a government bureaucracy. In addition to its political wing—a board of commissioners appointed by the governor—the APA also employed a staff of non-partisan, professional scientists. The two sides did not always work in tandem. In a comprehensive site analysis published in early 1977, agency scientists showed that far from being untouched wilderness primed for modernization, the reclassified site was a prized piece of the fabric of local life. The report noted that residents and tourists made frequent use of the tract, enjoying its picnic grounds and athletic fields; accessing trails to popular hiking and climbing spots; hunting game in the fall; watching for rare birds; camping under the stars; casting lines in its ponds and streams; and skiing across its powder during the winter. Camp Adirondack had even built a sanitary landfill on the property where incarcerated men helped manage the penitentiary's solid waste.[18]

APA scientists also revealed an energetic non-human environment at the future prison site. A forest of evergreen and deciduous trees, planted a century earlier, towered over its stream, pond, lake, and wetlands, whose fish were maintained through DEC stocking. Marshlands also provided refuge for the indigenous ring-necked duck and endangered osprey. Carefully maintained vegetation at the waters' edge supplied shade for aquatic organisms, stabilized the banks for use by fishing enthusiasts, and provided forage for wildlife. By storing excess water, wetlands on the property protected residents and visitors from springtime floods.[19] These and other seemingly pristine features masked the deeply entwined human and non-human habitats the property supported. This outward display of untouched nature, it seemed, had opened the door to BOP and LPOOC planners who saw the site as undeveloped real estate.

Though concerned about the potential environmental impacts, APA scientists did not call for the project's cancellation. Instead, they offered a non-binding construction plan designed to ensure the site's ecological and economic vitality. Concerned that excess rainfall might wash excavated soil and wood chips into nearby waterways, the scientists recommended building on the site's flat athletic fields and picnic grounds. The report also emphasized preserving existing vegetation. First, the agency highlighted the vital role of plant life in providing water storage, guarding against soil erosion, and preventing pollution. Second, mindful that a prison might not blend seamlessly with the local landscape, the agency noted that retaining trees and other plants would aid in maintaining aesthetic features prized by residents and visitors. Fearing the penitentiary might "be visible from several nearby peaks . . . and from the Ray Brook Road," APA scientists suggested BOP planners look to the wooded grounds of Camp Adirondack, which "operated without clearcutting around the buildings" as a model. Finally, the report underlined the necessity of vegetative screening along the perimeter as a hedge against the devaluation of nearby homes.[20] With the tract under federal control, however, review of the project's potential environmental impact began and ended with this report.

Besides the Park Agency scientists, few in positions of authority seemed interested in safeguarding Ray Brook's environment. In March 1977, LPOOC, APA, and BOP leaders met in Washington, D.C., to discuss the scientists' recommendations. Bureau officials estimated excavating and filling one million cubic acres of earth and cutting seventy-five acres of forest to satisfy regulations that required building federal prisons on flat, unobstructed terrain. The BOP argued that preserving the existing environment—a step agency scientists had never recommended—would both hinder incarceration and imperil public safety. One bureau leader commented, "You can't have any hills and valleys that might provide refuge for a prisoner. You can have little vegetation in the area. Those are the things you have to live with if you want to build a prison." Accordingly, BOP officials simply ignored the Park Agency recommendations. Local North Country politicians interpreted the APA report through the lens of anti-environmental politics. By 1977, winning elections in the Adirondacks required an ironclad opposition to a nonexistent, monolithic APA. As such, local officials could not acknowledge the agency's instrumental role in advancing the project. Such environmental heresy would bring certain electoral defeat. A seasoned politician such as Congressman McEwen surely understood the intricacies of APA governance, but he also knew what he needed to say to keep his job, thus, he falsely branded the Park Agency as a force "in this area . . . against job opportunities and the expansion of the economy," even though APA employees had worked to achieve the total opposite.[21] In a political environment where facts seemed increasingly unimportant, the fictional APA villain would live to see another election cycle.

While possible ecological degradation mattered little to project supporters, these same individuals were less sanguine about the facility's penal future. Public statements regarding the project often contained deliberate omissions, artfully worded descriptions, and outright lies that betrayed planners' discomfort with their plan to house Olympic athletes in a future penitentiary. In March 1977, McEwen declared the Ray Brook complex would "provide first class accommodations for the athletes in 1980," adding, "you'd never know it was a prison." For its part, the LPOOC misled the IOC about its housing plan, incorrectly claiming the new campus "would offer a permanent after-use as a state or federal facility," stating falsely that New York State had granted the land to Olympic organizers, vaguely reporting the buildings would be "turned over by the Organizing Committee to the Government of the United States for its long-term use," and avoiding any penal terminology in all cases.[22] Planners' deception revealed an implicit understanding of the perils associated with their plan as well as a sensitivity to the opinions of a public that thus far had been excluded from the planning process. LPOOC and BOP officials knew their scheme would attract condemnation that might spread worldwide. With groundbreaking scheduled for spring 1977, planners calculated that some mild fibbing could help them weather the inevitable political storm.

It did not take long for that storm to arrive. Journalists at the *Lake Placid News* were among the first to issue warnings about the potentially harmful impacts of penal expansion in the Adirondacks. While praising the federal penitentiary's potential to stimulate economic growth, the *News* criticized the exclusion of local input. Recognizing that the impacts of prison construction in Ray Brook extended beyond questions of employment or inclusive planning, the editorial waded into the racially charged politics of mass incarceration. By labeling New York City "a world of barely-chained violence," warning that penitentiaries would expose North Country residents to "state and national problems largely unfamiliar to Adirondackers," and that with the transportation of convicted men to Ray Brook, "no longer will distance and mountain winds silence the ghetto's scream," the *News* stoked the racial anxieties of a largely white park population unaccustomed to either diversity or unlawful activity.[23] Though unwelcome news to BOP and LPOOC planners anxious to control the project narrative, the editorial could not stop construction.

With little notice, deforestation and excavation work commenced in June 1977. Outraged residents criticized their exclusion from planning and fretted over decreased property values and possibly higher taxes in the future. However, their biggest source of anxiety sprang from environmental impacts. Nearby homeowners complained about elevated noise and artificial lighting at the construction site. Townspeople also assailed the removal of seventy-five acres of forest as "an environmental disaster" that "damaged the land" and "created a big scar." Further, with construction equipment barring access to the property, some residents asked plaintively, "How do you propose we get to our homes?" One homeowner even declared that while he was "not afraid of getting murdered in my bed by escaped prisoners," he was "upset by the impact of the prison itself on the surroundings," fearing "a trout will never be seen" in Ray Brook again. For its part, the *Lake Placid News* decried the "rape of the stripped and ravaged land" and, in questioning "why some things are worth protecting, and others aren't," asked, "why wasn't Jones Beach condemned?"[24] Planners must have been surprised to discover that many residents valued environmental protection more than economic development.

In a move that revealed the nearly limitless authority that came with federal ownership, BOP and LPOOC officials convened a public meeting only after construction began. For homeowners and visitors accustomed to the parcel in its original form, planners' promises to retain vegetation at the site and to install "a special type of lighting" to mitigate visual impacts proved insufficient. Assurances that property taxes would not increase, that construction noise would be temporary, and that the facility would resemble a "country club" and incarcerate nonviolent, "high class criminals," did nothing to alleviate concerns about environmental health.[25] It seemed that nothing short of the project's cancellation would satisfy residents. The nearly irresistible power of federal authority meant the BOP and LPOOC could safely ignore the public in whose name the prison was being built. One can only wonder how many opponents of the APA—an agency whose

FIGURE 4. Aerial view of early construction on the Olympic Village in Ray Brook, built for the 1980 Olympic Winter Games. Courtesy of the Lake Placid Olympic Museum.

environmental oversight included public input—had a change of heart once federal chainsaws and bulldozers began ripping Ray Brook apart.

Local rage only intensified once planners announced their proposal for collecting and treating prison waste. In August 1977, officials unveiled plans for a network of sewage "lagoons" adjacent to Ray Brook stream and close to a residential neighborhood. Homeowners expressed worries about potential air, water, and noise pollution, in addition to impacts on property values and scenery. Some Ray Brook residents even voiced fears about harmful effects on men incarcerated across the road at Camp Adirondack. With some locals threatening to move, exacerbating an ongoing exodus from the region, the *Lake Placid News* blasted prison planners' "lack of concern for Ray Brook's health and welfare," criticized officials who had tolerated its "legal rape," and praised homeowners for their "firm stand in opposing the siting of the 'fecal facility.'" Dozens of residents signed a petition outlining their commitment to environmental and public health, conditions they considered inextricably linked:

If on-site sewage disposal is used . . . there is potential for serious adverse impact upon values which we consider important citizens' rights—a healthy environment for our children and for ourselves; enjoyment of one's property without imposition of . . . nuisances such as foul odors, and visual degradation; and avoidance of new neighborhood development which causes serious property value reductions. Also . . . there is potential for significant negative impact of Prison on-site sewage disposal to Ray Brook stream, Oseetah Lake and Lake Flower. These are important outdoor recreational waterways which are heavily used for fishing and other water related activities . . . The piping of sewage to the Saranac Lake Village sewage treatment system . . . will largely avoid these stated negative impacts . . . To make a choice other than the Saranac Lake option is to disregard the health and welfare of Ray Brook citizens.[26]

Citizen activism prevailed, as officials in the nearby village of Saranac Lake offered to collect and treat federal prison sewage at their sanitary facility, already the recipient of sewage from Camp Adirondack, obviating the need for potentially damaging lagoons.[27]

Success in the sewage battle proved but a hollow victory for residents, whose exclusion from planning meant new and sometimes destructive surprises around every corner. Pressured to meet construction deadlines, contractors failed to secure the excavated soil and wood chips at the site; heavy rains in August 1977 unleashed four hundred tons of mud and construction debris into nearby waterways. Park Agency scientists reported that "drainage from the site began depositing substantial quantities of sediment in adjoining water bodies," just as their non-binding recommendations had predicted. Excessive sedimentation and siltation created new sandbars, befouled aquatic vegetation, and threatened wildlife populations. By September, homeowners noticed muddied waterways and discolored water coming out of their faucets, and faced restricted access to local swimming and fishing spots. APA scientists predicted the site would not recover for at least five years.[28]

For those unacquainted with the bureaucratic intricacies of building an Olympic Village destined to become a federal prison on federal land inside an inhabited state park, the disaster of 1977 provided some clarity. Nobody wanted to be responsible for the cleanup, because nobody knew who was responsible. Everyone involved, however, understood this was not 1845: threats to environmental and public health could not simply be ignored. The bureaucratic blame game began. The Economic Development Administration (EDA), responsible for managing and disbursing federal Olympic funds, accused contractors of ignoring directives to guard against runoff. The APA blamed the BOP for failing "to exercise precautions to prevent a serious environmental impact" and called on the United States Council on Environmental Quality to force the bureau to take "all possible measures . . . to restore the impacted resources." For its part, the BOP blamed the weather, arguing heavy rainfall alone had caused the destruction. Even the Environmental Protection Agency (EPA) disclaimed any responsibility, arguing the federal prison being built on federal land was not, in fact, a federal project. Instead, the EPA claimed it was the duty of the LPOOC—a state-chartered agency—to ensure eco-friendly construction practices. Blame aside, probable violations of New York water quality standards resulting from pollution of state waterways by federal debris prompted DEC litigation warnings to the BOP. Only when faced with EDA threats to withhold construction funding did the bureau agree to implement Park Agency recommendations to forestall further destruction. By November 1977, contractors had installed sediment basins, mulched loose dirt and wood chips, seeded recently cleared terrain, and placed jute mesh around the site. Even those measures proved insufficient, however, as heavy rains in October 1978 destroyed a thirty-five-foot embankment at the property, setting loose another 250 tons of mud into waterways only then beginning to recover. One APA official described the episodes, simply, as "the environmental tragedies of the Olympics."[29]

For two years, the actions of federal prison planners and their allies had repeatedly underscored the limitations built into existing environmental laws. At every turn, regulatory agencies and statutes charged with protecting the environment proved powerless to prevent its destruction. The lack of the "forever wild" status of Forest Preserve lands eliminated the possibility of DEC oversight. Federal condemnation had stripped the APA of its review powers, and the EPA denied responsibility for managing the project's ecological impacts. Its long-term use as a prison, its placement on federal land, and the fact that Justice Department appropriations—and not Olympic financing—funded its construction mattered little. For the EPA, the facility's first use as an Olympic Village provided sufficient cover to watch the destruction from the sidelines. Even after significant damage had occurred and New York State threatened to sue, prison planners pressed forward, brought to heel only by the specter of financial loss and a potentially unfinished complex. Complaints about the project that were so easily dismissed during its first year became difficult to ignore once local grievances morphed into an international controversy.

The "Olympic Prison": One Penitentiary, Two Oppositions

The Ray Brook complex elicited discomfort from nearly all quarters. While residents struggled with a transformed environment, even project supporters had trouble with the plans for the facility's long-term use. With construction underway, significant damage already done, and no indication that public input would figure in future planning, homeowners awaited the next disaster. In New York City, liberal activists anxious over Ray Brook's place in an expanding prison system sought to steal the Olympic spotlight and draw attention to their cause. Founded in March 1978, Stop the Olympic Prison (STOP) drew support from a variety of civil rights groups, including the American Civil Liberties Union, Fortune Society, National Association for the Advancement of Colored People, National Council of La Raza, and National Urban League, among others.[30] STOP launched a campaign highlighting the project's moral and environmental costs at a time when mass incarceration was in its infancy. Though successful in increasing awareness of a growing national crisis, STOP's inattention to local homeowners' more immediate, everyday concerns kept the opposition permanently separated.

STOP issued some of the earliest warnings about the perils of mass incarceration. The group assailed the Ray Brook facility as symptomatic of the nation's intensifying addiction to imprisonment. Politicians' persistent indifference to the social and economic inequalities that drove much lawbreaking—exacerbated by the recession of the 1970s—contributed to an acceleration in prison building that mirrored that of the early nineteenth century. As rates of unlawful activity increased—aggravated by a crackdown on narcotics possession—existing penitentiaries burst at the seams. STOP warned that by not addressing the problems underlying most unlawful activities, lawmakers' impulse to build new cells would feed an unsustainable cycle of overcrowding and prison construction. As such, Ray Brook's "Olympic Prison," a moniker coined by STOP, was a glaring example of the justice system's deep-rooted structural deficiencies.[31]

Supporters of STOP warned of the facility's potential to inflict political damage on the United States at home and abroad. The celebratory spirit of the Olympics, they worried, might be tarnished by the "grief, social failure and oppression" STOP members considered endemic to American prisons. STOP shamefully noted that once the athletes departed in February 1980, "their place will be taken by other young men brought there in chains and caged."[32] Deemed "a violation of human rights . . . by a land that proclaims them," the Olympic Prison was a challenge to the nation's self-proclaimed status as a bastion of liberty.[33] STOP members predicted an amplified geopolitical advantage for nations notorious for mass imprisonment, including the U.S.S.R. and South Africa. In particular, Soviet plans to convert athletes' housing to family apartments after the 1980 Summer Olympics in Moscow, STOP argued, only undermined the United States' tainted moral authority. Finally, project opponents stirred memories of the violent uprising at New York's Attica Correctional Facility in September 1971. Enraged by overcrowding, unsanitary quarters, racial discrimination, and inhumane treatment from the prison's white officer corps, Attica's predominantly African American and Latino incarcerated men had staged a revolt that killed dozens. STOP invoked Attica as a cautionary tale, warning that the federal penitentiary in Ray Brook might someday achieve notoriety as the "Attica of the Adirondacks."[34]

The facility's potential to aggravate class and racial tensions was a source of deep concern for STOP. The group viewed the 1980 Winter Olympics as akin to an affirmative action program for white Americans: wealthy elites enjoying winter sports; working-class men building the athletic facilities; and unemployed residents seeking prison jobs. The price of this white-uplift scheme extended beyond congressional appropriations and environmental impacts. From 1970 to 1977, the BOP had built eighteen prisons to incarcerate 6,000 convicted men. During that same time period, the number of African American and Latino men confined in the federal system grew by 6,700. Of the 600 medium-security convicted men in federal custody from New York—mainly African American and Latino—95 percent hailed from New York City. The Ray Brook prison's long-term viability thus depended on an unrelenting churn of men of color into federal confinement. Black and Brown New Yorkers would help pay for Lake Placid's Olympics with imprisonment, isolation, family separation, and income loss, among other burdens. STOP members also fretted over the potentially deadly dynamics of "poor, non-white, inner city, unemployed youthful males" being guarded by "rural white mountain folks in search of 'recession proof'" jobs in a region where whites comprised 99 percent of the population.[35] As pawns in a penal economic development scheme, poor New Yorkers—regardless of race or locality—might someday find themselves trapped in a cauldron of racial violence.

As the *Lake Placid News* had underscored only months earlier, these were problems most North Country residents knew only from news reports. Recognizing the region's increasing dependence on prison employment, STOP focused its appeal to locals on environmental issues. Project critics noted the facility's remote locale violated BOP standards mandating new prisons be built near convicted men's hometowns. Exile in the Adirondacks would thus undermine access to health care and educational, employment, and familial resources the bureau deemed essential to the well-being of incarcerated men. Accordingly, STOP urged the penitentiary's relocation to an urban setting to uphold BOP directives and to minimize recidivism.[36] However, by pushing bureau enforcement of its own policy, STOP unwittingly undermined its stated opposition to incarceration and missed a chance to attract the support of area residents who were either unconcerned with the facility's long-term use or whose economic fortunes were tied to its construction.

Undeterred in its campaign to garner local support, STOP seized on the Adirondack Park's history as an enclave protected for the "recreational and conservationist uses of all New Yorkers." Suddenly seeing virtue in the region's remoteness, opponents criticized the prison plan as "an affront to public intent" and intoned the area's "beautiful environment," its "big woods," and "clear lakes" as suitable only for recreation. Branding the institution as "alien to Lake Placid's traditions of recreation, health, and family fun," STOP warned of the penitentiary's potential to damage the tourist trade.[37] The group's focus on the park as only a site of leisure and recreation ignored the region's reality as a home, workplace, and site of incarceration. Further, STOP's rosy view of Adirondack tourism overlooked that industry's historically low pay and irregular hours, factors that contributed to unemployment, poverty, and depopulation. By labeling prisons as incompatible with the park, STOP both denied history and reinforced the privileges of the same whites earlier condemned as unworthy beneficiaries of Olympic largesse. Finally, the group's concentration only on how visitors valued and used the Adirondacks discouraged most Ray Brook residents from joining STOP's crusade.

These setbacks did not end STOP's efforts to unite the opposition. Addressing environmental and health impacts, STOP called the project antithetical to Ray Brook's history of promoting wellness. Again highlighting flawed notions of the Adirondacks as an unpeopled wilderness, critics lamented that "an environment of James Fenimore Cooper" had been replaced by "a modern *1984* facility, with all its symbolism." Instead of underscoring how environmental laws had permitted this destructive change, STOP focused instead on the buildings' tiny rooms and narrow windows, fearing that restricted cell space, in concert with the area's "long and cold winters," would create "embittered and more dangerous young people coming out of there." Supporters of STOP also dismissed time-worn beliefs in the supposedly healthful qualities of Adirondack nature, claiming, "Pure cold air and pine trees may cure tuberculosis, but not crime, else there would be no crime in the North Country." Unexpectedly, both STOP and the LPOOC expressed disgust with the facility's design. Olympic organizers feared its concrete-and-steel construction would create a "concentration camp atmosphere for some people from European countries." International sports executives condemned plans to lodge four athletes apiece in rooms designed to house only one incarcerated man. Cramped quarters, they feared, would inhibit rest and promote the spread of infectious disease.[38] While few disagreed about the facility's inherent unhealthfulness, STOP once again missed an opportunity to draw disaffected residents into the opposition.

Unable to prevent construction, STOP proposed a remedy it hoped might legitimize the facility's placement in the Adirondacks. STOP called for converting the complex to an Olympic training center whose emphasis on recreation closely matched prison opponents' understanding of the proper use of Adirondack nature.[39] This proposal only widened the chasm separating local residents from their putative STOP allies. Ray Brook homeowners shared few of STOP's concerns. Living near Camp Adirondack had not caused the harm that STOP had predicted the federal prison might inflict. Putting the facility to a non-carceral purpose, therefore, was of little concern to homeowners adjusted to having a prison next door. For residents, the complex whose construction had damaged their environment and threatened their health might never be welcome, no matter its use.

Nevertheless, STOP members continued their efforts to raise awareness of the trend toward mass incarceration. Scattered interviews, letters to the editor, and news stories eventually became an organized social justice machine. Throughout 1978, STOP spread its message through the distribution of anti-prison newsletters, brochures, fliers, letters, posters, and bumper stickers. They confronted Olympic organizers during a summer visit to Lake Placid; participated in courtroom battles with the United States Olympic Committee (USOC) over the use of Olympic symbols in STOP advertising; used speeches, publications, and news media appearances to stir doubts among bureaucrats, politicians, and local residents; and staged a December demonstration in Washington, D.C., to highlight Ray Brook's position in the expanding carceral state. Swift action in year one inspired STOP to keep fighting as Olympic planning entered its final months.[40]

With the Olympics one year away, efforts to derail the prison accelerated in 1979. At the local level, STOP's work triggered a minor schism among Christian denominational leaders, clerics, and congregations across the North Country. Though the project's potential economic impacts drew the support of the Roman Catholic Diocese of Ogdensburg and its bishop, Stanislaus Brzana, several individual Catholic parishes and most local religious organizations signed on to STOP's crusade. Lawmakers in Albany, meanwhile, threatened to make state Olympic funding contingent on abolishing the prison plan, and in Washington, D.C., countless phone calls, telegrams, and letters persuaded the House of Representatives to convene two days of hearings on the facility in March 1979. One month later, congressional Democrats mounted three failed attempts to scrap the plan, and in May, STOP held another rally in the nation's capital. Though STOP leaders made little headway at an October meeting with President Jimmy Carter's domestic policy advisers, they warned the White House of potentially disruptive protests in Lake Placid during the Olympics if their demands were not met. Capping an eventful year, in November 1979 local St. Regis Mohawk elders, citing eighteenth-century treaties, pressed their own legal claims to the prison site in Ray Brook.[41]

The effectiveness of STOP's campaign varied. Though stories on STOP and the Olympic Prison appeared regularly in news outlets both at home and abroad, it is difficult to assess reactions outside the core of self-identified stakeholders connected to the project. Only an organization with committed members and healthy finances could sustain such efforts as those STOP made. The full extent of STOP's appeal and its success in raising awareness

FIGURE 5. STOP bumper sticker. Courtesy of the Stop the Olympic Prison Collection, MSS-54, St. Lawrence University Libraries, Canton, New York.

about mass incarceration outside New York is hard to gauge. In the North Country, while STOP's social justice-oriented positions resonated with some in the religious community, its environmental arguments, relying on nineteenth-century conceptions of the Adirondacks as an unpeopled wilderness, fell largely on deaf ears. Though many visitors, second homeowners, and permanent residents likely appreciated STOP's defenses of tourism and recreation, the failure to understand Ray Brook as a home, workplace, and site of incarceration prevented collaboration with residents impacted by the prison's construction. While STOP might not have succeeded in building a groundswell of popular opposition, the group's persistence did force correctional planners and their supporters back on their heels.

Stopping STOP and Opening the FCI

From 1976 to 1978, the planners of Ray Brook's second prison operated largely without restriction. With environmental regulators sidelined, the project's most significant barrier was the public itself. Though residents had scored a victory in their battle against the sewage lagoons, the destruction unleashed in 1977 and 1978 underscored that planners had near absolute control over the project. The juggernaut of STOP's public relations machine, however, proved impossible to ignore. Sustained attacks on the project forced ordinarily imperious planners onto the defensive. Remarkably, counterarguments offered by prison supporters contained many of the same inconsistencies and misleading interpretations of local history as those advanced by members of STOP. In the end, those rebuttals did not matter. The real power in this battle had always rested in planners' hands. As February 1980 approached, project boosters were left with only two important tasks: deflect bad publicity and run down the clock until the facility's conversion to a federal prison.

As the controversy surrounding the Olympic Prison exploded, local residents attracted to its potential economic impacts jumped to the project's defense. Echoing words written over a century earlier about Clinton State Prison, supporters claimed men incarcerated in Ray Brook would benefit from the "purity of the air" and "meditative quality of the surrounding mountains." Cities, they argued, had "spawned the crimes" that made prisons necessary. If the Adirondacks were "good enough for tourists," then surely "the unfortunate souls who are society's transgressors" would also benefit. Incarceration in a non-urban environment, advocates claimed, would more than make up for the potentially harmful impacts of geographic and social isolation predicted by STOP. Reinforcing this decades-old belief in the inherently healthful qualities of Adirondack nature, Ronald MacKenzie, the first president of the LPOOC and a lifelong resident, confidently declared, "If I were a prisoner, I couldn't think of a better place to serve out my time than in the Adirondacks."[42] Missing from this argument, of course, was the fact that most of Ray Brook's federal convicted men would spend the majority of their time indoors, restricting their experience of Adirondack nature to occasional glimpses out their narrow cell windows.

Though many planners and boosters were unimpressed with the facility's design, most viewed the complex as appropriate both for the Adirondack environment and its long-term penal use. Defenders described the squat buildings as "attractive" and "modern," comparing the facility's layout to a campus that "would not be turned down by any university in this country." Indoors, planners promised brightly painted walls that, they argued, would promote rehabilitation, while outside, modern security features would perform double duty. During the Olympics, electrified fencing and razor wire would "keep potential terrorists out" and prevent the sort of violence that shattered the 1972 Summer Olympics in Munich. Once converted to a penitentiary, that same fencing would help "keep juvenile offenders in," thereby reducing the risk of escapes and harm to nearby homeowners. If incarcerated men at Ray Brook were confined behind razor wire on the flattened, deforested penitentiary grounds, how would they benefit from the supposedly healthful qualities found in Adirondack nature? Project advocates did not answer this question.[43]

Supporters also viewed the prison as an exclusively local concern whose broader implications did not matter. Even as Congress appropriated tens of millions of federal dollars to fund the project, advocates deployed rhetoric aimed at locally popular notions of home rule, exclaiming, "Government has done too little for Northern New York." Echoing the grievances of generations of permanent residents, boosters assailed STOP as but the latest in a long line of meddling outsiders bent on harming the Adirondack economy. Arguing that "people who live elsewhere, and barely ever heard of us" should not make "decisions about our future," project defenders urged spite as a sufficient cause for year-round homeowners to support the prison. Appealing to residents' sense of history, advocates labeled the facility a normal development for a region experienced in operating large residential institutions. If local control, spite, and tradition were not enough, boosters could always highlight the 230 well-paying jobs that, they argued, would help create a "new permanent industry" and spur economic recovery.[44] Once again, project advocates' inconsistencies mirrored those of their opponents. Without decades of government intervention and decisions made by outsiders, there would never have been state-run institutions, a tourist industry, or two Olympic Games in the Adirondacks. Though few were unaware of this paradox, almost no one in the conservative region was willing to accept it.

Project advocates were also silent on the problem of mass incarceration. Unable or unwilling to rebut STOP's analysis, planners and their allies instead deployed falsehoods. They claimed the project enjoyed widespread support garnered through thoughtful attention to local concerns, accused the BOP of forcing the prison upon Ray Brook, and claimed construction had inflicted no damage on the local environment. The LPOOC even solicited private donations on the false premise that taxpayer money was not funding the Olympics and that the Olympic Village would become an athletic training facility. Sensitive to the fallout from STOP's campaign, advocates pressured journalists to eschew the word "prison" in favor of "athletes' housing," "dormitories," or "Olympic Village." As the Winter Games approached, an exhausted Congressman McEwen remarked that it was "time the country moved on . . . instead of dwelling on what mistakes may have been made." After all, as one LPOOC bureaucrat pointed out, "We're sure as hell not experts on prisons."[45]

Contractors finished the Ray Brook complex in October 1979, and nearly two thousand athletes and coaches from thirty-seven nations were its first occupants. Members of STOP, for their part, followed through on promises to protest during the games by attempting to extinguish the Olympic flame as it traveled to Lake Placid. Police subdued the protesters and the torch reached its destination for the opening of the XIII Olympic Winter Games on February 13, 1980. Efforts to conceal the facility's future use continued, as the Olympic Village Guide provided to each complex resident stated, "the operational buildings and residences are arranged much like a modern university campus." Years of subterfuge ended once the games concluded on February 24. By March 1980, the athletes had gone home, the LPOOC had submitted a glowing review of the complex to the IOC, and the BOP had begun transforming the facility into a federal prison.[46]

The compound's $4 million carceral conversion proceeded through the spring and summer of 1980. To the surprise of many, some in the BOP began to voice skepticism about the project. In a speech to the Saranac Lake Chamber of Commerce, one bureau leader called Ray Brook "not an ideal site," yet claimed its design and security features made no other government use possible. Local journalists, meanwhile, did not share the BOP's glum assessment. The editorial board of the Plattsburgh-based *Press Republican* jumped on the prison bandwagon as opening day approached.

FIGURE 6. Aerial view of the Olympic Village in Ray Brook, New York. Courtesy of the Lake Placid Olympic Museum.

Misunderstanding the bifurcated nature of the prison opposition, the editors argued that diminished public criticism of the project since the Olympics ended indicated widespread local support. Amid a state budget crunch, the paper called for unanimous acceptance of the penitentiary as a vehicle for economic growth that would "keep . . . people off" New York's strained "public assistance rolls." The editors ended with a parting shot to remaining opponents: "The prison is going to become a viable industry in the North Country whether you like it or not."[47]

After numerous delays, including misplacement of the prison's keys, the Federal Correctional Institution-Ray Brook (FCI) opened on September 26, 1980. Congressman McEwen, Bishop Brzana, and BOP Director Carlson were guests of honor at a ceremony attended by 150 staff members, project supporters, and opponents. Carlson pledged a "modern" institution that would "offer hope instead of despair." For his part, McEwen remarked, "There is no facility whose completion gives me more satisfaction . . . in the heart of our picturesque Adirondacks." That same day, members of STOP held their final protests. Standing outside BOP headquarters in Washington, D.C., supporters of STOP handed out ersatz awards to individuals they considered most responsible for their movement's failure. For his embrace of a project that promised to perpetuate miserable prison conditions long condemned by Catholic prelates, STOP "honored" Bishop Brzana as "Turkey of the Year." STOP bestowed the "prize" for "Super-Turkey," meanwhile, on President Carter for betraying his commitment to human rights by refusing to support STOP's mission. Back in Ray Brook, a handful of opposition stalwarts in the audience expressed disappointment with the outcome but noted the controversy's value as "a good publicity tool" for the anti-prison movement.[48] As four years of debate ended, few could predict whose vision of Ray Brook's future—that of prison supporters or opponents—might someday come to pass.

Naturalizing Camp Adirondack

During the struggle over the Olympic Prison, across the road at Camp Adirondack, incarcerated men, prison staff, and residents forged partnerships that fortified the institution's place in the community. A culture of outreach and exchange took root, characterized by activities emphasizing social welfare, health, and education. An abundance of goodwill, however, could not forestall the escapes, violence, and unrest that provided constant reminders of the facility's carceral purpose. The cooperative spirit of the camp's early years did help preserve public support after it expanded into a medium-security penitentiary—renamed as Adirondack Correctional Facility (ACF)—in 1981. Existing relationships easily withstood the placement of razor wire around the old and familiar facility.

In the 1970s and 1980s, local residents, service organizations, and educational institutions fostered collaborative ties that facilitated a smooth transition for both facility and community. Their efforts, directed toward enhancing imprisoned men's health, neatly aligned with the institution's roots as a medical facility. North Country Community College in Saranac Lake offered undergraduate courses for incarcerated men and staff members. Over time, the prison education program helped the underfunded college achieve financial solvency.[49] Local residents raised money for and volunteered with music and literacy programs for incarcerated men, and area actors and musicians often traveled to the facility to entertain them.[50] Regional clergy, for their part, became active in ministry with both imprisoned men and corrections officers.[51]

Prison staff also worked to promote public involvement in the facility's development. In so doing, correctional leaders built on the work of residents, educators, and clergy to draw prison and community closer together. DOCS officials hosted open house events at the prison that became a fixture of Ray Brook's summer calendar. These gatherings featured tours of the facility guided by incarcerated men, outdoor barbecues, displays of artwork produced by imprisoned men, speeches by camp residents, prison administrators, politicians, and civic boosters, and even carnival rides and activities for children. While hundreds of residents got an inside view of prison life, facility administrators ventured into neighboring communities, delivering informational lectures to service organizations, displaying photographs of the camp, and answering questions about the facility. Administrators also reached out to the families of incarcerated men, sponsoring visits to the facility and hosting picnics and outdoor activities, including fishing trips to area ponds and streams.[52]

Incarcerated men also engaged in activities that promoted community acceptance of the facility. Music groups comprised of incarcerated men performed for children at recreational facilities, for patients in hospitals, and in concerts open to the public and held at the prison. Imprisoned men raised money for charity, including the American Cancer Society and for victims of the 1980s famine in Ethiopia. School administrators and service groups frequently enlisted incarcerated men to visit local schools to warn students against the dangers of alcohol and narcotics.[53] By continuing Ray Brook's tradition of promoting health, collaborations among staff, imprisoned men, and residents continually reaffirmed the facility's legitimacy in its new role as a prison.

The work of prison labor crews on projects dedicated to social welfare and outdoor recreation did the most to help maintain public support for the facility. Incarcerated workers' promotion of social welfare objectives began on an ad hoc basis in the 1970s. Camp residents, who earned on average between $1.10 and $4.20 per day in the labor program jointly operated by DOCS and the DEC, refurbished churches, renovated the offices of civic groups and governmental organizations, cleared vegetation at industrial sites, cut and stacked firewood for the poor, battled forest fires, and assisted with flood control.[54] By the 1980s, this social welfare work became characterized by formal relationships with local clients. In addition to their outdoor work, imprisoned men became quasi-regular employees of public schools, fire departments, senior centers, libraries, sports groups, and health organizations.[55] The region's many low-income families, in particular, came to depend on free Christmas toys built and repaired by incarcerated men.[56] In a region battered by poverty and unemployment, and during an era of austerity, deficits, and disinvestment in social programs, prison labor filled a gaping void for the area's vulnerable residents.

Incarcerated workers also aided in preserving the region's recreational resources and infrastructure. They helped build the bobsled run, cross-country trails, and downhill runs used during the 1980 Winter Olympics. Imprisoned men renovated parks, skating rinks, and athletic fields in local communities. Having demonstrated its value in the 1970s, prison labor on recreational projects acquired quasi-official sanction in the 1980s, as conservation and sports groups, philanthropic organizations, and local governments came to rely on incarcerated men as a dependable, low-cost workforce.[57] The most prominent of these semi-official agreements involved the Saranac Lake Winter Carnival, an event first held in 1897 to encourage outdoor activity for people diagnosed with tuberculosis. From 1977 to 1983, carnival organizers enlisted incarcerated men from Ray Brook to build the event's centerpiece Ice Palace.[58] For their part, more than a few imprisoned men valued the chance to work in the Adirondack Mountains. Incarcerated workers described a "feeling of freedom . . . being outdoors," and that "it feels free." Others labeled their work as "healthy" because "you're in the outdoors." Echoing nineteenth-century prison reformers and administrators, DOCS officials hoped exposure to the relatively unspoiled Adirondack environment might aid incarcerated men in their eventual reentry to free society.[59] By promoting wellness, the work of incarcerated men on social welfare and recreation projects continued Ray Brook's legacy as a health-oriented community and helped maintain public support for the institution in its new role as a penitentiary.

In assessing the facility's smooth penal transition, residents and staff gave much of the credit to incarcerated men. While some interpreted the men's hard work and discipline as a ploy to avoid transfer to more restrictive facilities like Clinton, many staff members viewed incarcerated men as partners in an experiment whose success depended on the good conduct of all. Administrators highlighted "a greater degree of trust" where there was "no need to enforce basic rules" because the men performed "work which they know has real value," often undertaking projects "no contractor would touch." Residents, for their part, called imprisoned men a "credit to the community," and considered them "part of our life in the Adirondacks." The prison superintendent, linking the facility's past and present, offered the ultimate endorsement when he stated, "We are still helping people to get well."[60]

The opening of Camp Adirondack, as it turned out, had not foreclosed its use for Olympic housing. In early 1977, DOCS had agreed to temporarily move the camp's two hundred incarcerated men to other facilities to make way for 1,300 Olympic security personnel. Lawmakers appropriated $6 million to renovate the facility for Olympic use, installing new water, electrical, and waste disposal systems, along with upgraded kitchen, laundry, and bathroom amenities. The camp superintendent praised the makeover, noting, "it indicates we're going to be here," a view confirmed in 1979 as Corrections predicted the facility would receive an additional one hundred incarcerated men after the Olympics. Averse "to see a facility like this go to waste," especially with an insufficient number of minimum-security convicted men to fill the refurbished camp, DOCS planned security upgrades once the Olympics concluded.[61]

As New York's prisons approached 100 percent capacity in 1980, Corrections moved to take full advantage of the modernized Ray Brook facility. Fears of idleness in a Ray Brook prison population predicted to swell from two hundred to five hundred spurred the creation of new vocational education programs. Seeking to capitalize on its investment and use all available space to confine a growing population of convicted men, DOCS announced Camp Adirondack's conversion to medium security in December 1980. To incarcerate a potentially more violent and unruly population, the camp quickly came to resemble a traditional prison, featuring a double security fence topped by razor wire and equipped with motion sensors, industrial factories for imprisoned workers, recreation and maintenance buildings, and new guardhouses. Contractors also removed the old tuberculosis cure porches, replacing them with classrooms and a law library. For its part, the APA conducted nonbinding advisory review of the upgrades, advising officials to plant trees and construct berms along the perimeter to mitigate visual impacts. A sign bearing the prison's new name, Adirondack Correctional Facility, appeared on Ray Brook Road in October 1981, and by December the penitentiary incarcerated 485 medium-security convicted men.[62]

FIGURE 7. Entrance to Adirondack Correctional Facility, Ray Brook, New York. Photo courtesy of the author.

Preserving the relationships forged between prison and community became a challenge amid heightened security. With the DOCS-DEC labor program available only at minimum-security facilities, imprisoned men accustomed to outdoor work found themselves restricted to prison grounds. As the facility's population expanded without its traditional work programs, Democratic Governor Mario Cuomo warned of "critical inmate idleness" that might threaten public safety. In response, lawmakers funded construction of a new visitor center, gymnasium, recreation yard, and vocational education facilities. At the same time, contractors barred the prison's windows, erected more fencing, installed security cameras, and built special cells for disruptive men. Legislators also authorized building a day care center for workers' children, an employee dining facility, and an interfaith chapel to mitigate the stresses of work in an increasingly crowded and confined environment.[63]

At Ray Brook and elsewhere, Corrections had become ensnared in a vicious cycle of expansion. To satisfy their security and space imperatives, planners built new prisons and enlarged existing ones. As prison populations swelled, DOCS hired more staff and planned more renovations. Between 1975 and 1999, the state prison population more than quadrupled, from 16,384 to 71,000. A system comprising thirty-two prisons in 1981 became a far-flung network of seventy by 1999. And overcrowding? Two decades of expansion left New York's prisons operating at 130 percent of capacity by 2000, the worst overcrowding in state history. The costs were staggering, as annual budgets at ACF jumped from $947,500 in 1977 to $14 million in 1997. A staff of eighty-one in 1977 grew to a cadre of 357 employees a decade later. The facility's population of incarcerated men, 80 percent African American and Latino and 18 percent white, increased from a total of 148 in 1976 to a peak of 713 in 1997.[64] So long as policies dedicated to mass incarceration remained ascendant, these cycles could not be broken.

Ray Brook's commitment to community-oriented rehabilitation could not preclude the disorder characteristic of many penal environments. The relatively light security of the early years did not help matters. Between 1976 and 1982, eleven incarcerated men escaped, prompting searches involving Corrections and state police officers, bloodhounds, roadblocks, and helicopters. Imprisoned men used the relatively uncontrolled minimum-security environment to their advantage, climbing out windows, walking away from work projects, and, in the process, undermining prison-

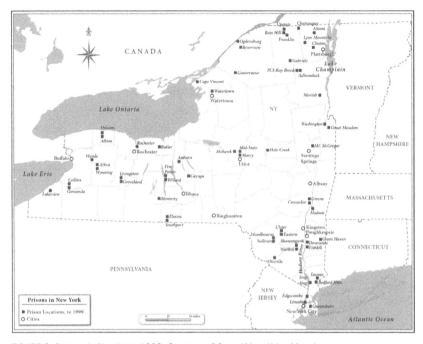

FIGURE 8. Prisons in New York, 1999. Courtesy of Gerry Krieg, Krieg Mapping.

community relations. However, the Adirondacks were as challenging in the 1970s as they had been in the 1840s; the unfamiliar environment proved both blessing and curse. While some planned well, including one escapee whose wife drove a getaway car from Long Island, most relied on luck. One man found refuge inside a nearby hunting camp, while another pair, disguised as hikers and toting stolen camping equipment, claimed membership in a nature club to thwart detection by three teenage boys. Many simply got lost, failing in their efforts to navigate rail lines, roads, and waterways as conduits to freedom, though one desperate fellow briefly imprisoned an elderly couple in their Saranac Lake home in exchange for transportation out of the area. Amid heightened security after 1981, incarcerated men not enamored of prison life redirected their energy into hostility toward their keepers and each other.[65]

Increased tension and violence among imprisoned men and facility employees accompanied the medium-security upgrade. Several incidents involved only incarcerated men, including brawls over television programs shown in common activity rooms. Imprisoned men also attacked staff members, posing constant risks to employees' health and safety.[66] The hazards of prison employment, however, were not restricted to the whims of wayward convicted men. Unionized corrections officers at Ray Brook struggled with facility administrators and state leaders. Often, salaries and benefits took a backseat to workplace safety and control. Shifts in union tactics and rhetoric closely paralleled the prison's transition from minimum to medium security. When AFSCME Council 82, the union representing New York correctional officers, struck the state's prisons in April and May 1979, nearly all of Camp Adirondack's unionized officers joined the picket line. Amid proposals to end seniority privileges, enforce the use of paid sick leave in place of workers' compensation for workplace-related injuries, and to reopen salary negotiations after one year, union leaders struck both to force higher pay and to preserve existing protections. While the state National Guard maintained security inside ACF, officers outside simultaneously picketed and performed their duties, surveilling the unfenced perimeter. Concerned for the region's economy, strikers permitted unionized construction workers to cross the picket line and continue pre-Olympic renovations. At the same time, employees who once declaimed affection for incarcerated men now decried their "lenient" treatment—characterized by generous vocational, educational, and recreational programs—at the "expense" of properly compensating officers and staff.[67]

After 1981, employees' struggles for improved benefits and working conditions involved severing the bonds linking incarcerated men to the community. The upgrade to medium security, which reduced public interaction with imprisoned men and increased vocational, educational, and recreational activities for convicted men on prison grounds, facilitated unionists' demonization of men once considered members of the community. Incarcerated men partaking in pricy, reform-oriented programs became scapegoats for officers engaged in bread-and-butter conflicts with the state. Unionists, however, found themselves in a trap of their own creation: When lawmakers heeded calls to reduce prison programming budgets, officers grudgingly acknowledged the vital role of educational, recreational, and work activities in minimizing unrest.[68] Similar attempts to scapegoat incarcerated men diagnosed with HIV/AIDS as public health threats foundered as understanding of the disease improved by the late 1980s.[69] Prison staff and residents who had once hailed convicted men as a "credit to the community" easily recast them as undeserving competitors in the contest for state largesse.

Believing public sentiment had shifted away from incarcerated men and toward staff, some officers tested the boundaries of their authority. Random drug testing led to numerous suspensions and arrests, one was convicted of sexually assaulting an incarcerated man in a bathroom, and an ACF superintendent faced forced retirement after embezzling $18,000 in unearned salary. The most egregious example of corruption came from abuses of ACF's shift-swapping program. For decades, New York prisons had allowed officers to trade shifts. An audit revealed ten ACF employees having never paid back swapped shifts and offering others only small sums to work for them. In 2001, four officers were arrested, one of whom had served as a local town supervisor, and charged with fraud and official misconduct. After pleading guilty, each paid restitution and faced a lifetime ban from public service.[70] Incidents of employee misconduct such as these paralleled the violence and unrest that flared after 1981. With heightened security, ACF seemed less secure from its days as a mere camp.

In 1987, dozens of former tuberculosis patients returned to Ray Brook for a reunion that included a tour of ACF. At a reception, the prison superintendent intoned the facility's past to rationalize its present, claiming, "It's not that different from when you were here. We too are giving people the opportunity to get better." Ironically, overcrowding and the weakened immune systems of incarcerated men diagnosed with HIV/AIDS created conditions that allowed tuberculosis to return to the Ray Brook facility in the early 1990s, raising anew health fears sparked by HIV/AIDS.[71] The anxiety that accompanied the return of tuberculosis mirrored the larger institutional challenges ACF faced following its medium-security upgrade. Though shaken by escapes, violence, unrest, corruption, and disease, residents' connections to the facility persisted. Notably, area homeowners never developed the same feeling of attachment to the federal prison across the road.

FCI-Ray Brook: A *1984* Facility

Area residents' alienation from the federal prison only deepened after its opening in 1980. Despite pledges to the contrary, FCI officials did little to encourage community involvement in the facility's development. Consequently, negative impressions formed in the 1970s hardened, especially as many of STOP's warnings came to fruition. Only after fifteen years of tension and unrest, punctuated by two failed attempts to build a second federal prison in Ray Brook, did FCI leaders develop a program of public participation in prison life. BOP leaders' initial indifference to homeowners' concerns about environmental and public health, followed by FCI administrators' reluctance to become good neighbors, condemned town and prison to a condition of permanent estrangement.

In contrast to the initiatives that harmonized relations between Camp Adirondack and its neighbors, similar efforts at FCI were sporadic and rarely involved incarcerated men. FCI officials held five sparsely attended open house events between 1980 and 1992, offering museum-like tours of the facility with no interactions between residents and imprisoned men. Most activities occurred irregularly and took place outside the penitentiary: employees held craft sales and holiday parties, a branch of the Jaycees run by FCI employees made periodic donations to local charities, staff instructors and professionals offered infrequent public lectures in surrounding communities on topics ranging from child psychology to women's history, and residents sometimes utilized prison facilities for family and social gatherings.[72] FCI's insubstantial, ad hoc attempts at integration in its first fifteen years—especially when compared to Camp Adirondack and ACF—did little to bridge the gap separating town and prison.

Further stymieing efforts at community outreach, the medium-security status of the men incarcerated at FCI-Ray Brook restricted their interactions with the public. Their earliest outreach activities were sporadic and not strategically designed to integrate town and prison. Imprisoned men raised money for playgrounds, Christmas bureaus, and the Red Cross; donated their own artwork for charity sales and auctions; and recorded books on tape for language students in public schools. Only in the mid-1990s did FCI develop a coherent program of prison–community collaboration. Officials launched a volunteer program for residents to work with incarcerated men on activities ranging from pre-release counseling to arts and crafts. FCI's Inmate Volunteer Corps, for its part, allowed imprisoned men to hone their talents on projects for charities, philanthropic organizations, and schools. Local high schools sent their students to FCI to hear incarcerated men lecture on the scourges of narcotics and alcohol abuse.[73] With their focus on projects emphasizing health, FCI efforts toward community integration unwittingly mirrored those of Camp Adirondack and validated project advocates' view that the prison was consistent with the North Country's history of promoting wellness.

We should take care, however, not to overstate FCI efforts to foster better relations with its neighbors. Its initiatives were never part of a broader strategy either to atone for past offenses or to improve ties with residents. If anything, activities linking town and prison seemed tangential to the facility's carceral and economic missions. Most men incarcerated at FCI spent their days working inside the penitentiary. While many toiled as cooks, custodians, groundskeepers, and in a slew of other unskilled positions, roughly half labored in Federal Prison Industries—also known as UNICOR—factories producing goods sold to federal agencies. Profits earned from FCI's glove, printing, and textile plants maintained production facilities, funded salaries, and paid for education programs. UNICOR workers earned from $0.44 to $1.10 per hour, and many either remitted their pay to family or saved it for shopping in the prison commissary. In the printing plant, workers learned typesetting, photography, and publishing skills used to produce annual reports, brochures, stationery, and accounting pads. Men working in the glove and textile plants produced gloves, military uniforms, linens, canteen pouches, and ammunition cases for the Department of Defense. By the early 2000s, FCI's UNICOR plants returned annual profits of $4 million.[74] By channeling the energies of imprisoned men toward jobs performed solely behind the razor wire, FCI administrators squandered an opportunity to improve town–prison relations.

As at ACF, population shifts at FCI closely mirrored state and national trends. Late twentieth-century wars on drugs and crime drove increasing narcotics-related convictions. While illegal drugs was the largest source of federal commitments by 1977, only 26 percent of men under BOP confinement were serving narcotics-related sentences. Harsher penalties enacted under Presidents Ronald Reagan and George H. W. Bush altered that balance. By 1990, more than half of FCI's population found themselves imprisoned for narcotics activity. Rapid population increase at FCI—swelling from 500 to 1,245 imprisoned men between 1980 and 2006—again disproved the notion that expanded cell capacity could solve overcrowding. The wars on drugs and crime generated a demographic revolution in the federal prison system. While 56 percent of men confined in BOP facilities in 1977 identified as white, changes were afoot by 1990. As FCI neared its tenth anniversary, 66 percent of its incarcerated population identified as either African American or Latino.[75] With its staff nearly all identifying as white, the racial imbalance between free and unfree risked sparking the unrest STOP had predicted.

Though FCI was overcrowded shortly after opening, neither its capacity nor its officer corps—which on average numbered 250—witnessed equivalent expansions. As a result, most incarcerated men found themselves double- and quadruple-bunked in the same tiny rooms that had lodged Olympic athletes, and there were often too few jobs available for all convicted men who wanted one.[76] As the population surged, administrators struggled to manage idle convicted men in tight quarters. FCI officials encouraged incarcerated men to use the facility's gymnasium, library, chapel, and wellness center.[77] Imprisoned men could enroll in high school, college, or vocational training courses offered at the prison.[78] Running FCI under such conditions drove the penitentiary's annual operating costs from $7 million in 1983 to over $20 million by 2005.[79] By the early 1980s, many of STOP's warnings had begun to materialize. By overcrowding the facility without commensurate increases in either staff or space, the BOP was simply warehousing convicted men. The value of educational, recreational, and work programs diminished amid cramped conditions and insatiable demand. Increasing tensions among imprisoned men and staff members confirmed STOP's warnings of a second Attica in the making. Exiled in a remote locale hundreds of miles from home, forced to share tight quarters with unpredictable cellmates, and afforded few opportunities to interact with the public, unrest became inevitable.

Imprisoned men planned and executed numerous escapes from FCI during its first quarter-century, testing BOP's promises of a safe facility. Though several managed to breach the fences, razor wire, and electronic sensors surrounding the prison, the Adirondack environment challenged even well prepared fugitives. Following a two-day manhunt involving police helicopters, bloodhounds, and roadblocks, officers apprehended FCI's first escapee in September 1982. Law enforcement, however, could not take total credit for the capture. A resident driving near Lake Placid called authorities to report an unusual sighting: an African American man dressed in hunting gear walking along the road. Racial profiling complete, officers arrived and apprehended the runaway. Other escapees took better care with their planning. In 1996, an incarcerated man crafted flower planters that were, in fact, ladders used to scale the fence. The fugitive entered a nearby home and ate a meal before stealing a truck and leading police on a high-speed chase that ended on a boat docked at a lakeside retreat. Some, however, were victims of circumstances beyond their control. Exploiting the light supervision over those incarcerated workers landscaping the prison's edge, four incarcerated men jumped into their friend's getaway car—driven from Brooklyn—and disappeared in 1983. Irreconcilable differences among the friends led to their being dumped in the Hamilton County hamlet of Indian Lake. As their friend headed back to New York City, a resident spotted and reported the men to authorities, who quickly picked them up. FCI's tight security prevented most would-be runaways from even leaving the grounds. Over the years, one hid in a storage building, another jumped toward a vehicle exiting the prison, a third was caught building a hang glider to fly out, and authorities thwarted the plan of one convicted spy from Hungary to break out, guns blazing, with a helicopter.[80]

With prison security and an unfamiliar environment likely deterring many potential escapees, most of FCI's incarcerated men channeled their anger through protests and violence behind the razor wire. Imprisoned men railed against narcotics and sentencing laws by engaging in work or meal strikes and setting small fires. They employed similar tactics to signal their disapproval of the actions of staff members, housing policies, food service, and even television and radio options. These episodes routinely prompted lockdowns and the transfers of men who were deemed disruptive.[81] Imprisoned men's grievances could also result in violence of the type STOP had anticipated. With the use of homemade knives and other makeshift weapons, fights among incarcerated men and staff members occasionally turned bloody. STOP's warnings materialized as incarcerated men battled numerous times in common recreation areas. One imprisoned man murdered another, while a handful died by suicide inside their cells. The most spectacular act of violence, however, came in 1992, when a convicted man set fire to the prison wellness center, burning the building to the ground.[82]

FCI staff also contended with hazards unrelated to the whims of disgruntled incarcerated men. Risks to employees' health were ever-present, ranging from slips and falls and kitchen fires to stress-induced heart problems that forced some into early retirement.[83] FCI provided few pathways to prosperity, contrary to the claims of project boosters in the 1970s. In addition to low salaries that compelled many to seek better paying jobs—sometimes at ACF—the nation's shifting political and economic winds also wreaked havoc with workers' livelihoods. The specter of congressional sequestration during the federal budget crisis of 1990, followed five years later by full-scale government shutdowns, traumatized employees convinced their jobs were safe.[84] Tension between administrators and officers often called into question the "modern orientation" promised in 1980. One FCI union leader asserted that facility bosses "ruled by intimidation," and a former employee spoke of a "snitch system" in which "the way to do well is to rat on your buddies." Workers' grievances sometimes engendered rogue behavior, including theft of federal property, importation of contraband, and sales of banned items, such as alcohol, to imprisoned men.[85]

Incarcerated men's attitudes confirmed the reality of FCI Ray Brook: a controlled environment in which managers struggled to maintain control. The only facets of prison life worthy of praise from imprisoned men were the opportunities to work and learn. One printing plant employee stated, "Someday . . . I'm going to step out on the streets and use this," while a colleague in the glove factory hailed "the chance to make some dollars that will help me when I get out." The value of prison employment extended to imprisoned men's loved ones; one worker noted the "need . . . to help your family's financial situation." Incarcerated men also commended educational and vocational programs as a chance to "do something constructive and earn your way out of jail."[86] Not all incarcerated men, however, held such views. While calling Ray Brook "a nice joint" and "beautiful," one imprisoned man described officers as "maniacs" and claimed the prison was "a ticking time bomb." FCI administrators, according to another, were "devious, vicious people" whose authoritarian tendencies made rank-and-file officers "so upset that they're ready to quit." A third imprisoned man accused officers of threatening the prison population "like what the Germans did to the Jews in World War II." One incarcerated man's observation seemed to confirm FCI's anti-modern, anti-progressive qualities: "Everything's a threat at Ray Brook. Instead of doing it the finesse way, it's, 'You do this or you're going to the hole,' or, 'If you don't do that, you're going to the hole.' If they'd just do it with finesse, like they do at other prisons, things would be ok."[87] Such turbulence quickly disproved the BOP's promise to promote hope over despair in this "modern" institution.

Residents' views of FCI mirrored those of many incarcerated men. Homeowners complimented imprisoned men's work for local charities, service organizations, and schools, while educators commended incarcerated men for excellence in the classroom and for their contributions to narcotics and alcohol education programs.[88] The contentious relationship forged between the BOP and its neighbors in the 1970s persisted long after the facility opened. Escapes were a sore point for residents unaccustomed to locking windows and doors. Fugitives made locals feel "uneasy," "imposed on," and "mad." One home-owner longed for the time when her family was "able to walk and pick berries and do anything we wanted." That had all changed. "Now," she claimed, "we are afraid." Another blasted escapees' ability "to hold a community in terror," and one area man called FCI "a school for crime" populated by "terrorists, rapists, and murderers" who were guarded by "novices with no experience or training in handling people or their problems."[89] The dysfunctional operation of FCI in its early years—outlined by its employees, imprisoned men, and neighbors—did not bode well for BOP plans to expand its Ray Brook oper-ations in the 1980s and 1990s.

Still contending with overcrowded penitentiaries, the BOP announced in April 1983 the construction of a $2.7 million, 150-bed minimum-security prison camp—along the lines of Camp Adirondack—on a parcel of unde-veloped federal land in Ray Brook. Residents once hobbled by the weight of federal power sprang into action. Claiming that property ownership and taxpayer status conferred local authority over developments, area home-owners mobilized as Concerned Citizens of Ray Brook (CCRB) and pres-sured the area's Republican Congressman, David O'Brien Martin, to stop the project. The prospect of a third penitentiary—despite Camp Adirondack's relatively warm reception—prompted some in CCRB to fear the hamlet was becoming "saturated with prisons." Critics worried that escapes—a perennial source of concern even before Camp Adirondack's medium-security upgrade—from a new, unfenced camp might again plague the community. While one young girl's family had acquired "two German shepherds . . . because sometimes prisoners escape," an older res-ident concerned about tourism feared more fugitives "would set publicity back years," especially as Lake Placid basked in the afterglow of the Olympics. Opponents who recalled the destruction of the 1970s warned of litigation if the bureau failed to safeguard the "human environment" against ecological harm. Even the reliably pro-prison *Press Republican* joined the opposition, warning the region might "be opening Pandora's

Box by accepting anything to increase its economic standing." Residents breathed a sigh of relief when the BOP cancelled the plan in May 1983. Though the Justice Department claimed a $200 billion federal budget deficit made the project untenable, CCRB took credit for saving Ray Brook from untold harm.[90]

In 1989, a swelling deficit proved no barrier to the bureau in reviving plans to build a prison camp in Ray Brook. Having lain dormant for six years, CCRB reemerged with a host of objections. Critics warned of harmful economic impacts, including diminished property values, increased taxes, higher water and electricity rates, and strain on schools and hospitals unprepared for an influx of new residents—incarcerated men and their relatives—moving to the region. Threats to environmental and public health lay at the forefront of CCRB's campaign. While some focused on quality of life concerns such as noise and fumes from automobiles, others trafficked in racial and sexual hysteria. In particular, CCRB stoked fears that additional incarcerated men living in Ray Brook—especially in an unfenced facility—risked introducing HIV/AIDS to residents and visitors. Though gauging the effectiveness of such claims—especially as public understanding of the disease improved—remains difficult, defending against "further damage" to the "fragile and beautiful ecosystem" of Ray Brook was a top priority for all CCRB supporters. Of particular concern was the aging and overused pipe connecting Ray Brook's prisons to the sewage plant in Saranac Lake. By 1989, ACF and FCI were sending a total of 250,000 gallons of sewage to Saranac Lake every day. The prospect of a third penitentiary prompted a reassessment of the sewage deal struck back in 1977. Saranac Lake officials notified the BOP that its contract with the village forbade any new construction without town approval. Few could have predicted in 1977 that the federal government might one day be waylaid by the same local leaders and residents it had once so blithely ignored. While the prison's future lay with the town board, supporters of CCRB took nothing for granted. Hundreds signed petitions and sent letters to Martin, imploring the congressman to intervene on their behalf. With officials in Saranac Lake poised to reject the bureau's plan and Martin threatening to block it in Congress, the BOP cancelled the project in 1990. CCRB interpreted its victory as a sign that "representative democracy really works."[91]

In contrast to ACF, whose efforts toward public engagement left primarily positive impressions with area residents, FCI leaders largely forsook outreach opportunities that might have mitigated the harm done by over-crowding, understaffing, escapes, protests, violence, and labor struggles. Instead, FCI administrators viewed these conditions as part of the normal functioning of a federal prison that need not concern the community. Once undertaken, efforts to bridge the many gaps separating town and prison were stonewalled by residents whose bitterness toward the institution had only deepened with the passage of time. The new, *1984*-style ecosystem built by the BOP in Ray Brook was, for many, an unacceptable substitute for the tract's once-abundant forests, wetlands, and wildlife.

IIIIIIII

Passing through Ray Brook, individuals unconnected to the prison system would be hard-pressed to locate the penitentiaries that upended life in this community in the last quarter of the twentieth century. Visitors driving to and from Lake Placid may be forgiven for missing them entirely. The wooden, rustic-style signs directing drivers toward the prisons on Ray Brook Road are so tiny as to be easily unseen by motorists. The penitentiaries, too, are barely visible. While the contrasting architectural styles of the buildings at ACF—from both the early and late twentieth century—remind passersby of that facility's long history as a residential institution, the many trees, shrubs, and other vegetation found on its grounds, though punctuated by steel fencing topped with razor wire, obscure clear views of the complex. Across the road, dense forest and tight security successfully block even the smallest glimpse of the only facility from the 1980 Winter Olympics never opened to the general public.

The prisons' invisibility mirrors a history that also remains hidden. The vegetative screens surrounding both Ray Brook facilities—as opposed to Dannemora's wooden stockade and high stone wall—show how environmental law and environmentalism, innovations unknown in the 1840s, shaped the penal system in the 1970s and beyond. However, the otherwise deforested landscape surrounding FCI reminds us of how even well-intentioned regulations designed to safeguard environmental and public health could also undermine the very conditions they were created to protect. The fact that there are not two federal penitentiaries in Ray Brook remains a testament to the role of citizen activists in conducting oversight that is typically reserved to government bureaucrats, particularly with regard to the pipe carrying prison sewage to Saranac Lake. The recreational infrastructure and public works—especially those used for the Olympics—that are the legacy of Camp Adirondack's labor crews bear no indication that incarcerated men played a hand in their creation. Similarly, the anguish of generations of New Yorkers—incarcerated and free—connected to Ray Brook's prisons may never be memorialized, and, quite possibly, never known.

Essex County congregational minister Jonathan Tetherly was among the group of STOP activists who visited the Ray Brook construction site in August 1978. In a letter to Congressman McEwen, Tetherly offered a prophetic vision of changes afoot in the Adirondacks:

> People in the North Country of New York are the keepers. We keep people at the very large Clinton Prison in Dannemora. We keep people in Camp Adirondack, in Ray Brook. And now we have an offer to keep more people in a federal prison in Ray Brook. In the North Country, our concept of black people is that they are prisoners; we see black people on television who are not prisoners, but our only personal contact with black people, nearly all of the time, is with prisoners.[92]

Though STOP had warned of the deadly consequences of operating correctional facilities divided by race and class, Tetherly underscored another potentially damaging outcome from building prisons in the Adirondacks; namely, that residents of the nearly all-white region would come to automatically associate people of color with criminality and imprisonment. As New York's prison population skyrocketed in the 1980s, cash-strapped correctional planners looked beyond Ray Brook to other park communities where prisons could be built quickly and cheaply. In the Franklin County hamlet of Gabriels, questions of race and class would become central to the planning and operation of yet another North Country prison.

CHAPTER THREE

"WHO IS GOING TO LIVE IN GABRIELS?"

Race, Class, and the Nature of Incarceration in Gabriels

Introduction

Five years after transforming Ray Brook's old tuberculosis hospital into a state prison, the Department of Correctional Services discovered an abandoned 233-acre compound of buildings in the Franklin County hamlet of Gabriels. Confronted with a growing population of convicted men, in 1981 DOCS proposed repurposing that facility—built in the 1890s as a Catholic tuberculosis hospital and used since the 1960s as a satellite campus of Paul Smith's College—as a minimum-security prison. That May, Corrections officials released a map of the planned penitentiary that labeled each building according to its intended function. One structure appeared simply as "chapel mosque." At a public hearing on the project convened by the Adirondack Park Agency in January 1982, a lawyer representing local prison opponents inquired about the mosque, to the exclusion of the chapel. When a Corrections official attending the meeting questioned the question's relevance, the attorney bridled, "The relevance is who is going to live in Gabriels."[1] The mosque's innocuous position on the map masked larger anxieties that had lain dormant until New York's prison system arrived in this particular corner of the Adirondack Park.

Gabriels is tucked away in a heavily forested area of Franklin County, twelve miles north of Ray Brook. Though tiny and thoroughly white, its population nevertheless reflected the socioeconomic diversity characteristic of many Adirondack communities. While the core of the prison opposition could be found among Gabriels' well-off seasonal homeowners and visitors, its middle- and low-income permanent residents provided the project an unshakeable base of support. While Gabriels served as a home, workplace, and recreational outpost, for elites its primary draw remained the wild and rugged terrain that seemed to embody the essence of the Adirondack Park. Many affluent locals also imbibed late nineteenth-century notions of the park—recently highlighted by members of STOP in Ray Brook—as an exclusive enclave for the pleasure of people like themselves. Possible incursions by the state's primarily poor, African American and Latino incarcerated men thus alarmed residents whose understanding of nature was entwined with ideas of racial and class superiority.

The creation of Citizens Against More Prisons in the Adirondacks (CAMPA), the resistance group formed by Gabriels elites, opened a new chapter in the history of anti-prison organizing in New York's North Country. While members of the Prison Association had worked to improve conditions for men incarcerated at Dannemora, and the Concerned Citizens of Ray Brook had curtailed correctional expansions that posed environmental risks, Citizens Against More Prisons in the Adirondacks borrowed a page from STOP's playbook in defending the Adirondack Park as a place dedicated solely to the promotion of health, leisure, and recreation. Accordingly, CAMPA members argued, building more prisons would undermine the park's historical character. Affluent Gabriels homeowners did not, however, share STOP's concerns about the challenge of mass incarceration, the plight of the urban poor, or the lives of imprisoned men, and any concern over possible prison-induced damage to woods, waters, and wildlife paled in comparison to the anxiety over the penitentiary's potential to diversify the primarily white and well-to-do community. Supporters of CAMPA used environmentalist rhetoric not merely to protest the possibly destructive construction of new infrastructure—rather, their paeans to protecting nature provided convenient cover for prison opponents' uniquely racist brand of environmentalism.

Driven by a well-financed and determined opposition, the debate over Gabriels' prison lasted more than a year. As with the conflicts surrounding Ray Brook's federal penitentiary, the struggle in Gabriels revealed both the powers and the limitations of ordinary people, elected officials, environmental regulators, correctional planners, and incarcerated men in shaping New York's carceral state. Unlike with Camp Adirondack, state leaders could not unilaterally convert Gabriels' former hospital to a penal institution. Because its location outside the public domain was never in doubt—as opposed to the site that became home to FCI-Ray Brook—government bureaucrats could not simply reclassify the tract and open a penitentiary. The Adirondack Park Agency, empowered to oversee private land developments, posed an additional significant obstacle to the property's sale and repurposing. Members of CAMPA discovered that the APA leadership equally shared their resistance to correctional expansion in the region. Thus, for the first time, formal environmental regulation would figure heavily in the planning of an Adirondack prison. Long accustomed to building in the Adirondacks without restriction, the Corrections Department found itself on the defensive.

The act of purchasing the Gabriels property and opening a penitentiary required approval neither from residents nor the APA. DOCS's power was absolute. However, Corrections had learned much from the BOP's experience in Ray Brook, where indifference to local concerns estranged townspeople from the prison. Without persuasive salesmanship—a skill heretofore absent from DOCS leaders' toolbox—ensuring both smooth community relations and a quick repurposing would prove challenging. Nowhere was this truer than in Gabriels, where elite worries about prison-induced demographic shifts superseded concerns about ecological damage or economic vitality. Unwilling to accommodate CAMPA's request to cancel the project, Corrections officials instead offered olive branches they hoped would soften the inevitable blow. Recognizing the value that residents placed on outdoor activities, DOCS pledged to remand any unused lands at the site to the Forest Preserve. Further, acknowledging the difficulty that depressed towns and villages faced in maintaining infrastructure spurred state leaders to make a second concession: Recalling the positive reception that incarcerated workers had received at Ray Brook, Corrections leaders promised Gabriels homeowners the free use of prison labor crews. Though neither proposal satisfied the opposition, each proved crucial in the penitentiary's long-term development and relationship with its host community.

For nearly three decades, men incarcerated at Gabriels toiled on public works and conservation projects in communities across the area. In particular, imprisoned workers spent much time repairing and maintaining recreational infrastructure without which the elites' enjoyment of the Adirondack Park might not have been possible. In the process, prison labor unwittingly helped preserve an environment whose shape and character perpetuated exclusionary nineteenth-century wilderness ideals. Affluent homeowners once opposed to the penitentiary soon measured the value of imprisoned men in terms of tax dollars saved on projects that facilitated *their* continued use of the park. However, the work completed by incarcerated men created neither racial nor social harmony. Their status as men of color and the type of low-paid, manual labor they performed—largely for the benefit of well-to-do whites—reinforced the sense of power and privilege that wealthy homeowners and visitors assumed was as natural to Gabriels as its woods, waters, and wildlife. The ability to preserve both vital infrastructure and longstanding inequalities helped a penitentiary that was once viewed as a threat become an integral component of the Gabriels environment.

Mass Incarceration and Gabriels

Correctional planners scouting new penitentiary sites in the early 1980s must have felt a sense of déjà vu upon discovering Gabriels. Both Ray Brook and Gabriels were remote, sparsely populated mountain communities long experienced in hosting and treating people diagnosed with tuberculosis. Each was located in a region notorious for high unemployment and systemic poverty, and both contained abandoned residential facilities that state officials viewed as a convenient remedy to New York's prison crisis. Though Ray Brook had taught DOCS the value of repurposing surplus properties for penal use, the ceaseless churn of new incarcerated men also served as a reminder that correctional facilities alone would not solve overcrowding. Nevertheless, nearly a decade of enforcing stringent narcotics and sentencing laws had created an unsustainably large population of convicted men. With few in government questioning the myriad costs of these developments, lawmakers and correctional planners followed their nineteenth-century predecessors in embracing an expensive program of prison expansion. When they assumed that Gabriels would be another Ray Brook, state leaders miscalculated.

The settlement of Gabriels began in 1892 with the construction of temporary housing for workers building the Adirondack and St. Lawrence Railroad. Also at that site, the Roman Catholic Sisters of Mercy opened the Gabriels Sanatorium in 1894 on land owned by wilderness guide, recreation advocate, and hotelier Paul Smith. The Sisters purchased the property in 1924 and operated the facility until the emergence of antibiotics and declining inpatient care for people diagnosed with tuberculosis forced its closure in 1963. Two years later, the diocese sold the site to Paul Smith's College (PSC) for use as a satellite campus, but low enrollments drove college officials to sell the property in 1979.[2] Likely inspired by a similar repurposing in Ray Brook, DOCS leaders in 1980 expressed interest in Gabriels. Lawmakers, however, sought carceral space that promised convenience, speed, and affordability. In March 1981, Republican Senate Majority Leader Warren Anderson proposed that DOCS lease an undeveloped portion of FCI-Ray Brook to house some of the state's convicted men, but with the federal penitentiary slated to reach its capacity of five hundred incarcerated men by summer, attention turned back to Gabriels. After meeting with PSC President Thomas Stainback in April 1981, Corrections officials remarked that the likely difficult process of converting private property for penal use inside the Adirondack Park made a prison in Gabriels unlikely. Desperate to lessen the college's financial burden, Stainback lamented he had "no indication that they [DOCS] are interested, and joked, 'I wish it were true.'"[3]

Penal overcrowding remained *the* factor driving continued correctional expansion in early 1980s New York. Nearly a decade of enforcing the Rockefeller drug laws and punishing multiple felony offenders pushed the state prison population past capacity. By July 1981, DOCS incarcerated 23,700 men in facilities designed to hold 22,700. Corrections Commissioner Thomas Coughlin III pressed lawmakers for new cells, and that same month, the Senate authorized $3.3 million to convert the Gabriels facility to a minimum-security prison for one hundred fifty incarcerated men to be transferred from the soon-to-be medium-security Adirondack Correctional Facility.[4] One month later, State Assembly and Senate lawmakers enacted a more robust correctional expansion plan, appropriating $11 million to build 650 cells at five new locations, including Gabriels, and over $24 million to expand capacity at existing facilities. Even with this spending, Governor Hugh Carey predicted the state would need at least 4,000 additional cells within five years. With future growth inevitable, Carey authorized a $500 million prison construction bond—the Security Through the Development of Correctional Facilities Bond Act—for inclusion on the November 1981 election ballot. Bond funds would provide $350 million for new construction and renovations to existing prisons, $125 million to expand and renovate local jails, and $25 million to increase the size of detention centers for convicted youth and people diagnosed with psychiatric ailments.[5] If approved, the bond would cement mass incarceration as New York's preferred remedy to its overcrowding crisis.

By the early 1980s, New York's political leaders had abandoned their slapdash approach to managing overcrowding—exemplified by the rapid conversion of the shuttered complex in Ray Brook—in favor of a coherent, well-funded program designed to meet current and future carceral needs. Lawmakers first had to convince voters to support the bond. In promotional literature, they noted that since 1978, New York had incarcerated 7,000 new convicted men. With limited capacity, overcrowding threatened the health and safety of individuals working inside the state's correctional facilities, but prison employees did not face this danger alone. Scarce funding and cell space, lawmakers warned, meant that not all who engaged in unlawful activity would end up behind bars. Violent and nonviolent individuals alike thus endangered the well being of *all* New Yorkers. While conceding their war on drugs had fueled the overcrowding crisis and that cheaper alternatives like probation, community service, drug treatment, and restitution operated successfully in towns and villages statewide, leaders in Albany viewed correctional expansion as the *only* solution. Seeking to capitalize on Reagan-era anathema toward taxes, state officials argued that "the taxpayers of today should not be burdened with the total cost of public improvements designed to last for generations." They urged voters to approve the bond—predicted to cost individual New Yorkers only six dollars per year during a thirty-year repayment period—to avoid the burden of tax hikes in a state notorious for its high cost of living. Echoing sentiments first expressed in Albany over a century earlier, lawmakers reminded voters of their duty to "remove violent criminals from [New York] communities."[6]

Corrections officials, who were under pressure to incarcerate a growing population of convicted men, could not wait for November. The successful repurposing at Ray Brook likely inspired Corrections to attempt a repeat performance in Gabriels. Plans to upgrade Camp Adirondack to medium security—necessitating the relocation of its minimum-security imprisoned men—neatly coincided with DOCS's discovery of Gabriels.[7] Corrections leaders hoped an equally eco-friendly hospital-turned-penitentiary in Gabriels would yield the same type of enthusiasm among area homeowners as had early efforts at Ray Brook. As Camp Adirondack's transformation into a larger and more restrictive penal environment proceeded in early 1981, DOCS Commissioner Coughlin offered Gabriels residents a preview of what might lay in their future. Focusing on changes to Camp Adirondack's physical environment, the commissioner noted that construction of new fencing, parking lots, and roads, as well as blasting to remove rocks and trees, would "not have a significant effect on the environment." Further, Coughlin argued that a community as thoroughly human-built as Ray Brook could not possibly be harmed by new construction.[8] With the built environments of Ray Brook and Gabriels sharing so much in common, Coughlin suggested that Gabriels residents had nothing to fear if a prison came to town. Unfortunately for DOCS, Ray Brook's experience could not be easily mapped onto Gabriels. Though separated by only a few miles, the two hamlets were worlds apart.

Citizens Against More Prisons in the Adirondacks

The proposal to open a prison in Gabriels activated racial and class divisions long-embedded in the hamlet's social fabric. For many affluent residents, the community's demographic profile—mainly white and well-to-do—was as natural as its waters, woods, and wildlife. A large number of residents had deep roots in the community, including some who claimed descent from the Adirondack Park's earliest residents and visitors. For them, the state's growing interest in the region as a site of incarceration represented a betrayal. Wealthy homeowners' understanding of the park—as a place designed to promote the health and recreational pursuits of New York's elite—closely mirrored that of its late nineteenth-century founders. Penitentiaries contradicted that ideal. Well-off residents could feel the ground shifting beneath them as the Corrections Department extended its footprint across the Adirondacks. The outcome that elites feared most entailed a restructuring of power relations wherein the interests of low-income whites hungry for correctional employment and poor men of color sentenced to a prison term might supersede their own. In opposing the penitentiary, Gabriels residents struggled to preserve an environmental ideal—if not an environment— squarely rooted in racial and class superiority.

News that lawmakers were considering a Gabriels prison spurred the creation of an organized resistance. In June 1981, a handful of local women began canvassing the area and circulating petitions against the proposal. In

July, the nascent opposition coalesced as Citizens Against More Prisons (CAMP), but was renamed Citizens Against More Prisons in the Adirondacks (CAMPA) two months later to avoid confusion with a national prison abolition group of the same name. Organizing two years before Concerned Citizens of Ray Brook, CAMPA became the Adirondacks' first homegrown anti-prison group.[9] CAMPA's arguments against the penitentiary underscored environmental impacts that were as much social and racial as they were ecological. As CAMPA emerged in July 1981, Diane Peterson, one of the organization's founders, previewed its coming campaign. She noted that while low-income locals might benefit from prison employment, affluent residents would suffer. Peterson stated she did not "think a prison upgrades your community at all," effectively dismissing whatever value her less-well-off neighbors might find in the institution. In predicting that a penitentiary would increase unlawful activity in the area, Peterson reinforced the commonly held view that all incarcerated men, regardless of the conditions surrounding their confinement, were equally prone to violence.[10] Peterson's apparent disinterest in potential ecological and public health impacts closely mirrored the similar lack of concern by Ray Brook residents back in 1976. After all, both residential institutions were community fixtures that had been constructed decades earlier. How damaging could conversion from medical to educational to correctional use possibly be? In worrying that a prison would *degrade* the community and endanger public safety, Peterson implicitly identified incarcerated men as a threat as severe as any earthmoving machine or chainsaw.

Aware of the simmering opposition, the Corrections Department convened a public meeting on the project in July 1981. Ironically, attendees had to pass through state police roadblocks set up after a man incarcerated at Camp Adirondack escaped that morning from a work detail in Saranac Lake. Over three hundred residents crowded into a Paul Smith's College auditorium that summer evening to learn about the proposed prison. DOCS Commissioner Coughlin appealed to homeowners' social conscience, arguing all New Yorkers had a duty to help solve the overcrowding crisis. In the same breath, Coughlin blamed New York City lawmakers for enacting narcotics and sentencing laws that had caused the crisis in the first place. For his part, PSC President Stainback emphasized the prison's potential to improve both the college's balance sheet and the local economy. He dismissed concerns about harmful impacts on tourism and second home-ownership, sectors he claimed were "not likely to improve" amid a nation-wide recession, which underscored the importance of diversifying Gabriels' economy and finding "growth avenues aside from the tourist industry." A petition delivered by CAMPA founder Peterson bearing the signatures of over two hundred prison opponents, however, illustrated the limited value of Coughlin and Stainback's message. Drawing on popular caricatures of Adirondackers as low-income, conservative anti-statists, Coughlin and Stainback had surmised that a promise of economic uplift mixed with contempt for downstate politicians might satisfy skeptics. To their chagrin, the mainly affluent men and women filling the seats that night neither subscribed to Reagan-era anti-government screeds nor required an economic boost.[11]

Shortly after that July meeting, members of CAMPA launched their campaign to stop the Gabriels prison. They flooded the offices of local periodicals, elected officials, and the Adirondack Park Agency with personal correspondence, telegrams, and telephone calls denouncing the prison proposal. Of ninety-eight letters mailed to the APA about the project, only three expressed support. Critics articulated a definition of environmental impact that concentrated on the prison's potential to effect economic, social, and racial change. Messages from supporters of CAMPA also underscored the influence second homeowners and visitors wielded in small, isolated settlements like Gabriels. Both return addresses and writers' own words revealed that more than half of all opposition correspondence sent to APA headquarters about the penitentiary came from seasonal property owners. Not surprisingly, many of these individuals claimed New York City and other urban centers—the hometowns of most of the state's incarcerated men—as their primary residence.[12] While CAMPA may have been the first homegrown anti-prison organization formed in the Adirondacks, the factors driving New York's high conviction rate—unemployment, poverty, and unlawful activity increasingly endemic to urban areas—were not unfamiliar to its members. The supporters of CAMPA resisted sharing their wilderness retreat with the same individuals they deemed responsible for the urban breakdown that drove their visits to the North Country in the first place.

Members of CAMPA spent the summer and fall of 1981 presenting their argument against the prison. Not surprisingly, their biggest fear concerned potential damage to tourism, outdoor recreation, and related industries in the Gabriels region. Critics worried a correctional facility would scare off visitors and individuals considering the purchase of a second home—people like themselves—and possibly endanger the livelihoods of restaurateurs, tavern keepers, wilderness outfitters, and the owners of sleepaway camps, grocery stores, and gas stations, among others. Shuttering such businesses, opponents argued, would diminish both the quality and quantity of the outdoor excursions prized so highly by well-to-do residents and tourists. Supporters of CAMPA also highlighted the investments vacationers and seasonal property owners made in the local economy, including consumer spending that contributed to generating over $4 million in sales taxes in Franklin County in 1979 alone. Many of these same critics warned that the penitentiary's opening would spell the end of their own trips to the Adirondacks, thus helping to unleash the very economic harm their correspondence predicted.[13]

A recurrent theme in opposition rhetoric concerned the perceived indispensability of affluent homeowners to the survival of Gabriels. In particular, wealthy residents believed their status as high-tax payers—much like their counterparts later on in Ray Brook—conferred special decision-making powers in community affairs.[14] They behaved accordingly, warning that if Corrections refused their demand not to open the penitentiary, they would sell their properties and withdraw much-needed tax revenue.[15] Critics also claimed that without their tax dollars, low-income residents would face tax increases to cover the cost of public services ranging from schools to snow removal. While this was possibly true, CAMPA members understood the limited value of such arguments in a region whose economic woes predated the arrival of either prisons or the rich. How, then, to draw less-well-off Adirondackers into CAMPA's mostly well-to-do ranks? Prison foes hoped that exploiting what they assumed was a shared antipathy toward people of color might do the trick. They warned that the impoverished dependents of incarcerated men might take up residence in Gabriels and drain already scarce public funds. While local schools, fire departments, and medical providers predicted no trouble in absorbing an influx of newcomers, officials in the Town of Brighton—of which Gabriels is a part—doubted their ability to accommodate a larger population. CAMPA deployed a campaign involving stereotypes of people of color that, by the early 1980s, had become tropes of modern conservatism. One member wrote: "In most cases there are children and wives and the amount of money to dependent children plus the easy life in prison is more attraction to the inmates than outside life. Conjugal visits are just enough to create another member of the family. We, the people, are supporting them, we should have something to say about where they are put."[16] The implicit assumption that people of color pursued welfare dependency and incarceration to avoid paid work both reinforced popular misconceptions and exploited the paranoia of a white, rural working class buffeted by decades of job loss. Race baiting, however, did not guarantee low-income whites would join a campaign organized by and for their elite neighbors. Forced to choose between stable government employment and the prospect of having Black or Brown people living next door, it is hard to imagine poor whites trapped in vicious cycles of poverty rejecting diversity in favor of penury.

Like the LPOOC a few years earlier, CAMPA had tasked itself with promoting an agenda likely to generate significant local backlash. They took a page from the LPOOC playbook and labored to control public opinion about the project through carefully crafted lies, half-truths, and exaggerations. Without evidence, they charged Corrections with overstating the scale of overcrowding, and accused the college of seeking to capitalize on that lie.[17] If there were no crisis, critics argued, it would be unconscionable to open new penitentiaries, especially in "such big old buildings in the Adirondacks" where heating costs were "exorbitant." At the same time, supporters of CAMPA noted that if new correctional facilities truly were necessary, the state should build them in accordance with existing penal policy "nearer the large urban areas" that were home to most incarcerated men and their families, though the best interests of imprisoned men and their loved ones were immaterial to CAMPA's position on prison site selection.[18] Critics next deployed misleading statements to dampen local enthusiasm, warning their low-income neighbors against unrealistic expectations should a penitentiary actually open. While opponents pointed out that seniority rules and transfer lists figured heavily in state hiring decisions, they conveniently omitted the fact that local residents would be eligible for DOCS jobs. CAMPA supporters also announced—without evidence—that several private employers planned to leave the area if the prison opened, further tightening an already difficult labor market. With private sector jobs disappearing and correctional employment apparently impossible to attain, critics reminded struggling homeowners that transplanted people of color might soon be competing with them for the region's increasingly scarce paid work and public services.[19] It is difficult to imagine easily verifiable misstatements such as these driving an uptick in CAMPA's membership. The role that falsehoods played in CAMPA's critique, on the other hand, is easy to decipher. The insecurities that prison opponents tried to sow in others were, in fact, their own. Unable to undermine the project's obvious appeal to their less-well-off neighbors, critics instead tried to frighten them into opposition, but because fear was not a viable solution to the area's economic woes, CAMPA would remain an exclusively elite endeavor.

Much like their STOP counterparts, members of CAMPA believed correctional institutions did not belong in the Adirondack Park. Critics claimed there were too many prisons in the region already.[20] Opponents warned the park risked becoming a penal colony known more for its penitentiaries than its aesthetic beauty and recreational opportunities.[21] Gabriels remained an attractive home and retreat precisely "because of the town's peaceful setting." The park, picnic area, playground, athletic fields, skating rink, waterways, and campsites were but a stone's throw away from the old sanatorium. The prospect of a penal institution intruding on such a calm environment conjured images of Clinton, the park's oldest prison. Supporters of CAMPA feared the construction of light towers, razor wire fencing, high concrete walls, and guard towers that could transform Gabriels into another Dannemora.[22] If such changes materialized, critics worried about resulting heightened threats to public safety—especially escapes—that could leave residents confined inside their homes. Critics who voiced these concerns urged Corrections leaders to open penitentiaries in urban areas, which afforded runaways fewer places to hide. The Adirondack wilderness, after all, had already proven tempting for generations of fugitives.[23] Fortunately for members of CAMPA, the institution planned for Gabriels contained none of the features that made Clinton the archetypical prison. Architectural design alone could not alter community life in the ways they feared. The foreboding image of a penitentiary served as a convenient proxy for the real object of critics' anxiety: imprisoned men of color.

As the foregoing evidence has shown, the poor men of color who would one day find themselves incarcerated in Gabriels were the single biggest source of anxiety for local prison opponents. CAMPA remains an outlier in the history of anti-prison organizing in the Adirondacks, as the adherents of no other resistance movement singled out this part of the imprisoned population in such harshly personal and racist terms. Gabriels' high concentration of affluent homeowners from urban areas—some of whom may have experienced unlawful activity themselves—provides a possible explanation for this variation. Given the ubiquity of this vitriol across the written record, however, a generalized feeling of racial and class superiority seems a more likely reason. Some critics' descriptions of incarcerated men were purely hateful. Opponents branded imprisoned men as "animals," "scum," "humanity's trash," "undesirables," and "the sordid element of our generation," among other epithets. These "blacks and Spanish speaking persons" were, in the eyes of CAMPA members, "the dregs of New York," and had no place in the Adirondack Park. One prison foe even compared incarcerated men to the toxic substances that were then destroying the park's aquatic environments: "We have suffered from acid rain long enough. Please don't introduce another poison into our area." This particular critic offered a solution: "Let's convert or rehab some of the buildings in New York [City] and keep those people where they originate from."[24] Such comments revealed that whenever members of CAMPA bemoaned the abstract "prison," their real targets were the poor men of color who would someday occupy its cells.

Recognizing their inability to singlehandedly stop the penitentiary, members of CAMPA appealed to the Adirondack Park Agency for help. It is instructive to consider the individuals and organizations that CAMPA did not turn to for support. The Republican politicians occupying most local elected positions favored the proposal, as did the majority of Democratic and Republican state lawmakers. Given its recent history shepherding the construction of both Ray Brook prisons, the APA might have seemed an odd choice. By the early 1980s, though, committed environmentalists and prison opponents filled the agency's political leadership. Moreover, CAMPA members knew that building on private land guaranteed Park Agency involvement in the project, and opposition leaders likely understood that aggressive environmental oversight might be the only way to scuttle the prison. However, in seeking an alliance with the APA, opponents betrayed both a misunderstanding of environmental law and Park Agency power. Members of CAMPA claimed the agency was obligated to "protect the forest preserve against intrusions and retain those public lands as a wild forest preserve." However, the Gabriels complex was situated outside the boundaries of state Forest Preserve lands under the exclusive control of the DEC, not the Park Agency.

Even if the compound had been within the Forest Preserve, the APA still would have lacked jurisdiction, as the agency's nonbinding regulatory power over state developments inside the park meant Corrections could open the prison with or without its consent. Heedless of this distinction, critics warned Park Agency officials that the penitentiary would unleash a wave of disasters.[25] Opponents wrote the prison would "destroy the land," "degrade recreational and living conditions," "destroy both a beautiful area and the surrounding community," and, simply, "be cruel to the environment." Of course, members of CAMPA knew the penitentiary would be confined to an existing facility on land that had been transformed decades earlier. The environmental costs of converting the complex to a correctional facility, as at Ray Brook in 1976, would be minimal at best. The destruction they feared was social, not ecological. In a telling turn of phrase, one critic wrote that building a prison would not be "in keeping with what the Adirondack Park means to us."[26] What did the park mean to supporters of CAMPA? Many viewed the region as a wilderness resort protected by the state constitution, an idea that captured the feeling of elite entitlement that infused the group's campaign.[27] As 1981 came to a close, it remained an open question whether the APA shared critics' view that potential demographic shifts constituted irreparable environmental harm.

Through the summer and fall of 1981, members of CAMPA rallied around an anti-prison message that added new dimensions to an environmentally oriented opposition first forged in the North Country's other prison towns. In identifying the proposed penitentiary as an environmental problem, supporters of CAMPA evoked critiques from residents of mid-nineteenth-century Dannemora and late twentieth-century Ray Brook. Prisons, like any large-scale infrastructure, inevitably impose ecological costs. While Dannemora property owners grumbled over state enclosure of a once-expansive commons, and Ray Brook residents organized to safeguard their community's environmental and public health, the wealthy residents of Gabriels held remarkably similar views. The prospective public transformation of privately held resources, along with the potential for harm to the community, worried Gabriels residents. However, members of CAMPA departed from their counterparts in Dannemora and Ray Brook in identifying incarcerated men and their dependents as specific environmental threats. The "prison" was no longer an abstract piece of infrastructure inflicting damage only during construction. Neither were wildlife, vegetation, air, soil, and water its only possible targets. To maintain Gabriels as the exclusive hamlet many believed it was, prison opponents needed a more inclusive definition of "environment." Reformulated along social and racial lines, CAMPA's understanding highlighted people of color as a unique source of harm whose exclusion was key to the community's survival. While CAMPA's fearmongering sowed doubts across the region, the project's supporters, though fewer in number, were equally fervent in their desire to see the prison built.

Defending and Planning the Gabriels Prison

As a project legally immune to the whims of public opinion, the penitentiary planned for Gabriels neither needed nor enjoyed an organized defense. Besides Park Agency review, little stood in the way of state leaders purchasing the property and building the prison. With decision-making power in the hands of Albany lawmakers and Corrections officials, rallying to the project's defense might have seemed unnecessary. The emergence of CAMPA, however, transformed a routine bureaucratic exercise into a conflict involving a variety of stakeholders. Compelled to defend a project under harsh public attack, the collective message of the project's loosely organized advocates constituted a rebuttal of CAMPA's doomsday scenarios. Leaders from DOCS, PSC, and local governments, along with a cohort of middle- and low-income residents, underscored the potential for a prison-induced economic boom. The focus on economic impact was so intense that it often overshadowed the correctional facility at the project's heart. For ordinary folks on the defense side, the penitentiary was about more than just jobs. For them, CAMPA's opposition represented an illegitimate power grab reminiscent of past class conflicts in the Adirondacks. This ideological warfare reached a climax in the fall of 1981 when the APA, pressured by CAMPA, undertook a formal review of the project. As the year ended, a conflict until then contested in the court of public opinion moved into the hearing rooms of the Adirondack Park Agency. For the individuals and organizations involved, at stake was nothing less than the future of New York's great north woods.

Echoing arguments first advanced over a century earlier, Corrections officials stressed the penitentiary's ability to invigorate the local economy. Operating in the realm of speculation, members of CAMPA had foretold a prison-induced economic catastrophe. By contrast, DOCS's data-driven arguments portrayed a correctional facility that would lift *all* boats. Officials' emphasis on facts and figures also helped distract from the penitentiary that drove CAMPA's creation in the first place. If the prison were out of sight, Corrections bureaucrats likely reasoned, it might exit critics' minds. A technocratic approach also allowed DOCS to avoid engaging with—and thus re-airing—CAMPA's venomous screeds. Corrections leaders turned instead to the topic of employment, noting the penitentiary's 101 full-time positions would help reduce Franklin County's high unemployment. In January 1981, joblessness stood at 17.3 percent, nine points above the state average. While unemployment dipped to 8.6 percent during the summer tourist season, that figure still outpaced the statewide rate by nearly two points. With more people holding permanent, full-time positions, DOCS predicted a boost in incomes for Franklin County families that routinely trailed the state average. Increased employment and rising salaries, Corrections hoped, would also stem the scourge of depopulation—the number of people living in Franklin County had dropped from 44,830 to 42,899 between 1950 and 1980—ravaging North Country communities. With more jobs, higher incomes, and a growing population, DOCS leaders anticipated that reduced poverty would yield a diminishing demand for public assistance. Corrections envisioned an outlook that diverged from CAMPA's prediction of economic devastation: increased consumer spending, higher tax revenues, and new private sector businesses opening across the region.[28] DOCS officials hoped that a thriving local economy might more than compensate for the demographic shifts so feared by members of CAMPA.

Corrections bureaucrats also responded to CAMPA concerns that a prison would prove financially burdensome to Gabriels residents. DOCS showed that, on the contrary, penal institutions could blend seamlessly into existing settlements. Corrections Department studies of prison towns across New York and elsewhere revealed that penitentiaries often lifted local property values. State research also uncovered no harmful impacts on new real estate developments either inside prison communities or in their surrounding regions, and, in addition, studies indicated no evidence of high turnover in local housing markets as a result of penitentiary construction. Regarding costs, DOCS officials noted that the Gabriels compound already had its own firefighting equipment, fresh water supply, and sewage treatment plant, thus requiring no expensive or potentially disruptive tie-ins to existing public systems. Corrections leaders further stated there was widespread cooperation from local public services: local politicians had consented to accepting prison refuse at county landfills, hospitals and public schools had signaled their readiness to admit new patients and students, and area law enforcement had agreed to help in the event of escapes or disturbances. Under such scenarios, CAMPA's prediction of tax hikes generated by a prison-induced exodus of elite homeowners might never come to pass. Indeed, by DOCS's own account, repurposing Gabriels for penal use might be as smooth as the 1976 transformation of the former hospital at Ray Brook into the minimum-security prison of Camp Adirondack.[29]

The prison's potential to revitalize a sputtering economy inspired an equally fervent defense from area political leaders. In a region known for its adherence to anti-statist ideologies, state intervention in the economy elicited little more than a shrug from its mainly conservative local authorities. After all, the same Reagan-era conservatism that lauded the supposed virtues of small government also emphasized preserving "law and order." Accordingly, local officials doubled down on DOCS's message of economic uplift. For Karl Griebsch, a member of the Adirondack Correctional Facility Board of Directors, the bodies of imprisoned men represented only dollar signs. According to Griebsch, it cost New York State $17,000 per year to incarcerate a single convicted man. The higher the incarcerated population, therefore, the greater the state investment. Compensating staff along with regular upkeep of buildings and grounds would necessitate even larger financial commitments. With millions of dollars flowing from Albany to Gabriels, Griebsch anticipated "most of that money" would be "spent right in this area."[30] Nelson Parker, an elected member of the Brighton Town Council, shared Griebsch's excitement over the potential to jumpstart business activity. With millions required just to open the penitentiary, Parker declared, "It's bound to bring some money into town." The ripple effects of such spending, especially from Correctional workers' salaries, would inevitably boost non-penal industries. Parker noted, "They've [DOCS employees] got to eat, they've got to have some place to live."[31] Also echoing the timeworn view of corrections as sustainable economic development, members of the Franklin County legislature in Malone unanimously endorsed the Gabriels plan.[32] By turns, then, area leaders deflected attention from the region's growing dependence on government largesse by focusing instead on its purportedly positive effects. In tough times, area leaders gambled that residents' desire for a more robust economy would trump the adherence to principles of limited government that formed the bedrock of their political identity.

Similar desires infused the thinking of President Stainback at Paul Smith's College. With many of his 180 employees opposed to the prison, Stainback hoped pragmatic considerations might diminish the power of CAMPA's emotion-laden appeals. Having learned from the July 1981 public meeting, in subsequent remarks Stainback avoided highlighting the economic impacts favored by his counterparts in state and local government. After all, most of his Paul Smith's constituents required no economic boost. Instead, the president hinted at possibly painful college budget cuts if the plan fell through. Stainback noted that maintenance costs on the abandoned complex were draining PSC resources. The buildings' deterioration, he warned, would eventually make them unsellable, inevitably driving the college deeper into the red. Suddenly, Gabriels' vaunted remoteness appeared a liability. With no one besides DOCS interested in purchasing the facility, Stainback claimed the college had no choice. To those troubled by the college's possible implication in the carceral state, Stainback pointed to PSC's past use of Camp Adirondack labor crews and its loan of faculty to teach courses to men incarcerated at FCI-Ray Brook. Finally, Stainback argued that the facility's environment made it naturally suited for a prison. His description would have made the Bureau of Prisons proud: "The terrain is in large part level and ideal for additional construction and, in part rolling to higher ground with mountain views . . . One could easily recognize that conversion for security purposes was always a potential for utilization."[33] Failing to convert such a site—seemingly molded by the hand of God for penal use—could be as catastrophic for Gabriels, Stainback suggested, as any of CAMPA's darkest predictions.

The prison also served as the catalyst for renewed hostilities between elite and working-class Adirondackers. The proposal unearthed tensions over power, place, and belonging that for decades structured social relations in many Adirondack communities. Not unlike elite members of CAMPA, the ties that bound many middle- and low-income residents to Gabriels conditioned their reactions to the project. Ordinary folks noted that Gabriels was not just a tourist destination, the Adirondack Park was not only a resort, and not everyone in town worked at Paul Smith's College. To the contrary, Gabriels was also a working-class community where many struggled to survive. For over three decades, young people had been leaving the area "because there are no good paying year round jobs to offer." In contrast to adherents of CAMPA, local advocates of the penitentiary worried that without the boost officials claimed it would provide, a community that was "slowly dying out" might someday disappear. Lower income residents indicated that in addition to providing them with new employment opportunities, the penal institution would also benefit North Country homeowners who were already working for DOCS. As Corrections Department rules often required new employees to begin their careers at penitentiaries far from their hometowns, project supporters noted a correctional facility in Gabriels would reunite many local families. The prospect of prison opponents selling their properties and leaving town did not trouble the hamlet's ordinary men and women. After all, the predicted influx of working-class residents back to Gabriels would create "more taxpayers," ensure "more taxes going back into the area," and offset any negative impacts from the possible withdrawal of elite tax dollars.[34] The suggestion that the interests of permanent, middle- and low-income residents should supersede those of seasonal homeowners and visitors closely mirrored CAMPA's equally exclusionary claims to power in the community. Coexistence, it seemed, did not mean a shared sense of belonging.

If only working-class, year-round residents truly belonged in Gabriels, then it followed that elite opposition to the prison was not legitimate. The efforts of ordinary folks to tarnish CAMPA's credibility demonstrated a commitment to exclusion matched only by the project's opponents. If there was any high ground in this conflict, neither side could rightfully claim it. Using a timeworn tactic of North Country class struggles, middle- and low-income homeowners highlighted the fact that most CAMPA members were neither permanent residents nor native-born Adirondackers. The notion that place of birth and length of residency conferred power also paralleled CAMPA's similarly restrictive views concerning wealth and taxpayer status. Further, noting that prison critics ignored the plight of the working class, supporters of the penitentiary complained that adherents of CAMPA did not care "for the economic welfare of us year-round residents," and that they "could care less whether we survive here or not." While the evidence surely pointed in that direction, rich and poor alike shared a mutual disdain for the well-being of the other. Local advocates of the project claimed that by laboring to stop the prison, members of CAMPA were actually "trying to destroy Paul Smith's College and the Town of Brighton."[35] The destruction they feared, though, closely matched that of their erstwhile foes in CAMPA. The high-, middle-, and low-income residents of Gabriels were all, in fact, united in their shared dread of degraded social status. While elites viewed the penitentiary as a threat to their long-assumed dominance, ordinary folks interpreted the same institution as a potentially liberating force for those struggling just to make ends meet.

Finally, ordinary men and women in Gabriels proudly defended the North Country's long history with incarceration. Their comments constituted a rebuke of CAMPA's fear-based vilification of correctional facilities and their occupants. Advocates of the project highlighted what they perceived as the positive bonds already forged among local communities and the Adirondacks' three existing penitentiaries. In addition to the economic support the institutions provided to thousands of residents, supporters of the proposal expressed gratitude for the work performed by incarcerated men from Camp Adirondack on infrastructure and conversation projects. They also called for compassion for the imprisoned population, including some who appealed to arguments regarding the supposedly healthful qualities inherent in Adirondack nature. Rosemarie Nopper, a survivor of tuberculosis who had received inpatient care at Gabriels beginning in 1948, argued that imprisoned men needed "the beauty, serenity, and spirit" of the Adirondacks to facilitate their reentry into free society.[36] While this rosy interpretation provided a sharp contrast with CAMPA's foreboding image, the prison system's checkered history in the North Country was no secret. Ecological destruction, social tensions, labor unrest, escapes, violence, and exploitation of prison labor each were features of the area's correctional facilities. And that was just in Ray Brook. Exaggeration and emotion, therefore, were not the exclusive province of CAMPA in the fight to determine Gabriels' future.

As the debate between supporters and opponents continued, officials from the Corrections Department and Paul Smith's College began planning the Gabriels prison. In the late summer of 1981, DOCS enlisted experts in environmental protection, food service, and security to assess future needs at the property. The department also contracted with the Ehrenkrantz Group, a New York City-based architectural firm, and environmental consultants at McKeown and Franz, also headquartered in New York City, to prepare an environmental impact statement prior to construction. These steps did not preclude DOCS Commissioner Coughlin from claiming emergency exemption from the State Environmental Quality Review Act (SEQRA) of 1975. Overcrowding in the prison system, Coughlin argued, made undertaking even the self-directed environmental reviews mandated by the law a burdensome distraction.

Converse Goddard, chair of the Paul Smith's College Board of Trustees, affirmed his commitment to the project, noting his "responsibility to maximize the use of college resources" by "selling the property so we will have the money to build other things." To those ends, the board empowered President Stainback to negotiate the sale with Corrections. In October, DOCS leaders unveiled their plan for converting the compound into a minimum-security penitentiary. Contrary to Coughlin's suggestion back in April, the prison would create significant impacts. Construction workers would demolish four unneeded buildings at the site, erect a new visitors' center, and renovate existing structures for education, housing, dining, and religious worship. As overcrowding made further delay untenable, that same month local newspapers carried notification from the APA of the state's intent to build.[37]

Opening the prison might have remained a routine bureaucratic exercise were it not for the emergence of CAMPA. Recalling government officials' indifference to residents' concerns during the planning and construction of FCI-Ray Brook, DOCS leaders labored to balance the competing interests of the project's supporters and opponents against their own need to meet the state's demand for new cells.[38] Recognizing the presence of an opposition in Gabriels, the department worked to minimize the risk of a potentially burdensome estrangement from the town. With opponents demanding the project's cancellation, DOCS officials understood they faced an uphill climb. Corrections administrators knew they could not prevent the demographic changes at the core of CAMPA's critique. Destined to disappoint the penitentiary's critics, DOCS leaders hoped that transparency and compromise—characteristics lacking at Ray Brook back in 1977—might foster community support. Accordingly, Corrections officials informed homeowners *before* building began that it would be impossible to open the penitentiary without imposing harmful environmental impacts. DOCS anticipated the removal of vegetation, adverse effects on migratory osprey and loon populations, and restrictions on the use of recreational infrastructure. Acknowledging the value many homeowners placed on outdoor play, Corrections offered to turn over most of the tract to the DEC for inclusion in the Forest Preserve, keeping it free from development and open for wilderness excursions.[39] In recognition of the challenging conditions under which many North Country homeowners lived and an awareness that insufficient public funding could leave vital infrastructure either unbuilt or unrepaired, worsening many residents' already difficult lives, Corrections took a page from its Ray Brook playbook and pledged to cash-strapped local governments the free use of prison labor on conservation, infrastructure, and public works projects.[40] Unfortunately for DOCS, while its promise of imprisoned work crews proved attractive to many from all income levels, its plan to expand the Forest Preserve did not match the environmental concerns identified by CAMPA. Not satisfied with simply more outdoor space, prison opponents hoped the APA might be more receptive to their concerns.

In the fall of 1981, the Adirondack Park Agency began what ordinarily might have been a mundane review of a state project inside the park. Like their counterparts at the Corrections Department, officials at the APA found themselves trying to satisfy the divergent concerns of Gabriels' affluent and less-well-off residents. As no law barred New York State from developing property purchased from a private owner, Park Agency leaders knew they could not stop the prison. APA counsel noted, however, that state developments on public lands inside the park were subject to Section 814 of the APA Act. Unfortunately for DOCS, the APA's non-binding review process involved several time-consuming steps. Before lawmakers could approve a budget for Gabriels, Section 814 required DOCS to file a notice of intent to build with the Park Agency. The APA would then determine whether it had enough information to proceed. Even then, Corrections would have to wait up to thirty days to begin work. If the APA determined the project would impose harm, public hearings "to provide full public disclosure and allow public opinion to be expressed" could be scheduled, requiring DOCS to wait an additional ninety days after the first hearing before breaking ground, though the review's non-binding nature ensured that the findings of any public inquiry could not stop construction. While local supporters of the prison would eventually achieve their objective, the Park Agency's constituency included all park residents, including members of CAMPA.[41] Recognizing their inability to stop the penitentiary, members of CAMPA opened the APA toolbox to disrupt its progress.

As DOCS and PSC moved toward making the prison a reality, CAMPA's leaders settled on gumming up the process any way they could. They began by pressuring the APA to schedule delay-inducing hearings on "this large and controversial project," warning they were "very serious in our concern," adding that their organization had "both the resources and the will to see that all of our concerns are properly addressed." To that end, the opposition hired a team of environmental consultants, scientific experts, and attorneys. Acknowledging their duty to represent all park residents, Park Agency leaders agreed in late September to hold public hearings.[42] CAMPA then worked to slow down the review itself. To their delight, opponents found kindred spirits within the political wing of the APA. Agency counsel Robert Glennon commented that "a clever lawyer" could find ways to drag out the time-consuming process. In late September one such Park Agency attorney announced he would need at least two months to process prison-related paperwork and proceeded to bombard Corrections with dozens of questions about the project. Meanwhile, APA Chair Theodore Ruzow cast doubt on DOCS's rationale for building the penitentiary, arguing that since prison overcrowding was "not a new or sudden development," it "could not be considered emergency conditions." Ruzow pushed still further, questioning the legitimacy of Coughlin's claim of exemption from SEQRA requirements. Arguing that "the public has the right to be heard," Ruzow solicited input on the proposal from Gabriels residents in October. As opposition correspondence began arriving at Park Agency headquarters, Executive Director Vincent Moore claimed his agency had "the weight of public opinion behind it" as the APA moved toward the first formal environmental review of an Adirondack prison in Gabriels.[43] With hearings on the horizon and mountains of Park Agency paperwork to complete, DOCS officials scuttled the prison's planned November 1 opening. For a project that neither organization was supposed to be able to stop, both CAMPA and the APA approached the hearings from a position of strength.

CAMPA became a potent counterweight to the prison proposal in the second half of 1981. No one connected to the project, it seemed, was immune to its members' loud and venomous screeds. Corrections officials and leaders from Paul Smith's struggled to respond to the group's unconventional environmental agenda. The fact that they responded at all shows that CAMPA's legal disempowerment in the planning process did not equate to lack of influence. Promises of economic uplift fell on deaf ears. So, too, did the prospect of an expanded Forest Preserve, enhanced recreational opportunities, and the free use of incarcerated labor. In contrast, the relatively muted defense of the penitentiary from ordinary folks in Gabriels—who understood their conflict with CAMPA as but the latest of the Adirondack Park's long-running class struggles—likely left the misleading impression of a community unified in opposition. Armed with time and financial resources not available to their less-well-off neighbors, adherents of CAMPA forged connections with Park Agency leaders that proved invaluable in their effort to stop the penitentiary.

Environmental Regulation(s) and the Opening of Camp Gabriels

Between November 1981 and August 1982, environmental regulators became, for the first time, central players in the planning of an Adirondack prison. Mounting pressure in the previous half-year had transformed a project that had been legally insulated from public opinion into a development whose future seemed increasingly uncertain. Oversight involving representatives from the Adirondack Park Agency, Department of Correctional Services, and Citizens Against More Prisons in the Adirondacks, along with permanent residents and seasonal homeowners, played out in three phases. The hearings that ran from November 1981 to January 1982 highlighted, as they had at Ray Brook, professional divisions within the Park Agency. While its non-partisan scientists testified to the potential for prison-induced destruction, the APA's political leadership, members of CAMPA, and officials from Corrections proposed only reduced visual impact as a remedy. Once the hearings ended, Agency leaders and adherents of CAMPA resumed their opposition campaign, concluding with the APA's non-binding rejection of the proposal in March 1982. This resulted in the end of Park Agency involvement, the property's sale, and the beginning of renovations; however, it did not spell the end of CAMPA. In the final, informal phase of the oversight process, opponents spent the spring and summer of 1982 pressing Corrections to complete SEQRA assessments—particularly an environmental impact statement (EIS)—that had been suspended months earlier. Critics hoped the possibility for ecological damage as first identified by APA scientists might also be discovered by private consultants under contract to DOCS. Members of CAMPA anticipated such evidence might be enough to scuttle the prison. Unfortunately for CAMPA, the real power in this fight had always rested with the

Corrections Department. DOCS bureaucrats reinforced this point in August 1982 by opening the penitentiary before completing the mandated environmental reviews. At that point, the battle over Gabriels was over.

The APA hearings began on November 16, 1981. The first session, held at the Harrietstown Town Hall in Saranac Lake, attracted over four hundred participants. Similarly large crowds composed primarily of penitentiary opponents packed hearing rooms at subsequent sessions held in Ray Brook, Saranac Lake, and Brighton. Difficult winter weather caused the six days of hearings—planned originally only for the month of November—to last until January 15, 1982. Public comment consumed the first two sessions, while the final four featured testimony from expert witnesses called by DOCS, the APA, and CAMPA. Attendees rehashed many of the arguments advanced both for and against the prison during the previous half-year. The acrimony that had characterized the relationship among CAMPA, the Park Agency, and Corrections during the second half of 1981 largely dissipated once stakeholders found themselves in the same room. Likely resigned to the prison's construction, members of CAMPA refined their definition of environmental impact to match a narrow interpretation offered by representatives from the APA and DOCS. With all three groups agreeing on the importance of limiting the facility's visual impact, the discussion of any other possible effects on the Gabriels environment vanished from public view.[44]

Since the penitentiary's real potential for environmental impacts concerned neither members of CAMPA nor the project's local supporters, calculating its ecological costs was left to the Park Agency's professional scientists. Their testimony served notice that, once again, correctional planners were seeking to build a prison in a fragile environment. The scientists' findings warned of possibly irrevocable damage to environmental and public health. James Hill, an APA soil and water engineering specialist, anticipated harm to local wetlands, wildlife, and water supplies, in addition to increased strain on area sewage and waste disposal systems. Betty Ann Hughes, a biological resources analyst for the agency, concurred with Hill's assessment that the Gabriels property, not unlike the site of FCI-Ray Brook, contained sensitive wetlands that would likely be damaged by construction. As an alternative form of development, Hughes recommended "uses such as hiking, hunting, and limited timber removal," which, she argued, "would be compatible" with the existing landscape. Michael DiNunzio, a Park

Agency ecologist, agreed with Hughes, arguing the penitentiary would create "severe conflict with the use of the Park's natural resources by the public by the very nature of its existence and function." DiNunzio went on to claim that the prison would not "exist in harmony with the relatively wild and undeveloped character of the Adirondack Park," and would constitute a "non-conforming use in the Park region."[45] The experts' analysis foretold the startling possibility of a Ray Brook-style disaster in Gabriels. However, their focus on questions surrounding the penitentiary's compatibility and conformity with the park environment conveyed an unmistakable message of support for CAMPA's cause.

Dire predictions from APA scientists carried only as much weight as the agency's political arm would allow. At the hearings, Park Agency lawyers and bureaucrats signaled a willingness to collaborate with Corrections and, in the process, undercut their scientist colleagues. Why would an agency committed to stopping the prison suddenly become its handmaiden? There are several possible explanations. Under the glare of the public spotlight, APA officials sought to cast their organization in the best possible light. Adopting CAMPA's hard line risked alienating DOCS employees, project supporters, and residents still on the fence about the agency's intentions. Park Agency leaders knew the hearings were political theater. Though Corrections and the agency held diametrically opposed positions, power rested entirely on one side. With the prison an inevitability, public squabbling would benefit no one. However, recalling the destruction at Ray Brook, some in the Park Agency likely felt a duty to at least minimize the risk of disaster, so APA officials adopted a definition of environmental impact narrow enough to satisfy any stakeholder not a scientist by training. That definition entailed a focus on visual impact. At the hearings, William Curran, the agency's principal project review specialist, expressed concern that Corrections had given no assurance "that the future visual character" of Gabriels would be preserved. During testimony, APA general counsel Robert Glennon asked DOCS Director of Facility Planning and Development Jeff Buck to promise that the prison would have sufficient "vegetative or topographic buffers" to shield it from public view. Buck promised that "natural growth," including shrubs, grass, and trees, would form a barrier separating the town from the prison.[46] Thus, a project whose social, racial, and economic dimensions had for months been the subject of intense debate now, in an instant, was reduced to a matter of aesthetics. It is difficult to imagine that Park Agency officials viewed their public compromise with Corrections as a permanent solution.

Though members of CAMPA remained opposed to the project, they accepted the interpretation of environmental impact as hashed out by DOCS and the APA. Supporters of CAMPA, like officials in the Park Agency, knew they could not stop the penitentiary. They understood the hearings for what they were: a stalling tactic that allowed opponents to publicize their cause. During the hearings, CAMPA leaders therefore followed their agency counterparts in eschewing the caustic language found in their written correspondence. A willingness to cooperate with DOCS, they likely surmised, might avoid further damage to their relationships with neighbors who were supportive of the prison. The questions regarding real concerns about environmental and public health that were raised by Park Agency scientists barely registered with CAMPA. By contrast, since visual impact *was* a stated opposition concern, it required little effort for CAMPA to accept the non-binding compromise of a vegetative wall. In his testimony, Gary Randorf, executive director of the Adirondack Council, a local environmental organization aligned with CAMPA, underscored the value that well-to-do homeowners placed on the area's wildness. Randorf expressed fear over further "encroachment into that area by any kind of man made structures or facilities," and worried about how increased artificial lighting might harm the community's wilderness character and its wildlife. Most CAMPA supporters present at the hearings, including Randorf, thus accepted screening the penitentiary from public view as the best outcome—short of scuttling the project entirely—they could hope for. The general apathy over the project's potential to harm environmental and public health that had characterized the debate's first half-year remained a fixture during the hearings. The presentation of expert, non-partisan research did nothing to alter those views. Park Agency bureaucrats and CAMPA leaders, who were worried mainly about matters of compatibility and conformity, it seemed, were more than willing to gamble with the community's ecological future.[47] Like their counterparts at the APA, members of CAMPA likely realized their fight would resume once the hearings concluded.

For the Corrections Department, too, the hearings were little more than a formality. Its dominant position in the debate meant that adjusting arguments, offering new solutions, and even telling the truth were unnecessary. DOCS official Ramon Rodriguez inexplicably commented in his testimony that "it is our history within this area, that we are good neighbors." Though the first five years at Camp Adirondack generally showed that to be true, making a similar claim about Dannemora would have been much more difficult. Nevertheless, Rodriguez repeated what had by then become Corrections Department gospel, underlining the penitentiary's potential to realize economic wonders the private market had never achieved. Jeff Buck noted that state leaders considered corrections "a very viable program in the North Country."[48] Left unanalyzed, of course, were the tight budgets, NIMBYism, and overcrowding that drove DOCS to the Adirondacks in the first place. Finally, Corrections officials used the hearings to repeat promises concerning environmental impacts. Public expressions of support from the APA and CAMPA for its visual impact scheme left little reason for DOCS to offer any new ideas on how to balance its need for cells with the preservation of environmental and public health. Corrections bureaucrats simply reiterated their plans to use existing vegetation to shield the facility from public view, to expand the Forest Preserve, and to deploy poorly paid incarcerated men on infrastructure, conservation, and public works projects.[49] While possession of the upper hand granted DOCS freedom unknown either to CAMPA or to the APA both before and during the hearings, it is important not to downplay the significance of the concessions Corrections made. While promises of a vegetative screen and prison labor crews evoked gestures made in Ray Brook, DOCS's commitment to adding land to the Forest Preserve represented tacit recognition of the role that area residents and environmental regulators had played in shaping the newest corner of New York's carceral state.

Neighborly gestures notwithstanding, incarcerating convicted men remained the Corrections Department's top priority. As the hearings ended in January 1982, the department's earlier eagerness to find common ground with its counterparts in CAMPA and the APA began to dissolve. Underscoring his belief that additional compromises in the area of environmental protection would not be possible, DOCS Commissioner Coughlin reminded APA Chairman Ruzow "that society's needs for prison space are immediate and critical." Having already made concessions to groups that DOCS legally could have ignored, Coughlin suggested that Corrections would be reassuming its lawfully protected position of dominance. After all, Coughlin was going to build the Gabriels prison no matter what. Ironically, only days after the hearings concluded, Governor Carey asked lawmakers for even more Corrections funding in his 1982 budget. The governor's request came after voters narrowly defeated the $500 million prison bond in the November 1981 election. Carey called for additional monies to operate packed penitentiaries in Dannemora and Ray Brook. By January 1982, the state incarcerated 2,700 men at Dannemora—109 percent of capacity—and employed over 1,300 workers in that facility. Adirondack Correctional Facility in Ray Brook held 290 convicted men and, following its medium-security upgrade, had witnessed a jump in its workforce from 120 to 310 employees.[50] Few, then, were under any illusion that a prison in Gabriels would make even a small dent in the state's worsening overcrowding crisis. If anything, news of correctional expansions beyond those planned only months earlier re-galvanized the opposition just as it was losing steam.

For CAMPA, professions of fealty to an environmental impact mitigation plan that excluded nearly all of its priorities proved short-lived. Recognizing the Gabriels prison might someday be as large and overcrowded as those at Dannemora and Ray Brook likely convinced some in CAMPA to resume their campaign. Success at this point would require a shift in tactics. Appealing to the APA would be a fruitless endeavor, especially as that agency's involvement reached its conclusion. With DOCS uninterested in further discussion with either the Park Agency or CAMPA, opponents' only hope would be exposing a potentially fatal technicality in the planning documents. To wit, at the end of January 1981, CAMPA filed suit against Corrections to compel the department's compliance with the State Environmental Quality Review Act. Opponents demanded DOCS prepare an environmental impact statement (EIS)—an action that had been delayed after Commissioner Coughlin's invocation of emergency exemption status months earlier—prior to acquiring the property. Such a document would provide a blueprint detailing the project's anticipated effects on both human and non-human nature. Prison critics, much like Chairman Ruzow, pointed to the still-unfinished prison as proof that the "emergency" Coughlin claimed did not exist.[51] CAMPA's real hope entailed the possibility that an EIS prepared by an outside firm might corroborate the predictions of ecological harm outlined by agency scientists. If so, opponents hoped that fear of a Ray Brook–style disaster might help kill the prison.

In March 1982, Park Agency officials ended their review. APA staff reviewed all hearing transcripts and documents related to the project, and on March 25 recommended the agency commissioners reject the prison.

That same day, Chairman Ruzow joined CAMPA in its renewed effort to stop the penitentiary, underscoring fears that had animated the opposition from day one. Ruzow painted a grim picture of what awaited Gabriels: "First, you get minimum security. Then come the wires, the walls and the gun turrets." Further correctional expansion, Ruzow warned, would turn the park "into a great big penal colony," which he called "a great big mistake." Labeling penitentiaries in the park "paradoxical" and "unfortunate," Ruzow lamented the legal constraints that prevented his agency from stopping the facility. The only weapon left to opponents, he noted, was "to marshal public opinion." At this late stage, however, popular discontent alone could not stop the prison.[52]

At its meeting on March 26, the commissioners of the APA voted 6–2 to reject the correctional facility in Gabriels. This action marked the first time in the Park Agency's history that its staff and commissioners had each turned down the development plans of a sibling state agency. By endorsing many of CAMPA's grievances, however, the staff recommendation to the commissioners rejected the idea that the Adirondacks were also a working-class wilderness:

> Parks are created to increase . . . opportunities for appropriate park-like activities and to limit certain other activities . . . The Adirondack Park exists because . . . the wild forest, water, wildlife and aesthetic resources of the Park and its open space character . . . [are] of national and international significance. Activities and enterprises which do not further these values and, in fact, insult them cannot be permitted or entertained. Otherwise, the Park will not remain dedicated to the tenets of the State Constitution . . . The acquisition of private lands for discordant public activities is yet another attempt to distort the wisdom and meaning of the legislation protecting the preservation of the Park . . . It is inconceivable that the Agency can fulfill its responsibility to the Park, its history and its people, by recommending construction of this facility. The . . . emerging image of the Park as a prime location for prisons cannot be tolerated or justified.

For his part, Ruzow agreed it was the APA's duty to arrest prison expansion in the Adirondacks. Echoing the anxieties of many homeowners, Ruzow commented, "The question comes to this: if this park accepts this [prison] . . . will that be an invitation for a fifth, a sixth or even a tenth prison in the park?" However, claims that penal institutions were incompatible with the Park relied on a narrow interpretation that excluded any development not connected to leisure or outdoor recreation. Arguing that prisons did not conform with the Adirondack environment effectively denied the area's history, diminished the importance many locals placed on correctional employment, and guaranteed that many middle- and low-income Adirondackers would continue to see the Park Agency as little more than an elite advocacy group. Corrections leaders simply ignored the Park Agency's conclusion and moved ahead with plans to open the penitentiary.[53]

Corrections moved quickly to get the prison built. In April, Paul Smith's sold its property to DOCS for $635,000. In its last action related to the project, Park Agency officials classified 92.6 acres of the now-state-owned tract as "State Administrative," with the remainder designated as "Wild Forest," which under the APA's classification schema restricted "land use to recreational and certain other activities which do not change the wild forest character." Following Corrections' much-touted promise, the Park Agency promptly asked the DEC to add the Wild Forest land to the Forest Preserve. Having completed nearly all the bureaucratic requirements necessary before construction, Corrections Commissioner Coughlin visited the area at the end of April and claimed victory. Coughlin chose the friendly setting of the Saranac Lake Chamber of Commerce for a lunchtime address. There, the commissioner again underscored the value of correctional services as an economic development model for the region. He noted, "Northern New York State has a future with the state service industry and I think we should take advantage of it," asking, "Why not provide services upstate that the state needs?" Of the opposition, Coughlin complained, "I don't understand why people raise such a fuss." Addressing Ruzow's charge that the park was becoming a penal colony, Coughlin stated, "No more prisons are being planned for the Park," but, seeking to reassure residents desperate for jobs, he declared, "We have never had to close a prison."[54]

One of the last steps required of Corrections before construction could begin involved preparation of an environmental impact statement. As had been the case since Coughlin requested an exemption, DOCS met this particular obligation on its own schedule. Not even the lawsuit filed by CAMPA could push Corrections to alter its timeline, again reminding stakeholders where real power rested in this struggle. In May 1982, after the Gabriels property was under its control, DOCS received a draft of an EIS for the project from its consultants in New York. In July, DOCS distributed copies of the draft—mainly a rehashing of data created before and during the hearings—to news media outlets, elected officials, and government agencies for comment. CAMPA leaders complained upon discovering Corrections had failed to send them a document they had pursued in court. Unfazed, DOCS only submitted a final EIS—effectively a facsimile of the draft—for public review in December 1982, three months after the prison opened, neutralizing any possible impacts its content might have had.[55] Even after the penitentiary opened, Corrections' disregard for the reporting requirements of state law, the formal legal complaints of its opponents, and the concerns of area residents reminded stakeholders that questions of environmental and public health were never high on the Corrections Department priority list. For an agency that sought to avoid comparisons to the BOP, DOCS came awfully close to matching the bureau's dismal record.

The shuttered complex at Gabriels entered its third phase of life in the summer of 1982. Continuing a practice first established in the early nineteenth century, New York deployed its imprisoned population to help build its newest correctional institution. In mid-July, men incarcerated at Adirondack Correctional Facility in Ray Brook began working under the supervision of private contractors to convert the compound for penal use. Imprisoned men mowed the lawns, installed new windows, scraped and applied coats of paint, and performed plumbing work, among other tasks. Corrections officials promised renovations, including the construction of four new buildings, would be complete by November. Worsening overcrowding instead drove DOCS to open the penitentiary—New York's thirty-sixth—on August 30, 1982, two years after the state had first expressed interest in Gabriels and before its construction had been completed. Planned as a minimum-security prison, Camp Gabriels, like Camp Adirondack before it, would incarcerate men completing sentences of twenty-four months or less and who, according to DOCS criteria, posed minimal security risks. Camp Gabriels' new superintendent welcomed the facility's first twenty-six convicted men as they arrived by bus from ACF, noting the penitentiary would reach its full complement of 153 incarcerated men by the end of the year. With the prison finally open, by the end of 1982 over 4,000 imprisoned men would be living in the park's one federal and three state penitentiaries.[56]

For over a year, the fate of the Gabriels prison hung in the balance as DOCS, the APA, and CAMPA engaged in what amounted to an extended piece of political theater. Two months of hearings proved to be little more than a combination of venting sessions, rehashing of old arguments, and public displays of false comity among advocates and opponents. Once the sessions ended, then, it came as little surprise that each side promptly reassumed their pre-hearing postures. By the spring of 1982, it was almost as if the hearings had never taken place. But this outcome was not unexpected. With decision-making power weighted so heavily on one side, it is little wonder the sessions had no lasting impact. For those paying attention, the entire oversight process served as a reminder—as at Ray Brook in 1976 and 1977—of the limitations built into APA oversight of state developments in the park. Even a well-oiled machine like CAMPA could not alter that reality. The months-long drama also provided residents and visitors a valuable education on how state agencies like Corrections could exploit agency rules for their own ends, potentially endangering environmental and public health in the process. The struggle also taught DOCS an important lesson. Having undergone APA review, Corrections now knew that more prisons in the Adirondacks, should they be necessary, could be built with or without the support of either local residents or the Park Agency. Concessions such as those granted in Gabriels, DOCS now understood, need not be part of future correctional planning.

Prison Labor and a Naturalized Prison

With the opening of Camp Gabriels, former critics and supporters awaited the transformations they had long anticipated. Unsurprisingly, few of the outcomes predicted during planning ever materialized. The penitentiary's biggest impacts ultimately appeared in areas few could have foreseen. While occasional escapes rattled homeowners, Gabriels remained as peaceful after the prison opened as it had been before. Though the penitentiary neither revived nor destroyed the local economy, the changes that did occur happened largely in spite of its presence. As time passed, the correctional facility became as much a community fixture as the sanatorium before it. Though wounds inflicted during the prison fight healed slowly, old class divisions remained. Area residents grew to appreciate the penitentiary for the variety of money-saving projects its incarcerated men completed, just as Corrections officials had predicted. However, DOCS could not have anticipated the influence its labor program would exert on local class relations. Performing manual labor for low pay under armed guard for the benefit of whites placed imprisoned workers, many of whom were poor men of color, at the bottom of the hamlet's rigid social hierarchy. Middle- and low-income homeowners received an unexpected boost in their social position while simultaneously reaping the free fruits of prison labor. The wealthy, never fans of the penitentiary or its occupants, came to a grudging acceptance of both. Through the renovating of recreational infrastructure, incarcerated workers unwittingly perpetuated elite interpretations of the Adirondack Park's purpose and character. Both the almost-servile status of imprisoned men in the community and the type of work they performed helped reinforce elites' sense of social dominance. For these reasons, affluent residents who were once opposed to the penal institution came to accept it and its imprisoned men as integral components of the Gabriels environment.

Contrary to what many in CAMPA had anticipated, Gabriels did not become a hotbed of violence and unlawful activity. In the 1980s and 1990s, incarcerated men did escape, and the roadblocks, bloodhounds, helicopter flyovers, and searches characteristic of modern manhunts became a regular feature of life in the Gabriels area. The lack of fencing around the facility, as at Camp Adirondack, only exacerbated the possibility of escapes. The camp's first pair of fugitives walked away from the compound in December 1982 and, by their own account, went into town for some beer. Following their apprehension, authorities stripped the duo of the privilege of camp confinement and transferred them to Dannemora for punishment. Between 1983 and 1986, the girlfriends of at least three other incarcerated men served as getaway drivers for their beaus. Traveling from Saratoga Springs, Watertown, and Oswego, the young women arrived in Gabriels, picked up their boyfriends, and smuggled them out. In all three cases, state police quickly detained and charged both the fugitives and their lovers with felony escape. As at Dannemora and Ray Brook, the rugged and unfamiliar terrain surrounding Gabriels could upend the plans of even the best-prepared runaway. In October 1986, an escapee from Gabriels managed to elude his captors for nearly a week while unwittingly hiding in a sanitary landfill—on the prison grounds. Three years later, in May 1989 an incarcerated man serving on a labor crew at a local campground walked away, got lost, and quickly stumbled across one of his pursuers.[57] Thus, while low rates of unlawful activity in Gabriels remained largely unchanged after 1982, the penitentiary's risk to public safety, as first identified by members of CAMPA, proved to be more than hyperbole. Though escapes were rare and nonviolent, the anxiety that was generated by a new, ever-present, and potentially deadly unknown likely filled more than a few former opponents with a sense of vindication.

The penitentiary also failed to unleash the economic transformations that advocates and critics had foretold. While many found work at the prison, and a small number of service-oriented businesses opened in the area, the lofty goals of reduced unemployment, higher incomes, and increased population went largely unfulfilled. Several factors help explain how and why Camp Gabriels proved a less potent economic force than many had predicted. First, the number of jobs at the prison was not unlimited, and, as opponents had pointed out, seniority rules and state transfer lists guaranteed some jobs would go to individuals from outside the area. Second, Gabriels' sparse population and remote locale had always been both a blessing and a curse. While the number of seasonal homeowners and visitors remained high, the generally lower-income permanent population could not sustain the panoply of new businesses anticipated by Corrections. Under such conditions, private investors' failure to deliver on DOCS's promise was not unsurprising. Finally, the area's population had never been high. If the few dozen jobs available at the penitentiary generated only minor ripple effects in the economy, then dreams of a higher year-round population would remain a fantasy. After all, Dannemora, home to the state's largest maximum-security prison, was itself only a small town.[58] Though CAMPA's darkest economic forecasts did not pan out, the relatively unchanged Gabriels economy after 1982 demonstrated the limited power of large infrastructure to effectuate significant change in an out-of-the-way, lightly populated area. The same could not be said, however, for Gabriels' crews of imprisoned workers.

Operating under the same rationale that inspired the creation of New York's prison system in the 1790s, camps like Gabriels, according to Corrections, were designed "to train the men in good work habits." If people living near the facility also benefited, so much the better. To those ends, crews of incarcerated workers completed projects designed to serve the practical needs of cash-strapped local residents, governments, and institutions. The vast scale of the work program demonstrated the need that permeated the area's depressed towns and villages. For nearly three decades, imprisoned men refurbished buildings, cleaned floors, repaired furniture, and crafted handmade plaques, awards, and outdoor signage for schools, municipal facilities, businesses, recreational sites, and service organizations. Incarcerated workers also spent time fighting forest fires, cutting firewood, mowing grass, shoveling snow, and maintaining cemeteries. Finally, poorly paid prison labor provided a valuable lifeline for the region's low-income homeowners, helping to install fiberglass insulation in the homes of low-income residents, harvest surplus crops from farms for area food banks, repair and craft Christmas gifts for poor children, and they donated hundreds of dollars from their meager earnings to help a struggling Little League team. Men incarcerated in Gabriels even tapped trees on the prison grounds and produced maple syrup that made its way into public school cafeterias and government offices statewide. The work of imprisoned men, therefore, produced a footprint that extended from Gabriels to all corners of New York State. Observing that "These are things that just wouldn't get done" without the men from Gabriels, Saranac Lake village manager Richard DePuy testified to the dilemma of chronically limited resources in the state's deindustrializing hinterlands.[59]

Recognizing the importance of tourism and outdoor play to residents, visitors, and the local economy, officials managing the prison labor program also deployed incarcerated men on projects designed to enhance the area's recreational appeal. Some of the earliest projects completed by imprisoned workers involved creating hiking trails on Forest Preserve land that had once been part of the prison property. This work generated a minor uproar in June 1983 when incarcerated workers accidentally cut trees protected as "forever wild." Minor mishaps like this did not diminish the value of prison labor in maintaining and preserving structures necessary for outdoor recreation. Most notably, imprisoned men became crucial to the success of the Saranac Lake Winter Carnival beginning in 1983—following Camp Adirondack's medium-security upgrade—when men from Gabriels cut blocks of ice from Lake Flower and assembled them into the carnival's Ice Palace. Imprisoned men also completed a variety of projects designed to guarantee the area's attractiveness as an outdoor destination, reinforcing an elite vision of the park first articulated by its nineteenth-century founders and reaffirmed by CAMPA and the APA. Projects included constructing buildings for a ski center in Saranac Lake, building trails for the Alpo International Sled Dog Races held every winter in Gabriels, helping erect the Adirondack Park Visitors' Interpretive Center in Paul Smith's, repairing trails and chair lifts at Big Tupper Ski Area in Tupper Lake, constructing public cross-country ski trails, cleaning up local beaches, cutting lumber to make cabins and lean-tos for state campgrounds, and raising pheasants on the prison grounds for donation to fish and game clubs for recreational hunting. Men incarcerated at Gabriels also set up summertime carnivals in area communities and prepared the Lake Placid Center for the Arts for its annual gala.[60] The very imprisoned men who had been the source of so much angst became instrumental in preserving the elite-oriented environment CAMPA had struggled to protect.

The work of Gabriels' incarcerated men generated warm reactions from once-hostile local homeowners. Grateful residents and politicians acknowledged their labor with citations, plaques, and formal receptions—to which imprisoned men did receive invitations—held in their honor. Many incarcerated men appreciated the work itself, and the opportunity to work outside the penitentiary. Matthew Quigley, a man incarcerated at Gabriels who helped build the Ice Palace in 1992, spoke highly of the labor program: "We're getting valuable training—which will be very helpful when we get out. It makes you feel proud to see something you built yourself." One of his co-laborers, Douglas Lowery, said he enjoyed working in the region, and thanked "the two women who faithfully continued to bring us coffee and donuts, every morning." Lowery added that he was touched by the fact that "civilians treated us as part of the community." Edwin Howell, another imprisoned man, agreed, noting that though he was paid only ninety cents per day, the work in local communities gave him "a chance to get in touch with outside people . . . I see some civilians, okay, they say 'Hi,' I greet them back. You know, it gets you ready for the free society, communicating with other people." Another incarcerated man, Raymond LaBarron, remarked simply, "There are a lot of nice people around here."[61]

Reaping the benefits of mass incarceration, of course, meant affluent whites had to reconcile feelings of racial and class superiority with the presence of poor, imprisoned men of color in the community. While many seasonal homeowners and visitors claimed permanent residence in densely populated metropolitan areas where contact with people of color could be both unavoidable and fleeting, the remote, compact environment of Gabriels guaranteed a close degree of interaction few could avoid. For the hamlet's well-to-do, the prison labor program proved a godsend. By consigning imprisoned workers to an almost-servile position, Corrections officials reinforced elites' perceived sense of social and racial dominance. It seems hard to imagine that the sight of incarcerated, poor men of color performing manual labor for low pay under the watchful eye of gun-toting white officers did not bring a measure of relief to homeowners for whom racial and class privilege defined the Gabriels environment. So long as Gabriels' incarcerated workers remained fixed in a subordinate role and completed projects critical to elite enjoyment of the park, then high-income homeowners could see the prison as compatible with Adirondack nature.

|||||||||

In the mid-1990s, rates of unlawful activity in New York began to decline, and lawmakers began to relax the narcotics and sentencing laws that had driven the overcrowding of the prior two decades. The state prison population, which in 1999 peaked at 71,000 people incarcerated in 69 penitentiaries, witnessed a steady decline by the early 2000s. Such conditions restricted the flow of new convicted men to places like Gabriels. By the mid-2000s, the camp was operating at less than half capacity, and a shrinking population made its continued operation difficult to justify. In January 2008, Democratic Governor Eliot Spitzer proved former DOCS Commissioner Thomas Coughlin wrong by announcing the prison's closure. In July 2009, after months of local lobbying to keep the once-hated institution open, Camp Gabriels closed its doors. Five years later, in March 2014, the State Office of General Services (OGS) approved the sale of the property for $166,000 to two Hudson Valley investors with plans to open a sleep-away camp and educational retreat, yet lawmakers' failure to transfer the ownership from New York State back to private hands—a matter complicated by some of the same environmental regulations that stalled the state's takeover in the first place—has kept the property's redevelopment on hold. Its fourth phase of life remains a mystery.[62]

Passing through Gabriels in the early twenty-first century, the wall of trees and shrubs that served as the compromise of the Park Agency hearings still stands, though finding the much-touted vegetative screen can be a challenge in a community where dense forests have always been the rule. One has to know the address of the former prison in order to locate this particular barrier. Even then, locked swing gates, security cameras, and large Facility Closed and No Trespassing signs bar access to the property. Ironically, the site is more restricted today than at any time in its history. Though hidden from view and closed to the public, the environmental legacies of Camp Gabriels can be found across the region. Most, as in Ray Brook, are hiding in plain sight. The thicket of vegetation surrounding the property, along with the nearby tract ceded by DOCS to the Forest Preserve, provide reminders that planning, building, and opening the prison was a question of environmental politics. It is fair to say that neither of these features would exist in their current form without the alliance of CAMPA and the APA. Indeed, without an opposition buttressed by state power, the penitentiary's footprint might have extended far enough to allow for expanded capacity, possibly preventing its closure. Without the work of incarcerated men, it is difficult to say whether Gabriels could have retained its status as a desirable wilderness retreat. Amid the austerity of the late twentieth and early twenty-first centuries, who else would have completed the renovations necessary to preserve the area's recreational infrastructure? Further, how would middle- and low-income residents have survived without the numerous lifelines that prison labor provided?

The homes of Gabriels' visitors and seasonal homeowners themselves provide an unusual reminder of the hamlet's history as a prison town. Like

FIGURE 9. Entrance to former Gabriels Correctional Facility, Gabriels, New York. Courtesy of the author.

the former prison, they can be difficult to spot amid the thicket of bushes and trees. Few members of CAMPA followed through on threats to sell their properties and move. Indeed, it likely took little time for former opponents to realize—and reap—the benefits of prison labor. With the penitentiary proving to be both less disruptive and more beneficial than predicted, there seemed little to reason to leave. The labor of incarcerated men likely kept property and school taxes low enough to enable high-income homeowners to enjoy the park much as they always had, an endeavor that was made even easier by prison labor. The ultimate irony of the Camp Gabriels story, then, lay in the fact that in the end, the prison did more to keep Gabriels frozen in time than either its opponents or supporters could have anticipated.

CHAPTER FOUR

"A POOR CHOICE"

Incarceration and the Legacies of Mining
in Lyon Mountain

Introduction

Two years after the hearings that preceded the opening of Camp Gabriels, the Adirondack Park Agency convened sessions on yet another North Country prison, this one planned for the Clinton County hamlet of Lyon Mountain. However, by the time of that March 1984 meeting, the minimum-security facility there had been open for three months. The turbulent experience of Gabriels had taught the Department of Correctional Services some important lessons. DOCS officials had a much better understanding of the value of identifying host communities unlikely to resist penal expansion. This time they chose an abandoned school in a depressed, working-class community as the site of their next penitentiary. Corrections had also learned that circumventing state environmental law was crucial to minimizing delays. Amid worsening overcrowding, DOCS claimed extraordinary power to open its new prison before the APA had its say. With the penitentiary a fait accompli, the one-day hearing garnered far less attention from Lyon Mountain residents than had the proceedings at Gabriels. Not a single homeowner attended. Residents' resignation, however, did not connote indifference to matters of environmental and public health. To the contrary, homeowner support for the prison hinged on help from Corrections in rebuilding a community shattered by corporate misrule.

Predating the creation of both the Forest Preserve and Adirondack Park, the business of iron mining dominated life in the Lyon Mountain region from the 1790s through the 1960s. The hamlet's industrialized landscape thus bore little resemblance to the aesthetically pleasing environments of places like Ray Brook and Gabriels. While visitors and seasonal homeowners traveled to the Adirondacks for outdoor recreation, generations of Lyon Mountain residents understood the North Country primarily as a place of hard and dirty work. For decades, they blasted holes, dug tunnels, and built shafts in mountainsides; cut and burned acres of forest; rerouted streams and filled wetlands; erected new towns; laid rail lines; and extracted tons of iron ore to feed the steel industry. The mines were a constant source of danger. Explosions, cave-ins, and other calamities could bring disease, disability, or death at any time. Over nearly two centuries, at least 162 workers died on the job, while thousands more contended with a variety of workplace-related injuries and ailments.[1] Corporate executives' focus on profits created an environment ill-suited to human health, comfort, and inhabitation.

In the sixteen years that passed between the mines' closure in 1967 and the prison's 1983 opening, Lyon Mountain, a powerhouse of the American steel industry, was witness to a spectacular fall. Failed efforts to attract new developers left the isolated community's dwindling population in a state of perpetual fear. By the 1970s and early 1980s, residents also contended with an environment marred by dilapidated public infrastructure, mountains of toxic ore tailings, polluted water, cutover forests, and crumbling industrial facilities. The near-simultaneous disappearance of corporate rule and rise of the environmental movement opened homeowners' eyes to the high ecological price that had been paid for their former prosperity. Not unlike their counterparts in Ray Brook, Lyon Mountain residents newly attuned to the bonds linking environmental and bodily health resisted potentially hazardous redevelopment schemes. Lyon Mountain's deindustrialization thus instigated a clash between conservative town board members determined to rebuild irrespective of environmental costs and a loosely knit coalition of working-class homeowners whose commitment to sustainable development outweighed their loyalty to conservative political ideologies.

Warding off the hamlet's collapse required new forms of employment guaranteed not to harm an already-compromised environment. With residents applying strict environmental litmus tests to redevelopment ideas, board members in 1982 proposed the seemingly eco-friendly conversion of Lyon Mountain's shuttered public school to a state prison. Responding warmly to the idea, a Corrections Department still burdened by overcrowding returned in 1983 to the mining district that had birthed the North

Country prison industry over a century before. Though a smaller complex than those at Ray Brook and Gabriels, the Lyon Mountain school satisfied the state's preference for repurposing surplus properties as correctional facilities, and, unlike Ray Brook and Gabriels, Lyon Mountain was a quasi-prison-town even before the penitentiary arrived. While generations of Lyon Mountaineers had worked twelve miles away at Clinton Correctional Facility in Dannemora, many not employed there had either family or friends who were. With its working-class residents already firmly ensconced within prisonland and even more dependent on DOCS employment after the mines' closure, Corrections leaders had to have anticipated a smooth transition in Lyon Mountain.

By the time Corrections arrived on its doorstep, Lyon Mountain was a shadow of its former self. Its population had fallen by more than 75 percent between 1887 and 1983, and 80 percent of its residents were retired. For those still hanging on, the correctional facility represented the hamlet's last hope of survival. Homeowners thus welcomed the spending necessary to repurpose and operate the former school as a prison. Viewed as a replacement for neither the school nor the mines, residents instead looked on the penitentiary as a catalyst for reversing their community's fortunes. Lyon Mountain homeowners would measure the prison's value not by its ability to revive a weak economy, but through its potential to restore their damaged environment. High-paying jobs, free prison labor, a constant flow of public funds, and a Corrections Department invested in its host community's well-being—or so locals hoped—might help undo the devastation wrought by two centuries of exploitation. Unfortunately, residents' expectations of a prison-induced reconstruction exceeded the strictly carceral goals of Corrections. With the lessons of Gabriels fresh in their minds, DOCS officials proved as indifferent to local concerns as Lyon Mountain's former corporate masters. Over time, however, the correctional facility proved to be a stabilizing force that aided Lyon Mountain's transition away from its mining past and toward the future, uncertain though it may be.

Mining Lyon Mountain

For much of its history, Lyon Mountain and the business of iron mining were inseparable. First identified in the late eighteenth century by individual prospectors as a potential source of riches, the area drew the attention

of state leaders following the Natural History Survey of the 1830s. As mining at Lyon Mountain expanded through the late nineteenth and early
twentieth centuries, its impacts on the area's environmental and public
health concerned neither corporate executives nor Albany lawmakers. The
passage of state environmental laws at the end of the nineteenth century
and the inclusion of Lyon Mountain in the Adirondack Park did nothing
to halt the region's destruction. Before the creation of the Adirondack Park
Agency in 1971, private landowners claimed unfettered power over their
park properties. The abrupt termination of operations at Lyon Mountain
in 1967 and coincidental birth of the environmental movement, however,
helped residents better appreciate the high ecological costs of mining.
Working-class homeowners once enamored of the high wages and benefits
of private-sector employment soon became the North Country's newest
and most unexpected advocates of sustainable development.

Situated in northwestern Clinton County, Lyon Mountain for nearly two
centuries attracted investors ranging from scrappy individual prospectors to
titans of industry, each grasping at the ore that lay in its mountains and
hillsides. While the American naval fleet had drawn ore from Essex County's
Lake Champlain shoreline during the revolution, it was not until the late
1790s that mining activities commenced in the Clinton County settlement
then known as Rogersfield. Through the mid-nineteenth century, the trade
involved a limited number of independent prospectors drawing small
amounts of ore from surface outcroppings in the Rogersfield area. From
there, entrepreneurs transported their discoveries for processing at privately
owned forges along the Saranac River. Ships then carried their wares over
Lake Champlain either north to markets in British Canada or south toward
Albany and New York City. Construction of new rail lines across the North
Country beginning in the mid-nineteenth century eventually helped transform a miniscule local business into an industry that connected the remote
Adirondacks to national and international markets.[2]

Interest in northern New York's untapped natural resources grew with the
rise of industrialization after the Civil War. Heightened nationwide demand
for steel drove a search for new sources of iron ore. In the Rogersfield area,
veins of ore threaded amongst thousands of acres of forest; dozens of freshwater lakes, rivers, and streams; and infant rail lines primed for future
expansion. Hoping to cash in on the lucrative steel market, in 1873 a consortium of investors established the Chateaugay Ore and Iron Company

(COIC). In short order, the firm controlled over 100,000 acres of land in Clinton and Franklin Counties, including Rogersfield and its mineral deposits. As a vertically integrated enterprise, COIC claimed authority over local rail and water transit networks. It quickly began erecting towns and industrial facilities across its territory, and, to maximize profits, consolidated production at Bellmont, a planned village built on the Chateaugay River in 1875. The firm's mining hub at Rogersfield—renamed Lyon Mountain by its new owners—began to grow, providing increasing amounts of ore for processing at the forge in Bellmont before making its final journey to the nation's expanding network of steel mills.[3]

Lyon Mountain and Bellmont soon became the twin axes on which COIC's industrial empire turned. The Delaware and Hudson Railway's (D&H) acquisition of majority control of the firm allowed for plant and machinery upgrades, more hiring, and increased mining to feed the steel industry. As its North Country footprint expanded in the late nineteenth century, COIC imposed enormous environmental harm. Deforestation to fuel the fires of COIC's forges and to construct private homes and industrial facilities sparked forest fires, exacerbated air pollution, and increased flooding along area waterways. Corporate indifference to environmental and public health allowed for the growth of overcrowded, unkempt, and unsafe company towns where infectious diseases and workplace-related injuries and fatalities proved to be all too common. For all of COIC's failings, however, by 1880 northern New York produced one-quarter of the nation's iron ore, and its Bellmont forge ranked as the world's largest. By the time Lyon Mountain's population peaked at 3,500 in 1887, the unsightly mining center had become a popular stop for tourists vacationing in the Adirondacks.[4]

The turn of the twentieth century proved a moment of transition for the firm and its host community. Lyon Mountain achieved international recognition when COIC received first prize for its high-quality iron ore at the 1893 World's Fair in Chicago. However, increasing competition from mining operations elsewhere in the United States, especially Minnesota's Mesabi Range, along with the economic meltdown of the 1890s, decimated the firm's balance sheet. A decade of financial turmoil took its toll, allowing the solvent D&H Railway to seize control of COIC in 1903. Subsequent investigations of northern Clinton County's extant mineral resources discovered vast untouched veins of ore lying deep inside Lyon Mountain itself. Accessing the ore required building one of the longest and deepest mine shafts ever dug in North America. COIC's new owners consolidated the firm's once-sprawling empire of forges, forests, and mines into a tightly organized operation centered in Lyon Mountain.[5]

In the first half of the twentieth century, Lyon Mountain became a prototypical company town. Corporate leaders lured immigrant labor from Europe, Canada, and Mexico, along with a small number of African Americans from the Deep South, to make the trek to Lyon Mountain. The promise of housing, educational, and medical benefits would, executives hoped, outweigh the low pay and dangerous working conditions. Lyon Mountain soon became the most diverse community in the North Country, save perhaps Dannemora. Segregated enclaves soon sprang up, fueling interethnic and racial conflicts both at work and in the hamlet's neighborhoods. Gangs formed, the Sicilian mafia established a foothold, and by the 1910s Lyon Mountain had a reputation as a profitable yet ungovernable community. With few law enforcement resources available in the hamlet's isolated and corporate-controlled setting, in 1919 the company hired John R. Linney, a former coal miner from Scranton, Pennsylvania, to serve as superintendent at Lyon Mountain. Through a mixture of authoritarianism and welfare capitalism, Linney's twenty-five-year tenure helped stabilize working and living conditions in the community through the 1940s.[6]

The Great Depression decimated both COIC and the D&H. Chicago-based Republic Steel acquired COIC's Lyon Mountain holdings in 1939.[7] Republic's timing could not have been better, as military contracts helped turn the hamlet into a boomtown once more, with facilities humming twenty-four hours a day throughout World War II. Yet wartime prosperity gave way to the familiar realities of hard work in a hazardous environment and painful truths that portended Lyon Mountain's slide toward oblivion.[8] Collective bargaining agreements and long strikes provided little protection against the layoffs and irregular employment that became common in the 1950s and 1960s.[9] Then just as Lyon Mountain's future became ever more uncertain amid the waning postwar demand for American steel, Republic decided to pump millions into modern mining equipment and upgrade the facilities in its North Country operations.[10] Still, contracts dwindled and the workforce plummeted. Local residents, politicians, and civic leaders began preparing for a once-unthinkable future.

Republic Steel announced the shutdown of its Lyon Mountain operations in April 1967. Having furnished ores used to construct the George Washington and Golden Gate Bridges, along with scores of consumer and industrial products, Lyon Mountain's mines succumbed to the pressures of a globalizing and increasingly consumption-oriented economy. Company executives blamed the closure on diminishing ore supplies, expanding foreign steel imports, falling prices, and rising costs. Anticipating a drastic cut in revenues, the D&H, sole carrier of Republic goods overland from Lyon Mountain to Plattsburgh, signaled its intent to end rail service in the area. Anxious residents petitioned public officials to ease the pain of their community's impending postindustrial transformation. Amid a tsunami of plant closings nationwide, however, cash-strapped politicians from Washington to Albany could counsel only self-help and individualism. A sense of foreboding accompanied the departure of Republic Steel's 250 workers as they exited the Lyon Mountain mines after the last shift on June 30, 1967. While some opted for early retirement, others transferred to Republic operations elsewhere, including one who decamped to a mine in Liberia. For those unable to move, there seemed little choice but to heed public officials' call to self-reliance.[11]

On July 1, 1967, Lyon Mountain residents awakened to a community stripped of its identity. Having succumbed to the irresistible vagaries of late capitalism, homeowners now inhabited a postindustrial setting that could not escape the environmental legacies of its industrial past. The abrupt withdrawal of private capital bestowed upon the Town of Dannemora—of which Lyon Mountain is a part—both the vast holdings of Republic and the task of repurposing that wealth for the greater good. With federal and state leaders counseling self-help amid a slow-moving, nationwide industrial collapse, local officials labored to determine the value of their new properties while seeking investors who might make old resources turn new profits. Corporate indifference to environmental and public health, long-term neglect of critical infrastructure, and new regulations governing developments inside the Adirondack Park greatly complicated this work. Nearly two decades after the mines' closure, Lyon Mountain would be no closer to reckoning with the legacies of its industrial history than on the day the mines shut down.

The Politics of Redevelopment and Reconstruction

Republic Steel's departure ignited a struggle over the future of Lyon Mountain's vast new public domain. The experience of deindustrialization significantly transformed residents' relationships with their environment. While local politicians wooed new capital investments as a hedge against economic ruin, residents resisted privatization efforts that either underpriced nature's value, threatened environmental and public health, or circumvented popular consent. The near-simultaneous enactment of APA regulations and the birth of the environmental movement in the early 1970s only exacerbated tensions between locals and their elected officials. Town board members' excoriations of Park Agency regulations met surprising indifference from homeowners whose adherence to conservative ideologies did not preclude concern for environmental and public health. Beginning in the late 1960s, Lyon Mountain residents formed a loosely organized though potent counterweight to local officials' pursuit of development at any cost. By the early 1980s, their resistance had helped convert previously anti-environmentalist board members into disciples of sustainable development.

Local politicians had worked for years to prepare Lyon Mountain for its post-mining future. Efforts to improve the delivery of public services such as fresh water, sewage removal, electric power, and sanitation began in the 1950s. As the Lyon Mountain region's wealthiest and largest property owners, COIC and Republic Steel had long maintained a base of power unmatched either by the town's political authorities or its private homeowners, meaning that any town board attempts to consolidate Lyon Mountain's hodgepodge network of privately installed water and sewage lines, septic tanks, and electrical connections into uniform districts first required the firms' blessing.[12] While a victory for rational planning, public districting during continued corporate rule neither improved the quality of delivery nor altered the climate of indifference that had created the hamlet's unreliable water, sewage, and electric systems in the first place. These attempts to make Lyon Mountain more livable—like districting—unfortunately coincided with corporate efforts to reinvigorate mining activities at the community's expense. Such was the degree of Republic Steel's disinvestment in Lyon Mountain as a home for its workers that by 1967 its water, sewage, and electrical systems were in no better shape than they had been before districting, leaving residents and political leaders to contend with the practical concerns of everyday living as well as the existential questions of a future without mining.

The once-disempowered populace and town board were suddenly granted full stewardship of the community, its natural resources, and its future.

Enticing private capital to fill Republic's shoes proved challenging in an isolated hamlet of fewer than a thousand mainly older residents; it boasted no
retail establishments and was plagued by dilapidated infrastructure. The
North Country's chronically high unemployment was not restricted only to
Essex and Franklin Counties. Local officials worried that joblessness in
Clinton County that had hovered between 7 and 12 percent in the late 1960s
might also alienate potential investors. Under such conditions, efforts by the
town board to attract other mining companies, resort developers, and enterprises ranging from wood and gun manufacturing to asphalt production
failed to gain traction.[13] Short-term employment opportunities recommended
by area politicians, including temporary work at the 1967 World's Fair in
Montreal, construction of a television transmission tower atop Lyon
Mountain, and the conversion (that was ultimately canceled) of the hamlet's
shuttered underground mines to air raid shelters, paled in comparison to the
relative bedrock of stability that mining had provided.[14]

The board's failure to reindustrialize Lyon Mountain in the late 1960s
and early 1970s was matched only by its inability to provide residents with
safe and reliable transportation, clean water, and sewage removal. The loss
of the $60,000 in annual property taxes Republic had deposited into town
coffers exacerbated the heavy burden of rebuilding infrastructure left to rot
by corporate executives. Chronically insufficient funds made reconstruction, particularly of crumbling roadways and sidewalks, a slow and drawn-
out affair.[15] These troubles paled in comparison to the task of repairing the
hamlet's waterworks. While aiding the collection of usage fees, the establishment of districting in the 1950s entailed no repairs to the decaying
nineteenth-century water system born of corporate indifference. The
relentless dumping of toxic ore tailings into wetlands had created the land
on which Lyon Mountain was built while making its groundwater unsafe
for consumption.[16] Most homeowners drew water from a rusting network
of underground pipes connected to an antiquated open-air reservoir. Raw
sewage was collected in belowground septic tanks connected to private
homes and businesses whose contents were discharged—also via disinte-
grating pipes—into area waterways.[17] Thus, when Lyon Mountain residents
were left with no functioning infrastructure in 1967, they came to better
understand environmental degradation, infrastructural decay, and threats
to public health as the significant legacies of corporate rule. Translating this
knowledge into a political agenda centered on sustainable development set

the stage for their clashes with a town board whose commitment to environmental and public health left much to be desired.

As Lyon Mountain worked on plans to upgrade the hamlet's rundown water and sewage systems, the town learned of the most promising private redevelopment idea that had been proposed since Republic's departure. Amid a national energy crisis, in May 1978 executives from Montreal-based Vibra Resources International announced plans to purchase twenty acres of former Republic Steel property in Lyon Mountain, including underground mines, to build an oil storage facility for the federal Strategic Petroleum Reserve. Promising to spend $110 million, Vibra planned the construction of an aboveground pipeline to move petroleum in and out of the mines, the creation of one hundred private-sector jobs, and an expanded area tax base. Members of the town board responded enthusiastically and offered purchase options to Vibra with an eventual final sale price of $25,000. Several local residents expressed fear that a rush to redevelop had blinded politicians to the potential for oil spills and other hazards to environmental and public health. Critics argued that board members, in their zeal to make Lyon Mountain great again, had also drastically undervalued the property's actual worth. For reasons unknown, and to the relief of many area homeowners, Vibra took no action for the next six years.[18] In an era of heightened awareness of the connections between environmental and bodily health, it seems likely that public pressure and the prospect of a binding APA review drove Vibra toward a face-saving postponement.

Though fixated on redevelopment, board members could not escape the rusting pipes, overflowing septic tanks, befouled waterways, and filthy reservoirs that comprised Lyon Mountain's aging waterworks. While strident, nonbinding resolutions opposing APA rules received board approval at meetings held throughout the 1970s, residents' equally persistent calls for sustainable reconstruction ultimately carried the day. One screed against the Park Agency's apparent complicity in preserving the Adirondacks "for only the Super Rich"—though consistent with the conservative tenor of North Country politics—offered no support to struggling homeowners. Years of frustration boiled over in the mid-1970s, when residents challenged the legality of existing water districts, disputed the board's claim to an exclusive right to sell local water, and displayed a jar of polluted drinking water during a town board meeting, with one resident telling officials, "If you want to drink that, go ahead. It's what I have to drink everyday." When the town supervisor asked, "Who has the right to sell the water if the town board doesn't?" the audience replied in unison, "the people." Unwilling to leave their fate to leaders unattuned to the ecological problems literally engulfing their community, Lyon Mountain homeowners demanded a referendum to settle outstanding water-related issues and that the town government do more to safeguard public health.[19] With few resources for such a massive undertaking, reconstruction of the water system would not begin for another decade.

With reconstruction and redevelopment stalled through the 1970s and early 1980s, homeowners and elected officials worked on other ways to rebuild a semblance of civic life in Lyon Mountain. In so doing, conservative members of the town board showed an uncharacteristic sympathy for matters of environmental and public health. Participation in monthly town board meetings, including debates over control and use of natural resources, reinvigorated a democratic process that in Lyon Mountain had long been dominated by corporate executives. While board members continued delivering anti-environmental missives, they also established a planning board and zoning rules to ensure public oversight of new developments. Community leaders responded to residents' health and quality of life concerns by installing new tennis courts, picnic areas, outdoor playgrounds, and athletic fields. The cash-strapped town government encouraged action by citizens as well: they urged homeowners to volunteer to replant local forests to help restore the area's ravaged landscape, and they hired schoolchildren to keep the hamlet's crumbling streets and sidewalks clear of debris. Finally, board members discovered a means by which they could simultaneously raise revenue and improve public health. In the mid-1970s, the board authorized the marketing and commercial sale of ore tailings left behind by Lyon Mountain's former corporate rulers. Profiting from the notoriously large piles of industrial waste, however, required barring access to some of the local youth for whom the mountains of ore sand had become the perfect spot to ride their all-terrain vehicles.[20] Although members of the board retained their conservative allegiances, an increasing appreciation for the pragmatic realities of life in a ravaged, postindustrial community facilitated politicians' slow conversion to an agenda focused on sustainable development by the early 1980s.

Inadvertent actions by local school district officials and the town board paved the way for the investments required to secure Lyon Mountain's future.

Faced with low student enrollments, the Northern Adirondack Central School (NACS) District closed the hamlet's fifty-year-old public school in the summer of 1981. In October the town board discussed offering the shuttered school for lease or sale, and simultaneously considered a request from Vibra for a three-year extension on its purchase options. Aware of recent penitentiary openings in Ray Brook and ongoing debates in Gabriels, board members in February 1982 approved a non-binding resolution proposing the conversion of the former school to a minimum-security state prison.[21] Though ostensibly these ideas were from the town board, the fingerprints of residents committed to preserving environmental and public health were unmistakable. While the board also approved a three-year extension on Vibra's purchase options, it did so with the knowledge that APA bureaucrats and the town's recently created planning board would have the final say. It seems likely that board members viewed their prison proposal as the type of development that would satisfy residents' demands for sustainable development, but as 1983 approached, whether Lyon Mountain would embrace a hazardous or eco-friendly future remained an open question.

Expanding Prisonland to Lyon Mountain

Relentless growth of New York's population of convicted men ultimately drove correctional planners to Lyon Mountain. Increasing public criticism in the early 1980s of the state's heavy reliance on incarceration did nothing to curb lawmakers' obsessive pursuit of new cells. A Corrections Department freshly aware of its dominant position in planning prisons had to have looked on Lyon Mountain's shuttered public school—especially compared to the complex at Gabriels—as mere child's play. However, unlike the opening of penitentiaries at Ray Brook and Gabriels, the sale of Lyon Mountain's school first required a referendum of district voters. For the first and only time in the history of prison building in the Adirondacks, existing law afforded local residents a central role in deciding whether to allow a prison in their community. Once again, the Corrections Department's inattention to a host community's history, population, and the nuances of land classification threatened to derail its expansion plans. Though publicly ambivalent about the penitentiary, homeowners' ultimate endorsement recognized not its potential to revive the economy, but to help rebuild their broken community.

As at Ray Brook and Gabriels, news of New York's interest in building a prison reached Lyon Mountain through unconventional means. During a Sunday homily at St. Bernard's Roman Catholic Church in Lyon Mountain in June 1983, Father Howard McCasland accidentally leaked contents of a recent conversation wherein local Republican State Senator Ronald Stafford had signaled the impending arrival of a correctional facility. Three weeks later, the Corrections Department confirmed its plan to spend $10 million to convert Lyon Mountain's former school to a minimum-security prison designed to incarcerate 150 convicted men. DOCS indicated construction would require hiring 200 local workers, and that 126 full-time employees would staff the facility at an annual budget of $3 million. At a public meeting in July, Corrections officials informed residents that most staff members at the new penitentiary would transfer from Clinton Correctional Facility in Dannemora, an unsurprising revelation given the two communities' close proximity. Department leaders also foretold daily routines at Lyon Mountain closely mirroring those at Gabriels. While some incarcerated men would labor on area infrastructure, conservation, and public works projects, others would partake of educational and labor programs on the prison grounds. Corrections seemed to be fully in control of the situation as usual, but in this case they were not. While the APA's non-binding advisory review would resemble the process recently completed in Gabriels, existing law also required a referendum on the sale of school district property. Thus, it was the voters in the Northern Adirondack Central School District—not DOCS, not the APA, and not the town board—who were in charge, and who would have final say on whether a penitentiary came to Lyon Mountain.[22]

Having endured over a year of delays at Gabriels, Corrections anticipated smoother planning at Lyon Mountain. The hamlet had not been DOCS's first choice. Only after community opposition in May 1983 scuttled plans to build a penitentiary at the New York City Police Department's shuttered retreat in the Greene County village of Platte Clove did Corrections turn northward once more. Lyon Mountain's closeness to Dannemora, its long-standing ties to Clinton Correctional Facility, and the town board's endorsement likely calmed DOCS's fears of a CAMPA-style resistance. The Lyon Mountain school, unlike the deteriorating compound in Gabriels, had undergone renovations just prior to closing. The primary reason that Corrections leaders had reason to be optimistic about Lyon Mountain was due to their recent experience twenty-one miles away in the Clinton County village of Altona. In April 1983, voters in the Northern Adirondack Central School District had participated in a referendum and approved, with 96 percent support, selling the forty-two-acre campus of Altona's shuttered public school to DOCS for $623,000. As the town was located outside the Adirondack Park, a Corrections Department unencumbered by APA review was able to move quickly to open a medium-security prison designed to incarcerate three hundred convicted men. By the time DOCS indicated interest in Lyon Mountain in June, renovations totaling $14 million were already underway at Altona.[23] Though Lyon Mountain's position inside the park made APA oversight impossible to avoid, Corrections leaders had to have hoped that instead of repeating the experience of Gabriels, Lyon Mountain might simply be another Altona.

New York State's longtime reliance on expanding prison capacity as a solution to overcrowding intensified in the mid-1980s, making penitentiaries in places that were once little known like Altona and Lyon Mountain a real possibility. In 1983, the state's correctional facilities incarcerated 30,324 residents and operated at 116 percent of capacity. With revisions to narcotics and sentencing laws not up for debate, lawmakers predicted steadily increasing prison populations far into the future. To satisfy DOCS's insatiable demand for cells, legislators approved annual appropriations that ballooned from $150 million in 1971 to $550 million by 1983. In addition to the $10 million earmarked for Lyon Mountain, lawmakers allocated $100 million to build a new maximum-security prison in the Bronx designed to incarcerate 1,000 convicted men. Legislators also approved $90 million to fund the construction of medium-security annexes—each designed to incarcerate 500 convicted men—at existing maximum-security penitentiaries in Attica and Great Meadow, and at the medium-security women's prison in Albion. In the North Country, by 1983 state prisons in Dannemora, Ray Brook, and Gabriels carried a combined annual budget of just under $49 million, held over 3,000 incarcerated men, and employed nearly 1,700 workers.[24] With new penitentiaries on the horizon, New York was quickly realizing Robert McEwen's dream of establishing corrections as a permanent local industry.

The rapid growth of New York's prison system was not an uncontested phenomenon. In addition to residents and organizations that resisted the placement of penitentiaries in their communities, groups such as STOP had issued some of the earliest warnings against mass incarceration. In the early

1980s, influential figures in state government began to sound alarms over New York's heavy reliance on imprisonment. In July 1982, one month before the opening of Camp Gabriels and less than a year before DOCS announced plans to build in Lyon Mountain, Governor Hugh Carey's Executive Advisory Commission on the Administration of Justice, chaired by state judge Arthur Liman, cautioned against New York's continued use of incarceration as a remedy to overcrowding. Underscoring the reality that "the public wants prisoners locked up, but not in their own neighborhoods," Liman warned the state was "drifting toward disaster." Echoing STOP, Liman anticipated a "repetition of the bloodshed at Attica" could come at any time. Calling for alternatives such as probation and drug treatment, Liman evoked the message of New York's nineteenth-century prison reformers, arguing, "The best hope for eliminating the crime problem is to eliminate the social conditions that create crime." Liman acknowledged such an approach would "be difficult and expensive and cannot be expected to succeed in this generation," but, he argued, "the effort to achieve social justice cannot be abandoned by any civilized nation."[25] The twin burdens of mandatory minimum sentences and an electorate enamored of law-and-order politics compelled the state's new Democratic governor, Mario Cuomo, to shelve Liman's recommendations and accelerate the penal expansions initiated by his predecessor. Thus, Lyon Mountain became but the latest New York community to find itself in the Corrections Department's crosshairs.

Both the Liman Report and recent opposition to penitentiaries planned for Gabriels and Platte Clove demonstrated that not all New Yorkers were as serious about solving prison overcrowding as Corrections might have hoped. Increasing criticism of the state's relentless and expensive pursuit of cells encouraged DOCS to adopt a new and possibly less controversial approach to incarceration. In addition to recycling empty complexes in rural areas, Corrections would attempt to incarcerate convicted men inside existing state residential facilities. To wit, in 1983 DOCS announced plans to expropriate part of the Marcy State Psychiatric Center near Utica to incarcerate 1,200 convicted men. This action prompted a lawsuit from both the facility's board of directors and family members of people housed there concerning the legality of imprisoning convicted men at a psychiatric institution, as well as the state's years-old claim of a prison overcrowding emergency. In July 1983, the state Court of Appeals—New York's highest judicial authority—unanimously approved DOCS's plan for a mixed penal-psychiatric facility at Marcy. Judge Solomon Wachtler's opinion turned the Liman Report on its head, ensuring packed penitentiaries in perpetuity by endorsing incarceration as the only solution to both lawbreaking and over-crowding. With all three branches of state government in its corner, Corrections could build almost wherever and whenever it pleased. Free to ignore the public as never before, DOCS moved forward with its plan for Lyon Mountain.[26]

The legal and political dramas surrounding New York's tightening embrace of incarceration seemed worlds away at Lyon Mountain in the summer of 1983. Since the mines had closed, residents had adjusted to a peace unknown during the hamlet's boom years. The Lyon Mountain environment, despite its sorry state, closely resembled those of Ray Brook and Gabriels before the building of their respective prisons. Surrounding the eleven-acre school campus were clusters of private homes, paved road-ways, churches, a gas station, streams, ponds, forests, and a twenty-three-acre protected state wetland. Wildlife including whitetail deer, coyote, beaver, muskrat, and mink also lived nearby, and wetland habitats hosted a variety of waterfowl and fish. The 3,830-foot-high Lyon Mountain, sur-rounded by unsightly piles of ore tailings, rusted mining equipment, abandoned shafts, and industrial buildings, and topped by the transmission tower, literally overshadowed the future prison site. Of the town's 43,000 acres of forestland, over half belonged to the Forest Preserve or to state forests open to commercial logging. With almost no business activity or vehicular traffic, the atmosphere was quiet. Residents enjoyed pastimes such as hunting, fishing, and ice skating, among other activities. The onset of a postindustrial serenity marked an unprecedented shift for this once-bustling industrial hub.[27]

Demographic and economic changes that occurred in the wake of Lyon Mountain's industrial collapse were equally difficult not to notice. Though the hamlet's population dropped from 1,000 to 800 between 1967 and 1983, this decline proved to be an anomaly in a county that was an outlier in a rapidly depopulating region and state. Between 1950 and 1980, Clinton County's population grew from 53,622 to 80,750, while from 1970 to 1980, New York State's population dropped by four percent. The main drivers of the county's economy—the State University of New York at Plattsburgh, Clinton Correctional Facility, and Plattsburgh Air Force Base—accounted for much of this increase. The county's modern auto, air, and rail infrastructure, its less isolated settlements, and an array of employment opportunities helped prevent the exodus plaguing nearby Franklin and Essex Counties. By the early 1980s, over 5,500 students were enrolled full-time at the university, 10,000 Air Force personnel and their dependents worked and lived in Plattsburgh, and at the prison in Dannemora, an incarcerated population that stood at 960 in 1970 had swelled to 2,100 by 1982. With 1,250 employees, Clinton Correctional Facility had also become one of the region's largest employers. Nevertheless, Clinton County was no stranger to the unemployment and poverty endemic to upstate New York. From 1970 onward, joblessness in the county fluctuated between 8 and 13 percent, staying roughly three points above the national average. In 1981, 53 percent of households in the county earned a gross income of less than $15,000 per year, leaving most families with no disposable income at the end of each month. This ambiguous picture of population growth amid economic stagnation mirrored the equally mixed experience of life in postindustrial Lyon Mountain. Despite a drop in the number of permanent homeowners, most of the hamlet's working-age residents had full-time employment, including a large number working at Clinton. With many of those DOCS employees destined for transfer to Lyon Mountain, Corrections did not fear the formation of an opposition group like STOP, CCRB, or CAMPA.[28]

Unlike Ray Brook and Gabriels, where powerful constituencies resisted penal expansion, Lyon Mountain's position within prisonland yet outside the orbit of the park's tourist economy ensured a relatively muted local response to the state's proposal. However, Corrections Department claims that residents were "strongly in favor" of the prison exaggerated a complex reality: Though organized opposition did not materialize, the prospect of a penitentiary proved unimpressive for many homeowners. The editorial board of the *Press Republican,* a staunch supporter of the corrections industry, flatly rejected the Lyon Mountain plan, reprising fears first articulated at Gabriels that the North Country was becoming a penal colony. Evoking both STOP and CAMPA, the *Press* warned that continued acceptance of prisons might threaten the region's image as a family-friendly resort. The *Press* feared that without strong resistance, more sinister forms of development—including radioactive waste storage—might be impossible to stop in the future. A small number of residents joined the dissent, rebuking the town board and lamenting area politicians' lack of "intestinal fortitude" in the face of correctional expansion. According to these critics, board members had done little to challenge state officials who viewed North Country homeowners as little more than "country bumpkins" seemingly desperate to have prisons "dumped in their front yards." Some feared a penitentiary would make Lyon Mountain as chaotic as it was before 1967, abruptly terminating their moment of postindustrial serenity. Others warned that a correctional facility might demoralize young people yearning for a brighter future, perpetuate an industry notorious for hazardous working conditions, and consign Lyon Mountain to a Dannemora-style future, defined solely by its prison.[29] Though opposition voices were few, their presence underscored the contested nature of the state's carceral enterprise and injected a dose of unpredictability into what Corrections had assumed would be smooth planning.

More common reactions among residents ranged from ambivalence to lukewarm support. After all, there was little chance the facility would significantly alter either social or economic relations in Lyon Mountain. Corrections would be the equivalent of neither COIC nor Republic Steel, and homeowners understood that a prison employing 126 workers would neither restore Lyon Mountain's former glory nor raise its population to industrial-era levels. Nearly everyone realized its impacts would, at best, be modest. Residents currently employed at other penitentiaries would simply be able to work closer to home. Further, there was no shock value in a prison coming to a community that had grown up under Clinton's shadow. While a small number of homeowners offered support, including one who viewed the penitentiary as "the best thing that's ever happened . . . since the mines came in," most were simply relieved that the school would be reused. The facility's likely neutral impacts thus led many residents to concur with homeowner Pat Golovach, who stated simply, "I'm not against it and I'm not for it." With no organized opposition and little need for public debate, in September 1983 Northern Adirondack Central School District voters decided whether to sell the abandoned school to Corrections. DOCS officials breathed a sigh of relief when residents approved the sale for $322,000 by a vote of 383 to 23.[30]

The result of the September 1983 referendum effectively sealed Lyon Mountain's fate as the newest corner of the North Country prisonland. With no organized opposition, the only remaining barrier standing in DOCS's way was an APA review whose findings would not alter the final outcome. Though the path Lyon Mountain traveled to reach this point was shorter and faster than many of its sibling institutions, we should misread neither the speedy process nor the vote itself as evidence of local enthusiasm. In terms of speed, it was the *Marcy* decision and the full backing of state government that gave Corrections the confidence necessary to move with Ray Brook-style quickness in Lyon Mountain, not necessarily the support of residents. Many Lyon Mountain residents did not require the economic uplift that had become a trope of DOCS salesmanship campaigns, and while they were familiar with the prison system, many had expressed concerns about accepting a penitentiary in their community. Yet most voted to sell the school to DOCS, seemingly in favor of the project. Why? First, the school district included communities outside Lyon Mountain for whom new jobs likely were a concern. Second, there were individuals who favored any development over none at all. And, finally, more than a few Lyon Mountain residents were frustrated by years of inaction yet hopeful that correctional planners would be as interested in helping to rebuild their new host community as they were in the prison itself. Thus, for some an affirmative vote may well have been a roll of the dice, anticipating that a warm welcome for DOCS might yield an equally friendly gesture from Corrections. Unfortunately for Lyon Mountain residents, the state's interest in the hamlet remained strictly carceral.

Nature, Incarceration, and the Politics of Civic Renewal

With the school under its control after the September referendum, Corrections moved aggressively to open the prison by the end of 1983. The Adirondack Park Agency review remained the only hurdle DOCS had left to cross. To meet its own compressed timetable, Corrections took the unprecedented step of suspending APA oversight and beginning the project before the completion of any environmental assessments. DOCS then unveiled plans for a prison whose footprint would extend far beyond the schoolhouse grounds. Corrections planned a penitentiary comprised of multiple new structures spread across the eleven-acre school campus plus a sixteen-acre tract located in a residential neighborhood and atop protected state wetlands. As the Department ignored homeowners' concerns, any hope that DOCS might help rebuild its host community vanished. Instead, Corrections promised benefits—jobs, prison labor crews, and vegetative screening—sought neither by residents nor board members. Displaying a degree of indifference to local needs matched only by Lyon Mountain's former corporate rulers, DOCS risked alienating residents who should have been natural allies.

The backing of both the entire state government and school district voters had encouraged Corrections to test the boundaries of its power. With Park Agency review the only barrier separating DOCS from opening the prison, department leaders determined to avoid Gabriels-style delays asserted their dominance in an unusually aggressive manner. In so doing, DOCS again underscored the limitations built into agency authority. In the fall of 1983, APA Commissioner Theodore Ruzow acceded to DOCS Commissioner Thomas Coughlin's request to suspend the agency's non-binding advisory review. Citing the overcrowding emergency, Coughlin went beyond his 1981 suspension of SEQRA reporting requirements at Gabriels, anticipating that freedom from all environmental regulation would permit Lyon Mountain's partial opening by year's end. By Coughlin's estimation, the first phase of construction, requiring the conversion of classrooms into cells, would allow for the arrival of seventy incarcerated men by December 1983. Phase two would involve more significant transformations not included in the state's original proposal, including the construction of fencing, a program and support services building, recreation facilities, garage, parking lots, access roads, pedestrian paths, and a sewage treatment plant built on a separate piece of privately owned property. DOCS planned upgrades of the school's heating, electricity, telephone, and lighting systems; conversion of its gym and auditorium for use as a library and craft shop; placement of bars over the windows; and planting of a vegetative screen to mitigate visual impacts. With building complete, Corrections predicted the penitentiary's full complement of 150 incarcerated men and 126 full-time employees would be in place by July 1984.[31]

Of the projects planned for Lyon Mountain, the sewage treatment plant attracted the most attention from residents and board members. With the hamlet's aging and run-down sewage removal system unable to meet the needs of Lyon Mountain's 800 full-time residents, accommodating an additional 276 users would be impossible. Accordingly, DOCS purchased a sixteen-acre property—a tract larger than the prison site—in a neighborhood south of the school to build its new sewage plant. Lyon Mountain residents hoped the prison's plant—a state-of-the-art facility equipped with modern filtration and treatment technologies—could serve both the penitentiary and its host community. In addition, local politicians anticipated a new source of revenue could be gained by selling town water to the prison.[32] Unfortunately for homeowners and their elected leaders, DOCS did not share their view of the prison as a vehicle for Lyon Mountain's revitalization. The new plant would be only for the prison, its occupants, and its employees, but, situated in the middle of a residential neighborhood, the new facility would provide a constant reminder of Corrections' indifference to the well-being of its beleaguered host community.

Nor was that the end of the indifference. While Lyon Mountain homeowners had welcomed DOCS's stated commitment to sustainable development, the department's words ultimately did not match its actions. Of particular concern were the twenty-three acres of protected state wetlands managed by the Department of Environmental Conservation abutting the prison property. Building on lands adjacent to fragile ecosystems was no problem for DOCS officials unencumbered by organized opposition or environmental regulation. Corrections announced plans to destroy seven percent of Lyon Mountain's wetlands and to restrict access to the rest. DOCS had learned from poor decisions made by its BOP counterparts in Ray Brook. Unfortunately, the department's plans for preventing a Ray Brook-style disaster—including obtaining wetland building permits, erecting fences to prevent intrusion on sensitive areas, and using berms, mesh netting, and other equipment to protect remaining wetlands—did not change the fact that the larger plan posed significant risks to environmental and public health. The environmental protections DOCS did offer—building a wall of trees around the penitentiary and not posting a sign indicating its location—fixed problems that existed only in the minds of correctional planners. The one thing that DOCS did fear was that piles of ore tailings on Lyon Mountain might hinder the penal experience of both incarcerated men and prison employees—as opposed to the real threats that industrial waste posed to environmental and public health—which reinforced a growing sense of local alienation from both the prison and its planners.[33]

Aware that its destructive plans might drive away otherwise supportive residents, Corrections planned a penitentiary whose daily operations might compensate for whatever damage the facility would cause. As at Ray Brook and Gabriels, only convicted men not considered security risks, with clean behavior records, and who were within two years of release would be incarcerated in Lyon Mountain. To the benefit of local homeowners, most imprisoned men would spend their days laboring on public works, conservation,

and infrastructure projects outside the prison. The remainder of the incarcerated population would participate in work, educational, recreational, and
vocational training activities on the facility grounds. Echoing the views of
nineteenth-century correctional planners and reformers, DOCS promised a
penal experience at Lyon Mountain conducive to instilling "regular work
habits" in incarcerated men, and anticipated that the area's "forested hills,
terrain and wetlands" would "contribute to a peaceful, rural character" free
of escapes or other disturbances. Corrections predicted these factors, combined with new employment opportunities, increased tax receipts, and outreach activities linking residents and incarcerated men might smooth over
any rough patches created during planning.[34]

Following a weeks-long suspension, Park Agency officials finally began
their non-binding advisory review of Lyon Mountain at the end of 1983.
For its part, DOCS remained determined not to allow delays like those
experienced in Gabriels, and, as the properties were already under department control and there was no organized opposition, the only potential
roadblock to a speedy opening was the Park Agency itself. Though the two
sides pledged mutual cooperation in public, the *Marcy* decision had greatly
inflated DOCS's sense of its own power. Flexing its newfound muscle,
Corrections effectively dictated terms to the APA. DOCS expected the
agency to use its power under Section 814 of the APA Act to rule the new
prison consistent with the natural, scenic, aesthetic, and historic features of
the park. In addition, Corrections anticipated prompt reclassification of
the prison properties as State Administrative under Section 816 of the APA
Act. Finally, the department pressed the Park Agency to issue a building
permit—required by New York's Freshwater Wetlands Act of 1975—allowing
construction on protected state wetlands. After issuing its demands,
Corrections short-circuited the review process once again by opening the
penitentiary before the agency's work was completed. Coughlin did promise Ruzow that DOCS would take no action after the completion of phase
one "which irrevocably leads to the conversion of the . . . School to correctional use." Coughlin's promise, however, was ambiguous. Was he pledging
to await completion of APA review before commencing phase two? Or was
the commissioner flashing his usual sarcasm, aware that the arrival of incarcerated men constituted "correctional use"? Assuming the latter, Park
Agency leaders reached the limits of their patience. Bombarding DOCS
with a flood of questions and document requests, the APA proved that

Corrections was not the only state agency that had learned from Gabriels. In the winter of 1983 to 1984, both sides settled in for a drawn-out, Gabriels-style struggle.[35]

Three months passed between the arrival of Lyon Mountain's first incarcerated men in December 1983 and the APA hearing in Dannemora in March 1984. In contrast to the crowds packed in for the sessions on Gabriels, not a single local resident attended the hearing on Lyon Mountain, and while the Park Agency had received nearly one hundred pieces of correspondence about Gabriels, just one area homeowner bothered to write in about Lyon Mountain. A feeling of resignation in the face of irresistible DOCS power likely was behind the nonexistent turnout that day. Representatives from the Adirondack Park Agency, however, stood in for Lyon Mountain's residents at the hearing: agency staff skewered the state's penchant for building prisons in fragile ecosystems, warned of damage to environmental and public health, and argued that DOCS was turning the Adirondacks into a penal colony. They complained that the penitentiary's highly visible structures situated inside a residential area—as opposed to facilities in Ray Brook and Gabriels—risked further damage to an environment marred by decades of corporate neglect. Park Agency leaders reiterated a grievance first issued by STOP, reminding Corrections that incarcerating men hundreds of miles from their loved ones risked undermining its supposedly rehabilitative objectives. Finally, APA leaders urged DOCS to expand the capacity of its sewage treatment plant to help improve Lyon Mountain's environmental and public health. Prison politics made for strange bedfellows, as the conservative town supervisor concurred with the Park Agency's analysis, excoriating Corrections for refusing town access to the plant, thus depriving residents of a service more valuable than jobs. At the end of the hearing, APA officials labeled Lyon Mountain, simply, "a poor choice" for correctional expansion. More than a few Lyon Mountain residents likely agreed.[36]

As at Gabriels two years earlier, the Lyon Mountain prison revealed fissures within the Park Agency, but conditions specific to Lyon Mountain helped generate very different responses from the agency's scientific and political wings. While DOCS's augmented power in the wake of *Marcy* likely tempered some of the agency's anti-prison voices, for others in the APA, Lyon Mountain's aesthetically displeasing environment and its mainly retired, working-class residents likely appeared inconsistent with their image of the Adirondacks. The Park Agency's ambiguous findings on Lyon Mountain reflected those possibilities. In April 1984, APA staff—including its non-partisan scientists—recommended that agency commissioners reject the penitentiary as inconsistent with Section 814. The Agency's partisan commissioners, however, rejected the staff report, endorsed the penitentiary, reclassified the properties as State Administrative, and granted permits to build in protected state wetlands. Armed with the Park Agency's blessing, Corrections moved on to phase two. Then, in an episode eerily reminiscent of the disasters inflicted on Ray Brook in 1977 and 1978, heavy rains in May 1984 damaged a filtration system at the new sewage treatment plant, polluting local wetlands and raising fears of increased harm to environmental and public health. Corrections, however, would allow nothing to alter its timeline. Contractors moved quickly to finish construction so that five hundred local residents could participate in tours of the new prison—guided by incarcerated men—as it opened in July 1984.[37]

Fulfilling the wish of every New York prison advocate since the early nineteenth century, Vibra Resources International, lured by the potential of a prison-induced boom and still holding its purchase options, proposed a new development scheme for Lyon Mountain. In 1985, the firm announced plans to invest $100 million to purchase land, mineral rights, and shuttered mines in Lyon Mountain. Vibra proposed storing compressed air underground and using it to produce electricity. Rumors quickly spread that Vibra planned to stockpile toxic waste in the abandoned mines, fueling fears of possible explosions and threats to environmental and public health. Locals also assailed the low $25,000 sale price as a craven form of corporate welfare in a community still reeling from decades of private-sector neglect. Though contractually obligated to sell to Vibra, by the mid-1980s sustainable development had become a pillar of town planning and there was little enthusiasm for investment that might pose additional harm to a still-ravaged environment. The board authorized a referendum on the Vibra sale, which town residents rejected by a vote of 235 to 49 in July 1986. While Vibra's perplexed CEO could not comprehend resistance to the prospect of 260 jobs, town board members followed up by creating new rules mandating referenda preceding either the sale or development of town properties.[38] The destructive consequences of mining and, more recently, incarceration, had taught residents and politicians alike that no developer could be trusted to protect the hamlet's environmental and public health.

Though a shared commitment to sustainable development helped protect Lyon Mountain from possibly devastating private-sector schemes for nearly two decades, by the mid-1980s the hamlet's built and unbuilt environments still carried the scars from decades of corporate neglect. Indifference from the Corrections Department and an Adirondack Park Agency that was willing to sacrifice even its non-binding moral authority had inflicted additional harm on both Lyon Mountain's environment and its collective psyche. With few options for repairing either their damaged environment or crumbling infrastructure, local homeowners must have wondered what had gone wrong. It was their misfortune to encounter a DOCS leadership availed of new power, having learned that attention to local concerns, no matter how reasonable, distracted from the objective of incarceration. Further, Corrections likely saw in Lyon Mountain a community that, unlike Gabriels, might blindly accept its proposals. Unfortunately for DOCS, Lyon Mountain residents' devotion to sustainable development included any project—like a prison—that might endanger environmental and public health. DOCS's unwillingness to facilitate an ecologically sensitive, prison-induced reconstruction proved disappointing for many homeowners. Over time, however, the Lyon Mountain Correctional Facility itself, like those in Ray Brook and Gabriels, became an integral component of the local environment.

The Prison and Lyon Mountain's Struggle to Rebuild

Though Lyon Mountain adjusted to its status as a prison town, it could never shake the harmful legacies of its industrial past. Residents' familiarity with the correctional system eased the task of integrating the penitentiary into the community. Crumbling infrastructure and an ecologically compromised landscape were challenges that even the labor of incarcerated men could not solve, and so the difficulties that had plagued the hamlet before 1967 persisted after 1984. To survive as a community, homeowners and board members committed to sustainable development re-heeded the calls to self-reliance first issued back in 1967. No sooner had Lyon Mountain discovered the solution to its environmental and infrastructural woes did the state prison population begin to contract, endangering the viability of the very institution whose presence helped bridge the gap between a destructive past and a still-uncertain future.

In the months and years following the penitentiary's opening, Lyon Mountain settled into routines already familiar to the area's other prison towns. As at Camp Adirondack and Camp Gabriels, administrators at Lyon Mountain created a penal environment devoted less to discipline and more to helping incarcerated men adjust to post-prison life. At Lyon Mountain, imprisoned men moved about the penitentiary without constant surveillance. To lessen the risk of recidivism, prison leaders encouraged incarcerated men to complete high school, vocational training, and college courses, study in the facility library, and receive assistance from on-site professionals in obtaining documents necessary to secure employment, housing, and education upon release. Moreover, DOCS permitted imprisoned men to take furloughs both to visit family and to look for jobs. Facility administrators also attended to incarcerated men's physical and emotional health, allowing them to work out in the prison gym, relax at night watching television, or work in the art studio.[39] Imprisoned men, penitentiary staff, and residents also engaged in a variety of outreach activities designed to foster positive relations between town and prison. The penitentiary hosted public health informational programs, musical concerts, and charity fundraisers open to homeowners and incarcerated men alike. Local nonprofit groups held parties for imprisoned men and aided them in growing vegetable gardens on the prison grounds, among other activities. Incarcerated men even recruited the popular rock singer Jon Bon Jovi to host a public session at nearby Saranac High School in 1986 warning young people against the dangers of narcotics use. Then, at long last, members of the town board discovered a sustainable way to redevelop part of its public domain and to forge even better connections with the hamlet's newest and largest employer by leasing former mining lands to Corrections for use as a firing range for one dollar per year.[40]

Corrections' continued faith in the rehabilitative power of manual labor required Lyon Mountain's incarcerated men to spend most of their time at work. Half of Lyon Mountain's 150 incarcerated men served on poorly paid labor crews that by the 1980s had become ubiquitous across the North Country. However, because Lyon Mountain was not organized as a prison *camp,* its incarcerated men completed fewer of the environmentally themed projects commonly undertaken by men imprisoned at Ray Brook and Gabriels. Instead, their work focused mainly on renovating a wide range of public spaces in the area's cash-strapped towns and villages. Thus, prison labor proved crucial to beginning Lyon Mountain's long-awaited reconstruction. From the 1980s through the 2000s, incarcerated men fixed up and built playgrounds, athletic fields, fairgrounds, skating rinks, and holiday toys for low-income families; spruced up churches, libraries, public schools, fire departments, and medical facilities; landscaped and helped build other local prisons; and assisted with recycling programs, flood control, surplus crop gleaning, and post-storm debris removal.[41] Earning the same low wages paid in Ray Brook and Gabriels, Lyon Mountain's incarcerated workers saved local governments untold sums on projects that might otherwise have never been completed and, in the process, helped draw town and prison closer together. Even with the contributions made by the penitentiary's labor crews, repairing a community and environment laid waste by decades of corporate abuse was a challenge whose scale and cost exceeded New York's seemingly unlimited corrections budget.

The prison's relatively seamless integration into its host community did not provide relief for those still struggling to fund expensive infrastructural and environmental repairs. Voters and board members had rejected market-oriented reindustrialization in the 1986 referendum. In keeping with the hamlet's commitment to sustainable development, board members in the early 1990s reauthorized the marketing and sale of ore sand left sitting in massive piles since the 1960s. The ore tailings that had long been considered waste—and an eyesore by Corrections—acquired new value as raw materials for entrepreneurs producing asphalt and roofing shingles, among other consumer goods. To safeguard these now-precious resources, board members reissued warnings to recreational vehicle enthusiasts whose rides atop the piles threatened a reliable source of hard cash. To lure buyers willing to sign long-term contracts, town officials offered low, fixed rates based on tonnage. While generating only a small stream of revenue, limited development schemes such as these took important steps toward protecting Lyon Mountain's environmental and public health as well as helping restore at least part of a landscape still suffering from decades of corporate indifference.[42]

There were still other aspects of Lyon Mountain in need of development. Rebuilding its transportation infrastructure, for instance, would require sums exceeding both the town's and the Corrections Department's budgets. With limited resources for undertaking such a task, board members ultimately settled on using the labor of incarcerated men when possible, along with exploring federal and state grant funding opportunities. While construction grant money arrived slowly through the 1980s and 1990s, the hamlet's crumbling pedestrian pathways and roadside curbing remained a perennial source of complaint. Board members exasperated by the slow pace of progress attempted to disclaim responsibility for maintaining local roadways, arguing that the area's many state-owned highways were, in fact, New York's to fix. Residents awaited news on the status of grant applications and legal battles over the ownership of public infrastructure while area streets and sidewalks continued to decay. With few other options, the town board in the 1980s and 1990s again recruited low-paid schoolchildren to keep the hamlet's transit networks clear of debris.[43] The construction of Lyon Mountain's prison and the reconstruction of the hamlet thus proceeded along separate tracks. While handsomely paid contractors created a modern penal environment, poorly compensated children and incarcerated men worked on projects that many homeowners had hoped would be funded and completed by Corrections. Self-help ruled the day.

The modernization of Lyon Mountain's freshwater and sewage removal systems, meanwhile, met mixed results after 1984. The prison's advanced waterworks inspired the construction of a parallel system for residents. Board members proposed the creation of new water districts and sought grant and loan opportunities to clean up polluted waterways. However, residents frustrated by two decades of delays and no doubt unhappy about Corrections' indifference to their infrastructural needs refused to cooperate. Homeowners resisted returning water district surveys and prevented town-owned equipment from entering their properties for the environmental cleanup they had requested. With few options for improving the delivery of fresh water, the town deployed incarcerated men to spruce up open-air reservoirs that had not been cleaned in decades. When local residents in 1985 complained of ruptured septic tanks and pipes, board members irritated by residents' earlier resistance told them to find a solution on their own. Ultimately, neither homeowners nor elected officials could avoid repairing the sewage system forever. In 1988, the Department of Environmental Conservation invited Lyon Mountain to participate in its aptly named Self-Help Program. The state would help the town secure workers and building materials to construct a sustainable wastewater treatment system, but the town had to find the money to build the system. This required a new round of research and grant applications. In 1990, the Department of Housing and

Urban Development (HUD) agreed to fund a modern sewage removal system for Lyon Mountain contingent on the erection—using DEC-funded workers and building materials—of a low-income senior citizens' housing complex. Thus, a quarter-century after the mines closed and nearly a decade after the prison opened, Lyon Mountain had finally resolved most of its major infrastructural woes. In the years following 1990, however, board members denounced their DEC benefactors for imposing new development restrictions in area wetlands, and screeds against the APA again became regular features of the board's monthly meetings. Anti-regulatory bluster aside, without big government filling the role that big business had vacated in 1967, the reconstruction of Lyon Mountain's vital infrastructure might never have occurred.[44]

The quarter-century following the prison's opening provided constant reminders of the hamlet's industrial past. While the penitentiary and its unfree occupants proved an unobtrusive and often helpful presence to residents, its leaders' indifference to the needs of its host community left Lyon Mountain still struggling to survive. Incarcerated men played a central role in maintaining public and private infrastructure, but the time and expense required to rebuild the hamlet's decaying roadways and waterworks proved too high for Corrections. With private investment effectively dead after 1986, homeowners and board members again heeded the call of self-reliance. However, this time locals had to navigate government bureaucracies whose complexity mirrored the very infrastructure their funds were intended to rebuild. With improvements to their freshwater and sewage removal systems finally complete, the hamlet's decades-old consensus on sustainable development began to break apart. By the mid- to late 1990s, Lyon Mountain residents and their elected leaders had reverted to bashing the very government whose largesse had ensured the community's survival.

|||||||||

For much of its twenty-seven-year existence, the Lyon Mountain Correctional Facility was remarkable for its adherence to Corrections' original plan. Unlike local penitentiaries that struggled with overcrowding, Lyon Mountain's population of incarcerated men rarely exceeded 150; its twenty-seven-acre campus did not expand; and the relative peace that enveloped the hamlet after 1967 remained largely intact. When compared to disturbances witnessed at Dannemora, Ray Brook, and Gabriels, Lyon Mountain's prisonland experience could seem relatively bland. The penitentiary's only escape occurred in August 2009, when an incarcerated man walked out of the facility before the evening headcount. Authorities quickly launched a search operation featuring helicopter flyovers, state police dogs, and highway roadblocks. The local environment once again proved both blessing and curse. After spending twelve hours hiding in the woods, the runaway began walking along Route 374. About three miles from the prison, an off-duty corrections officer spotted an individual wearing a green DOCS uniform. After he ignored commands to surrender, the state police shot and recaptured twenty-three-year-old Scott Adkins. Following conviction for felony escape, Adkins explained his bid for freedom. Like many other convicted men, economic survival had originally driven Adkins to engage in unlawful activity; in his case, burglary. Mass incarceration had also facilitated Adkins's downward spiral. At his sentencing, Adkins told of struggles he faced when his primary caregiver was incarcerated while Adkins was a young man, and of suffering from depression since arriving at Lyon Mountain in 2008.[45] The rosy picture of town-prison relations trumpeted by Corrections officials and residents masked a likely widespread feeling of despair shared by many of Lyon Mountain's imprisoned men.

This singular interruption of the hamlet's postindustrial calm occurred only months before Democratic Governor David Paterson announced the penitentiary's closure in January 2010. New York's prison population had declined steadily since peaking at 71,538 in December 1999, leaving fewer than 59,000 incarcerated men in the system by 2010. A 30 percent drop in unlawful activity since 2000, combined with legal reforms featuring reduced sentences, early releases, and increased use of residential treatment for individuals convicted of narcotics-related offenses, led to a diminished need for cells. Moreover, with belt-tightening a priority amid the Great Recession, state leaders predicted closing Lyon Mountain would save taxpayers $7.2 million in annual operating costs and $950,000 in planned construction. Corrections promised its ninety-one Lyon Mountain employees equivalent positions in other penitentiaries. Correctional facilities elsewhere would absorb the hamlet's 135 incarcerated men, withdrawing a vital labor force from the area's struggling communities.[46] Though the prison had attracted little more than a shrug from homeowners when it opened, reactions to its closure prompted a harsher response.

The shuttering of Lyon Mountain's prison represented the fatal blow residents had long feared. Their criticisms of the decision evoked the same old anxieties as when the mines closed. With more than eighty percent of its population retired, town leaders worried about tax increases once Corrections ceased paying its annual $28,000 water bill and withdrew the labor of its incarcerated men. Homeowners were caught up in what amounted to grieving over the prison's closure, alternatively attacking and praising both DOCS leaders and the facility's incarcerated men. Angry residents accused Corrections of privileging the desires of incarcerated men to be closer to their hometowns at the expense of the North Country economy, but these same homeowners also took credit for teaching incarcerated men valuable work and vocational skills. Almost in the same breath, residents resurrected nineteenth-century arguments concerning the supposedly healthful qualities inherent in Adirondack nature, suddenly claiming to care for incarcerated men whose desire to be closer to their families they had so easily dismissed. Finally, homeowners were determined not to allow Corrections simply to skip town as Republic Steel had done in 1967. If DOCS insisted on abandoning Lyon Mountain, residents demanded compensation from lawmakers to mitigate the economic harm sure to come with the facility's closure.[47]

Though a crowd of two hundred residents stood in the winter cold to protest Lyon Mountain's closure, the state shuttered the facility in January 2011. Much like the school it had replaced in 1983, the penitentiary had received $3 million in upgrades five years earlier, and as of 2010 had an assessed value of $5 million. Two and a half years after its closure, New York auctioned off the penitentiary in the same Dannemora Town Hall where the APA hearing had been held, amid a sea of empty chairs, thirty years before. Bidding began at $140,000, and the only interested party in the room that day, a businessman from Québec, won the twenty-seven-acre facility, including its twenty-three buildings, several acres of undeveloped land, and the sewage treatment plant that had once been the subject of so much local angst. While the former prison's future remains a mystery, residents and board members are still contending with the hamlet's industrial past. The closure prompted the board to investigate new sources of revenue for a community with no major employer for the first time in nearly four decades. With prison redevelopment on hold and new private investments unlikely, town leaders raised tonnage rates on the sale of their still-abundant supplies of ore sand.[48] Still overshadowing the now-shuttered penitentiary, the tailings piles provide a constant reminder that Lyon Mountain may never escape the destructive consequences of its industrial past.

Lyon Mountain is more quiet today than it has been since the first ore prospectors arrived in the 1790s. Though the Lyon Mountain Mining and Railroad Museum—housed inside the hamlet's shuttered train depot—attracts a steady trickle of summertime visitors, Lyon Mountain's days serving as either a tourist attraction or active workplace have long since passed. However, as at Ray Brook and Gabriels, incarceration has created an indelible imprint in the Lyon Mountain landscape. Public and private infrastructure built and renovated by incarcerated men stand in enduring legacy to the central role of unfree labor in supporting the area's struggling economy. In contrast, the continued presence of rusting mining equipment, ore sand piles, and crumbling industrial structures provide a constant reminder of the limitations of correctional policy and environmental law

FIGURE 10. Shuttered Lyon Mountain Correctional Facility, Lyon Mountain, New York. Photo courtesy of the author.

in repairing postindustrial communities. Situated far from the prison, such features of Lyon Mountain's environment were of little concern to DOCS bureaucrats who were focused only on incarceration. With no new developments on the horizon, neither DEC nor APA oversight will compel the removal of human-made structures located on town property that pose unknown risks to a public granted unrestricted access to former industrial sites. Perhaps the most innocuous yet enduring legacy of Lyon Mountain's short history with corrections is Mountain Top Senior Housing—a complex funded and built by the DEC and HUD. Having served as the catalyst for building the hamlet's long-awaited modern sewage system, Mountain Top continues to provide affordable apartments to low-income residents. The former prison stands in the center of town, shielded from view by neither trees nor fencing. Unlike the complex in Gabriels, the owner of Lyon Mountain's shuttered penitentiary has left the facility open to curious visitors and vandals alike. The once-modern penitentiary is now deteriorating in much the same way as the mining facilities that once dominated the village. With the compound's future still up in the air, it seems likely that the postindustrial serenity that overtook Lyon Mountain after 1967 and reemerged to settle over the town after the departure of the prison in 2011 will become the community's defining characteristic far into the future.

CHAPTER FIVE

"THIS TOWN WILL DIE"

Pro-Prison Organizing and Environmental
Politics in Tupper Lake

Introduction

From the road, it is difficult to catch a glimpse of the collection of buildings that sits south of the Franklin County village of Tupper Lake. Turning off the highway, a gravel road leads to an asphalt lot where employees and visitors park their vehicles. Thick vegetation obscures the compound entrance, which is reached by walking down a paved path. Inside, security personnel are stationed in a large sunlit hall with long corridors veering off to the left and right. Visitors must wear identification badges while inside, and there are limits on the times and days of the week outsiders may enter. A complex ecosystem encircles the facility, which sits astride the Raquette River, New York's second longest. In many ways, this human-built institution seamlessly blends with the natural environment of the area long known by residents and visitors alike as the "Heart of the Adirondacks."

The facility in question is the Natural History Museum of the Adirondacks—popularly known as the Wild Center—that opened in 2006. The museum's construction was the unintended outcome of a nearly two-decade-long campaign to bring a correctional facility to Tupper Lake. Galvanized by the collapse of the area's logging industry and the successful opening of penitentiaries elsewhere, a coalition of homeowners and elected officials led by a committee known unofficially as the Tupper Lake Prison Task Force represented the most substantial pro-prison organizing effort in the history of the Adirondacks. If the Task Force had prevailed, the South Franklin Correctional Facility, a state maximum-security prison designed to incarcerate 1,500 convicted men and employ 400 staff, might now be operating on a tract of commercial forestland in Tupper Lake owned by International Paper (IP). The Task Force enjoyed support from both the North Country's growing number of DOCS employees as well as influential local politicians. However, challenges not faced by penitentiary advocates in the area's other prison towns undermined many of Tupper Lake's bids. One particular source of pressure well known to supporters and critics alike—potential harm to environmental and public health—ultimately doomed Tupper Lake's prison dream.

Like many Adirondack communities, Tupper Lake was home to middle- and low-income working people as well as a cohort of well-to-do homeowners and visitors who valued the area for leisure and recreation. For over a decade, the mainly affluent membership of Tupper Lake Concerned Citizens (TLCC) successfully prevented the village's penal transformation. TLCC's resistance evolved over time, representing the influence of circumstances beyond its control as well as issues critical to anti-prison organizing in other North Country communities. Legislative efforts to rein in New York's ballooning debt proved a valuable gift to opponents, as they helped to scuttle prison bids in the 1980s and early 1990s. Most importantly, the experience of earlier opposition campaigns finally taught correctional planners—burdened by a growing population of convicted men—the value of obstacle-free planning. As frugality, speed, and ease acquired heightened significance in prison site selection, arguments that had failed to stop penitentiaries elsewhere—including possible harm to environmental and public health—found a higher chance of success in Tupper Lake. Even a Corrections Department with unlimited power now shuddered at the prospect of delay-inducing environmental oversight. With communities outside the park now competing to host correctional facilities, DOCS had little incentive to grant Tupper Lake its potentially time- and money-consuming prison wish.

Whether intentional or coincidental, TLCC's successes only galvanized the project's advocates. After enduring a string of defeats and watching prisons open elsewhere, Task Force supporters rejoiced when in the summer of 1997 lawmakers awarded a penitentiary to Franklin County. Though Corrections had passed on Tupper Lake throughout the 1980s and early 1990s, the stars eventually aligned. Confronted with the worst prison overcrowding in New York history, DOCS found in the Tupper Lake region a supportive local population—with many residents already employed at local penitentiaries—that valued the jobs correctional facilities created. The overall growth in Corrections's North Country footprint throughout the 1980s helped diminish the influence groups like TLCC might otherwise have enjoyed. The influence of environmentalist groups also waned with the 1994 election of Republican Governor George Pataki, which ushered in less environmentally friendly governance at both DOCS and the APA. Providing uncharacteristic support to its longtime Corrections adversary, the Park Agency both abetted and overlooked legally dubious prison planning that eventually prompted the intervention of environmentalists. Amid predictions of catastrophic harm to environmental and public health, DOCS for the first time in the history of Adirondack prisons abandoned a project in the name of environmental protection and moved the planned Tupper Lake facility outside the park to the Franklin County village of Malone. In doing so, Corrections unwittingly endorsed the notion that penitentiaries did not belong in the Adirondack Park.

Prison Battles, 1981–1992

Between 1981 and 1992, Tupper Lake leaders waged five campaigns to attract a correctional facility to their community. Spurred on by high unemployment and poverty and unwilling to wait for Corrections to find them first, town officials created a Prison Task Force to undertake this unusual assignment. The Task Force faced difficulties that were largely unknown to penitentiary advocates in other North Country communities. Even with a swelling population of convicted men, support from the area's growing number of DOCS employees, and the endorsement of influential local politicians, Task Force members struggled to achieve their objective. Problems securing land for the prison, heightened public scrutiny of the high cost of incarceration, and competition from other prison-seeking communities posed challenges beyond supporters' control. The potential risks to environmental and public health highlighted by members of Tupper Lake Concerned Citizens stirred just enough doubt to send oversight-averse Corrections officials looking elsewhere. Pressured on multiple fronts, Task Force members throughout the 1980s and early 1990s repeatedly failed in their efforts to deliver the village its long-awaited economic salvation.

Much like Lyon Mountain, Tupper Lake in the early 1980s was a shadow of its former self. The silent reminders of empty storefronts, abandoned homes, and an aging and shrinking population lent the place an aura of despair. However, life had not always been so gloomy. Fur trappers first trekked into the region in the early nineteenth century, and by the turn of the twentieth, the dense, old-growth forests surrounding Tupper Lake were fuel for a resurgent logging trade. The Sunmount Veterans Administration Hospital for individuals diagnosed with tuberculosis opened in 1924, providing a valuable source of employment for residents. After World War II, the area's increasing popularity with visitors and seasonal homeowners spurred an expanded service sector. By the 1950s, Tupper Lake counted thirty-nine bars and restaurants, numerous retail outlets, a dozen hotels, and daily passenger rail connections. Economic decline, however, came quickly. While the veterans hospital closed in 1965, it quickly reopened as the state-run Sunmount Developmental Center and, with seven hundred workers, became the village's largest employer. By the mid-1970s, market forces and APA rules had decimated what remained of the logging industry, and tourists turned off by postindustrial blight increasingly bypassed Tupper Lake in favor of Lake Placid, driving many small businesses and homeowners into bankruptcy.[1] With unemployment and poverty threatening the village's future, Tupper Lake's leaders followed other North Country communities in seeking more reliable forms of economic development.

Having been likely inspired by the opening of penitentiaries twenty-four miles away in Ray Brook, Tupper Lake's political and business leaders embraced corrections as a potential solution to their woes. Village officials hoped a prison might revive the logging industry and introduce a stable source of employment that would presumably be immune to the vicissitudes of the capitalist economy. In 1981, area leaders learned that two state agencies were seeking space to build new facilities. The Power Authority of the State of New York (PASNY) planned a wood-fired electrical plant to provide steam power to businesses and homeowners struggling with high energy bills. The Department of Correctional Services was continuing its search for new and inexpensive cells as it contended with overcrowded penitentiaries. Local politicians informed PASNY and DOCS that Tupper Lake's "abundant wood supply" would make the village an "excellent location" for both institutions. Area officials also predicted that "the two projects [might] go hand in hand," noting the electric plant could also power the prison. Local Republican Assemblyman Glenn Harris said the plan "would certainly be a much-needed shot in the arm for the North Country in terms of new jobs, a potential savings in fuel consumption, and a general boosting of the economy." For reasons unknown, however, Tupper Lake's proposal to marry correctional services to electric power and revive the logging trade never came to fruition.[2]

The opening of prisons in Gabriels, Altona, and Lyon Mountain likely generated a heightened sense of urgency in Tupper Lake by the mid-1980s. Though the town was lacking an easily convertible surplus property, awaiting DOCS's discovery of their community was not an option for residents and officials desperate for economic relief. Therefore, Tupper Lake leaders launched a tightly focused pro-prison organizing campaign in 1986. Democrat Dean Lefebvre had won the election for supervisor of the Town of Altamont—of which Tupper Lake is part—in November 1985 while pledging to bring a prison to the community. After taking office in January 1986, Lefebvre received endorsements from the local board of education, chamber of commerce, and numerous town and village boards; he enlisted area corrections officers to lead petition drives in support of the campaign; and he created the Tupper Lake Prison Task Force, a body comprised of area business and political leaders charged with crafting a bid package and lobbying state leaders. In December 1986, Corrections signaled its interest in property identified by Task Force members—a 4,500-acre tract of commercial forestland owned by International Paper—as suitable for a penitentiary. Aware of DOCS's penchant for repurposing existing facilities, Task Force members knew that building a prison from scratch on private land would be a tough sell. Accordingly, they streamlined the village's complicated 1981 proposal: Instead of the prison serving as but one component of a multipronged development scheme, the penitentiary would operate solely for the Corrections Department and its unfree charges.[3]

Not everyone, however, was enthused about Tupper Lake becoming a prison town. The first rumblings of resistance emerged following an October 1986 escape from Gabriels. With a fugitive again threatening public safety, a group of residents gathered to discuss the Task Force proposal. In January 1987, they organized as Tupper Lake Concerned Citizens. Articulating a vision of the Adirondack Park free of prisons and preserved only for leisure and recreation, members of TLCC crafted an agenda nearly indistinguishable from that presented by CAMPA. Economic concerns figured prominently among their grievances, with critics warning of damage to property values, housing markets, tourism, and public services. TLCC also identified incarcerated men—particularly those diagnosed with HIV/AIDS—as a singular threat to environmental and public health. Opponents also feared that the families of incarcerated men—many of them low-income urban people of color—might either visit or resettle in Tupper Lake, potentially disrupting the racial and class privileges the group deemed essential components of the local environment. With Moriah, Malone, and Dannemora each vying to host a correctional facility, the formation of TLCC threw a wrench into the Task Force's plans.[4] Eager for a show of unity, Lefebvre scheduled public hearings on the project.

Town officials convened two public meetings on the Task Force proposal. The first, in October 1986, featured members fielding a mixture of softball questions and unvarnished praise from a room filled with project supporters. By 1987, however, the Task Force faced an organized opposition that no doubt stirred memories of struggles at Ray Brook and Gabriels. Unlike Corrections, the Task Force could not simply ram the prison through irrespective of public opinion. If anything, inattention to local concerns might sabotage its chances. While a frustrated Lefebvre called public involvement "unnecessary" and "a waste of taxpayers' money," he also seemed to appreciate the value of face-saving gestures, organizing a second meeting in March 1987. Attendees heard from a Task Force whose membership—including local prison leaders, a hospital administrator, newspaper publisher, chamber of commerce executive, and nonprofit and political officials from neighboring communities—suggested broad local support. Addressing TLCC's economic fears, Task Force members predicted state investment and well-paying prison jobs would pump $22 million per year into the area economy. Project boosters also anticipated a housing boom resulting from a prison-induced spike in property values. Their forecast for an improved economy predicted a prison would increase tourism and second-home ownership. Finally, supporters pledged to mitigate potential environmental impacts by using existing trees to shield the facility from public view.[5] Unfortunately for the Task Force, economic revival and vegetative screens proved as unimpressive for TLCC as they had been for CAMPA.

Members of TLCC did not go to the March hearing to talk about jobs, tourism, or trees. To the contrary, they zeroed in on threats to environmental and public health. In particular, members of TLCC focused on the unknown risks posed by incarcerated men diagnosed with HIV/AIDS.

Seeking to capitalize on lingering doubts about the disease's origins and modes of transmission, opponents warned that razor wire alone might not contain the pathogens potentially lurking inside the bodies of imprisoned men. Members of TLCC highlighted recent protests by officers at Adirondack Correctional Facility, where one picketing employee had held a sign asking, "How would you like to work with downstate men with AIDS?" Chip Brieant, a former respiratory therapy technician at Saranac Lake General Hospital and supporter of TLCC, testified having "lost count at 15 (on) the number of ones who died with AIDS, all of them prisoners." While ACF Superintendent and task force member James Racette acknowledged the existence of HIV/AIDS in his facility, he argued the disease did not affect "the community, except for the prison . . . and the hospital." Moreover, Racette informed critics that because men incarcerated at ACF had contracted the disease through intravenous drug use and not sexual activity, residents faced a miniscule risk of infection. Racette called AIDS "a scary disease," but reminded critics that "all the information says you can't get it by casual contact." Though Racette claimed that imprisoned men diagnosed with HIV/AIDS posed no threat to public health, he also indicated Corrections was negotiating with Saint Clare's Hospital in New York City to both incarcerate and treat convicted men diagnosed with the disease.[6] Racette's less-than-definitive claims, TLCC likely hoped, might sow just enough doubt to broaden its base of support and kill the prison.

In June 1987, DOCS rejected building a penitentiary in Tupper Lake. Corrections's announcement happened to coincide with the publication of a study commissioned by the Task Force on the facility's potential impacts. Its results closely mirrored the predictions of economic revival central to pro-prison organizing in other Adirondack communities. The study predicted a hypothetical medium-security penitentiary designed to incarcerate 700 convicted men would infuse $62 million into the area economy during construction. Further, the report anticipated that state investment along with salaries and benefits paid to the facility's 380 employees would generate an additional $23 million per year in economic impact. In addition, the prison could not help but spur private sector improvements that, the study argued, would include new small businesses and at least 380 jobs. For its part, DOCS cited IP's refusal to sell its property as the reason for passing on Tupper Lake.[7] Though its activities seemed not to have figured in Corrections's decision, members of TLCC rested comfortably knowing a penitentiary would not be coming to town.

Two years later, Governor Mario Cuomo requested more prison cells. The Task Force was encouraged enough to try again. Cuomo told lawmakers that stiffer penalties for crack and cocaine possession, along with more effective policing, had created a larger population of convicted men. With New York's fifty correctional facilities operating at 118 percent of capacity, in June 1989 legislators appropriated $887 million to build twelve new penitentiaries designed to incarcerate 7,100 convicted men. Lawmakers approved the construction of four large prisons, six smaller facilities designed to incarcerate 200 drug- and alcohol-addicted men apiece, and two penal institutions to be built in the future. With the North Country communities of Chateaugay, Champlain, Ellenburg, and Chesterfield also bidding for a prison, Tupper Lake again faced competition. Hoping to avoid a repeat of 1987, the Task Force made the purchase of the IP tract its top priority. Members asked the Franklin County legislature for a $50,000 grant to purchase the property. For good measure, they enlisted local Republican State Senator Ronald Stafford "to pull in some favors" done for IP to ease the tract's acquisition. After inspecting several other properties, in June 1989 Corrections approved a one-hundred-acre parcel in the center of the IP property as suitable for construction. IP officials expressed doubt over the wisdom of building a penitentiary in the middle of their forestland, highlighting the parcel's proximity to "some valuable recreation property"; but ultimately the firm pledged to cooperate and "be good corporate citizens." Stafford reminded Lefebvre that the land issue would have to be "squared away," because "that was the problem Tupper Lake has had in the past."[8]

The launch of Tupper Lake's third prison bid prompted the reemergence of TLCC. At a March 1989 public hearing, one critic reminded an audience filled with project supporters that "there is still some active opposition." TLCC leader Christine Randolph went further, stating, "This idea of broad-based support is not true. It's really a special-interest group (prison guards), supported by the town officials." Randolph highlighted the emergence of corrections employees as a distinct constituency in the Adirondacks, though her analysis minimized that group's influence in a region where DOCS's footprint was only expanding. Nevertheless, such reasoning guided TLCC's resistance in 1989. Critics wagered that racial and class hysteria couched as threats to environmental and public health might widen their ranks. Members of TLCC warned that a penitentiary would "overwhelm" Tupper Lake, "adversely affect its rural, small-town atmosphere," and irrevocably alter its "feeling" by introducing "a lot of the problems associated with a city." Class-conscious homeowners also feared what might happen once Tupper Lake acquired "the reputation as a prison town." In April, TLCC cheered when the North Elba Town Board declined Lefebvre's request for an endorsement, with one official complaining, "We've got better things to do . . . than bring in another prison." TLCC then broached an alliance with the APA. Park Agency Executive Director Robert Glennon voiced sympathy for TLCC and lamented his limited power over public projects in the park: "If a prison moves in here, it means the state sets up rules and regulations, but can break them whenever it pleases." Glennon did note, however, that IP would require an agency subdivision permit to sell part of its property to DOCS.[9] Without the permit, building a prison would be next to impossible.

In June 1989, Corrections again passed on Tupper Lake. Though failing to acquire the IP land was a major factor, DOCS also highlighted the budding alliance between TLCC and the APA as adequate reason to build elsewhere. Corrections's rejection of every Adirondack Park prison bid in 1989 underscored its increasingly wary view of both organized opposition and environmental oversight. No longer forced to open prisons in hostile locales, DOCS could now choose from among a slew of contenders clamoring to host a correctional facility. The only North Country community awarded a prison that year was Chateaugay, a Franklin County hamlet located outside the park. While TLCC expressed relief and indicated its "long term objective is to make sure Tupper Lake never gets a prison," the Task Force continued its pursuit. In November 1989, Lefebvre won a second term as town supervisor while still promising to secure a penitentiary. That same month, IP agreed to sell two hundred acres of its holdings for penal use.[10] Members of TLCC, meanwhile, had unexpectedly seized the upper hand in Tupper Lake's ongoing prison drama. With penitentiary NIMBYism all but dead and Corrections fielding more bids than it could handle, simply sowing doubt and inducing fear might be enough to keep the village penitentiary-free.

Tupper Lake launched its fourth prison bid in January 1990. Confident in the face of repeated defeat, Lefebvre stated, "We still feel that we have the best site in the state," and, somewhat misleadingly, "We know that this community wants a correctional facility." Shortly thereafter, IP formalized its pledge to sell two hundred acres of its property—should Corrections ever choose Tupper Lake. With the land issue settled, the Task Force planned a hypothetical medium-security prison designed to incarcerate 1,000 convicted men and employ 566 workers. Just as Tupper Lake seemed to have solved one of its biggest problems, the high cost of incarceration caught up to leaders in Albany: Concern over the state's $1.5 billion budget deficit made the massive DOCS appropriations of years past increasingly untenable. In 1990, Governor Cuomo requested only $282 million to fund a growing correctional system. Cuomo's bid for a third term that year prompted unusual Republican resistance to even minimal Corrections spending. Hoping to unseat Cuomo in November, the Senate's Republican majority wooed voters with promises of tax cuts at the expense of penal expansion. Facing budget cuts, DOCS requested only 3,000 new cells be built at five existing prisons. Republican State Comptroller Edward Regan countered with a proposal to cut Corrections staff to reduce the deficit, effectively shelving DOCS's modest expansion plans. In the end, a nationwide recession, unsustainable debt, and the fracturing of New York's once-solid pro-prison consensus made new construction impossible. Two years went by before Corrections announced plans to build another North Country penitentiary, this time an $18 million alcohol- and substance-abuse facility in the St. Lawrence County hamlet of Brasher Falls. Upon discovery of that site's location within a State Reforestation Zone, however, DOCS moved it to Tupper Lake. Stafford acknowledged his role in the switch, stating, "We wanted to keep that facility in the North Country." Alas, the aforementioned state budget woes meant there was no money to build the prison. As close to securing a penitentiary as at any time since 1981, area politicians dutifully endorsed Tupper Lake's unfunded future prison.[11]

In the spring of 1992, all that stood between Tupper Lake and its prison dream was an improved state budget. TLCC and its supporters were remarkably quiet. Peter Day, a Tupper Lake business owner and member of TLCC, explained the group's unusual silence, noting that the growing local influence of corrections employees as a constituency, a phenomenon confronted by no other North Country anti-prison group, was impossible to miss. Day claimed the Task Force had used the area's large population of DOCS workers to intimidate the opposition. He also feared penitentiary advocates might exploit TLCC's absence to make exaggerated claims of broad public support for the project. Day misleadingly argued, "The majority of our citizens don't want these types of facilities," and—deploying the coded language of racial and class hysteria—he continued, "the problems they will bring to our community . . . as we become the dumping grounds for the state." While Day called for more public hearings, Lefebvre argued there had been enough, claiming possession of a petition containing eight hundred signatures in favor of the penitentiary and stating that phone calls to his office ran fifty-to-one in support. Ever confident, members of the Task Force traveled to Chateaugay in May 1992 to visit the two-year-old alcohol- and substance-abuse correctional facility for a preview of what might lay in their future.[12]

Between 1981 and 1992, Tupper Lake's efforts to join prisonland reflected important shifts in New York's carceral state. The opening of penitentiaries in communities targeted by correctional planners inspired towns and villages not chosen for penal expansion to try their hand at pro-prison organizing. As deindustrialization tore through New York's rural hinterlands in the early 1980s, hollowed-out settlements actively pursued corrections-based development. NIMBYism all but dead, remote communities competed for a share of New York's widening prison pie. These factors combined meant that local difficulties once grudgingly tolerated by Corrections officials desperate for space—including land acquisition, organized opposition, and environmental oversight—could now be avoided simply by building outside the park. With DOCS expanding its footprint across the North Country, corrections employees acquired influence unknown just a few years before. However, state debt acquired during two decades of relentless correctional expansion forced a reckoning in Albany, shattering the prison dreams of communities like Tupper Lake and undermining the notion of DOCS's immunity to shifting economic winds. Until New York's budget picture improved, Task Force members withheld declarations of victory while TLCC plotted its next move.

Final Campaigns, 1996–1997

The troubles afflicting New York's prison system only worsened as the twentieth century ended. As correctional facilities strained under unprecedented overcrowding, Tupper Lake's working-class residents staggered under the weight of poverty, unemployment, and depopulation. With funding still not secured, Task Force members waited four more years for a penitentiary some thought might never materialize. Then, in 1996, a brighter economic outlook encouraged boosters to try again. One year later, lawmakers both approved and funded a penitentiary in Franklin County. Dormant for nearly a decade, TLCC quickly reemerged. With the prison close to becoming reality, TLCC abandoned attempts at local outreach in favor of an alliance with the Park Agency. Forced to reintroduce themselves after an extended absence, opponents repeated some familiar arguments and advanced new positions drawn from two decades of experience with the correctional system. Aware of the risks of APA oversight, the Task Force and its supporters also lobbied the agency with arguments that, like those of TLCC, drew from both the recent and distant past. As in other prison towns, Park Agency involvement all but guaranteed that the planning process would turn on questions of environmental and public health.

Budget woes had prevented the opening of Tupper Lake's prison in 1992. The following year, Lefebvre campaigned for a third term, still promising to get the penitentiary built. The likelihood of Tupper Lake hosting a correctional facility improved as the economy recovered from an early 1990s recession. Growth in the population of convicted men and a chronic lack of cell space also proved critical to Tupper Lake's chances. In 1996, the task force embarked on its final campaign, though it did so amid waning enthusiasm for the project. In May, the ordinarily supportive Harrietstown Town Board in Saranac Lake rejected Lefebvre's request for an endorsement. While board member Peter Donnelly agreed that a penitentiary might carry "great growth potential" and that Tupper Lake "needed economic help," he also did not "necessarily want another prison." Donnelly predicted that DOCS employees "moving into the area to work at the prison won't have a tremendous impact" on an economy already saturated with prisons. Local resident Shirley Colin told Lefebvre that with "private enterprise . . . already being killed" across the region, she feared that "everybody . . . trying to make the Adirondacks a prison community" would scare off entrepreneurs. With board members expressing uncharacteristic skepticism, town supervisor Bill Gallagher tabled the motion.[13] Though it was a stinging rebuke, Lefebvre had already learned that the value of such endorsements paled in comparison to sound planning free of delays and opposition.

Preparing its final campaign, the Task Force labored to neutralize TLCC's potentially harmful influence. Having learned from the experience of Gabriels and from their own 1989 defeat, Task Force members sought to foster a cooperative relationship with the previously hostile Adirondack Park Agency. To that end, in the summer of 1996—with no indication that Tupper Lake would

ever host a correctional facility—the Task Force requested Park Agency officials study a penitentiary's potential environmental and public health impacts.
In its report, an APA staff biologist reported that IP's Tupper Lake tract,
much like other North Country properties chosen for prison construction,
contained protected state wetlands. In the case of Tupper Lake, the property
hosted a total of sixty-seven acres of wetlands that would face irreparable
harm from building and operating the facility.[14] This small but important
detail, tucked away in a confidential memorandum sent to Task Force members, remained out of public view for over a year. With the community's
viability seemingly hanging in the balance, Task Force members were willing
to leave nothing to chance.

In January 1997, New York's correctional system incarcerated nearly
70,000 convicted men and operated at a record 130 percent of capacity.
With a penal population predicted to hit 84,000 by 2002, Republican
Governor George Pataki asked lawmakers for $635 million to build three
new maximum-security prisons designed to incarcerate 1,500 convicted men
apiece, along with adding 2,500 new cells to existing penitentiaries. That
same month, the Franklin County legislature acceded to Lefebvre's latest
request for an endorsement, praising the potential $18 million payroll and
$27 million in annual economic impact a Tupper Lake prison might bring.
The Task Force anticipated the village would "be in for some good times,"
as the prison "would bring back to the North Country some of our corrections officers" compelled by seniority rules to work far from home. Sixteen
years of organizing paid off when in July 1997, the legislature approved
construction of a 750-cell maximum-security penitentiary designed to incarcerate 1,500 convicted men in Franklin County. Senator Joseph Bruno, the
Republican majority leader of the State Senate and ally of Senator Stafford,
personally chose the site. Stafford acknowledged the prison as a gift from an
old friend: "I worked hard; I put a lot of effort into this. I've known Joe
Bruno since 1966 when I had a primary and he was a young Republican who
supported me. He made the decision . . . It came my way and I am most
appreciative." Though the bill named only Franklin County—not Tupper
Lake—as its location, the Task Force pointed to lawmakers' 1992 selection
of Tupper Lake in declaring victory. Lefebvre exulted, "It'll be about the
biggest economic change here in about 70 years. It's a great day for Tupper
Lake and the north country!"[15]

Unlike the area's other penal institutions, Corrections planned a prison in Franklin County designed to discipline men convicted of unlawful activities committed while incarcerated at other penitentiaries. Men imprisoned at the maximum-security Green Haven Correctional Facility near Poughkeepsie would manufacture the prison's concrete-and-steel cells before loading them on to flatbed trucks. Upon the arrival of the prefabricated sections in Franklin County, local incarcerated men and private contractors would then piece them together to form the two-story penitentiary. Solitary confinement would be the norm for 80 percent of its imprisoned men. While 300 incarcerated men would work in service jobs on the prison grounds, the remaining 1,200 would be confined to their cells twenty-three hours per day. Two imprisoned men would share each 105-square-foot cell containing a toilet, shower, and sink. For one hour each day, men in solitary could access the individual fenced recreation yards, one attached to each cell and accessible through an interior, electronically operated door. Upon completion of their disciplinary confinement, incarcerated men would leave Tupper Lake to continue serving their original sentences in their home penitentiaries. If all went according to plan, Corrections anticipated opening the facility by June 1999.[16]

Though thousands of North Country residents had become the beneficiaries of mass incarceration, the struggles that afflicted area homeowners before 1976 still persisted two decades later. The exodus of unemployed and under-employed residents that accelerated after World War II continued as the century drew to a close. The town of Altamont's population dropped 2 percent between 1980 and 1990, while the village of Tupper Lake lost nearly 27 percent of its residents between 1940 and 1990, going from a high of 5,451 residents to 4,000 five decades later. The poverty rate in Franklin County stood at 16 percent in 1990, three points above the state average. A draft of an environmental impact statement prepared in advance of the prison's construction illustrated Tupper Lake's bleak economic picture:

> The proposed facility is located in a sparsely settled region that is primarily a mixture of small villages, rural areas, and a mountainous wilderness. With a strong linkage to the summer recreational season, a lack of major employers and a limited transportation network, the area has substantial seasonal swings in job and unemployment levels throughout the year, with unemployment rates generally higher than the statewide average. . . . The region has double-digit unemployment rates in the winter months and rates below the statewide average in the summer.

Despite its increasingly heavy local footprint the Corrections Department had not showered its benefits on all North Country homeowners. With many locals mired in irregular and low-paying private-sector jobs, household incomes in Franklin County remained below the state average. The obviously limited economic benefits to locals after two decades of growth in the corrections sector failed to prompt a reevaluation of the Task Force plan. If anything, project supporters believed a penitentiary was all that separated Tupper Lake from a more prosperous future.[17]

With the Task Force's work complete, DOCS engaged in a salesmanship campaign reminiscent of past prison-building projects. Though most residents were likely already on board, Corrections hoped the penitentiary's predicted economic impacts might convert some opponents. As in other prison towns, DOCS promised a correctional facility would help revive the local economy. While there would be no incarcerated workers laboring on conservation, public works, and infrastructure projects outside the prison, Corrections did pledge the creation of 367 well-paying, full-time jobs at the facility. DOCS also predicted paying out $56 million in wages and salaries during construction and an annual payroll of $12 million once the penitentiary opened. Corrections further anticipated that state investments and higher incomes would help resuscitate the area's private sector, enabling small businesses to reopen their long-shuttered doors. With young people no longer forced to move in search of employment, DOCS predicted an increased tax base enabling local governments to provide vital services in a timely and reliable manner. For Tupper Lake's beleaguered residents, it must have sounded like a dream.[18]

However, just as the Task Force neared the end of its long journey, TLCC resurfaced. With the penitentiary all but assured, members of TLCC understood that tactics deployed in past prison fights—especially the sowing of racial, class, and sexual hysteria—might not be enough this time. In the eight years since TLCC's last campaign, DOCS had expanded its North Country footprint, drawing more residents and communities into its orbit. Under such conditions, TLCC gave up on changing local minds and instead appealed to the Park Agency. In dozens of letters delivered to APA headquarters in the summer and fall of 1997, members of TLCC reminded agency authorities that despite their recent silence, opposition to the prison was alive and well.[19] Highlighting Lefebvre's refusal to hold public hearings, TLCC argued that state leaders building a correctional facility with taxpayer money had an obligation to ensure fair and inclusive planning.[20] Moreover, members of TLCC pointed to actions taken by penitentiary supporters in an attempt to intimidate critics, namely threatening letters and phone calls, harassment at town board meetings, and acts of petty retribution, including an episode where a prison opponent discovered their freshly washed laundry thrown from a clothesline into the mud. Critics warned that failure to accommodate the concerns of all local residents would impel delay-inducing litigation, which TLCC hoped the APA might

FIGURE 11. Prison opposition ad, *Tupper Lake Free Press*, 1997. Courtesy of the *Tupper Lake Free Press*.

join.[21] Opponents were not merely seeking a seat at the planning table, however—their goal was the project's cancellation.

As in other North Country communities, the prison debate in Tupper Lake unearthed longstanding tensions surrounding the use and meaning of Adirondack nature. Members of TLCC reminded officials that in their view, the missions of the correctional system and Adirondack Park remained incompatible. Like their counterparts in Gabriels, Tupper Lake's well-to-do residents agreed that promoting leisure and recreation—not incarceration—would always be the park's top priority. Because they used the park in ways that reaffirmed its putative historical purpose, affluent locals believed control of Tupper Lake's future should rest exclusively in their hands.[22] As in Ray Brook and Gabriels, wealthy homeowners in Tupper Lake couched their class and racial anxieties as concerns about environmental and public health. Members of TLCC again warned the Park Agency that a facility incarcerating mainly low-income men of color threatened Tupper Lake's vaunted status as a wilderness retreat.[23] Inevitable reductions in property values, they argued, would drive away the very tourists and seasonal homeowners on whose spending and taxes the local economy depended. Viewing themselves as indispensable to the region's survival, TLCC expected the agency would be as receptive to its pleas as it had been for CAMPA.[24]

Not all of TLCC's environmental concerns, however, related to questions of racial and class privilege. TLCC also warned of threats to both human- and non-human nature. Evoking images of Ray Brook in 1977, opponents predicted disastrous consequences from removing two hundred acres of forest and constructing a facility on previously unbuilt land containing protected wetlands. Nearly two thousand individuals inhabiting and working at the site, critics feared, would endanger fragile ecosystems and overwhelm freshwater and sewage removal systems.[25] TLCC feared that the construction of prison-related infrastructure—including new electric power lines, sewage pipes, light poles, and paved roads—posed unpredictable risks to environmental and public health as well as immeasurable harm to the rugged aesthetic that for many embodied the park's essence. Though the conveniences of modern infrastructure could be found across Tupper Lake, their expansion posed a particularly dire threat for TLCC. Increased artificial light and more vehicular traffic, opponents worried, might place Tupper Lake and the park on a path toward a suburban and possibly urban future.

For members of TLCC, safeguarding against such threats required an unyielding opposition to further correctional expansion.[26]

While members of TLCC held many of the same concerns about environmental and public health as those outlined in past prison debates, two decades of penal expansion had furnished lines of attack largely unavailable to their predecessors. In particular, TLCC worked to show that mass incarceration was working neither for New York State nor for the North Country. With the state's penitentiaries more overcrowded in 1997 than they had been in 1976, opponents noted that building more prisons had created a vicious cycle that only justice reform could fix. TLCC used Corrections' own planning documents to argue that penitentiaries were not the economically and socially transformative institutions DOCS claimed. As the draft of the environmental impact statement attested, the unemployment and poverty afflicting Adirondack communities proved as stubborn in the late 1990s as they had been twenty years before.[27] TLCC's critique of mass incarceration applied only to communities within the Adirondack Park, reinforcing the self-interest central to so much local anti-prison organizing. Though opening new prisons had neither stemmed overcrowding nor revitalized the local economy, members of TLCC were concerned only about their community. If lawmakers wanted to build another penitentiary, critics could think of no better place than Malone. After intense local lobbying, Malone had welcomed two medium-security correctional facilities designed to incarcerate seven hundred convicted men apiece: Franklin in 1986, and Bare Hill in 1988.[28] With two successful pro-prison organizing campaigns under its belt, seemingly few concerns about environmental or public health, and located in a non-park environment that was not primarily valued for its aesthetic qualities, Malone seemed the obvious choice. And, since the bill authorizing the penitentiary listed Franklin County as its location, leaving Tupper Lake would be simple.[29] Right?

The rebirth of TLCC reminded Task Force members that until it opened, South Franklin Correctional Facility was not a foregone conclusion. In the summer and fall of 1997, Lefebvre and his allies embarked on yet another campaign to promote a project that many assumed was a done deal. Advocates solicited new endorsements from politicians, business leaders, and corrections officers. They repeated promises of economic revival.[30] Supporters worked to discredit the opposition by cultivating ties with the Park Agency. In correspondence delivered to APA officials, local periodicals, and other state leaders, backers of the penitentiary argued that social class, length of residency, and the manner in which one used the park conferred neither privilege nor power. In the eyes of supporters, nearly two decades of effort entitled Tupper Lake to a correctional facility. Ann Seymour of Tupper Lake wrote that residents had "worked very hard . . . to be selected as a site," and implored the Park Agency not to "let our hard work go to waste." Scores of advocates echoed these sentiments, with many asserting the penitentiary belonged to the village. Donna Lonergan summed up the feelings of many by demanding that state officials "give us our prison."[31] Task Force members worked a wider angle, charging that in its efforts to stop the penitentiary, TLCC was circumventing the will of voters who had elected pro-prison candidates. Supporters of the facility thus urged APA leaders to ignore critics whose motives, apparently unlike their own, were rooted purely in self-interest.[32] The penitentiary, it seemed, had been bought and paid for by the Task Force; therefore, it was the state's duty to build.

In their correspondence, project advocates also reminded state leaders that, contrary to TLCC claims, Tupper Lake was not only a wilderness retreat. Much like Gabriels, it was also a working-class community blighted by business closure, population loss, unemployment, and poverty. As in many other North Country communities, homeowners seeking economic security had been fleeing Tupper Lake since the 1960s, leaving behind a smaller, older population whose tax dollars proved insufficient for maintaining public services and infrastructure. Supporters argued the prison would be central to Tupper Lake's revival as it would provide the jobs needed to allow young people to return and future generations to remain.[33] The local tax base might be further boosted by local corrections officers— they were compelled by seniority rules to work in other parts of the state, but with a prison in Tupper Lake, they might be able to live and work in their hometown. Without the penitentiary, project advocates feared that their village, containing "a Main St. with no business, houses for sale everywhere you look," along with "failed businesses, empty stores," and "for sale signs" as far as the eye could see, might never recover. Local resident Gary Levesque put it bluntly, stating, "This town will <u>die</u> without the prison."[34]

The debate that consumed Tupper Lake in the summer and fall of 1997 showed that while both sides remained committed to their earlier positions, supporters and opponents had both learned several valuable lessons. Members of TLCC came to accept that Corrections exerted an unmistakable influence over North Country life. Recognizing their limited base of support, prison critics forged an alliance with a Park Agency whose leadership had yielded dividends in the past. By this time, however, TLCC likely understood that while paeans to racial and class superiority might have worked in the early 1980s, they carried less weight in a late 1990s political culture more attuned to the legacies of racial discrimination. Opponents accordingly downplayed the social aspect of their arguments and instead emphasized the prison's potential ecological threats. Task Force members, too, learned that far from being an anti-development bugaboo, the Adirondack Park Agency could prove to be a valuable partner. Though its powers remained non-binding, Park Agency assent to DOCS and Task Force plans might permit speedy construction. An alliance between the Task Force and the APA might even blunt the influence of opponents blessed with seemingly unlimited financial resources and valuable political connections that could imperil the project. With the Park Agency involved, the outcome of Tupper Lake's final prison fight would inevitably turn on questions of environmental and public health.

Prisonland's End

The final battle over Tupper Lake's prison ran from September 1997 to January 1998. A quarter-century of restrictive narcotics and sentencing laws left New York's correctional system as overcrowded as it had been at any time in the past two centuries. Eager to build quickly and cheaply, DOCS forged close ties with the ordinarily adversarial APA. Caught in the middle of an escalating conflict between the Task Force and TLCC, Corrections and the Park Agency labored to pacify both sides while using legally dubious means to build the penitentiary. As the APA accelerated its normally plodding oversight, DOCS began transforming property still owned by IP, and members of the Task Force rubbed their hands in glee. Scrutiny from environmentalists soon prompted an increasingly risk-averse Corrections Department to scrap its own plan. Paeans to anti-environmentalism, class resentment, and home rule offered by the project's supporters could not obscure the prison's actual threats to environmental and public health. By moving the facility to Malone, DOCS assured compliance with its own construction timetables. It also reaffirmed the view of anti-prison activists that the park was no place for penitentiaries.

Corrections moved quickly in the summer and fall of 1997. The urgency to expand penal capacity was as great as ever. While unlawful activity had fallen 25 percent since 1995, longer prison sentences along with new restrictions on parole and early release enacted under Governor Pataki only worsened the already record-breaking overcrowding. DOCS labored to add new cells while simultaneously pacifying the belligerents doing battle in Tupper Lake. Members of TLCC breathed a sigh of relief when Corrections announced a willingness to build outside the park as well as its intention not to open in Tupper Lake without Park Agency approval. Yet they shuddered when DOCS Commissioner Glenn Goord implicitly identified Tupper Lake as the site, pledging a penitentiary consistent with "the unique nature of the Adirondacks," including unobtrusive light poles, water towers, and buildings, along with vegetative buffers to screen the facility from view. Further, opponents had to have been shocked when DOCS, possessing neither title to the land nor APA consent, commenced pre-construction fieldwork in September and October. State historians, archaeologists, and scientists excavated two thousand shovel test pits to hunt for rare artifacts, drilled well tests for water and soil samples, studied satellite imagery of the site's topography, and floated tethered balloons above the property to analyze visual impacts. Despite having taken seemingly irreversible steps toward opening in Tupper Lake, Goord nevertheless disappointed Task Force supporters by mandating delay-inducing public involvement through "every step of this process."[35] Corrections' vacillation reflected its inability to reconcile the intransigent demands of competing local interests against its own carceral needs. Undertaking legally suspect fieldwork on private property, however, proved that DOCS's equivocation was purely rhetorical. Operating under emergency conditions in a community that valued its presence, Corrections tested the limits of its power in new and unprecedented ways.

Confronted with similar pressure from the Task Force and TLCC, the APA also sought a middle path through the intensifying controversy. As Park Agency officials spoke openly of compromise, they simultaneously worked to ease the prison's construction. Penitentiary supporters must have cheered when the agency took the unusual steps of placing Tupper Lake on a heretofore-unknown oversight "fast track" and of commencing its non-binding advisory review before the land was transferred to public ownership. In turn, members of TLCC must have been pleased when agency leaders promised the sped-up project would "get a thorough review," including public involvement, and that it would be planned "in such a manner as not to occupy or disturb any freshwater wetlands." Finally, in a sign of their own uncertainty about the project, APA leaders concurred with DOCS in stating, "There are no plans certain it will be located in the Tupper Lake area."[36] Caught between rival constituencies expecting unfettered loyalty, the Park Agency mimicked Corrections' paeans to consensus, but this willingness to circumvent its own rules and to overlook possible DOCS offenses showed that for the first time in its history, the APA was actively promoting the building of an Adirondack prison.

Public assurances of fair planning could not obscure the fact that both DOCS and the APA had begun building the penitentiary. Though lawmakers funded, planned, and constructed new infrastructure ostensibly for the public good, politics always lurked beneath the surface. State-sponsored projects remained as vulnerable to New York's shifting political winds as they had been in the nineteenth century. To wit, Republican appointees to both Corrections and the Park Agency under Governor Pataki fostered warmer ties between the historically adversarial bureaucracies. Tupper Lake's early planning stages demonstrated this unusually close relationship. In October, APA officials expressed anger after Corrections delivered an incomplete building permit application and seemed baffled by claims that the facility would carry "no significant potential for environmental impact." As a remedy, agency leaders merely requested that DOCS submit responses to unanswered questions. Watching from the sidelines, local environmentalists interpreted the agencies' unprecedented cooperation and legally questionable actions as evidence of a possible conspiracy to build the penitentiary outside established legal frameworks. Determined not to permit potentially destructive construction without proper oversight, prominent environmentalists entered the Tupper Lake prison debate. In October, officials from the Adirondack Council, an environmental group founded in 1975, described the site selection process as "a sham," asserting that Corrections had done nothing "to look outside the park for a site." The Adirondack Mountain Club, a recreational advocacy organization formed in 1922, criticized the APA's attempt "to short-circuit . . . the review process" by ignoring legally dubious fieldwork and by promising to "fast track" oversight of the project. The Association for the Protection of the Adirondacks, established in 1901 and the area's oldest environmental group, joined with the Albany branch of the Sierra Club in accusing DOCS and the Park Agency of rushing construction without adequate review. Unless the Agency performed each step of its legally mandated non-binding advisory review—including public hearings—the four organizations threatened a delay-inducing lawsuit.[37] Much to the chagrin of TLCC, environmentalists were interested only in ensuring adherence to existing law and not, as its members hoped, in stopping the prison entirely.

As proponents of sustainable development, most environmental groups in the Adirondack Park in the 1990s were not reflexively anti-prison. Early on, many of the organizations had committed to staying out of the Tupper Lake drama. In August 1997, representatives from Albany-based Environmental Advocates (EA), the Adirondack Council, and the Residents' Committee to Protect the Adirondacks (RCPA), a group founded in 1990, had promised not to oppose the facility. Interestingly, the revelations of both questionable fieldwork and accelerated APA oversight prompted a reevaluation only from EA, one of the few non-local organizations monitoring the project. Labeling the penitentiary "a step backwards for the community," EA argued the area's natural resources should be harnessed "to boost the economy without this prison." Echoing TLCC, leaders of EA also warned that correctional facilities were "notorious for pollution problems," and voiced concern that the state would "make the Tupper Lake area so dependent on this prison that it will have a long-time negative effect on the community." Local environmentalists, driven either by the acknowledgement of DOCS's extensive North Country footprint or by a sense that resistance might prove futile, remained largely supportive through the summer and early fall. Leaders of RCPA held fast to claims that a penitentiary posed few risks because "the site is not near a natural resource" and, in reference to commercial logging, "the area is already in industrial use." Leaders of the Adirondack Council concurred, noting that building a prison was "no different from siting any other major industrial facility," adding the matter was best left to residents and their elected representatives.[38] Maintaining credibility with a diverse—and sometimes hostile—local population required environmentalists to craft an approach to development that balanced ecological and economic concerns. Yet whenever government agencies tasked with preserving this balance ignored their own responsibilities—as in Tupper Lake—environmentalists were ready.

The arrival of environmentalists to the prison debate delighted members of TLCC. Their involvement proved especially gratifying after penitentiary opponents lost their once-reliable APA ally. In letters to state officials, TLCC echoed environmentalist demands that the Park Agency and DOCS permit the hearings and public involvement that both bureaucracies had deemed crucial to the project's completion. Critics also demanded the agency cancel the project outright, an outcome neither permitted by statute nor desired by most environmentalists, who sought only bureaucratic adherence to existing law. Unfortunately for TLCC, the agency had already adopted an accommodationist approach to Corrections. Though the APA maintained a public posture of neutrality, its leaders continued guiding the penitentiary toward a smooth opening. Under such conditions, complaining to the Park Agency, which had helped delay past prison-building projects, might prove ineffective. With the APA, DOCS, and the Task Force arrayed against them, members of TLCC deposited their trust in better-funded and more prominent environmentalists who, while not fully aligned with the opposition cause, represented the last remaining hope of keeping Tupper Lake prison-free.[39]

The indifference the Park Agency and Corrections showed to lawsuit threats from environmentalists only increased the pressure. In October, critics demanded the APA reject DOCS's incomplete building permit application. Simply resubmitting the documents with complete answers, it seemed, would be unacceptable. For its part, the Adirondack Council reiterated that it was not opposed to incarceration, though council leaders argued the Park Agency's legally suspect decision to "fast track" oversight of the prison, refusal to schedule public hearings, and complicity in possibly illegal fieldwork on private land had undermined public trust in the planning process. Council Executive Director Timothy Burke charged a conspiracy among Corrections, the Park Agency, and the Task Force to build the penitentiary outside the boundaries of existing law. After attending the APA's October meeting in Ray Brook, Burke described what he considered the scheme's vital elements:

> The presentation and [DOCS building permit application] to the APA weren't even mentioned in the APA's October meeting agenda, which was handed out to the public just minutes before the meeting began. If someone came to the APA the day of the meeting to see if the APA was considering the prison, he would never have known it would be discussed at all. That shows a callous disregard for the rights of the public on the part of both agencies. In addition, it is completely inappropriate

for the APA to hand over sole authority on whether a public hearing will be held to [its chair] who is a political appointee beholden to the Governor for his job. That only makes it easier for the public to assume the fix is in. It would be only natural for the public to expect that they will have no voice whatsoever in the decisions about where the prison will be located and how it will be constructed. That's just plain wrong.

Following this meeting, the council upped its pressure, calling on the APA to suspend its review and urging DOCS to move the facility outside the park. Even the RCPA, which only weeks earlier had labeled the penitentiary as risk-free, noted in mid-October that its members were "very concerned" about the project. RCPA leaders stated, "Such a facility—and development of this magnitude—may have a deleterious effect on the environment of the Adirondack Park." The Residents' Committee promptly joined the council's call for the prison's relocation in order to avoid "an adverse impact on the environment or rural community character of the Adirondack Park." Council leaders concurred: "This is a Park. It should never be our first choice for the site of a prison, let alone the only place considered."[40] By demanding the facility's removal from the park, environmentalists inadvertently cast their lot with a most appreciative TLCC.

The involvement of environmentalists transformed the debate over Tupper Lake's penitentiary in ways that opponents could only have dreamed about. In addition to revealing what appeared to be an inter-bureaucratic, pro-prison conspiracy, environmentalists uncovered proof of potentially illegal activity undertaken by Corrections and seemingly blessed by the Park Agency. In late October 1997, officials from the Adirondack Council flew over the Tupper Lake property to inspect for possible damage from DOCS-sponsored fieldwork. The council captured photographs showing extensive grading and excavation work, including the removal of trees and vegetation. Confronted with evidence that it had begun construction while lacking title to the land and official APA consent, Corrections confirmed its workers and bulldozers had gone on to the tract "to identify boundaries and wetlands," acknowledging previously undisclosed activity on the site beyond the fieldwork conducted in September and October. Burke's reaction was incredulous:

Why on earth would anyone need a bulldozer to find a wetland? APA has been delineating wetlands for decades, but not with a bulldozer. And I have never heard of anyone using a bulldozer to mark a boundary line in a forest. Surveyors normally use little flags and a hatchet to clear limbs when marking a boundary. There already appears to be a political bulldozer behind this proposal. We don't need a real one making things worse. APA regulations . . . do not allow an applicant to begin bulldozing in preparation for the project's construction and they do not allow for any major disturbance of the site connected to its proposed new use. The Corrections Department seems unaware, or unwilling to recognize, that this is a Park and must be treated with the respect it deserves. Following the rules on development is more important here than in any other part of New York State. Yet the department continues to act as if the APA's review was simply a formality.

Armed with seemingly irrefutable proof of unlawful activity, in early November the council ratcheted up the pressure, insisting the APA investigate DOCS for undertaking work on private land without required building permits, and warning the Park Agency would have to terminate its review in the event it discovered Corrections had broken any laws.[41]

With mounting evidence implicating both DOCS and the APA in possibly illegal activity—and with no indication either would relent—environmentalists in mid-November enlisted the larger, wealthier, and more influential Sierra Club to lead its fight. Club officials brought in former Park Agency Executive Director Robert Glennon, a veteran of past North Country prison conflicts, to serve as lead counsel and work "on behalf of the Club and local residents." Other environmentalists praised the choice, with Eric Siy of Environmental Advocates noting, "If there's any individual capable of stopping this prison, it's Bob Glennon; that's a fact. Nobody knows the agency's rules and regulations better than he does." At the outset of its involvement, it remained unclear what changes the Sierra Club could expect from DOCS and the APA. Whether the club would align its agenda with the area's other environmentalists—and, by extension, TLCC—was also a mystery. Club leaders proved as apathetic about incarceration and the placement of penitentiaries in the park as other environmentalists, arguing that inclusive planning alone might have prevented unnecessary destruction while preserving public trust. Recognizing that environmentalists' pressure had yielded movement from neither Corrections nor the Park Agency, the Sierra Club appealed directly to Governor Pataki, a known advocate of environmental protection and regular park visitor. Club officials implored the governor to force the APA to do "its job to protect the Adirondack forests, lakes and wetlands, from the Department of Corrections bulldozer." The Sierra Club also requested Pataki devote more "attention and resources on promoting a healthy timber economy . . . instead of . . . bringing 1500 of the most violent felons in New York State to Tupper Lake."[42] Scrutiny from both the nation's oldest environmental organization and the state's chief executive would, once again, redraw the boundaries of Tupper Lake's never-ending prison drama.

The Corrections Department blinked first, though neither the Sierra Club nor Governor Pataki prompted its turnabout. With its activities under increasing scrutiny, in late October DOCS began scouting alternative sites for the penitentiary. Mayor Joyce Tavernier of Malone said that while her community was "not in competition with Tupper Lake," she was more than "willing to take this prison if the Tupper Lake site is no longer viable." Corrections officials approached Richard LaVigne, a Malone businessman who had helped bring two correctional facilities to the village in the 1980s, inquiring about possible sites in case plans in Tupper Lake fell through. Describing Malone as the state's "insurance policy," LaVigne guided DOCS leaders to two potentially suitable properties, where officials conducted surveying and test drilling and discussed possible purchase prices. In November 1997, Corrections announced it was pursuing a move to Malone, with one DOCS administrator commenting, "We're not married to that site [Tupper Lake]. We just need a prison." Corrections leaders stated the penal system, still operating at 130 percent of capacity, could tolerate no further delays in expanding. As always, prison politics made strange bedfellows, as leaders of the Sierra Club welcomed DOCS as an ally, arguing, "a prison in Tupper Lake [would] have a much greater environmental effect than many people realize." Club leaders also agreed with Corrections that Malone was a much better choice, especially since it had already "adjusted to prisons."[43] With DOCS seemingly aligned with the Sierra Club, local environmentalists, and TLCC against its own project, the Task Force suddenly found itself alone in the corner once occupied by the penitentiary's small band of opponents.

The prison's supporters reacted to this sudden shift in fortune with attempts at rationality tempered by rage. They at first attempted to reason with their DOCS and Sierra Club enemies. In particular, supporters labored to turn critics' most prominent arguments on their heads. Proponents claimed their status as year-round park residents conferred special knowledge of local environments available only to people like themselves. Accordingly, Task Force allies argued a correctional facility would pose no harm to environmental or public health. In fact, backers of the prison asserted that since the IP tract had long been zoned industrial and used for commercial logging, it was no longer actually "nature," thus negating the possibility of harmful impacts. In the event the facility did cause harm, however, advocates noted that penitentiaries were ecologically benign forms of development. To underscore this point, they littered their descriptions of the project with the word "clean."[44] Corrections' abrupt withdrawal of support for Tupper Lake hit project supporters like a punch to the gut. Watching years of effort slip away, many backers of the facility resorted to the class-laden rhetoric that was by then a familiar staple of area development fights. In correspondence, advocates castigated environmentalists—their newest antagonists—as "arrogant," "extremists," "tree-huggers," "intruders," "zealots," "militants," and "radical oppressionists," among other epithets.[45] Supporters also attacked the "powerful" and "wealthy" members of TLCC and environmental groups possessed of "mountains of money" whom, they believed, were conspiring to keep the area's working-class residents mired in poverty.[46] Boosters also assailed the APA, conflating the heretofore pro-prison agency with the same environmentalists working to bring the facility down.[47] Supporters went so far as to express the fear that the Sierra Club's underlying motivation was the eventual depopulation of the Adirondack Park and the area's conversion into a playground for the rich.[48]

In an attempt to demonstrate the depth of Tupper Lake's continued support for the penitentiary, Task Force leaders organized a pro-prison rally for late November. On the Saturday after Thanksgiving, nearly 1,500 project advocates and elected officials packed into the local high school gymnasium to send a message to leaders debating the facility's fate. Journalists carried coverage of the event to television, radio, print, and internet outlets statewide. After hearing addresses from members of the Task Force and area officials, however, the event transformed from a well-planned show of force into a public venting session. Attendees holding anti-environmentalist placards chanted denunciations of the project's opponents, repeating many of the claims and epithets contained in their written correspondence. Though many remained hopeful that Corrections might yet build in Tupper Lake, none could deny the department's interest in Malone.[49] Intended as an opportunity to demonstrate loyalty to DOCS, the event instead became a public funeral for all the hopes of Tupper Lake that had been bound up in its bid for a prison.

The rally had no measurable effect on a Corrections Department inching toward building in Malone. In early December, Lefebvre complained that DOCS's continued indecision was "sending mixed messages to this town" and that residents were becoming "nervous and antsy." Aware that environmentalists had gained the upper hand, some project advocates attempted to maintain a stiff upper lip in the face of near-certain defeat. Tim Larkin, a local businessman and Task Force ally, sought to minimize the prison's past and potential future environmental impacts. In so doing, Larkin underscored the prevailing sense among Task Force members that local knowledge outweighed that possessed by affluent homeowners or environmentalists, commenting, "If the prison is an environmental problem here, then it's an environmental problem anywhere." However, Franklin County legislator Paul Maroun understood a reality that few were ready to accept; namely, that quick and inexpensive construction meant more to Corrections than loyalty to a potential host community. Maroun noted, "If environmentalists file a lawsuit against the state, then Corrections wants to be able to move rapidly in Malone."[50] While likely true, in the end, the mere intervention of environmentalists was all it took to scuttle Tupper Lake's final prison bid.

Though moving to Malone would solve its dilemma, Corrections seemed averse to blindsiding a community that had spent nearly two decades working to secure a penitentiary. DOCS needed a scapegoat that would allow it to let Tupper Lake down gently and escape responsibility for the outcome. Thus a department for whom environmental regulation had always been a bugbear suddenly converted to the religion of sustainable development. Since evaluating a project's compliance with SEQRA remained a requirement of all state-sponsored building projects, the DEC undertook an assessment of the Tupper Lake site. Having cited emergency overcrowding to circumvent SEQRA review in the past, DOCS now welcomed environmental oversight that might permit a smooth exit. In December 1997, DEC general counsel Frank Bifera announced his department's findings. Bifera predicted high risks of soil and chemical runoff into area waterways and wetlands both during and after construction. He noted the presence of two large aquifers adjacent to and under the site, warning that "there will be a significant impact on this water resource which may be needed for future potable water supplies." For these reasons, Bifera labeled Tupper Lake "both environmentally and legally problematic," arguing, "the State Environmental Quality Review Act demands the alternative site be chosen," adding that "it does not

appear . . . that similar problems would be encountered at the Malone site."
Corrections Commissioner Goord gratefully accepted Bifera's findings, stating, "With these issues now being identified, environmental protection requires that I build elsewhere." Environmentalists rejoiced, with John Stouffer of the Sierra Club exclaiming, "We feel vindicated."[51] But Tupper Lake's prison advocates were not finished yet.

Penitentiary supporters reacted to the DEC's decision with another spasm of rage. Reasserting the supposed primacy of local environmental knowledge, Lefebvre claimed Bifera's conclusions were "totally in direct opposition to what I have been told by people over the last four months. Everybody feels the site here is as good or better than they have in Malone." The more common response entailed a mixture of anti-environmentalist screeds and paeans to home rule that had long been a staple of North Country politics and that by the late 1990s had become planks of modern conservatism. Maroun claimed residents felt "tricked by the environmentalists," while Task Force member Dan McClelland asserted, "There's something quite un-American about environmentalists coming in and telling us what we can and cannot have." Lefebvre agreed, accusing state leaders of giving "in to the environmentalists" who "don't want good jobs." McClelland concurred, expressing a widely held fear that "Tupper Lake is on the beginning of a decline into nothing." Prison advocates then channeled their anger into action. Lefebvre proposed that Tupper Lake and other Franklin County communities inside the park separate from the non-park northern half of the county—home to Malone—and create a new county. Lefebvre argued that as a separate county, towns and villages inside the park could save money by not contributing tax dollars to public services and infrastructure—including the new prison—located outside its boundaries. Local officials also demanded lawmakers compensate Tupper Lake for its years of wasted effort and for the loss of economic impact from the penitentiary's removal. Some even threatened to sue the Sierra Club for facilitating the village's "loss of economic opportunity." Town leaders removed a plaque from the town hall that had been placed years earlier by a group of second-home owners marking Tupper Lake's centennial. Presumably officials could no longer bear the sight of a monument symbolizing friendships once forged between permanent residents and the "outsiders" they blamed for losing the prison.[52] Some reactions were outlandish, but—still hoping a penitentiary might come their way—no one in Tupper Lake dared critique the Corrections Department.

In January 1998, the Task Force made a final attempt to secure a penitentiary. Prison supporters had never been comfortable with the DEC's December findings. Confident in their knowledge of Adirondack nature and determined to prove environmentalists wrong and force the facility's return, project advocates studied maps provided by the federal Department of the Interior. Much to their delight, the maps indicated neither wetlands nor aquifers at the Tupper Lake site. However, the maps did show an aquifer close to the tract in Malone. Overnight the Task Force became the area's newest and most unexpected disciples of sustainable development. Lefebvre argued, "The state needs to study the environmental impact on the Malone site. Obviously, more environmental damage will occur in Malone than in Tupper Lake." He noted the Malone site's proximity to the Salmon River and to private homes dependent on freshwater wells. In the same breath, though, Lefebvre remarked, "It's time the environmentalists stop lying to the public. If they don't want a prison in Tupper Lake, then they should just say that." Hoping for a reversal, Lefebvre and his counterparts mailed copies of the maps to journalists and state leaders along with a final round of letters to Senator Stafford, one of which read, in part:

> What about the aquifer on the Malone site? Why is it that this aquifer is not a problem in Malone and yet an aquifer was supposed to have been such a big problem in Tupper Lake? The question now is whether you will do something to bring the prison back to us in Tupper Lake or not . . . Senator, you must use every bit of influence that you have to win back the prison.

Penitentiary advocates' conversion to environmentalism, unfortunately, was both too little and too late. In January 1998, the Park Agency absolved Corrections of any possible illegal activity committed at the Tupper Lake site, bringing an end to the department's long and tortured relationship with that community. To ensure Lefebvre and his allies understood, one DOCS official bluntly stated, "That prison is definitely not going to Tupper Lake."[53] After nearly two decades, Tupper Lake's hopes for a prison were dead.

As Corrections planned Malone's third penitentiary, leaders in Tupper Lake embraced a new development plan based on recreation and tourism that no doubt warmed the hearts of the affluent homeowners and visitors whose opposition had helped kill the prison. By February 1998, local officials had opened discussions about building a natural history museum to attract the sort of investment many had hoped a correctional facility might generate. Eight and a half years later, that vision became reality. Still, when the penitentiary that was supposed to be theirs—Upstate Correctional Facility—opened in Malone in July 1999, only eighteen months after Tupper Lake's prison hopes expired, former Task Force members and their allies must have grimaced.[54] Unbeknownst to many at the time, Upstate would be the last penitentiary built in the North Country, and, amid shrinking demand for cell space in the early twenty-first century, one of the last new prisons built in New York State.

Tupper Lake's final prison bid succumbed to state planners and Task Force boosters whose disregard for environmental protection proved no match for the heightened influence of environmentalists. Still possessed of nearly unlimited authority, in 1997 Corrections also enjoyed the backing of an ardently law-and-order Republican administration determined to sustain New York's "get tough" approach to policing, prosecution, and imprisonment. Aided by a less environmentally minded Park Agency and the loyalty of local DOCS employees, seemingly nothing stood in Corrections' way. Believing a compliant APA and supportive local populace would countenance legally questionable activity, DOCS pushed the limits of its own power in new and unprecedented ways. Unlike in the area's other prison towns, however, environmentalists fortified by a growing public appreciation for environmental protection stood ready to enforce the laws that state bureaucracies seemed willing to break. Unwilling to endure delay-inducing litigation, Corrections showed no hesitation in moving to a non-park locale neither prized by environmentalists nor subject to strict environmental scrutiny. In moving to Malone, DOCS also reinforced elite understandings of the Adirondack Park long espoused by the department's fiercest opponents. However, it is important to understand DOCS's late-hour conversion to sustainability in context: Its actions in Tupper Lake and the potential for damage in Malone proved, once again, that Corrections remained more than willing to endanger environmental and public health to achieve its objectives.

||||||||

Though a community where Corrections never put down roots, Tupper Lake waged the sort of campaign to become a prison town that yielded an

indelible local legacy. Featured prominently in "I Love NY" tourism advertising, The Wild Center—the result of Tupper Lake's fallback plan of a
natural history museum—has become renowned as a stop for visitors and
local public school students alike eager to learn about the Adirondack
environment. That tract of commercial forestland owned by International
Paper remains as wooded as it was before Corrections began transforming
it in the fall of 1997. Any evidence that this site once served as the nexus of
a battle over economic development, environmental protection, and mass
incarceration has long since faded from view. As for Tupper Lake itself,
aside from a handful of small businesses, the village is as quiet today as it
was before its fight to secure a penitentiary. The facility that was the area's
largest employer half a century ago, Sunmount Developmental Center,
holds that title to this day. How South Franklin Correctional Facility would
have altered these realities remains unknown.

The most important legacies of this chapter in Tupper Lake's history are
not even located in the village. Upstate Correctional Facility can be found
nearly sixty miles north in Malone. Thirteen miles east of Malone is the
Franklin County village of Chateaugay, also located in the county's non-
park northern section. Chateaugay held the distinction as the only North
Country community awarded a penitentiary during the penal expansion of
1989. Having passed over Tupper Lake that year, lawmakers' choice of
Chateaugay made the tiny farming community an unexpected beneficiary
of TLCC organizing.

Like their counterparts in Tupper Lake, Chateaugay's prison boosters
spent years urging correctional planners to build in their community. After
being rejected three times between 1983 and 1988, Chateaugay continued
to press ahead. Ultimately, Chateaugay's location outside the park proved
its biggest selling point. Unencumbered either by local opposition or Park
Agency review, Corrections built the facility on one hundred acres of former farmland in Chateaugay. Opening in 1990, the penitentiary's seventeen
new buildings housed and treated 250 incarcerated men and gave work to
159 full-time employees. Unlike the region's other penal institutions, DOCS
planned Chateaugay Correctional Facility to provide counseling, therapy,
and treatment to men convicted of alcohol- and narcotics-related offenses.
After six months in Chateaugay, convicted men would report to state-run
work release centers and continue court-mandated substance abuse treatment. Though a progressive institution, the state's declining prison popu-

lation and budget troubles forced Democratic Governor Andrew Cuomo to announce its closure in 2013, with the penitentiary shutting its doors for good in 2014. Chateaugay residents, much like their counterparts in Gabriels and Lyon Mountain a few years earlier, unsuccessfully resisted the state's decision. One corrections officer framed the issue in terms that Tupper Lake's Prison Task Force would have understood: "It's not about saving the jail, it's about saving the community." After the complex lay dormant for four years, New York's Office of General Services auctioned it off in July 2018. The property sold in November 2018 to a Brooklyn-based firm for $451,000, though its future remains uncertain.[55] More than a few of Tupper Lake's former prison boosters have likely breathed a sigh of relief that their community, unlike some of their North Country neighbors, has not been saddled with one of the state's growing number of empty correctional facilities.

CONCLUSION

Shortly after midnight on Saturday, June 6, 2015, two men incarcerated at Clinton Correctional Facility wriggled their way through an underground steam pipe, pushed open a manhole in a nearby Dannemora neighborhood, and emerged into the cool, pre-summer darkness.[1] Their getaway driver having bailed at the last minute, Richard Matt and David Sweat embarked on a path into the Adirondack wilderness first blazed by Clinton escapees in June 1845. Dannemora's first runaways had exploited the new prison's lax security to make their escape, only to be quickly undone by the unfamiliar and unforgiving wilderness surrounding the penitentiary. One hundred seventy years later, hundreds of officers, miles of razor wire, motion sensors galore, and an imposing stone wall proved as vulnerable to penetration as Clinton's roughhewn, wooden stockade had been so many decades before. Moreover, as in countless other escapes from North Country prisons, the concept of the rugged terrain of the Adirondack Mountains did not deter fugitives committed to pursuing freedom. Unfortunately for Matt and Sweat, the reality of experiencing the North Country environment proved as challenging in 2015 as it had been nearly two centuries earlier.

While the Adirondack wilderness may not have deterred escapees, it did pose a significant challenge to New York's vast arsenal of law enforcement tools and technologies. For three weeks, Matt and Sweat successfully evaded search party officers armed with sophisticated surveillance equipment and heavy weaponry, along with helicopters, dogs, an alert local population, and reporters tracking the manhunt's every move. Lost in the woods and fighting off biting insects, unquenchable thirst, and insatiable hunger, the fugitives found in the Adirondack Mountains a valuable, albeit uncomfortable, ally. The area's thick vegetation, swampy wetlands, hunting camps, and tree stands proved more than sufficient for keeping their well-outfitted trackers at bay.[2] That environment, of course, was not primeval wilderness. Its shape and character, like all lands inside the Adirondack Park, was the result of over a century of careful state planning. Though homeowners and businesspeople had built a community in the decades after 1845, much of the Dannemora area remained wild and rugged. With few local employers besides the penitentiary, the village's population had remained relatively stable, protecting much of the surrounding landscape from the pressures of modern development. Thus, the environment into which Matt and Sweat slipped that cool night bore a striking resemblance to the ground trod by Clinton's first escapees.

Though the Adirondack wilderness known by generations of residents, visitors, and fugitives remained largely intact, as of 2015 the North Country's prisonland had witnessed significant change. The network of chronically overcrowded correctional facilities from the turn of the twenty-first century had become a shrinking collection of mothballed penitentiaries, prisons operating with smaller populations, and facilities teetering on the brink of closure. Though its North Country footprint has diminished, corrections remains the lifeblood of towns, villages, and families across the region. And although criminal justice reform has proven to be a rare point of bipartisan cooperation at the federal level, mere rumors of prison closings prompt swift rebukes from Democratic and Republican politicians in northern New York.[3] With thousands of local families dependent on the jobs penitentiaries provide, elected officials attuned to their constituents must defend what remains of the Adirondack prisonland for as long as possible. If the shutdowns of Gabriels, Lyon Mountain, and Chateaugay are any indicator, the area's future may well be prison-free. Though the North Country's correctional facilities may one day fade into oblivion, their histories and environmental impacts will remain. The question then arises of how to publicly memorialize their place in local history and their numerous contributions to the shaping of local environments.

Acknowledging the role of prisons in Adirondack history is a fraught enterprise. Corrections lacks the romantic imagery inherent in logging, mining, institutional health care, and tourism. Artistic renderings of prisons, corrections officers, and incarcerated men evoke neither warm nor positive emotions. Nevertheless, public memorialization is necessary. First, recognizing the role of correctional facilities in North Country history helps dispel the notion that the Adirondacks are either pristine wilderness or "forever wild," mischaracterizations advanced by prison opponents that persist to this day. As we know, state lawmakers, correctional planners, environmental regulators, organized environmentalists, local residents, affluent visitors, and imprisoned men each left indelible environmental legacies. Second, high-lighting the place of prisons may also help retire the idea that the Adirondacks exist only for leisure and recreation, a notion reinforced by the continued dominance of tourism and the relative invisibility of penitentiaries them-selves in the landscape. Finally, including corrections as a significant chapter in the history of northern New York rightly complicates the stereotypical image of the Adirondacks as the birthplace of American conservation. While that is perhaps true, it is equally important to acknowledge the area's involve-ment in New York's carceral state, a historical development that predated the enactment of the state's first environmental laws and proved critically import-ant to the shape and character of the Adirondacks' public and private lands.

Though it is necessary, publicly memorializing the history of incarceration in northern New York will not be easy. Despite the system-wide contractions of the 2000s and early 2010s, corrections remains one of the region's largest employers and plays a significant role in the local economy. Many area towns and villages still depend on poorly paid incarcerated men completing vital conservation, public works, and infrastructure projects.[4] As such, the prison industry remains a subject as sensitive for residents and politicians today as it was in the 1970s. Historical inquiries into the North Country's role in the growth of mass incarceration, a phenomenon that leaders from both parties now agree posed irreparable harm to communities of color, will inevitably raise uncomfortable questions many locals would likely rather avoid. The almost total lack of public monuments to the Adirondacks' long history with corrections stands out amid the veritable cornucopia of roadside plaques and museums honoring mining, logging, and institutional health care—industries that, like corrections, have not completely disappeared—along with memo-rials to battles fought during the French and Indian War, American Revolution, and War of 1812. Even Champ, the mythical sea creature that supposedly lurks in the depths of Lake Champlain, has his own markers. Though corrections will join a crowded roster of memorials, historical accu-racy requires some public recognition of Adirondack prisons.

To date, the only public memorial to North Country prison history may be found in a tile mosaic entitled *Clinton County History through the Eyes of its Children* installed at the Clinton County Government Center in Platts-burgh in 2009. Tiles crafted and painted by local schoolchildren capture many of the prominent individuals, moments, and innovations that shaped the county's past.[5] Included among these are depictions of incarcerated miners at Clinton State Prison. While a lovely piece of public art, this portion of the mosaic raises more questions than it answers. First, details included in the written description accompanying the mosaic lack context important for understanding the conditions under which prison mine work was performed. Second, the focus on penitentiary-based mining obscures the plethora of jobs Clinton County imprisoned men have performed—and continue to perform—in areas far removed from the prison grounds. Third, without a more robust and detailed explanation of the work being performed, observers— whether local or from out of town—might assume men wearing the stereotypical black-and-white striped prison uniforms represent a relic of the region's past. Indeed, they might also believe incarcerated men only performed mining work, leaving the region's development largely in the hands of free labor. Finally, as but one part of a display that measures 342 square feet, the tiles representing Clinton could be easily overlooked by viewers

FIGURE 12. *Clinton County History through the Eyes of its Children*, Plattsburgh, New York. Photo courtesy of the author.

drawn to oversized renditions of a nineteenth-century battleship and Samuel de Champlain. Despite its flaws, however, the mosaic's focus on imprisoned men's outdoor work underscores the environment's pivotal role in the growth of incarceration in northern New York.

The question then becomes, which chapters of the North Country's prison history should and should not be publicly memorialized? Since correctional facilities exerted environmental impacts far beyond the prison walls, it will be important to acknowledge the many locations across the Adirondacks where imprisoned workers completed conservation, public works, and infrastructure projects. The places where battles over the building of prisons played out, including local town halls, APA headquarters, and even private homes, might also be appropriate candidates for recognition. Converting one of the area's shuttered penitentiaries into a museum serves as a good beginning, but, like the mosaic in Plattsburgh, might obscure the pervasive impacts of incarceration on environments far beyond the penitentiary grounds, and, in an effort to draw visitors, a prison museum could end up emphasizing the more sensational chapters of a facility's history, potentially leaving its environmental significance by the wayside. Therefore, a network of prominently displayed roadside plaques marking sites of incarcerated labor, current and former correctional facilities, and places where penitentiary advocates and opponents waged war would be an important first step toward recognizing the immense environmental legacies created by New York's Adirondack prisonland.

Such a public history project, however, is not only about recognizing a heretofore-unacknowledged chapter of North Country history. Just as the area's prisons never operated in isolation from the local environment, it is impossible to either live or play in the Adirondacks without touching the handiwork of incarcerated men. As the foregoing chapters have shown, the North Country environment is, in large measure, the product of poorly paid imprisoned workers. On a deeper level, it is also the result of criminal justice policies whose impacts disproportionately harmed communities of color in New York and beyond. Without the wars on drugs and crime waged at the state and federal levels in the last quarter of the twentieth century, Clinton Correctional Facility might have remained the Adirondacks' only penitentiary. In a region afflicted by chronically high unemployment, poverty, depopulation, and a dwindling tax base, it is hard to imagine how the hundreds of projects completed by incarcerated men would have ever seen the light of day. Who else would have accepted the low pay, long hours, and

FIGURE 13. Tiles depicting iron mining at Clinton State Prison, in *Clinton County History through the Eyes of its Children,* Plattsburgh, New York. Photo courtesy of the author.

untold hazards associated with those jobs? Thus, publicly recognizing the labor of imprisoned men in building and maintaining the Adirondack environment is not only about correcting historical inaccuracies. Instead, it acknowledges the collective debt every resident and visitor owes to the primarily African American and Latino men whose hard work continues to help preserve the beauty and majesty of New York's great north woods.

NOTES

Abbreviations

ADE	*Adirondack Daily Enterprise*
CR	*Chateaugay Record*
LPN	*Lake Placid News*
NYPL	New York Public Library
NYT	*New York Times*
NCC	*North Country Catholic*
NC	*North Countryman*
PR	*Press Republican*
TLFP	*Tupper Lake Free Press*
WDT	*Watertown Daily Times*

Note on Sources

I have made extensive use of articles originally published in the *Adirondack Daily Enterprise*, *Chateaugay Record, Lake Placid News, North Country Catholic, North Countryman,* Plattsburgh *Republican, Press Republican,* and *Tupper Lake Free Press* to craft the narrative that follows. The New York State Historic Newspapers (NYSHN) project houses these newspapers in its digital archive located at https://nyshistoricnewspapers.org. The Northern New York Library Network https://nnyln.org and the Empire State Library Network https://www.esln.org are co-sponsors of the NYSHN.

Introduction

1. "North Country Towns Compete for Prisons," *Lake Placid News* (hereafter *LPN*), Mar. 26, 1987.
2. David Rothman, "Perfecting the Prison: United States, 1789–1865," 100–16, and Edgardo Rotman, "The Failure of Reform: United States, 1865–1965," 151–77, both in Norval Morris and David Rothman, ed., *The Oxford History of the Prison: The Practice of Punishment in Western Society* (New York: Oxford University Press, 1998).
3. Connie Chiang, *Nature Behind Barbed Wire: An Environmental History of the Japanese*

American Incarceration (New York: Oxford University Press, 2018); Volker Janssen, "When the 'Jungle' Met the Forest: Public Work, Civil Defense, and Prison Camps in Postwar California," *Journal of American History* 96, no. 3 (Dec. 2009): 702–26; Peter Redfield, *Space in the Tropics: From Convicts to Rockets in French Guiana* (Berkeley: University of California Press, 2000).

4. Jonathan D. Anzalone, *Battles of the North Country: Wilderness Politics and Recreational Development in the Adirondack State Park, 1920–1980* (Amherst: University of Massachusetts Press, 2018); Philip G. Terrie, *Forever Wild: A Cultural History of Wilderness in the Adirondacks* (Syracuse: Syracuse University Press, 1994); Philip G. Terrie, *Contested Terrain: A New History of Nature and People in the Adirondacks* (Syracuse: Syracuse University Press, 1997).

5. Marc Mauer and Ryan King, "Uneven Justice: State Rates of Incarceration by Race and Ethnicity" (Washington, D.C.: The Sentencing Project, 2007), 1–2; Sarah Lawrence and Jeremy Travis, "The New Landscape of Imprisonment: Mapping America's Prison Expansion" (Washington, D.C.: Urban Institute Justice Policy Center, 2004), 8; Public Safety Performance Project, "Public Safety, Public Spending: Forecasting America's Prison Population, 2007–2011" (Washington, D.C.: Pew Charitable Trusts, 2007), ii–iii; Eric Schlosser, "The Prison-Industrial Complex," *Atlantic Monthly* (Dec. 1998), 51–77.

6. W. David Lewis, *From Newgate to Dannemora: The Rise of the Penitentiary in New York, 1796–1848* (Ithaca: Cornell University Press, 1965); W. David Lewis, "Newgate of New York: A Case History (1796–1828) of Early American Prison Reform, *New-York Historical Society Quarterly* 47, no. 2 (1963): 137–72; W. David Lewis, "Fiasco in the Adirondacks: The Early History of Clinton Prison at Dannemora, 1844–1861," *New York History* 49, no. 3 (1968): 284–305.

Chapter One: "This Great and Important Experiment"

1. "The Clinton State Prison," *United States Magazine and Democratic Review* 17 (Nov. 1845), 351–52.

2. Ibid.

3. Colin Calloway, *The Western Abenakis of Vermont, 1600–1800: War, Migration, and the Survival of an Indian People* (Norman: University of Oklahoma Press, 1990); Guy Omeron Coolidge, *The French Occupation of the Champlain Valley from 1609 to 1759* (Fleischmanns, NY: Purple Mountain Press, 1938/1999), 8–9; Philip Terrie, "The New York Natural History Survey in the Adirondack Wilderness, 1836–1840," *Journal of the Early Republic* 3, no. 2 (Summer 1983): 185–206; *The Opening of the Adirondacks* (New York: Hurd and Houghton, 1865), 16–17, 23, 54–57, 59, 61–64, 69.

4. James Darlington, "Peopling the Post-Revolutionary New York Frontier," *New York History* 74, no. 4 (Oct. 1993): 340–81; Glenn Harris, "The Hidden History of Agriculture in the Adirondack Park, 1825–1875," *New York History* 83, no. 2 (Spring 2002): 165–202; John Stilgoe, "Fair Fields and Blasted Rock: American Land Classification Systems and Landscape Aesthetics," *American Studies* 32, no. 1 (Spring 1981): 21–33; Philip Terrie, *Forever Wild: A Cultural History of Wilderness in the Adirondacks* (Syracuse: Syracuse University Press, 1994), 4; Philip Terrie, *Contested Terrain: A New History of Nature and People in the Adirondacks* (Syracuse: Syracuse University Press, 1997), 20–23, 28, 32–33.

5. Lloyd Irland, *The Northeast's Changing Forest* (Petersham, MA: Harvard University Press for Harvard Forest, 1999), 186–87; Jane Eblen Keller, *Adirondack Wilderness: A Story of Man and Nature* (Syracuse: Syracuse University Press, 1980), 114; Edward Pessen, *Jacksonian America: Society, Personality, and Politics* (Homewood, IL: Dorsey Press, 1969), 66; Terrie, "New York Natural History Survey," 185–86, 195–98; Terrie, *Forever Wild*, 7; Terrie, *Contested Terrain*, 13–14, 16.

6. Charles Brumley, *Guides of the Adirondacks: A Short Season, Hard Work, Low Pay* (Glens

Falls, NY: North Country Books, 1994); Ellen Damsky, "A Way of Life: Saranac Lake and the 'Fresh Air' Cure for Tuberculosis" (PhD diss., SUNY Binghamton, 2003); Karen Ann Dietz, "A Home in the Woods: Summer Life in the Adirondacks" (PhD diss., University of Pennsylvania, 1992); Craig Gilborn, *Adirondack Camps: Homes away from Home, 1850–1950* (Syracuse: Syracuse University Press, 2000); Harold Hochschild, *Life and Leisure in the Adirondack Backwoods* (Blue Mountain Lake, NY: Adirondack Museum, 1962); Stilgoe, "Fair Fields and Blasted Rock," 27; *Opening of the Adirondacks*, 66.

7. W. David Lewis, *From Newgate to Dannemora: The Rise of the Prison in New York, 1796–1848* (Ithaca: Cornell University Press, 1965), 7, 10, 12, 13, 15–17, 19; Michel Foucault, *Discipline and Punish: The Birth of the Prison* (New York: Pantheon Books, 1977); Rebecca McLennan, *The Crisis of Imprisonment: Protest, Politics, and the Making of the American Penal State, 1776–1941* (Cambridge: Cambridge University Press, 2008).

8. Lewis, *From Newgate to Dannemora*, 29, 32–33, 37–39, 41, 44, 54–55, 61.

9. M. J. Heale, "The Formative Years of the New York State Prison Association, 1844–1862: A Case Study in Antebellum Reform," *New-York Historical Society Quarterly* 59, no. 4 (1975): 320–47; Lewis, *From Newgate to Dannemora*, 63, 70, 117–18, 126–27, 133, 136, 153, 182–83; Roger Panetta, "Up the River: A History of Sing Sing Prison in the Nineteenth Century" (PhD diss., CUNY Graduate Center, 1999); Pieter Spierenburg, "From Amsterdam to Auburn: An Explanation for the Rise of the Prison in Seventeenth-Century Holland and Nineteenth-Century America," *Journal of Social History* 20, no. 3 (1987): 439–61.

10. John Conley, "Prisons, Production, and Profit: Reconsidering the Importance of Prison Industries," *Journal of Social History* 14, no. 2 (Winter 1980): 257–75; W. David Lewis, "Fiasco in the Adirondacks: The Early History of Clinton Prison at Dannemora, 1844–1861," *New York History* 49, no. 3 (1968): 284–305; Lewis, *From Newgate to Dannemora*, 179, 181–83; Anne Mackinnon, "Welcome to Siberia," *Adirondack Life* 28 (Nov./Dec. 1997): 40–51.

11. Tyler Anbinder, *Five Points: The Nineteenth Century New York City Neighborhood that Invented Tap Dance, Stole Elections and Became the World's Most Notorious Slum* (2001; repr., New York: Plume, 2002); Herbert Asbury, *The Gangs of New York: An Informal History of the New York Underworld* (New York: Hippocrene, 1989); M. J. Heale, "Humanitarianism in the Early Republic: The Moral Reformers of New York, 1776–1825," *Journal of American Studies* 2, no. 2 (Oct. 1968): 161–75; Randolph Roth, *American Homicide* (Cambridge: Belknap Press of Harvard University Press, 2009).

12. Conley, "Prisons, Production, and Profit," 259; Lewis, "Fiasco in the Adirondacks," 288–89; Mackinnon, "Welcome to Siberia," 46.

13. Lewis, *From Newgate to Dannemora*, 198; Mackinnon, "Welcome to Siberia," 46; Terrie, "New York Natural History Survey," 198; Terrie, *Contested Terrain*, 16.

14. Sven Anderson and Augustus Jones, "Iron in the Adirondacks," *Economic Geography* 21, no. 4 (Oct. 1945): 276–85; Robert Gordon, *American Iron, 1607–1900* (Baltimore: Johns Hopkins University Press, 1996), 1, 28; Douglass North, *The Economic Growth of the United States, 1790–1860* (New York: Norton, 1966), 164–65.

15. Report of Ransom Cook to the Legislature, Jan. 28, 1843, New York Public Library, Stephen A. Schwarzman Building, New York, New York.

16. "The New York State Prison Bill—Movements of the Mechanics," New York *Daily Tribune*, Mar. 29, 1844; "The State Prison Bill," New York *Daily Tribune*, May 1, 1844; "The Clinton State Prison," *United States Magazine and Democratic Review* 17 (Nov. 1845), 345–52, 347; "These Are Your N.Y. State Correctional Institutions . . . Clinton Prison, Part I," *Correction* 14, no. 2 (Feb. 1949), 3–13. Duane H. Hurd, *History of Clinton and Franklin Counties, New York* (1880; repr., Plattsburgh: Clinton County Bicentennial Commission, 1978), 48.

17. Ransom Cook, Agent of Clinton State Prison, First Report to the Legislature, 1845, NYPL. *Opening of the Adirondacks,* 20–21; Hurd, *History of Clinton and Franklin Counties,* 304. "The Clinton State Prison," 348; Lewis, "Fiasco in the Adirondacks," 290; Mackinnon, "Welcome to Siberia," 46–47.
18. Amendment to May 1844 bill establishing Clinton State Prison, passed Apr. 16, 1845, Sections 5–8, reprinted in Plattsburgh *Republican,* Apr. 26, 1845 (hereafter *Republican*). New York State, Inspectors of State Prisons, *Annual Report of the Inspectors of State Prisons* (Albany: New York State Senate, 1849), 288, in Lloyd Sealy Library, John Jay College of Criminal Justice / CUNY, New York, New York.
19. "New State Prison," *Republican,* Jun. 7, 1845.
20. Untitled article, *Republican,* Aug. 16, 1845.
21. Untitled article, *Republican,* Nov. 22, 1845.
22. Annual Report of the Agent of the Clinton State Prison to the Legislature, *Republican,* Jan. 30, 1847; "Clinton Prison," *Republican,* Mar. 6, 1847.
23. New York State, *Annual Report* (1849), 282, 288–89, 294; New York State, Inspectors of State Prisons, *Second Annual Report of the Inspectors of State Prisons* (Albany: New York State Senate, 1850), 35–36, 266; New York State, Inspectors of State Prisons, *Eleventh Annual Report of the Inspectors of State Prisons* (Albany: New York State Senate, 1859), 10; New York State, Inspectors of State Prisons, *Thirteenth Annual Report of the Inspectors of State Prisons of the State of New York* (Albany: New York State Senate, 1861), 200; New York State, Inspectors of State Prisons, *Fifteenth Annual Report of the Inspectors of State Prisons, of the State of New York* (Albany: Comstock and Cassidy, Printers, 1863), 293; New York State, Inspectors of State Prisons, *Seventeenth Annual Report of the Inspectors of State Prisons of the State of New York* (Albany: Charles Van Benthuysen, Printer, 1865), 138; New York State, Inspectors of State Prisons, *Eighteenth Annual Report of the Inspectors of State Prisons of the State of New York* (Albany: C. Wendell, Printer, 1866), 136.
24. On the arrivals of new incarcerated men, see untitled articles, *Republican,* Jun. 7, 1845, Jun. 19, 1852, Dec. 18, 1852, Aug. 11, 1855, Jun. 5, 1858, Feb. 23, 1861, Apr. 6, 1861, Apr. 29, 1865. On appropriations for salaries and construction, see untitled articles, *Republican,* Dec. 18, 1847, May 5, 1849, Mar. 23, 1850, Aug. 9, 1851, Jul. 1, 1854, Jul. 28, 1855, Jun. 18, 1859, Jul. 9, 1859, Jul. 30, 1859. "Clinton Prison," *Republican,* Oct. 8, 1859.
25. Annual Report of the Agent of the Clinton State Prison to the Legislature, *Republican,* Jan. 30, 1847; "Clinton Prison," *Republican,* Feb. 6, 1847; "Clinton Prison," *Republican,* Mar. 6, 1847. New York State, *Annual Report,* (1849), 280–81, 285; New York State, Inspectors of State Prisons, *Third Annual Report of the Inspectors of State Prisons* (Albany: New York State Senate, 1851), 34.
26. New York State Prisons, Annual Report of State Prison Inspectors, *Republican,* Mar. 11, 1854.
27. Untitled article, *Republican,* Sept. 2, 1854; "Fire at Clinton Prison," *Republican,* Jun. 28, 1856.
28. "An Award against the State of $59,239.61—A Matter which Demands Investigation," *Republican,* Oct. 15, 1859.
29. On hotels, see "Cadyville Hotel," *Republican,* Aug. 30, 1845; "West Plattsburgh Hotel," *Republican,* Jan. 10, 1846; untitled advertisement, *Republican,* Oct. 1, 1859; untitled advertisement, *Republican,* Jul. 20, 1861. On stage lines, see "Accommodation Stage," *Republican,* Apr. 24, 1846. On roads, see "Clinton Prison Plank Road," *Republican,* Aug. 17, 1850; untitled article, *Republican,* Mar. 10, 1855; "Special Notice," *Republican,* Jul. 2, 1864. On small businesses, see "New Boot And Shoe Store," *Republican,* Dec. 8, 1855; untitled article, *Republican,* May 22, 1858; "Clinton County Lime!" *Republican,* Nov. 26, 1859; untitled article, *Republican,* Apr. 11, 1863. On land, see "Mortgage Sale," *Republican,* Mar. 17, 1849; "Sheriff's Sale," *Republican,* Feb. 23, 1850. One example of each is cited here. Foreclosures and land sales featured prominently in the pages of

the newspaper throughout the 1840s, 1850s, and 1860s. New York State, *Third Annual Report*, 35–36, 264, 266; New York State, *Thirteenth Annual Report*, 200; New York State, *Eighteenth Annual Report*, 136.

30. Untitled article, *Republican*, Sept. 20, 1845; untitled article, *Republican*, Oct. 11, 1845; "Notice!," *Republican*, Jan. 24, 1846; untitled article, *Republican*, Mar. 7, 1846; untitled article, *Republican*, Oct. 24, 1846; untitled article, *Republican*, Dec. 29, 1846; untitled article, *Republican*, Jul. 17, 1847; untitled article, *Republican*, Sept. 11, 1847; untitled article, *Republican*, Dec. 18, 1847; "Beef! Beef!" *Republican*, Mar. 30, 1850; "Clinton Prison Plank Road," *Republican*, Aug. 17, 1850. New York State, *Annual Report* (1849), 286; New York State, *Third Annual Report*, 33.

31. New York State, *Eleventh Annual Report*, 15; New York State, Inspectors of State Prisons, *Twelfth Annual Report of the Inspectors of State Prisons* (Albany: New York State Senate, 1860), 4.

32. New York State, *Annual Report* (1849), 284–85; New York State, *Third Annual Report*, 36, 265; New York State, *Eleventh Annual Report*, 10, 152–53; New York State, *Twelfth Annual Report*, 171.

33. "Clinton Prison Plank Road," *Republican*, Aug. 17, 1850; untitled advertisement, *Republican*, Oct. 4, 1851; "New Boot And Shoe Store," *Republican*, Dec. 8, 1855; untitled advertisement, *Republican*, May 15, 1858; "Clinton Prison Convict Labor," *Republican*, Dec. 24, 1859; "Proposal for Convict Labor," *Republican*, Nov. 29, 1862; untitled article, *Republican*, Apr. 11, 1863; "Proposals for Convict Labor," *Republican*, Oct. 1, 1864; "Proposals for Convict Labor," *Republican*, Mar. 4, 1865. New York State, *Thirteenth Annual Report*, 9; New York State, *Fifteenth Annual Report*, 292.

34. Untitled article, *Republican*, Aug. 16, 1845. "The Clinton State Prison," 351; *Opening of the Adirondacks*, 31; Hurd, *History of Clinton and Franklin Counties*, 49; Mackinnon, "Welcome to Siberia," 42.

35. Untitled article, *Republican*, Aug. 16, 1845.

36. Prison Association of New York, *Fourth Report of the Prison Association of New York* (New York: The Association, 1847–1848), 3–5, in NYPL.

37. Prison Association of New York, *First Report of the Prison Association of New York* (New York: Jared W. Bell, 1845), 3, 6–7, 13, 15, 20, 23, 27, 40.

38. Prison Association of New York, *Second Report of the Prison Association of New York* (New York: The Association, 1846), vol. II, iii–vi, 68, 76, 84, 97, 102; Prison Association of New York, *Third Report of the Prison Association of New York* (New York: The Association, 1847), 9.

39. Prison Association, *Second Report*, 149–50; Prison Association, *Third Report*, 43, 59, 112, 114, 117–26. New York State, *Annual Report* (1849), 344.

40. Prison Association, *Fourth Report*, 207–209, 214. New York State, *Annual Report* (1849), 344.

41. Untitled article, *Republican*, Jan. 29, 1848.

42. "Meeting at Clinton Prison," *Republican*, Feb. 12, 1848.

43. Prison Association, *Fourth Report*, 207–14. New York State, *Annual Report* (1849), 344.

44. "$50 Reward!" *Republican*, Jun. 12, 1847; "$100 Reward!" *Republican*, Sept. 25, 1847; untitled article, *Republican*, Apr. 8, 1848; "Clinton Prison Bill," *Republican*, Apr. 22, 1848; untitled article, *Republican*, Jun. 3, 1848; "Cruelties at Clinton Prison," *Republican*, Aug. 5, 1848; untitled article, *Republican*, May 5, 1849; "Transfer of Prisoners," *Republican*, May 12, 1849; "Fifty Dollars Reward!!" *Republican*, Sept. 13, 1851.

45. "Cruelties at Clinton Prison," *Republican*, Aug. 5, 1848; unsigned letter to the editor, *Republican*, Aug. 12, 1848; untitled article, *Republican*, May 5, 1849; untitled article, *Republican*, May 12, 1849.

46. Prison Association of New York, *Ninth Report of the Prison Association of New York* (Albany: Charles Van Benthuysen Printers, 1854), 25, 156–60.

47. Prison Association of New York, *Tenth Report of the Prison Association of New York* (Albany: Charles Van Benthuysen Printers, 1855); Prison Association of New York, *Eleventh and Twelfth Reports of the Prison Association of New York* (Albany: Charles Van Benthuysen Printers, 1857), 21–22; Prison Association of New York, *Sixteenth Report of the Prison Association of New York* (Albany: Charles Van Benthuysen Printers, 1862), 16–17.

48. "Ore Bed on the State Lands at Clinton Prison," *Republican*, Apr. 16, 1859; untitled article, *Republican*, Jul. 9, 1859; untitled article, *Republican*, Jul. 30, 1859; "Clinton Prison," *Republican*, Oct. 8, 1859; "New York State Prisons," *Republican*, Mar. 11, 1854; "Clinton Prison," *Republican*, Dec. 21, 1860; untitled article, *Republican*, Sept. 28, 1861. New York State, *Eleventh Annual Report*, 10, 153; New York State, *Twelfth Annual Report*, 4; New York State, *Thirteenth Annual Report*, 9.

49. "Christmas at the Prison," *Republican*, Jan. 1, 1859.

50. "Convict Shot at Clinton Prison," *Republican*, May 20, 1854; untitled article, *Republican*, Aug. 5, 1854; "Escapes from Clinton Prison," *Republican*, Aug. 23, 1856; untitled article, *Republican*, Nov. 5, 1859; untitled article, *Republican*, May 12, 1860; untitled article, *Republican*, Jun. 16, 1860; untitled article, *Republican*, Apr. 6, 1861; "Desperate Attempt of Prisoners to Escape," *Republican*, Apr. 20, 1861; "Attempted Escape at Clinton Prison," *Republican*, Aug. 2, 1862; "An Escaped State Prison Bird Caught in Troy—The Vagabond Resists and Makes an Effort to Shoot," *Republican*, Apr. 1, 1865.

51. Untitled article, *Republican*, Oct. 11, 1856; untitled article, *Republican*, Jan. 17, 1863.

52. "Three Hundred Dollars Reward," *Republican*, Jul. 13, 1861; "Terrible Murder at Clinton Prison," *Republican*, Jul. 13, 1861; untitled article, *Republican*, Jul. 20, 1861; untitled article, *Republican*, Oct. 19, 1861.

53. "The Criminal Trials at the Late Circuit," *Republican*, Feb. 15, 1862.

54. Untitled article, *Republican*, Nov. 16, 1861.

55. Untitled article, *Republican*, Nov. 4, 1865.

56. New York State, *Eighteenth Annual Report*, 17.

57. Anthony D'Elia, *The Adirondack Rebellion: A Political, Economic, and Social Expose of the Adirondack State Park, 1880–1980* (Onchiota, N.Y.: Onchiota Books, 1979), 8–25; Frank Graham Jr., *The Adirondack Park: A Political History* (Syracuse: Syracuse University Press, 1978), 23–52, 79–87; Karl Jacoby, *Crimes against Nature: Squatters, Poachers, Thieves, and the Hidden History of American Conservation* (Berkeley: University of California Press, 2001), 26–28; Keller, *Adirondack Wilderness*, 130–61; David Stradling, *The Nature of New York: An Environmental History of the Empire State* (Ithaca: Cornell University Press, 2010), 96–100; Terrie, *Contested Terrain*, 61–82.

58. D'Elia, *The Adirondack Rebellion*, 14–15, 17–21; Graham, *The Adirondack Park*, 88–95; Jacoby, *Crimes against Nature*, 24–26; Keller, *Adirondack Nature*, 77–110, 175–78; Stradling, *The Nature of New York*, 100–102; Terrie, *Contested Terrain*, 83–87, 106–16.

59. D'Elia, *The Adirondack Rebellion*, 22–25; Graham, *The Adirondack Park*, 65–78, 96–132; Jacoby, *Crimes against Nature*, 11–25, 29–78; Keller, *Adirondack Nature*, 161–70, 173–85; Stradling, *The Nature of New York*, 102–105; Terrie, *Contested Terrain*, 87–105.

60. Andrea Guynup, "The Largest Maximum Security Prison in New York," *All Points North Magazine*, Aug. 2006; Ron Roizen, "The 'Courts' of Clinton Prison," New York Correction History Society, http://www.correctionhistory.org/northcountry/dannemora/html/courts00.htm#list.

61. D'Elia, *The Adirondack Rebellion*, 26–32; Graham, *The Adirondack Park*, 143–49, 184–96, 208–18; Keller, *Adirondack Nature*, 186–209; Terrie, *Contested Terrain*, 118–65.

62. D'Elia, *The Adirondack Rebellion*, 26–41, 48–60; Graham, *The Adirondack Park*, 219–63; Keller, *Adirondack Nature*, 213–24; Terrie, *Contested Terrain*, 166–75.

Chapter Two: "Attica of the Adirondacks"

1. "STOP Opposing Prison Concept," *Press Republican* (hereafter *PR*), Aug. 4, 1978. Stop the Olympic Prison (S.T.O.P.), meeting minutes, Aug. 3, 1978, in S.T.O.P. (Stop the Olympic Prison), St. Lawrence University, Owen D. Young Library, Frank and Anne Piskor Special Collections Department, Canton, New York (hereafter STOP Records), (MSS 54).

2. "Lake Placid Wins 1980 Winter Games," *Adirondack Daily Enterprise* (hereafter *ADE*), Oct. 23, 1974; "Moscow, Lake Placid Awarded '80 Olympics," *New York Times,* Oct. 24, 1974 (hereafter *NYT*). Ronald MacKenzie, "Lake Placid, 'Olympic City,'" (Lake Placid, N.Y.: Lake Placid Olympic Organizing Committee, 1977), 84.

3. New York State Legislature, One Hundred Twenty Third Session, Chapter 416, "An Act to Establish a State Hospital in Some Suitable Location in the Adirondacks for the Treatment of Incipient Pulmonary Tuberculosis, and Making an Appropriation Therefor," enacted April 12, 1900, Lake Placid Olympic Museum Archives, Lake Placid, New York (hereafter LPOOC Records), Box 6-2-6: Lake Placid Olympic Organizing Committee (LPOOC) Records, Folder: Athletes' Housing: Federal Condemnation.

4. "Ray Brook," *ADE,* Feb. 1971; "Ray Brook Future Remains Uncertain," *ADE,* Apr. 8, 1971; "Ray Brook Probers Hit Facility's Location," *ADE,* Nov. 20, 1975; "S.I.C. and Ray Brook," *ADE,* Dec. 2, 1975; "Carey Says Ray Brook to Close," *ADE,* Dec. 16, 1975.

5. John Maxwell, Raymond Richardson, and Patricia Olin, "The Economic Impact on the Lake Placid Area of Hosting the 1980 Olympic Winter Games" (Plattsburgh, N.Y.: Technical Assistance Center, 1974), 5–8; Stephen Papson and Alan Schwartz, ed., "Lake Placid and the 1980 Olympic Games: Community Attitudes and the Planning Process" (Canton, N.Y.: St. Lawrence University Environmental Studies Program and North Country Research Center, 1977), 1–4.

6. House of Representatives, 93rd Congress, 2nd Session, *Report No. 93–1182, Endorsing Lake Placid, N.Y., as the Site of the 1980 Winter Olympic Games* (Washington, D.C.: U.S. Government Printing Office, 1974), 9; United States Senate, 93rd Congress, 2nd Session, *Report No. 93–771, 1980 Winter Olympic Games at Lake Placid, N.Y.* (Washington, D.C.: U.S. Government Printing Office, 1974); House of Representatives, 93rd Congress, 2nd Session, *Hearing before the Subcommittee on International Organizations and Movements of the Committee on Foreign Affairs, on H. Con. Res. 443 and H. Con. Res 444, Expressing the Sense of Congress in Support of Lake Placid, N.Y., as the Site of the 1980 Winter Olympic Games,* May 8, 1974 (Washington, D.C.: U.S. Government Printing Office, 1974), 1–4.

7. "College May Use Games Buildings," *ADE,* Oct. 30, 1974; "Ray Brook Proposed for Olympic Village," *ADE,* Sept. 30, 1975; "Ray Brook Drug Center May Be Olympic Village," *PR,* Jan. 14, 1976. LPOOC, "Information on the 1980 Olympic Winter Games Prepared by the Lake Placid Olympic Organizing Committee for the Congress of the United States" (Lake Placid, N.Y.: LPOOC, 1975), 55. Gray Twombly to Robert McEwen, Oct. 14, 1975; Helen McDonald to Jacob Javits, Nov. 10, 1975, in Robert McEwen Papers, Owen D. Young Library, Frank and Anne Piskor Special Collections Department, St. Lawrence University, Canton, New York (hereafter McEwen Papers), (MSS 25), Box 95–27, Folder: 1980 Olympics, to 1977—Ray Brook Facility Correspondence.

8. "Prison System to Be Expanded," *ADE,* Nov. 11, 1975; "Drugs, Booze Traded for Favors, Ray Brook Inmate Tells Hearing," *PR,* Nov. 19, 1975; "SIC Recommends Closing Ray Brook Rehab Center," *ADE,* Nov. 26, 1975; "Ray Brook Drug Unit May Close," *PR,* Dec. 17, 1975; "Carey Seeking Other Agencies to Reopen Ray Brook Facility," *ADE,* Jan. 13, 1976; "NCCC Trustees Urged to Accept Ray Brook for Campus Expansion," *ADE,* Jan. 14, 1976. Judith Green and Mark Mauer, "Downscaling Prisons: Lessons from Four States" (Washington, D.C.: The Sentencing Project, 2010). Ernest Drucker,

"Population Impact of Mass Incarceration under New York's Rockefeller Drug Laws: An Analysis of Years of Life Lost," *Journal of Urban Health: Bulletin of the New York Academy of Medicine* 79, no. 3 (Sept. 2002): 1–10.

9. "Ray Brook Drug Center May Be Olympic Village," *PR*, Jan. 14, 1976; "Olympics Affect Ray Brook," *ADE*, Apr. 12, 1976; "Ray Brook May Be Olympic Center; USOC Considering Site for Training," *ADE*, May 11, 1976; "Corrections Taking over Ray Brook," *ADE*, Aug. 13, 1976; "State Plans Prison Camp for Ray Brook Center," *PR*, Aug. 14, 1976.

10. "Prison No Bar to '80 Housing," *LPN*, Aug. 19, 1976; "Camp Adirondack Relocates in Ray Brook," *ADE*, Sept. 2, 1976; "Ray Brook Campmen Tuned to Mountain Air," *LPN*, Sept. 15, 1976; "Triple Play at Ray Brook: Camp to Village to Prison?" *LPN*, Sept. 22, 1976.

11. "Camp Adirondack Relocates in Ray Brook," *ADE*, Sept. 2, 1976; "Camp Adirondack Is Good News for the Area," *ADE*, Sept. 13, 1976.

12. "Ray Brook Age Called an Issue, Site Is Good," *ADE*, Jun. 2, 1976; "Ray Brook Roomers: Felons or Athletes?" *LPN*, Jun. 3, 1976; "Ray Brook: Another Tour," *LPN*, Jun. 24, 1976; "Ray Brook Prison Plan Hatched in Casual Chat," *ADE*, Feb. 23, 1977. Gary Mote to Bob Honsted, Jun. 7, 1976; Gary Mote to Bob Honsted, Jun. 16, 1976; Gary Mote to Bob Honsted, Jun. 23, 1976, McEwen Papers, Box 95–27: Folder—Winter Olympics Youth Correction Center, Ray Brook Memos, Info—Folder 95–27/2168.

13. "Olympic Village Sited at Ray Brook," *LPN*, Dec. 1, 1976; "Fregoe on U.S. Prison: 'We Want to See It,'" *LPN*, Jan. 12, 1977; "No Bars—and No Place to Put Them," LPN, Mar. 31, 1977. 94th Congress, 2nd Session, *Public Law 94–427, Olympic Winter Games Authorization Act of 1976* (Washington, D.C.: U.S. Government Printing Office, 1976). LPOOC, "Fifth Report of the Lake Placid 1980 Olympic Winter Games Organizing Committee, for the Executive Committee of the International Olympic Committee" (Lake Placid, N.Y.: LPOOC, 1976), 9.

14. "McEwen Eyeing '80 Olympics as an Incumbent," *PR*, Feb. 16, 1977; "Congress Acts to Speed Olympic Funds," *LPN*, Feb. 17, 1977. Senate Committee on Appropriations, Statement of Norman A. Carlson, Director, Bureau of Prisons, before the Senate Committee on Appropriations for the Department of Justice, Feb. 7, 1977; House Subcommittee on Appropriations, Statement of Norman A. Carlson, Director, Bureau of Prisons, before the Subcommittee on Appropriations for the Department of Justice, House of Representatives, Feb. 9, 1977; Statement of Robert C. McEwen before House State, Justice, Commerce, and Judiciary Subcommittee on Appropriations, Feb. 9, 1977, McEwen Papers, Box 95–27: Folder—Winter Olympics Youth Correction Center, Ray Brook Memos, Info—Folder 95–27/2168.

15. Robert Glennon to Anthony Conde, Jul. 23, 1981, Camp Gabriels Records, Adirondack Park Agency Records Office, Ray Brook, New York (hereafter Gabriels Records), SP 81-15.

16. Richard Thibedeau to APA senior staff, Dec. 7, 1976; Robert Glennon to Herman Cole, Norman Hess, and J. Langdon Marsh, Jan. 6, 1977; memo from Robert Glennon to Olympic Village File, Jan. 17, 1977, LPOOC Records, Box 6-2-6, Folder: Athletes' Housing: Federal Condemnation.

17. "Several Problems Persist for Olympics Planning," *PR*, Jan. 22, 1977; "No Word from 2 Groups on Olympic Litigation" *PR*, Jan. 29, 1977; "Olympics Land Filed for," *PR*, Jun. 8, 1977. Robert Glennon to Anthony Conde, Jul. 23, 1981, Gabriels Records.

18. APA, "Site Analysis of the Proposed Site of the Olympic Village," APA Staff Evaluation Report (Ray Brook: APA, Feb. 1977), 4–5, McEwen Papers, Box 95–27, Folder: 1980 Olympics, to 1977—Ray Brook Facility Correspondence.

19. APA, "Site Analysis," 1–4, McEwen Papers.

20. Ibid., 6–9, McEwen Papers.

21. "Construction Program Outlined," *PR*, Mar. 2, 1977; "U.S. Prison Officials Go Flat Out to Stop Escapes," *LPN*, Mar. 24, 1977.

22. "Spring Brings Olympic Greening," *LPN*, Mar. 31, 1977; "Olympic Organizers Present Fifth Report," *LPN*, Apr. 7, 1977.

23. "For Humanity, Dignity and Equal Opportunity," *LPN*, Apr. 4, 1977.

24. "Soft Cell at Ray Brook," *LPN*, Jun. 9, 1977; "A Needless Waste of Beauty," *LPN*, Jun. 9, 1977; "Prison Site," *ADE*, Jun. 14, 1977. Joan Potter, "The 'Olympic Prison': An Obvious Choice or a 'Chilling Idea?'" *Corrections Magazine* (Jun. 1978), 26, 30; "Games and Other Games: The New Olympic Prison," *frying pan* (Sept. 1978), 23–24, STOP Records.

25. "Soft Cell at Ray Brook," *LPN*, Jun. 9, 1977. Potter, "The 'Olympic Prison,'" 26, 30; "Games and Other Games," 23–24.

26. "Federal Prison: An Arrogant Intruder," *LPN*, Aug. 18, 1977. Potter, "The 'Olympic Prison,'" 30. Warner Deitz to Wiley Lavigne, Aug. 15, 1977; Warner Deitz to Robert McEwen, Aug. 19, 1977; Richard McCormick to Robert McEwen, Aug. 16, 1977, McEwen Papers, Box 95–27, Folder: 1980 Olympics, to 1977—Ray Brook Facility Correspondence. PETITION from Ray Brook Citizens to the Economic Development Administration, 1977, McEwen Papers, Box 95–27, Folder: 1980 Winter Olympics, Ray Brook Correspondence, 1978.

27. "Hearing Set on Prison Sewage Line; APA to Challenge Olympic Projects," *ADE*, Jul. 25, 1978. John F. Cullen, Memo Re: Meetings Relative to Olympic Sewerage, Nov. 30, 1977; Warner Deitz to David Bochnowich, Feb. 22, 1978; Warner Deitz to Robert McEwen, Mar. 29, 1978; four additional letters, McEwen Papers, Box 95–27, Folder: 1980 Winter Olympics, Ray Brook Correspondence, 1978.

28. "Construction Impact Concerns Berle," *LPN*, Sept. 21, 1977; "Prison Site Erosion Repair to Take 5 Years," *PR*, Sept. 23, 1977; "380 Tons of Mud," *LPN*, Sept. 28, 1977. "Adverse Environmental Impacts of the Construction of the Federal Correctional Facility at Ray Brook, New York: Evaluation and Recommendations: A Special Report Prepared by the State of New York, Adirondack Park Agency," Sept. 22, 1977, 1–6, McEwen Papers, Box 95–27, Folder: 1980 Olympics, to 1977—Ray Brook Facility Correspondence.

29. "Construction Impact Concerns Berle," *LPN*, Sept. 21, 1977; "380 Tons of Mud," *LPN*, Sept. 28, 1977; "Federal Agency Bears Olympic Financial Burden," *ADE*, Oct. 19, 1977; "Update on Olympic Construction," *LPN*, Nov. 3, 1977; "Prison Sand Bank Washes into Brook," *ADE*, Oct. 16, 1978. David Bochnowich to J. Bernard Fell, Sept. 16, 1977; Robert Flacke to Charles Warren, Sept. 22, 1977; Robert F. Messmer to Philip Gitlen, Sept. 23, 1977; Norman Carlson to Robert Hall, Sept. 29, 1977, McEwen Papers, Box 95–27, Folder: 1980 Olympics, to 1977—Ray Brook Facility Correspondence. Ronald MacKenzie to David Bochnowich, Nov. 8, 1977, LPOOC Records. Dick Persico, interview by Elizabeth Morrison, Apr. 19, 1979, tape transcription, in XIII Olympic Winter Games Oral History, 1980 Winter Olympic Games, St. Lawrence University, Owen D. Young Library, Frank and Anne Piskor Special Collections Department, Canton, N.Y. (hereafter Winter Games Oral History), (MSS 90).

30. STOP, "Update on STOP Activities," Sept. 1, 1978, STOP Records.

31. "STOP Opposing Prison Concept," *PR*, Aug. 4, 1978; "Opposing a Prison at Lake Placid," *NYT*, Jan. 17, 1978. STOP, "An Olympic Prison: Is This for Real?," 1978, STOP Records.

32. Graham Hodges, letter, *LPN*, Apr. 21, 1978; Graham Hodges, letter, *ADE*, Apr. 24, 1978; "Prison Use Comes under Attack," *LPN*, Nov. 22, 1978; "Anti-Prison," *LPN*, Nov. 23, 1978. STOP, "An Olympic Prison"; National Moratorium on Prison Construction, "Repression Replaces Celebration: The 1980 Winter Olympic Prison" (Washington,

D.C.: National Moratorium on Prison Construction, Mar. 1978), 5–8; STOP, meeting minutes, Apr. 5, 1978, 1; STOP, meeting minutes, Apr. 18, 1978, 1–2, STOP Records.

33. "The Challenge of Corrections," *LPN,* Mar. 2, 1978; "Olympics, Yes! Prison, No!" *LPN,* Aug. 10, 1978; Graham Hodges, letter, *LPN,* Oct. 25, 1979. STOP, pamphlet, 1978; *Jailbrake: Newsletter of the New York Moratorium on Prison Construction* (Syracuse, N.Y.: Spring 1978), 4–5; Graham Hodges to Terence Cardinal Cooke, Apr. 18, 1979; Graham Hodges, comments on the prison, Jun. 1, 1979, STOP Records.

34. Graham Hodges, letter, *ADE,* Apr. 24, 1978; "Olympics, Yes! Prison, No!" *LPN,* Aug. 10, 1978; Graham Hodges, letter, *LPN,* Oct. 25, 1979. Graham Hodges to Terence Cardinal Cooke, Apr. 18, 1979; "Moscow Olympic Village Rises amidst Mud," *Sunday Gazette-Mail,* Oct. 15, 1978, STOP Records.

35. Graham Hodges, letter, *LPN,* Apr. 21, 1978; Graham Hodges, letter, *ADE,* Apr. 24, 1978; "Being Taken," *LPN,* Jun. 29, 1978; Graham Hodges, letter, *LPN,* Jun. 1, 1979; Graham Hodges, letter, *LPN,* Oct. 25, 1979. National Moratorium on Prison Construction, "Racist Nature of Juvenile Facilities, Jails and Prisons in the United States," (Washington, D.C.: National Moratorium on Prison Construction, Feb. 1978); STOP, meeting minutes, Apr. 5, 1978; Graham Hodges to Terence Cardinal Cooke, Apr. 18, 1979, STOP Records. *Census of Population: 1980, Vol. 1, Characteristics of the Population, Chapter B: General Population Characteristics, Part 34, New York, PC80-1-B34* (Washington, D.C.: U.S. Government Printing Office, 1982), Table 14, 34-12, Table 14-A, 34-25, Table 15, 34-33, and Table 15-A, 34-46.

36. Graham Hodges, letter, *LPN,* Apr. 21, 1978; Graham Hodges, letter, *ADE,* Apr. 24, 1978; "Prison Use Comes under Attack," *LPN,* Nov. 22, 1978; "Urban Prisoners Should Have Urban Environment," *LPN,* Jan. 25, 1979. STOP, "An Olympic Prison," Apr. 1978; STOP, meeting minutes, Apr. 5, 1978, 1–2, STOP Records. House of Representatives, 96th Congress, 1st Session, Bureau of Prisons Fiscal Year 1980 Authorization, *Hearings before the Subcommittee on Courts, Civil Liberties, and the Administration of Justice of the Committee on the Judiciary,* Mar. 21 and 23, 1979, Serial No. 7 (Washington, D.C.: U.S. Government Printing Office, 1979) 18–19, 59–65, 82–84, 86. Elizabeth Minehan, interviewed by David Casier, Apr. 17, 1979, Winter Games Oral History.

37. "STOP Opposing Prison Concept," *PR,* Aug. 4, 1978; "Olympics, Yes! Prison, No!" *LPN,* Aug. 10, 1978; Graham Hodges, letter, *LPN,* Oct. 25, 1979. STOP, meeting minutes, Aug. 3, 1978; Graham Hodges, letter on the Olympic Prison, Jun. 1, 1979; Graham Hodges to Hugh Carey, Jun. 27, 1979, STOP Records. *Hearings before the Subcommittee on Courts,* Mar. 21 and 23, 1979, 18–19, 59–65, 78–79, 82–84, 86. Minehan, interviewed by Casier, Apr. 17, 1979, Winter Games Oral History.

38. Graham Hodges, letter, *LPN,* Apr. 21, 1978; "Being Taken," *LPN,* Jun. 29, 1978; Graham Hodges, letter, *LPN,* Oct. 25, 1979. STOP, "An Olympic Prison"; STOP, meeting minutes, Aug. 3, 1978; "Skiers May Snub Olympic Village," *St. Louis Globe-Democrat,* Feb. 22, 1979; William Oscar Johnson, "The Olympic Getaway," *Sports Illustrated,* Apr. 6, 1979, 22; "Complaints on Housing for Games," *Newsday,* Apr. 13, 1979; Graham Hodges to Hugh Carey, Jun. 27, 1979, STOP Records. *Hearings before the Subcommittee on Courts,* Mar. 21 and 23, 1979, 18–19, 59–65, 82–84, 86. Minehan, interviewed by Casier, Apr. 17, 1979, Winter Games Oral History.

39. "Opposition to Ray Brook Mounts," *PR,* Feb. 21, 1978; "Being Taken," *LPN,* Jun. 29, 1978; "Prison Use Comes under Attack," *LPN,* Nov. 22, 1978; "Anti-Prison," *LPN,* Nov. 23, 1978; "Lake Placid People Talk: Should the Olympic Village Become Prison?" *LPN,* Mar. 28, 1979; "Lake Placid Is for Athletes, Not Convicts," *NYT,* Apr. 22, 1980. "Stop the Olympic Prison," *Jericho* 1, no. 1 (Feb.–Jun. 1978), 1–2; STOP, meeting minutes, Aug. 3, 1978, 2; STOP, "The Olympic Prison," Winter 1979, STOP Records. *Hearings before the Subcommittee on Courts,* Mar. 21 and 23, 1979, 61–62, 78–79. Minehan, interviewed by Casier, Apr. 17, 1979, Winter Games Oral History.

40. "Prison Suit Possible," *LPN,* Apr. 5, 1978; "Placid Prison Fight Expands to Carter," *Watertown Daily Times* (hereafter *WDT*), May 13, 1978; "Athlete Housing Opposed," *LPN,* Jun. 29, 1978; "STOP Tours Prison Site," *ADE,* Aug. 4, 1978; "Olympics, Yes! Prison, No!" *LPN,* Aug. 10, 1978; "U.S. Attorney General Discusses Olympic Village After Use, APA," *PR,* Sept. 12, 1978; "S.T.O.P. Protestors Hold Rally," *PR,* Dec. 8, 1978. United Church of Christ, New York Conference, "Resolution on the Olympic Prison," 1978; *Jailbrake,* Spring 1978, 4–5; STOP, meeting minutes, Mar. 22, 1978; STOP, meeting minutes, Apr. 5, 1978, 1–2; STOP, meeting minutes, Apr. 18, 1978, 1–2; United Methodist Church, "Resolution on the Proposed Use of the Olympic Village Facility as a Federal Prison," Northern New York Conference, May 31–Jun. 2, 1978, 1–3; United Presbyterian Church in the United States of America, "The Olympic Athlete Housing and Lake Placid Youth Prison," Jun. 1978; Jonathan Tetherly to North Country Committee Against the Olympic Prison, Jul. 21, 1978; STOP, meeting minutes, Aug. 3, 1978; Jonathan Tetherly to Graham Hodges, Aug. 4, 1978; STOP, "Update on STOP Activities," Sept. 1, 1978; STOP, "Olympic Prison Poster," Sept. 1978, 1–3; STOP, flier on USOC lawsuit, Sept. 1978; *Stop the Olympic Prison v. United States Olympic Committee,* Civil Action in United States District Court for Eastern District of New York, Oct. 5, 1978; Eugene Turner to Stanislaus Brzana, Nov. 9, 1978; STOP, "Olympic Prison Poster," Nov. 14, 1978, 1–3; Virginia Mackey to Charles Tobin, Dec. 4, 1978, STOP Records. Edwin Potter to Robert McEwen, Mar. 8, 1978; Thelma Graziano to H. Douglas Barclay, Oct. 12, 1978; James Bailey to Robert McEwen, Dec. 14, 1978; three additional letters, McEwen Papers, Box 95–27, 1980 Winter Olympics, Ray Brook Correspondence, 1978.

41. "Lawmakers Try to Stop Funds for Olympics," *LPN,* Feb. 22, 1979; "Sign Statement Opposing Prison," *North Country Catholic* (hereafter *NCC*), Feb. 22, 1979; "Olympic Housing Hearings Scheduled," *PR,* Mar. 10, 1979; "Mohawks Plan Olympic Demonstrations," *LPN,* Nov. 29, 1979; "STOP Seeks Permit for Placid Protest," *LPN,* Dec. 13, 1979. Allen Wollenberg to James Hanley, Jan. 26, 1979; "Statement of Conscience on the Lake Placid Olympic Prison by North Country Clergy," Feb. 1979; Eugene Turner to Mark Rohrbaugh, Feb. 9, 1979; "News from Senator Carl McCall: Legislators to Offer Amendment to Stop Olympic Village Construction," direct-mail flyer, Feb. 13, 1979; North Country Clergy Concerned about the Lake Placid Olympic Prison, "Leading North Country Clergy Ask Change in Use of Olympic Dormitories," Feb. 15, 1979; "Another Ray Brook Delay Attempt Expected Today," *WDT,* Apr. 4, 1979; "House Committee Defeats Ray Brook Delay Moves," *WDT,* Apr. 5, 1979; "Moynihan Changes Opinion on Prison," *WDT,* May 2, 1979; "Prison Troubling White House Staff," *WDT,* Oct. 18, 1979, STOP Records. *Hearings before the Subcommittee on Courts,* Mar. 21 and 23, 1979, 18–19, 59–65, 78–79, 82–84, 86. Margaret Kesler to Robert McEwen, Jan. 22, 1979; A.R. Hall to Robert McEwen, Feb. 1, 1979; Maile Fowler to Robert McEwen, May 23, 1979; and three additional letters, McEwen Papers, Box 95–27, Folder: 1980 Winter Olympics Correspondence, Jan.–Jun. 1979. Phillip K. Shinnick, "Natural Sport, the Olympic Prison, and the Fight for Sovereignty Rights of the Mohawks," *Journal of Ethnic Studies* 9, no. 1 (Spring 1981): 43–52.

42. "Depressing?" *ADE,* Jan. 19, 1978; "Reply to Prison Opposition, Part I," *ADE,* Mar. 3, 1978; "Clergy Issue Statement of Support for Ray Brook Prison," *NCC,* Oct. 4, 1978; "Supports Prison Plan," *NCC,* Nov. 22, 1978; "Misguided Urban Arguments about Ray Brook Prison," *LPN,* Jan. 18, 1979; "Prison Protest Is Grandstanding," *ADE,* Feb. 16, 1979; "Bishop Brzana's Statement on Ray Brook Prison Plan," *NCC,* Feb. 21, 1979. "Prison Opposition Is Un-Christian," *WDT,* Jun. 22, 1978, STOP Records. *Hearings before the Subcommittee on Courts,* Mar. 21 and 23, 1979, 10–11, 17, 37–38, 43–44, 56–57.

43. "Church Criticism of Ray Brook Prison Blasted; McEwen Says 'Attempt to Embarrass U.S.,'" *PR,* May 20, 1978; "McEwen Airs Views on Olympic Village Use," *LPN,* Jul.

26, 1978. Daniel Patrick Moynihan to Graham Hodges, Sept. 28, 1978, STOP Records. *Hearings before the Subcommittee on Courts*, Mar. 21 and 23, 1979, 44–45, 48–50, 52–53, 56–57.

44. "Locals Favor Ray Brook Prison," *PR*, Feb. 22, 1978; "Harrietstown Supports Prison Concept for Olympic Village," *PR*, Feb. 27, 1978; "Church Criticism of Ray Brook Prison Blasted; McEwen Says 'Attempt to Embarrass U.S.,'" *PR*, May 20, 1978; "Ray Brook Prison Needed, McEwen Says," *LPN*, May 31, 1978; "McEwen Airs Views on Olympic Village Use," *LPN*, Jul. 26, 1978; "Ray Brook Prison to Provide Jobs," *PR*, Apr. 2, 1979; "Saranac Lake Supports Prison," *PR*, Apr. 4, 1979; "Village Board Backs Prison Plan," *PR*, Apr. 12, 1979. Potter, "The Olympic Prison," 28, 31; Daniel Patrick Moynihan to Graham Hodges, Sept. 28, 1978, STOP Records. *Hearings before the Subcommittee on Courts*, Mar. 21 and 23, 1979, 43–44, 52–53, 56–57. IKON (Dutch Television), Robert McEwen, interview by Freke Vuyst, Jun. 27, 1978; Gerald Oxford to Robert McEwen, Aug. 17, 1978, McEwen Papers, Box 95–27, Folder: 1980 Winter Olympics, Ray Brook Correspondence, 1978.

45. "Church Criticism of Ray Brook Prison Blasted; McEwen Says 'Attempt to Embarrass U.S.,'" *PR*, May 20, 1978; "Ray Brook Prison Needed, McEwen Says," *LPN*, May 31, 1978; "McEwen Airs Views on Olympic Village Use," *LPN*, Jul. 26, 1978; "Olympics 'A Steal at Any Price,' McEwen Says," *PR*, Apr. 18, 1979. LPOOC, "A Special Opportunity for Friends of Good Causes and the American Way of Life," flyer, 1978; Daniel Patrick Moynihan to Graham Hodges, Sept. 28, 1978, STOP Records. *Hearings before the Subcommittee on Courts*, Mar. 21 and 23, 1979, 10–11, 17, 37–38, 43–45, 48–50, 56–57. Dereck Williamson, "Olympic Village: A Special Place," *Lake Placid Olympian* 2, no. 11 (LPOOC: Lake Placid, Aug. 1979), 4, 8.

46. "Internationals Examine Olympic Village," *The North Countryman*, May 23, 1979; "Athletes' Village Prepares for Grand Opening," *LPN*, Jan. 24, 1980; "Some Lesson on Protest from the 1980 Olympics," *San Francisco Chronicle*, Mar. 31, 1980. LPOOC, *Final Report: XIII Olympic Winter Games, February 13–24, 1980* (Lake Placid, N.Y.: LPOOC, 1980), 155–62; LPOOC, *Olympic Village Guide* (Lake Placid: LPOOC, 1980), 5.

47. "Olympic Prison to Open in August," *LPN*, Mar. 13, 1980; "No Inmates at Federal Prison till February 1981," *PR*, Jun. 17, 1980; "New Prison to Provide 110 Local Jobs," *LPN*, Aug. 14, 1980; "Warden in, Readies for Opening," *PR*, Sept. 17, 1980; "Work Progresses," *PR*, Sept. 17, 1980.

48. "Prison Keys Gone," *ADE*, Sept. 3, 1980; "Protest of Prison Fails to STOP Dedication," *PR*, Sept. 27, 1980; "New Federal Prison Opens in Ray Brook," *LPN*, Oct. 2, 1980. Program, FCI Ray Brook Opening Ceremony, Ray Brook, New York, September 26, 1980; "STOP Welcomes You to the Olympic Prison Counter-Dedication"; STOP, pamphlet on prison opening, STOP Records. Remarks by Rep. Robert C. McEwen at the Dedication of the Ray Brook Federal Correctional Facility, Ray Brook, Sept. 26, 1980, McEwen Papers, Box 95–27, Folder: Ray Brook Dedication, 9/26/1980.

49. "Campmen Take NCCC Courses," *ADE*, Feb. 16, 1977; "Prison Employees to Be Trained through Program at Local College," *PR*, Feb. 22, 1984; "NCCC Enrollment Up; Budget Back in Black," *PR*, Oct. 1, 1985.

50. "Saranac Lake Students Donate to 'Camp,'" *PR*, Dec. 12, 1977; "Scholarship Club Gives 2 Grants," *PR*, Feb. 23, 1978; "Grassroots Program Brings Arts into Area Schools," *PR*, Apr. 26, 1978; "Thank You, Camp Adirondack," *ADE*, Jun. 13, 1978; "Jailhouse Rock," *PR*, Dec. 21, 1982; "Onchiota Woman Helps Inmates Break out of Prison Illiteracy," *ADE*, Nov. 5, 1984; "Prison Literacy Program Earns Praise," *ADE*, Feb. 15, 1985; "Pendragon Draws Actresses from NYC," *PR*, Aug. 30, 1985; "Rhythm and Blues," *ADE*, Feb. 9, 1990.

51. "Prison Visit," *NCC*, Mar. 26, 1986; "Father Muench Says Prison Mass," *NCC*, Jul. 16, 1986; "Inmates Concerned," *ADE*, Oct. 11, 2001.

52. "350 Visitors Tour Camp Adirondack," *ADE*, Jun. 13, 1977; "In Favor of Campmen," *ADE*, Jun. 17, 1977; "Camp Adirondack Marks 1st Year," *PR*, Sept. 2, 1977; "A Prison Superintendent Who Should Stay as Top Man," *LPN*, Sept. 8, 1977; "Thank You, Camp Adirondack," *ADE*, Jun. 13, 1978; "Camp Adirondack Hosts Open House," *PR*, Jun. 14, 1978; "Community Praises Camp Residents," *PR*, Sept. 2, 1978; "Camp Man Honored," *PR*, Sept. 2, 1978; "Annual Picnic," *PR*, Sept. 13, 1978; "Open House," *ADE*, Feb. 20, 1979; "Racette Says Camp Adirondack Is Still Helping People Get Well," *PR*, Mar. 2, 1979; "Prison Slide Show Offered," *ADE*, Apr. 11, 1979; "Adult Center Schedules Events," *ADE*, Apr. 16, 1979; "Camp Adirondack Holds First of Three Family Days," *ADE*, Jul. 9, 1979; "Camp Adirondack Plans Open House," *PR*, Aug. 21, 1979; "A Walk through Camp," *PR*, Sept. 5, 1979; "New Vocation," *LPN*, Sept. 3, 1987.

53. "Camp Adirondack Inmate Group Named 'Time,' Gave Kids Good Time," *ADE*, Jun. 29, 1977; "Carmelites Celebrate 25th Anniversary," *NCC*, Sept. 14, 1977; "Singing for a Captive Audience," *ADE*, Apr. 14, 1982; "Explaining the Do Nots of Drugs," *PR*, May 8, 1982; "Inmates Warn Students away from Alcohol, Drugs," *PR*, Nov. 15, 1982; "Elks Set Program on Drug Abuse," *PR*, Nov. 12, 1983; "Inside Help," *ADE*, Nov. 15, 1984; "Inmates Aid Starving Ethiopians," *ADE*, Feb. 19, 1985; "Inmate Expresses Gratitude," *ADE*, Mar. 8, 1994.

54. "Blocking Out," *PR*, Aug. 26, 1977; "Tree Surgery," *PR*, Sept. 8, 1977; "Heave Ho!" *ADE*, Oct. 13, 1977; "Campmen Provide Service to Area," *PR*, Nov. 11, 1977; "Village Completing Dam Construction," *PR*, Jun. 21, 1978; "Thursday's Rain Aids Volunteers in Forest Fire," *PR*, Jul. 29, 1978; "Woodcutting," *ADE*, Nov. 27, 1978; "Contracts for Plumbing, Construction Awarded," *PR*, Mar. 27, 1979; "The Finishing Touch," *PR*, Apr. 5, 1979; "Area Forest Fires under Control," *PR*, Oct. 25, 1979.

55. "Adult Center to Settle Down on Broadway," *PR*, Jan. 15, 1980; "Camp Adirondack Inmates Enjoy Work Outdoors," *PR*, Feb. 26, 1980; "Stacking Up," *PR*, Mar. 6, 1980; "DOT Field Work Begins; Use Again Considered," *PR*, May 16, 1980; "Clearing the Brush," *PR*, Aug. 1, 1980; "Dig It," *ADE*, Oct. 8, 1980; "An Attempt," *PR*, Feb. 12, 1981; "Waters, Requests for Red Cross Aid on the Rise," *PR*, Feb. 19, 1981; "Camp Adirondack Commended," *ADE*, Jun. 11, 1981; "Inmates Working on Bridges in Jay," *PR*, Jul. 25, 1981; "Bloomingdale Field Day Attracts Many," *PR*, Sept. 8, 1981; "Finishing Touches," *ADE*, Nov. 3, 1981; "Lettermen," *ADE*, Nov. 27, 1981; "It's a Frame," *ADE*, Jun. 15, 1982; "Blooming Berkeley," *ADE*, Jun. 30, 1982; "Handicapped Children Aided," *ADE*, Sept. 23, 1982; "Work on Walkway Begins," *ADE*, Oct. 13, 1982; "Recognition for Project Sought," *PR*, May 25, 1983; "Industrial Site," *PR*, Jul. 1, 1983; "New Look for Hubbard Hall," *PR*, Oct. 6, 1983; "Library Holds Open House," *PR*, Oct. 17, 1983; "Inmates Spruce Up NCCC's Hubbard Hall," *PR*, Jul. 11, 1984; "Library Will Open Monday: Inmates Helped with Renovations," *ADE*, Oct. 5, 1984; "Toys to Help Athletes," *ADE*, May 9, 1986; "Time Donated to Project," *ADE*, May 13, 1986; "Camp Crews Do Community Work," *LPN*, May 22, 1986; "Inmates Join Farmers in Franklin County Haylift," *PR*, Aug. 18, 1986; "New Prison Shops Busy," *PR*, Dec. 15, 1986; "Prison Crew Helped Airport," *ADE*, Sept. 1, 1987; "Toys Help Athletes," *PR*, Jan. 9, 1987; "Advertisement: PBS Channel 57 Arts Auction," *PR*, Jun. 2, 1987; "Helping Hands," *ADE*, Jun. 17, 1987; "Hard at Work," *ADE*, Feb. 4, 1988; "Streamlined Signs," *ADE*, Sept. 11, 1992; "Gardening for Needy," *PR*, Jun. 20, 1995; "Saying Goodbye," *ADE*, Jul. 15, 2002; "New Girl Scouts Recycling Bin," *ADE*, May 9, 2007; "Adirondack Art Chair Preview Party to be Held May 31," *ADE*, May 23, 2008.

56. "Santa's Jukebox Donors," *ADE*, Dec. 21, 1976; "Campmen Give Toys New Life," *PR*, Dec. 18, 1978; "Jackets, Mittens Given to Elks by Youngsters," *PR*, Dec. 19, 1978; "Lions Deliver Toys to Camp for Repair," *PR*, May 12, 1979; "Street Scenes," *PR*, Nov. 6, 1979; "Cubs Hold Holiday Party," *PR*, Jan. 17, 1980; "At Camp Adirondack: Repairing Toys," *ADE*, May 13, 1980; "Helping Santa Helps Campmen," *ADE*, Dec. 24, 1980; "Santa's

Helpers," *ADE*, Dec. 9, 1981; "About Town," *ADE*, Apr. 22, 1982; "Gearing Up for Christmas," *ADE*, Apr. 23, 1982; "Toys for Christmas," *ADE*, Dec. 21, 1982; "Toy Program Plaudits," *ADE*, Feb. 25, 1983; "Helping with Toy Program," *ADE*, Jan. 25, 1984; "Toy Savers," *LPN*, May 17, 1984; "Inmates Create Kids' Christmas Toys," *LPN*, Dec. 12, 1985; "International Buffet to Aid 'Holiday Helpers,'" *ADE*, Sept. 16, 1986; "Santa Cutout Inmates' Gift to the Community," *PR*, Dec. 15, 1986; "Santa's Helpers Get Aid," *ADE*, Dec. 26, 1986; "Holiday Helpers' International Buffet a Success," *ADE*, Oct. 27, 1988; "Spirited Holiday Helpers Made Christmas Bright," *ADE*, Jan. 13, 1989; "Flowers Net Cash for Toy Program," *ADE*, May 11, 1989; "Holiday Helpers," *ADE*, Nov. 21, 1989; "Volunteers Help Provide Holiday Gifts," *PR*, Dec. 3, 1989; "Holiday Helpers," *ADE*, Dec. 19, 1989.

57. "Land-Clearing Starts for Two Softball Fields," *PR*, Jun. 25, 1977; "School's Tax Rate to Decrease," *PR*, Aug. 24, 1977; "Trail Work," *ADE*, Oct. 12, 1977; "Ski Club Fund-Raising Continues," *PR*, Oct. 27, 1977; "Appreciation Shown," *PR*, Nov. 2, 1979; "Girl Scouts Cite Work of Camp Adirondack Crews," *PR*, Nov. 2, 1979; "Prisoners Save Olympics Thousands in Labor Costs," *The Day* (New London, CT), Dec. 13, 1979; "Intervale Ski Site to Open as Summer Tourist Stop in May," *PR*, Apr. 10, 1980; "Students Hike in the Woods; It's Just in Their Nature," *PR*, Jul. 8, 1980; "Plans for Triangle Park Outlined," *PR*, Oct. 9, 1980; "Clearing the Way," *PR*, Oct. 22, 1980; "Ski Hut to be Constructed," *PR*, Jul. 11, 1981; "VIS Plants Flowers, Fixes Up Parks," *PR*, Jul. 23, 1981; "Essex County to Open Its 133rd Fair Tuesday," *PR*, Aug. 7, 1981; "Prisoners Help in Rescue of Man from Haystack," *ADE*, Aug. 12, 1981; "Many Are Involved in Ski Trail Project," *PR*, Jan. 28, 1982; "With a Little Help," *PR*, May 14, 1982; "Public Skating Rink in Village Eyed," *PR*, Oct. 13, 1982; "Stairway Added at Beaver Park," *PR*, Oct. 15, 1982; "Town Funds Sought for Ice Rink," *PR*, Dec. 13, 1982; "Cross Country Ski Building and Lighted Trails Dedicated," *ADE*, Dec. 22, 1982; "A Gift to the Skaters," *PR*, Feb. 14, 1983; "Field Work," *PR*, Jun. 2, 1983; "Clearing the Bases," *LPN*, Jun. 16, 1983; "Inmate Crews Improving Ski Trails," *PR*, Dec. 8, 1983; "Renovation Team," *PR*, Dec. 15, 1983; "VIS to Plant Cedar Hedge," *PR*, Dec. 12, 1984; "Inmates at State Prison Construct Furniture for Interpretive Center," *LPN*, Aug. 31, 1988; "New Playground," *ADE*, Oct. 11, 1988; "New Building Delivered to Base of Mt. Pisgah," *ADE*, Nov. 26, 1990; "Piecing Together the Bandshell," *ADE*, May 23, 1991; "A New Place to Skate," *ADE*, Jan. 9, 1992; "Floral Work Detail," *ADE*, Jun. 6, 1997; "One Step at a Time," *ADE*, Jun. 9, 1998.

58. "Streets Cleaned by Campmen for Carnival," *ADE*, Feb. 16, 1977; "The Icemen Make Their Deliveries," *PR*, Feb. 10, 1978; "Awaiting Construction," *PR*, Jan. 19, 1979; "Ice Palace in the Mud," *PR*, Jan. 19, 1980; "Ice Palace Takes Shape," *PR*, Jan. 28, 1981; "Saranac Lake Parade Highlights Ongoing 1981 Winter Carnival," *PR*, Feb. 14, 1981; "A Job Well Done," *PR*, Feb. 17, 1982; "Palace Beauty Warms Winter Chill," *ADE*, Feb. 10, 1983; "Camp Adirondack Carpenters," *ADE*, Dec. 11, 1984.

59. "Camp Adirondack—Where Realists Get Along," *LPN*, Apr. 13, 1977; "Camp Adirondack: Unique, but It Works," *ADE*, Nov. 8, 1977; "Camp Adirondack: Prisoners Like It Here," *ADE*, Apr. 2, 1979; "Camp Adirondack Inmates Enjoy Work Outdoors," *PR*, Feb. 26, 1980; "Helping Santa Helps Campmen," *ADE*, Dec. 24, 1980; "Inmates Spruce Up NCCC's Hubbard Hall," *PR*, Jul. 11, 1984; "Camp Crews Do Community Work," *LPN*, May 22, 1986; "Riding the Perimeter," *ADE*, Feb. 18, 1988; "Inmates at State Prison Construct Furniture for Interpretive Center," *LPN*, Aug. 31, 1988.

60. "Camp Adirondack—Where Realists Get Along," *LPN*, Apr. 13, 1977; "All Have Sinned," *ADE*, Jun. 13, 1977; "Newspaper Chronicles Prison Life," *LPN*, Sept. 29, 1977; "Camp Adirondack: Unique, but It Works," *ADE*, Nov. 8, 1977; "Campmen Provide Service to Area," *PR*, Nov. 11, 1977; "Camp Adirondack Hosts Open House," *PR*, Jun. 14, 1978; "Community Praises Camp Residents," *PR*, Sept. 2, 1978; "Racette Says Camp

Adirondack Is Still Helping People Get Well," *PR*, Mar. 2, 1979; "Camp Adirondack Inmates Enjoy Work Outdoors," *PR*, Feb. 26, 1980; "Camp Adirondack Commended," *ADE*, Jun. 11, 1981; "Field Work," *PR*, Jun. 2, 1983; "Handicapped Children Aided," *ADE*, Sept. 23, 1983; "Library Will Open Monday: Inmates Helped with Renovations," *ADE*, Oct. 5, 1984; "Keene Schools Thank Prison," *LPN*, Jul. 4, 1985; "Time Donated to Project," *ADE*, May 13, 1986; "Camp Crews Do Community Work," *LPN*, May 22, 1986.

61. "Troopers to Ensure Olympics Security," *PR*, Aug. 26, 1977; "Projects on Tap for Area," *PR*, Apr. 1, 1978; "Supplemental Budget Has Funds for Local Projects," *PR*, Sept. 30, 1978; "Camp Ad'k Getting $3.9 Million Redo," *ADE*, Oct. 5, 1978; "Camp Adirondack Getting Facelift," *ADE*, Jun. 8, 1979; "Olympic Quarters Called Unsafe," *PR*, Nov. 30, 1979; "Camp Adirondack Population to Swell," *ADE*, Mar. 7, 1980; "Prison Inmates, Staff Members Returning to Ray Brook Facility," *PR*, Mar. 10, 1980.

62. "Local Prison Plans to Expand," *ADE*, Nov. 12, 1980; "Camp Adirondack to Double Population," *LPN*, Dec. 11, 1980; "Area Residents Hired for Camp Adirondack," *PR*, Dec. 31, 1980; "Camp Adirondack to Become Medium Security," *LPN*, May 7, 1981; "Prisoners' Arrival Precedes Security," *ADE*, May 8, 1981; "Local Prison Gets State Overflow," *PR*, Jul. 3, 1981; "Camp Adirondack Becomes Medium Security," *LPN*, Aug. 13, 1981; "Camp Becomes Secure Prison," *ADE*, Oct. 15, 1981. SP80-016 and SP81-001, Camp Adirondack Records, Adirondack Park Agency Records Office, Ray Brook, New York.

63. "Prison in for $3 Million of Construction Work," *PR*, Dec. 21, 1982; "More Funds Targeted for North Country Prisons," *PR*, Feb. 1, 1983; "$1 Million Bid Let for New Cells at Camp Adirondack," *ADE*, Jun. 2, 1983; "Prison Change Fosters Renovations to Grounds," *PR*, Sept. 26, 1983; "$1.5 Million Building Bid at State Prison," *LPN*, Nov. 1, 1984; "Camp Adirondack to Install Wood-Burning Heat System," *LPN*, Jan. 23, 1986; "New Prison Shops Busy," *PR*, Dec. 15, 1986; "Budget Plan Has Plums, Prunes for North Country," *ADE*, Jan. 15, 1988; "Tendercare Tot Opening Gives Working Parents More Options," *ADE*, Oct. 23, 1990; "FCI Ray Brook, Camp Ad'k to Share Composting Facility," *ADE*, Dec. 11, 1995; "A View Inside the Prison Walls," *ADE*, Nov. 11, 1997; and, "Interfaith Chapel Dedicated at Adirondack Correctional," *ADE*, Sept. 20, 2002. SP 83-002, P83-049, P85-25-A, P93-224, P96-216, and P2005-133, Camp Adirondack Records, Adirondack Park Agency Records Office, Ray Brook, New York.

64. "Camp Adirondack Relocates in Ray Brook," *ADE*, Sept. 2, 1976; "State Prison Expansion Accounts for $11 Million," *PR*, Jan. 8, 1977; "Camp Population to Double," *LPN*, Jun. 16, 1977; "Camp Adirondack 'To Stay as It Is,'" *ADE*, Nov. 8, 1978; "Camp Adirondack Population to Swell," *ADE*, Mar. 7, 1980; "Prisoner Population to Increase," *ADE*, Aug. 28, 1980; "Camp Adirondack Due for Inmate Expansion," *PR*, Dec. 4, 1980; "Area Residents Hired for Camp Adirondack," *PR*, Dec. 31, 1980; "Camp Adirondack Inmate Population Expanded," *PR*, May 7, 1981; "State Prison Population at Record Level," *PR*, Jul. 1, 1981; "More Guards Headed for Camp Adirondack," *PR*, Sept. 19, 1981; "Officials, Businessmen Assess Impact of Prisons on Tri-Lakes," *ADE*, Jan. 26, 1982; "Prison in for $3 Million of Construction Work," *PR*, Dec. 21, 1982; "Prisons throughout Region Boost Economy with 2000 Employees," *PR*, Jan. 27, 1983; "$1 Million Bid Let for New Cells at Camp Adirondack," *ADE*, Jun. 2, 1983; "Massive Expansion to Cut Overcrowding," *ADE*, Oct. 31, 1983; "Cuomo Budget Includes More Monies for Area," *ADE*, Jan. 15, 1986; "N. Country Towns Compete for Prisons," *LPN*, Mar. 26, 1987; "Camp Ad'k Population Up," *ADE*, Sept. 10, 1987; "A View Inside the Prison Walls," *ADE*, Nov. 11, 1997; "Inmates Concerned," *ADE*, Oct. 11, 2001.

65. "Camp Adirondack Escapee Found in Wilmington Camp," *ADE*, Oct. 22, 1976; "'Camp' Escapee Captured with Shot in the Air," *PR*, Jul. 6, 1977; "Camp Adirondack Escapees Caught," *PR*, Aug. 23, 1977; "Campman Surrenders after Holding Couple," *ADE*, May 15, 1978; "Escaped Campman Found near Keene," *ADE*, Sept. 8, 1978; "Convicts Escape; Guards Protest," *ADE*, Jun. 9, 1980; "Escapees Nabbed in Keeseville," *PR*,

Jun. 17, 1980; "Ray Brook Escapee Nabbed," *PR*, Aug. 12, 1981; "Inmates Escape from Bus; Are Injured, Captured," *PR*, May 1, 1982; "Inmates Escape; Are Caught," *ADE*, May 3, 1982; "Escaped Convict Caught Saturday," *PR*, Jun. 2, 1982; "This Trooper's Bite Worse than His Bark," *PR*, Jul. 6, 1983.

66. "Inmate Slightly Hurt in Prison Fight," *ADE*, May 2, 1983; "Camp Adk. Inmate Cut, Battered," *ADE*, Jul. 26, 1983; "Inmate Convicted of Assaulting Local Guard," *ADE*, Dec. 17, 1991; "Prison Brawl Erupts over Television," *ADE*, Sept. 28, 1992; "Cook Clocked," *ADE*, Feb. 23, 1999; "Inmate Indicted for Assaulting Guards," *ADE*, Nov. 21, 2001.

67. "Emotions Running High at Ray Brook Walk-Out," *PR*, Apr. 21, 1979; "Guards Man Picket Lines in Strike's Sixth Day," *PR*, Apr. 24, 1979; "Ray Brook Strikers Direct Anger at Carey," *PR*, Apr. 24, 1979; "Prison Guards' Strike Enters Second Week," *LPN*, Apr. 26, 1979; "Guards Vow to Stay on Strike," *LPN*, May 3, 1979; "Accord Reached in Prison Guards Strike," *LPN*, May 10, 1979.

68. "Prison Guards Deplore Conditions," *ADE*, Jun. 9, 1980; "Guard Union Calls for Pro-Safety Picketing," *PR*, Jul. 18, 1984; "Prison Guards Protest Understaffing; AIDS a Concern," *LPN*, Mar. 26, 1987; "Ray Brook Prison Guards Upset," *ADE*, Feb. 4, 1988; "No More Cuts," *ADE*, Dec. 19, 1990; "Prison Bigs May Get Pink Slips," *ADE*, Feb. 26, 1991; "Corrections Dept. Not Ruling Out Further Cutbacks," *ADE*, Mar. 17–19, 1995; "Prison Protest," *ADE*, Apr. 7, 2000; "Closure of Special Units Protested," *ADE*, Oct. 10, 2002.

69. "Disease Kills Inmate, Another Hospitalized," *ADE*, May 11, 1983; "AIDS Kills Inmate at Clinton," *PR*, Oct. 22, 1983; "Prison Officials Detail Care of AIDS Patient," *PR*, Jul. 18, 1984; "The View from Inside the Wall Is Not So Pretty," *ADE*, Sept. 30, 1985; "AIDS-Stricken Inmate Remains Hopeful," *ADE*, Sept. 30, 1985; "Prison Guards Protest Understaffing; AIDS a Concern," *LPN*, Mar. 26, 1987.

70. "2 COs Suspended, Others Back on Job after Drug Testing," *ADE*, Nov. 30, 1994; "Tupper Lake C.O. Arrested for Sodomizing Inmate," *ADE*, Sept. 17, 1998; "Corrections Officers Illegally Swapped Shifts," *ADE*, Jul. 13, 2001; "Shift-Swapping Guards Plead Guilty," *ADE*, Jul. 25, 2001; "Shift-Swapping Guard Sentenced," *ADE*, Nov. 21–22, 2001; "Prison Guards Convicted of Misconduct," *LPN*, Dec. 29, 2001; "Former Ad'k Correctional Superintendent Pleads Guilty to Petit Larceny," *ADE*, Feb. 11, 2004.

71. "Former Cure Center Now a Prison," *PR*, Aug. 24, 1987; "TB Test Results Finished for NY Guards, Inmates," *ADE*, Feb. 11, 1992; "Debate Sparks Concern over Prison TB," *ADE*, May 24, 1996; "Second Inmate Tests Positive for TB at Adirondack Correctional Facility," *ADE*, Nov. 19, 1998; "Adirondack Correctional Facility Officials Search for Tuberculosis Carrier," *ADE*, Nov. 20, 1998.

72. "Prison Plans Open House," *LPN*, Dec. 4, 1980; "FCI Auxiliary to Meet Nov. 9," *LPN*, Nov. 4, 1982; "FCI Christmas Dinner," *LPN*, Dec. 18, 1982; "FCI Open House Features Visit by Sen. D'Amato," *ADE*, Oct. 24, 1984; "A Look Behind the Walls of Ray Brook's Federal Prison," *LPN*, Nov. 1, 1984; "From Inside the FCI," *LPN*, Nov. 8, 1984; "Life Flight Donation," *LPN*, Nov. 22, 1989; "FCI Ray Brook Sets Anniversary Open House," *PR*, Sept. 17, 1990; "FCI Recognizing Hispanic Month," *ADE*, Oct. 15, 1990; "Parents Come Despite War," *ADE*, Jan. 18, 1991; "Program to Honor Women's History," *ADE*, Mar. 8, 1991; "FCI Ray Brook Sets Open House," *ADE*, Aug. 25, 1991; "Gifts from FCI," *ADE*, Nov. 26, 1991; "Helping the Community," *ADE*, Jul. 7, 1992; "FCI Ray Brook Holds Open House," *PR*, Oct. 4, 1992.

73. "Prison Is Proud of Inmate Organization," *LPN*, Oct. 4, 1989; "FCI Inmates, Employees Raise Hurricane Funds," *PR*, Sept. 6, 1992; "Prisoners Help LP Elementary School Students Learn to Read," *LPN*, May 12, 1993; "Jukebox Plays On," *ADE*, Dec. 6, 1993; "Art Show Describes Hopes and Fears Trapped behind Bars," *LPN*, Nov. 16, 1994; "FCI Open House," *ADE*, Jan. 30, 1996; "FCI Inmates Giving to the Community with

Flower Donations," *ADE*, May 31, 1996; "A Field Trip to Prison," *PR*, Oct. 4, 1996; "'Kids at Risk' Program Continues with SLHS Students at Ray Brook," *ADE*, Feb. 18, 1997; "FCI Dares to Scare Kids off Drugs," *ADE*, Mar. 15, 1997; "Inmate Warns Kids of the Harsh Realities of Drug Use," *PR*, Apr. 24, 1997; "Sight-Seeing Tour through Hell," *PR*, Apr. 28, 1997; "FCI Ray Brook Hosting Fourth Volunteer Fair / Open House Today," *ADE*, Mar. 26, 1999; "Making a Difference," *ADE*, Apr. 7, 1999; "FCI Hosts Volunteer Open House Today," *ADE*, Mar. 24, 2000; "Daily Calendar: Today," *ADE*, May 4, 2001; "Ray Brook's Inmate Volunteer Corps Named Point of Light," *ADE*, Oct. 16, 2001; "Ray Brook Program Gets NEA grant," *LPN*, Aug. 30, 2002; "Corrections Staff Donates to Habitat," *ADE*, Nov. 4, 2002; "Ray Brook FCI to Hold Volunteer Fair and Open House Thursday," *ADE*, May 14, 2003; "FCI Citizen Program Awarded," *ADE*, Jun. 9, 2003; "FCI Ray Brook Makes Volunteers Feel Special," *ADE*, Jun. 24, 2003; "Kiwanis Contribution," *ADE*, Jul. 7, 2005.

74. "Inmates Work at FCI to Learn Skills, Decrease Tension," *LPN*, Jul. 28, 1983; "Prison Jobs: From Rewarding to Boring," *LPN*, Jul. 28, 1983; "From Inside the FCI," *LPN*, Nov. 8, 1984; "Federal Prison Ceases Money-Losing Industry," *PR*, Sept. 25, 1988; "Prison Study Shows Work and Vocational Training Helps Prisoners after Release," *LPN*, Jan. 8, 1992; "Inmates Make Soldiers' Pouches," *ADE*, Apr. 14, 2005.

75. "Population of Prison Slowly Grows," *PR*, Mar. 23, 1981; "Ray Brook Federal Prison Overcrowded," *ADE*, Jan. 19, 1983; "Prison Shows Changes from Olympic Village," *PR*, Oct. 25, 1984; "A Look Behind the Walls of Ray Brook's Federal Prison," *LPN*, Nov. 1, 1984; "More Inmates for Overcrowded Prison," *ADE*, Jul. 15, 1986; "Ray Brook Federal Prison Almost Double Capacity," *ADE*, Oct. 9, 1986; "FCI Ray Brook Doubles Capacity in First 10 Years," *LPN*, Oct. 3, 1990; "New FCI Warden Wants Inmates, Staff Involved in Community," *ADE*, Apr. 25, 2005; "FCI Lockdown Lifted, but Rescue Call Today Could Change That," *ADE*, Aug. 30, 2006. BOP Reports: Inmate Profile (Confined Population), as of Sept. 30, 1977; The Percentage of Population Confined to Institutions by Offense, FY '67 and FY '77; Bureau of Prisons Institution Based Population, 1971–1982; Federal Prisoners Confined, 1973–Present; Offenders Under Federal Supervision—1977; Relative Use of Probation, Fine and Other as a Percent of Total Convictions, FY 1966–1977; Use of Probation by Crime Type, FY 1977; Institution Based Population vs. Capacity, 1970–1990; Questions Posed Concerning Ray Brook Facility, McEwen Papers, MSS 25, Box 95–27: Folder—Winter Olympics Youth Correction Center, Ray Brook Memos, Info—Folder 95–27/2168.

76. "FCI Ray Brook: Federal Prison Employs 87 Guards, Others," *PR*, Jan. 27, 1983; "Ray Brook Federal Prison Almost Double Capacity," *ADE*, Oct. 9, 1986; "FCI Employees Complain about Prison Policies," *LPN*, May 7, 1987; "FCI Awaits Budget Talks," *ADE*, Sept. 5, 1990; "FCI Ray Brook Doubles Capacity in First 10 Years," *LPN*, Oct. 3, 1990; "New FCI Warden Wants Inmates, Staff Involved in Community," *ADE*, Apr. 25, 2005.

77. "Big Warehouse Planned for Federal Prison," *ADE*, Sept. 28, 1983; "A Look Behind the Walls of Ray Brook's Federal Prison," *LPN*, Nov. 1, 1984; "FCI Ray Brook Doubles Capacity in First 10 Years," *LPN*, Oct. 3, 1990; "Prisoner/Teacher Seeks Root of Problems," *PR*, Aug. 27, 1992; "FCI Ray Brook Holds Open House," *PR*, Oct. 4, 1992; "FCI Ray Brook, Camp Adk to Share Composting Facility," *ADE*, Dec. 11, 1995; "Ray Brook Program Gets NEA Grant," *LPN*, Aug. 30, 2002.

78. "A Look Behind the Walls of Ray Brook's Federal Prison," *LPN*, Nov. 1, 1984; "From Inside the FCI," *LPN*, Nov. 8, 1984; "Ray Brook Inmates Hold Commencement," *PR*, Jul. 12, 1985; "A Former Dropout, Inmate Goes to Head of His Class," *PR*, May 14, 1987; "Student Inmates Get No Vacation," *PR*, Aug. 27, 1992; "A Year after Cuts, Inmate Education at a Standstill," *ADE*, Sept. 13, 1996.

79. "Prisons throughout Region Boost Economy with 2000 Employees," *PR*, Jan. 27, 1983; "N. Country Towns Compete for Prisons," *LPN*, Mar. 26, 1987; "FCI Ray Brook Braces

for Federal Budget Cuts," *PR*, Sept. 27, 1990; "New FCI Warden Wants Inmates, Staff Involved in Community," *ADE*, Apr. 24, 2005.

80. "Massive Search Still on for Prison Escapee," *PR*, Sept. 30, 1982; "Police Tipped, Nab Escapee," *PR*, Oct. 2, 1982; "Ray Brook Escapees Nabbed at Indian Lake," *PR*, May 14, 1983; "Feds Foil Spy Prison Escape Plan," *PR*, Dec. 10, 1983; "FCI Inmate Attempts Escape," *ADE*, Jul. 14, 1988; "Ray Brook Inmate Failed in Escape Attempt," *PR*, Dec. 30, 1988; "Inmates Caught after High-Speed Chase," *ADE*, Jul. 22, 1996; "Feds Give More Details of Planned FCI Escape," *ADE*, Jan. 22, 1997; "FCI inmate Sentenced on Jail Break-Related Charges," *ADE*, Apr. 18, 1997; "Inmate Escapes from FCI Ray Brook," *ADE*, Aug. 24, 2003; "Prison releases details about inmate escape," *ADE*, Aug. 30–31, 2003.

81. "Prison Beefs Up Security after Protest by Inmates," *PR*, Oct. 27, 1983; "Fires Set by Inmates Prompt FCI Probe," *ADE*, Feb. 21, 1984; "Inmates Call Enterprise; Disgruntled Inmates Transferred," *ADE*, Mar. 1, 1984; "FCI Inmates Go on Food, Work Strike," *ADE*, Jul. 16, 1991; "FCI Official Says Sentencing Rules the Root of Inmate Work Stoppage," *ADE*, Jan. 13, 1993; "Still in Lockdown, FCI Officials Probe Cause of Inmate Work Strike," *ADE*, Jan. 11, 1994; "FCI Ray Brook Lockdown Gradually Coming to an End," *ADE*, Oct. 28, 1995.

82. "Former Ray Brook Inmates Indicted," *PR*, Feb. 25, 1985; "Suspect Isolated after Stabbing Incident at FCI," *ADE*, Mar. 31, 1986; "Ray Brook Prison Inmate Hangs Himself," *PR*, Feb. 27, 1987; "Inmate's Death Apparent Suicide," *ADE*, Dec. 23, 1987; "Inmate's Death Termed Suicide," *ADE*, Mar. 28, 1988; "FCI Removes 38 Prisoners following Racial Stabbing," *ADE*, May 2, 1990; "Inmate Stabbed at FCI over TV Room Mishap," *LPN*, Jun. 6, 1990; "Fire Streaks through FCI Facility, Causing Massive Damage," *ADE*, Jul. 2, 1992; "Inmate Held in Wake of FCI-Ray Brook Blaze," *PR*, Jul. 10, 1992; "80 Inmates Moved after FCI Brawls," *ADE*, Aug. 7, 1992; "One Suspect Identified in Assault on Guard," *ADE*, May 8, 1996; "Two Inmates at FCI Ray Brook Are Dead," *ADE*, Jun. 1, 1999; "FCI Incident; Another Inmate Stabbed at Ray Brook Facility," *ADE*, Jul. 3–4, 1999; "Federal Prison in Lockdown in Wake of Fight," *ADE*, Jul. 29, 2005; "Fight, Lockdown at FCI Ray Brook," *ADE*, Aug. 29, 2006; "Police and Fire Calls," *ADE*, Dec. 7, 2007.

83. "Rescue Calls," *ADE*, Apr. 21, 1981; "FCI Fire Damage Estimated at $15,000," *ADE*, Mar. 7, 1988; "FCI Ray Brook Gets a Bit of a Scare," *ADE*, May 14, 1999; "Powder Faces Quarantine," *ADE*, Nov. 3–4, 2001.

84. "Low Salaries Push Patrolmen to Look Elsewhere for Work," *PR*, Apr. 11, 1986; "Federal Prison Losing Guards to State," *ADE*, Apr. 22, 1987; "FCI Awaits Budget Talks," *ADE*, Sept. 5, 1990; "FCI Ray Brook Braces for Federal Budget Cuts," *PR*, Sept. 27, 1990; "Area FCI Workers Dodge Budget Axe," *ADE*, Oct. 1, 1990; "FCI Workers Feel Impact of Shutdown," *ADE*, Dec. 29, 1995.

85. "Ray Brook Workers Questioned; FBI Probing Wrongdoing at U.S. Prison," *ADE*, Mar. 19, 1982; "Prison Union Leader Fired; Claims Activism Cost Him," *ADE*, Apr. 30, 1987; "FCI Head Denies Mass Exodus to State Prisons," *ADE*, Apr. 30, 1987; "FCI Employees Complain about Prison Policies," *LPN*, May 7, 1987; "FCI Union President Answers Letters," *LPN*, Jun. 4, 1987; "Guard at FCI in Ray Brook Faces Extortion, Bribery Charges," *ADE*, Mar. 21, 1988; "Ex-FCI Ray Brook Garage Foreman Indicted for Theft," *ADE*, Dec. 22, 1988; "Former Worker at FCI Sentenced," *ADE*, May 10, 1989.

86. "Prison Jobs: From Rewarding to Boring," *LPN*, Jul. 28, 1983; "Ray Brook Inmates Hold Commencement," *PR*, Jul. 12, 1985; "Christmas Lonely, Depressing Time for Inmates," *PR*, Dec. 27, 1986; "A Former Dropout Inmate Goes to Head of His Class," *PR*, May 14, 1987; "Federal Prison Ceases Money-Losing Industry," *PR*, Sept. 25, 1988; "Prisoner/ Teacher Seeks Root of Problems," *PR*, Aug. 27, 1992; "A Field Trip to Prison," *PR*, Oct. 4, 1996; "Inmate Warns of the Harsh Realities of Drug Use," *PR*, Apr. 24, 1997.

87. "Fires Set by Inmates Prompt FCI Probe," *ADE*, Feb. 21, 1984; "Inmates Call Enterprise; Disgruntled Inmates Transferred," *ADE*, Mar. 1, 1984.

88. "Student Inmates Get No Vacation," *PR*, Aug. 27, 1992; "Prisoners Help LP Elementary School Students Learn to Read," *LPN*, May 12, 1993; "FCI Inmates Giving to the Community with Flower Donations," *ADE*, May 31, 1996; "A Field Trip to Prison," *PR*, Oct. 4, 1996; "Inmate Warns Kids of the Harsh Realities of Drug Use," *PR*, Apr. 24, 1997; "Tupper Lake Students May Visit Ray Brook Prison," *ADE*, Jun. 7, 2006.

89. "Residents Fearful with Inmate at Large," *PR*, Oct. 1, 1982; "Search Continues for Federal Prison Escapees," *PR*, May 7, 1983; "Origins of Sewer Gas Odor Still Remains a Mystery," *ADE*, Jul. 29, 1987; "After Ultimatum, Ray Brook Prison Solves Sewer Odor Problem," *PR*, Nov. 16, 1987; "School for Crime," *PR*, Sept. 11, 1988; "Nightmarish Odor on Pine Street Returns to Village," *PR*, May 18, 1989; "ESCAPED," *PR*, Jul. 21, 1996; "Sentence OK," *PR*, Jul. 15, 1998; "DEC Finds No Serious Problems at Prison Firing Ranges," *ADE*, Jan. 17, 2003; "DEC: No Lead Poisoning Problem near Firing Ranges," *LPN*, Jan. 24, 2003.

90. "FCI Expansion Faces Opposition," *LPN*, Apr. 21, 1983; "Funding for Prison Expansion Is Denied," *ADE*, May 16, 1983. David O'Brien Martin to Norman Carlson, Mar. 23, 1983; Concerned Citizens of Ray Brook, "A Sketch Map of the Area around the Indicated Location of a Proposed Satellite Camp at the Federal Correctional Institution, Ray Brook, New York, April 1983"; Sandra and W. Cole Campbell to David O'Brien Martin, May 3, 1983; David O'Brien Martin to Sandra and W. Cole Campbell, Jun. 7, 1983; eleven additional letters, David O'Brien Martin Papers, F. W. Crumb Library, Special Collections Department, State University of New York College at Potsdam, Potsdam, New York (hereafter Martin Papers), (SC-90001).

91. "Group Is Formed to Oppose New Prison Plan in Ray Brook," *PR*, Oct. 3, 1989; "Reasons for Fed Prison Camp Opposition Outlined," *ADE*, Oct. 1989; "Ray Brook Warden Defends Plan for New Prison," *PR*, Oct. 31, 1989; "N. Elba Board Says No to Prison Expansion," *ADE*, Nov. 15, 1989; "SL Board Supports Prison Expansion," *ADE*, Dec. 11, 1989; "Board Defers Prison Opinion," *ADE*, Dec. 27, 1989; "Saranac Lake May Hold Key to Prison Expansion," *PR*, Dec. 28, 1989; "Prison Expansion Needed for Health of Economy," *ADE*, Jan. 24, 1990; "Expand Local Jail Facility," *PR*, Jan. 28, 1990; "Ray Brook Citizens Air Concerns over FCI Prison Expansion," *LPN*, Jan. 31, 1990; "Prison Officials Withdraw Plans for Addition to FCI Ray Brook," *PR*, Mar. 21, 1990; "Martin, Residents Drive Off Prison Expansion," *LPN*, Mar. 28, 1990. Sandra and W. Cole Campbell to David O'Brien Martin, Jun. 14, 1989; Memo to file, Sept. 5–6, 1989; Owen Peacock to David O'Brien Martin, Oct. 28, 1989; FCI Ray Brook, N.Y.: Federal Prison Industries/UNICOR, Local Purchases from 10/01/88–11/10/89, Nov. 1989; Institution Fact Sheet, Nov. 1989; CCRB, petition, Nov. 1989; FCI Community Advisory Board, meeting minutes, Nov. 1, 1989; General Hospital of Saranac Lake, petition, Nov. 7, 1989; WNBZ, Lake Placid radio station, report on FCI decision, Mar. 23, 1990; CCRB to David O'Brien Martin, Mar. 26, 1990; twenty-eight additional letters, Martin Papers.

92. Jonathan Tetherly to Robert C. McEwen, May 22, 1978, McEwen Papers, Box 95–27, Folder: 1980 Winter Olympics, Ray Brook Correspondence, 1978.

Chapter Three: "Who Is Going to Live in Gabriels?"

1. DOCS, Application for Permit, (Albany: DOCS, May 1981); APA, "In the Matter of Proposed New Land Use in the Adirondack Park by the Department of Correctional Services: Camp Gabriels," Jan. 14, 1982, 147–48, Gabriels Records, SP 81-15.

2. "Gabriels Campus," *Post Script* (Paul Smith's College) 34, no. 3 (Nov. 4, 1981), 3, Joan Weill Adirondack Library, Historic Publications Collection, Paul Smith's College, Paul Smith's, New York.

3. "Rental at Ray Brook Asked; Gabriels Considered Too," *ADE,* May 20, 1981; "Hearing on Prison Draws Crowd," *PR,* Jul. 25, 1981; "Questions about Camp Gabriels," *ADE,* Aug. 21, 1981; "Changes Loom for Gabriels as Prison Nears," *PR,* May 20, 1982; "A Look Inside Minimum-Security Camp Gabriels," *ADE,* May 7, 1994. "Abstract of Title to Parts 77 and 78, Township 18, Town of Brighton, Franklin County"; Thomas Stainback to William Curran, Dec. 4, 1981, Gabriels Records.

4. "Rental at Ray Brook Asked; Gabriels Considered Too," *ADE,* May 20, 1981; "150-Inmate Prison Likely for Gabriels," *PR,* Jul. 10, 1981; "Prison Hearing Draws Hundreds," *ADE,* Jul. 24, 1981. DOCS, "1980–1985 Correctional Services Master Plan" (Albany, N.Y.: DOCS, Jan. 1981). Correctional Association of New York, "The Prison Population Explosion in New York State: A Study of Its Causes and Consequences with Recommendations for Change" (New York: Correctional Association of New York, March 1982).

5. State of New York, Hugh L. Carey, Governor, Press Release, Aug. 4, 1981, Gabriels Records.

6. State of New York, "The Bond Issue: Questions and Answers," 1981; New York State Senate, "More Prison Space for a Changing Decade," 1981, Gabriels Records.

7. APA, "Public Notice: Notice of Project Application Pending: Proposed Improvement to Camp Adirondack," Mar. 12, 1981, Gabriels Records.

8. "Rental at Ray Brook Asked; Gabriels Considered Too," *ADE,* May 20, 1981.

9. "Public Hearings Eyed on Gabriels Prison Plan," *PR,* Sept. 16, 1981.

10. "Senate Funds 'Camp Gabriels,'" *ADE,* Jul. 10, 1981.

11. "Prison Hearing Draws Hundreds," *ADE,* Jul. 24, 1981.

12. "Anti-Prison Group Started in Gabriels," *ADE,* Jul. 28, 1981; "And Against the Prison," *ADE,* Jul. 30, 1981; "Prison Protesters Voice Misgivings," *ADE,* Jul. 31, 1981; "Citizens Mount Campaign to Stop Gabriels Prison," *PR,* Aug. 1, 1981; "Reader Opposes Another Prison," *PR,* Aug. 5, 1981; "Group: State Using Double Standard with Prison," *PR,* Aug. 15, 1981.

13. Mildred Hooker Duncan to William Curran, Oct. 7, 1981; Barbara O'Neill to William Curran, Dec. 7, 1981; A. Moreland Lazier to Vincent Moore, Jan. 19, 1982; fifteen additional letters, Gabriels Records.

14. Diane Griffin to William Curran, Oct. 9, 1981; Drs. James and Lynn Kurtz to Vincent Moore, Nov. 9, 1981; Gulian Hook to Vincent Moore, Nov. 30, 1981; nine additional letters, Gabriels Records.

15. Joseph Reiners Sr. to Vincent Moore, Nov. 11, 1981; Mr. and Mrs. Max Klose to APA, Dec. 1981, Gabriels Records.

16. Lucien LeDuc to William Curran, Nov. 9, 1981; Joseph Reiners Jr. to Vincent Moore, Nov. 9, 1981; Stanley Tyler to William Curran, Nov. 11, 1981; Arthur Miller to William Curran, Nov. 13, 1981; John Murphy to William Curran, Nov. 13, 1981; Mr. and Mrs. Philip Weld to Vincent Moore, Nov. 14, 1981; Ernest Seifried to William Curran, Nov. 16, 1981; E. J. Lawless to William Curran, Nov. 16, 1981; Neil Suprenant to Vincent Moore, Dec. 3, 1981; "Anna" to Vincent Moore, Dec. 5, 1981; Thomas Sloan to Vincent Moore, Dec. 7, 1981; Mr. and Mrs. Max Klose to APA, Dec. 1981, Gabriels Records.

17. Catherine Mack to William Curran, Oct. 8, 1981; Mr. and Mrs. S. Leonard Kent to Vincent Moore, Nov. 9, 1981; Carol and James Mitchell to Vincent Moore, no date, Gabriels Records.

18. Sylvia Diller to Vincent Moore, Nov. 2, 1981; Donald Coogan, Jr. to William Curran, Nov. 30, 1981; Natalie LeDuc to William Curran, Dec. 1981; nine additional letters, Gabriels Records.

19. N.V.V.F. Munson to Vincent Moore, Nov. 4, 1981; Deborah Fletcher to APA, Dec. 8, 1981; Virginia West to Vincent Moore, Dec. 11, 1981; three additional letters, Gabriels Records.

20. Harrison Garrett to Vincent Moore, Nov. 4, 1981; Suzanne Snyder to William Curran, Dec. 5, 1981; Jean Garrison to Vincent Moore, Jan. 12, 1982; twenty-three additional letters, Gabriels Records.

21. Anonymous to APA, Aug. 29, 1981; Gulian Hook to Vincent Moore, Nov. 30, 1981; Beulah and George Biddlecombe to William Curran, Dec. 3, 1981, Gabriels Records.

22. Pauline Mayhew to William Curran, Oct. 7, 1981; Sandra Fisher to Vincent Moore, Nov. 13, 1981; Marian Rettger to Vincent Moore, Dec. 18, 1981; fifteen additional letters, Gabriels Records.

23. Joseph Reiners Jr. to Vincent Moore, Nov. 9, 1981; Nancy Crowley to William Curran, Dec. 5, 1981; Joyce Warner to William Curran, Dec. 14, 1981; nine additional letters, Gabriels Records.

24. Anonymous to APA, Aug. 29, 1981; "Baynon" to Vincent Moore, Oct. 8, 1981; Rosalind Baynon to Vincent Moore, Nov. 1, 1981; C. Minot Dole Jr. to Vincent Moore, Nov. 6, 1981; James Cameron to Vincent Moore, Nov. 7, 1981; Drs. James and Lynn Kurtz to Vincent Moore, Nov. 9, 1981; Beulah and George Biddlecombe to William Curran, Dec. 3, 1981; Judith Allen to APA, Dec. 10, 1981; Marian Rettger to Vincent Moore, Dec. 18, 1981; A. Moreland Lazier to Vincent Moore, Jan. 19, 1982; "Brandon" to Vincent Moore, no date, Gabriels Records.

25. "Group Opposes Proposed Prison," *ADE*, Aug. 11, 1981; "The Prison and the College," *ADE*, Aug. 26, 1981; "Camp Director Distressed," *ADE*, Aug. 31, 1981; "Prefers Status Quo," *ADE*, Sept. 9, 1981.

26. M. H. Duncan to William Curran, Oct. 7, 1981; Sandra Fisher to William Curran, Oct. 8, 1981; "Baynon" to Vincent Moore, Oct. 8, 1981; Donald Sweeney to APA, Oct. 9, 1981; D. Griffin to William Curran, Oct. 9, 1981; Justina Ortlieb to APA, Oct. 10, 1981; Harrison Garrett to Vincent Moore, Nov. 4, 1981; Marjorie Hull to Vincent Moore, Nov. 6, 1981; Arthur and Betty Staebell to Vincent Moore, Nov. 9, 1981; "Kents" to Vincent Moore, Nov. 9, 1981; Sandra Fisher to Vincent Moore, Nov. 13, 1981; Virginia Volkman to William Curran, Nov. 13, 1981; Marshall Peterson to Vincent Moore, Nov. 17, 1981; D. Coogan Jr. to William Curran, Nov. 30, 1981; Gulian Hook to Vincent Moore, Nov. 30, 1981; Patricia Castine to William Curran, Dec. 7, 1981; Jeffrey Wilkins to Vincent Moore, Dec. 11, 1981; Ernest Keet to William Curran, Dec. 12, 1981; Marian Rettger to Vincent Moore, Dec. 18, 1981; Mr. and Mrs. Max Klose to APA, Dec. 1981; Lee Robert to APA, Dec. 1981; "Brandon" to Vincent Moore, no date, Gabriels Records.

27. Catherine Mack to William Curran, Oct. 8, 1981; Marjorie Hull to Vincent Moore, Nov. 6, 1981; Jeffrey Wilkins to Vincent Moore, Dec. 11, 1981; twenty-four additional letters, Gabriels Records.

28. DOCS, "Answers to Interrogatories Posed by the Adirondack Park Agency in the Matter of Camp Gabriels" (Albany: DOCS, 1981), 5–7, 10–11; see major sections of interest: "Impacts and Benefits of Proposed Facility," no page numbers, "Demographic Characteristics," no page numbers, "Direct Economic Impact of Camp Gabriels Facility," no page numbers, "Taxation Impacts," no page numbers, Gabriels Records.

29. DOCS, "Answers to Interrogatories," see sections entitled "Adjoining and Nearby Land Uses," 52–53, "Sales Values and Turnover Rates," 53–55, "New Developments," 57–61, "Local Government Services," 16–18, "Service Impacts—Summary," n.p., Gabriels Records.

30. "Prison Hearing Draws Hundreds," *ADE*, Jul. 24, 1981.

31. "Senate Funds 'Camp Gabriels,'" *ADE*, Jul. 10, 1981.

32. "Public Hearing Set on OTB," *ADE*, Jul. 28, 1981.

33. Thomas Stainback to William Curran, Dec. 4, 1981, Gabriels Records.

34. "Public Hearing Set on OTB," *ADE*, Jul. 28, 1981; "Anti-Prison Feelings Unfounded," *PR*, Jul. 29, 1981; "For Prison," *ADE*, Jul. 30, 1981; "Supports Gabriels Prison," *PR*, Jul. 31, 1981; "Pro-Prison, *ADE*, Aug. 4, 1981; "Gabriels Prison, More Facts Needed,"

ADE, Sept. 3, 1981; "College in Jeopardy," *ADE,* Sept. 4, 1981; "Brighton Seeks Prison Study," *ADE,* Dec. 11, 1981. Frederick and Eleanor Klein to William Curran, Nov. 11, 1981, Gabriels Records.

35. "For Prison," *ADE,* Jul. 30, 1981; "Speaking Out for the Gabriels Prison," *ADE,* Jul. 31, 1981; "Pro-Prison," *ADE,* Aug. 4, 1981; "College in Jeopardy," *ADE,* Sept. 4, 1981; "In Favor of Prison," *ADE,* Sept. 4, 1981.

36. "For Prison," *ADE,* Jul. 30, 1981; "Speaking Out for the Gabriels Prison," *ADE,* Jul. 31, 1981; "College in Jeopardy," *ADE,* Sept. 4, 1981; "Prison Ground Sanctified," *ADE,* Sept. 22, 1981. Stanley Ingison to William Curran, Nov. 12, 1981, Gabriels Records.

37. "Anti-Prison Group Started in Gabriels," *ADE,* Jul. 28, 1981; "Another Group Plans Prison Opposition," *ADE,* Aug. 24, 1981; "State Moving Fast on Gabriels Prison," *ADE,* Oct. 1, 1981. Thomas A. Coughlin to Robert Flacke, Sept. 10, 1981; DOCS, Application for Permit (DOCS: Albany, May 1981), Gabriels Records.

38. Ramon Rodriguez to Vincent Moore, Oct. 15, 1981, Gabriels Records.

39. "Corrections Offers Land to DEC," *ADE,* Nov. 24, 1981; "State Prisons Agency Changes Land-Buy Plan," *PR,* Jan. 6, 1982. DOCS, Environmental Assessment Form (EAF), Sept. 29, 1981, Attachment B, "Site Description: Existing Conditions," 2, Attachment C, "Impact on Open Space and Recreation", Attachment G, "Energy Use: Electricity & Heating", Attachment I, "Impact on Visual Resources", Attachment K, "Community Issues," 6; George Glassanos to Vincent Moore, Oct. 13, 1981; Ramon Rodriguez to William Curran, Oct. 16, 1981; George Glassanos to John Banta, Nov. 6, 1981; DOCS, "Department of Correctional Services Recommendation for Classification of Gabriels Acquisition," Dec. 16, 1981, Gabriels Records.

40. DOCS, EAF, Sept. 29, 1981, Attachment K, "Community Issues," 9–10, Gabriels Records.

41. "Anti-Prison Group Started in Gabriels," *ADE,* Jul. 28, 1981; "Public Hearings Eyed on Gabriels Prison Plan," *PR,* Sept. 16, 1981. Robert Glennon to Anthony Conde, Jul. 23, 1981, Gabriels Records.

42. "Public Hearings Eyed on Gabriels Prison Plan," *PR,* Sept. 16, 1981; "Hearings on Gabriels Prison Set," *PR,* Sept. 23, 1981; "Notice Is Filed; Prison Set for Gabriels Site," *PR,* Oct. 2, 1981. Robert Glennon to J. Reiners Jr., Aug. 6, 1981; D. Peterson and L. LeDuc to Vincent Moore, Sept. 15, 1981; Vincent Moore to D. Peterson and L. LeDuc, Sept. 28, 1981, Gabriels Records.

43. "Hearing on Gabriels Prison Set," *PR,* Sept. 23, 1981; "Notice Is Filed; Prison Set for Gabriels Site," *PR,* Oct. 2, 1981; "Landfill Use Sought for Proposed Prison," *ADE,* Oct. 9, 1981; "APA's Moore to Schedule Prison Hearings," *PR,* Oct. 19, 1981. Vincent Moore to George Glassanos, Oct. 1, 1981; William Curran to APA Members and Designees, Oct. 8, 1981; APA, Notice of Agency Intent to Proceed to Public Hearing, Oct. 20, 1981; Vincent Moore to Thomas Coughlin, Oct. 21, 1981; Robert Glennon to George Glassanos, Oct. 28, 1981; APA, Notice, "To Owners of Land Near the 'Camp Gabriels' Site,'" Oct. 29, 1981; APA, "Notice of Public Hearings on Proposed 'Camp Gabriels' Project and on Related Amendments to the Master Plan for the Management of State Lands Pursuant to Sections 814 and 816 of the Adirondack Park Agency Act," Oct. 29, 1981; APA, "Notice of State Agency Intent Pending Proposed Acquisition and Improvements to Camp Gabriels, Adirondack Park Agency Project Number SP 81–15," no date; Vincent Moore to George Glassanos and William Kissel, Nov. 2, 1981, Gabriels Records.

44. "Prison Opposition Voiced," *ADE,* Nov. 17, 1981; "Public Hearing Focuses on Prison at Gabriels," *PR,* Nov. 18, 1981; "Prison for Gabriels Debated at Meeting," *ADE,* Dec. 15, 1981. APA, "In the Matter of the Proposal by the New York State Department of Correctional Services, to Undertake New Land Use and Development in the Adirondack Park: Camp Gabriels," Transcript of Proceedings (hereafter APA Hearing), Nov. 16, 1981, Dec. 14, 1981, Gabriels Records.

45. APA Hearing: Testimony of James Hill and Betty Ann Hughes, Jan. 5, 1982, 2–4, 2–8; Testimony of Michael DiNunzio, Jan. 15, 1982, 171–74, Gabriels Records.

46. APA Hearing: Testimony of William Curran, Jan. 5, 1982, 12–13; APA, Jan. 5, 1982, 102–104, Jan. 13, 1982, 60–63, 102–104, 125–26, Gabriels Records.

47. APA Hearing: Statement of Gary Randorf, Jan. 5, 1982, 209–14; Statement of Leroy Roberts, Jan. 13, 1982, 27–29; Statement of Ray Fadden, Jan. 15, 1982, 136–37; Statement of Diane Peterson, Jan. 15, 1982, 195–205; APA, Jan. 13, 1982, 199–201, Jan. 14, 1982, 138–41, 147–48, 236–37, 251–54, 288–89, Gabriels Records.

48. APA Hearing: Statement of Ramon Rodriguez, Nov. 16, 1981, 31–32; Statement of George Glassanos, Jan. 5, 1982, 40–41; Statement of Jeff Buck, Jan. 13, 1982, 161–63, 191; APA, Dec. 14, 1981, 47–49, 66–68, Gabriels Records.

49. APA Hearing: on Visual impact, Jan. 13, 1982, 60–67, 102–104, 125–26, Jan. 14, 1982, 251–54; on Forest Preserve, Jan. 5, 1982, 38–42; on Prison labor, Jan. 5, 1982, 173–75, Jan. 13, 1982, 56–57, Jan. 14, 1982, 218, 220, Gabriels Records.

50. "Prison Bond Wins in Photo Finish," *PR*, Nov. 5, 1981; "'Alliance' Cited in Bond Issue Win," *PR*, Nov. 5, 1981; "New York Expects to Expand Prisons Despite Bond Vote," *NYT*, Nov. 28, 1981; "Carey Aims to Add Housing in Region," *PR*, Jan. 20, 1982; "New Prison Eyed for Franklin County Site," *PR*, Jan. 28, 1982; "Clinton Facility a Major Force in Economy," *PR*, Jan. 28, 1982.

51. State of New York, Supreme Court, County of Franklin, *Citizens against More Prisons in the Adirondacks (CAMPA), the St. Regis Property Owners Association, Lucien LeDuc and Natalie LeDuc, Kirk Peterson and Diane Peterson, Floyd Hogan and Arlene Hogan, Petitioners, against, New York State Department of Correctional Services, Thomas A. Coughlin, III, Commissioner of the New York State Department of Correctional Services, Respondents,* Notice of Petition, Jan. 26, 1982; William Kissel to Robert Glennon, Jan. 28, 1982, Gabriels Records.

52. "Gabriels Prison on APA Agenda," *ADE*, Mar. 15, 1982; "More Evidence Wanted in Camp Gabriels Case," *PR*, Mar. 22, 1982; "APA Chief: Adirondacks May be 'Penal Colony,'" *ADE*, Mar. 25, 1982; "APA Chief Warns against Prison," *PR*, Mar. 25, 1982; "APA Committee Fails to Reach Decision on Camp Gabriels Plan," *PR*, Mar. 26, 1982.

53. "No to Gabriels Prison—APA," *PR*, Mar. 27, 1982; "State Pushes Ahead on Camp Gabriels," *LPN*, Apr. 8, 1982. "Gabriels Agreement Signed," *Post Script* 34, no. 9 (Apr. 23, 1982), 1, 7. "Proposal by the New York State Department of Correctional Services to Undertake New Land Use and Development in the Adirondack Park: Camp Gabriels: SP 81–15," APA Staff Recommendation, Mar. 25, 1982; APA, minutes, Mar. 26, 1982; "News from the NYS Adirondack Park Agency," Mar. 29, 1982, Gabriels Records.

54. "Camp Gabriels Closer to Reality," *PR*, Apr. 17, 1982; "Coughlin Sees Prisons as Big Employer in Region," *PR*, Apr. 29, 1982; "Gabriels Contract Signed," *ADE*, Jun. 15, 1982; "State to File Impact Statement on Prison," *PR*, Jun. 17, 1982; "Renovation to Start on Gabriels Camp Site," *ADE*, Jul. 8, 1982; "Camp Gabriels May Be Operating by November," *PR*, Jul. 8, 1982. "News from the NYS Adirondack Park Agency," Apr. 26, 1982, Gabriels Records.

55. "State to File Impact Statement on Prison," *PR*, Jun. 17, 1982; "Prison Opponents Riled at Not Receiving Report," *PR*, Aug. 27, 1982; "APA, Prison Opponents File Protest Statements," *PR*, Aug. 28, 1982. DOCS, "Camp Gabriels Correctional Facility: Draft Environmental Impact Statement," McKeown and Franz, Inc., Environmental Consultants, and the Ehrenkrantz Group, P.C., Architects and Criminal Justice Planners (Albany: DOCS, May 1982); DOCS, "Camp Gabriels Correctional Facility: Final Environmental Impact Statement," McKeown and Franz, Inc., Environmental Consultants, and the Ehrenkrantz Group, P.C., Architects and Criminal Justice Planners (Albany: DOCS, Dec. 1982), Gabriels Records.

56. "Camp Gabriels May Be Operating by November," *PR*, Jul. 8, 1982; "Renovation to

Start on Gabriels Camp Site," *ADE*, Jul. 8, 1982; "Report Says Camp Gabriels to Help with Overcrowding," *ADE*, Jul. 21, 1982; "Gabriels Opens Monday, Warden Named," *PR*, Aug. 28, 1982; "Camp Gabriels Opens," *ADE*, Aug. 30, 1982. "Gabriels Agreement Signed," *Post Script*. DOCS, "Final Environmental Impact Statement: Camp Gabriels Correctional Facility," Dec. 1982, Gabriels Records.

57. "Gabriels Residents Express Prison Concerns," *ADE*, Dec. 2, 1982; "Gabriels Convict Walks out of Jail," *ADE*, Mar. 14, 1983; "Escapee's Girlfriend Arrested for Driving Him out of Area," *ADE*, Mar. 15, 1983; "Study Details Prison Escape Data," *PR*, May 23, 1983; "Police Capture Camp Gabriels Escapee," *ADE*, Apr. 29, 1985; "Search for Camp Gabriels Escapee Fruitless," *ADE*, Oct. 21, 1986; "Prisoner Stayed Nearby," *ADE*, Oct. 28, 1986; "Gabriels Inmate Is Found after Short Search," *ADE*, May 17, 1989; "Ingolia Gets Probation in Camp Gabriels Case," *ADE*, Sept. 14, 1994; "Gabriels-Area Officials React to Escape," *ADE*, Sept. 6, 1995; "The Bids for Freedom by Inmates," *ADE*, Sept. 6, 1995.

58. "Final Environmental Impact Statement: Camp Gabriels Correctional Facility," Parts 2–4, 11, 16, Gabriels Records.

59. "Camp Gabriels Opens," *ADE*, Aug. 30, 1982; "Inmate Labor at Camp Gabriels Keeps Construction Costs Down," *PR*, Mar. 1, 1983; "Camp Gabriels Prisoners Bail Out Matty League Team," *ADE*, Jun. 24, 1983; "Firefighters Control 10-Acre Blaze near Derrick," *ADE*, Aug. 14, 1985; "'Toys' Christmas Project Gets Underway," *ADE*, Oct. 18, 1985; "Inmates Make Maple Syrup," *PR*, Mar. 20, 1989; "Thanking the Prison Leaders," *ADE*, Nov. 25, 1991; "A Look inside Minimum-Security Camp Gabriels," *ADE*, May 7, 1994; "Work Crews Involved in Array of Projects," *ADE*, Summer 1996; "Correctional Officers Cite Flexibility of Less-Restrictive Facility," *ADE*, Summer 1996; "Urban Inmates Find Work in the Wild," *ADE*, Feb. 9, 2007.

60. "Massive Sled Dog Effort Underway; Area Crews Pitch in to Move Snow to Track," *ADE*, Jan. 21, 1983; "S.L. Rescue," *ADE*, Jun. 12, 1984; "Killian's Korner: Bird-Hunting Prospects Excellent," *PR*, Sept. 28, 1984; "Camaraderie Warms Icy Work of Building Palace," *PR*, Jan. 27, 1986; "Pheasants Growing up behind Prison Walls," *PR*, Jun. 18, 1986; "Big Tupper Gets Prison Help," *ADE*, Jun. 27, 1986; "Happy Trails," *ADE*, Feb. 2, 1988; "Inmate Cuts Off His Arm," *ADE*, Oct. 27, 1988; "Getting Ready for the Big Day," *ADE*, Jul. 17, 1991; "Prisoners Do the Brunt of the Ice Palace Work," *LPN*, Feb. 12, 1992; "A Look inside Minimum-Security Camp Gabriels," *ADE*, May 7, 1994; "Prison Crew Violates Tree-Cutting Policies," *ADE*, Sept. 11, 1995; "Work Crews Involved in Array of Projects," *ADE*, Summer 1996; "Correctional Officers Cite Flexibility of Less-Restrictive Facility," *ADE*, Summer 1996; "Urban Inmates Find Work in the Wild," *ADE*, Feb. 9, 2007. L. LeDuc to Edward Lynch, Apr. 25, 1983; George Glassanos to Paul Herrmann, Jul. 12, 1983; Vincent Moore to L. LeDuc, Sept. 14, 1983; three additional letters, Gabriels Records.

61. "Camaraderie Warms Icy Work of Building Palace," *PR*, Jan. 27, 1986; "Pheasants Growing up behind Prison Walls," *PR*, Jun. 18, 1986; "Prison's Ice Palace Workers Aspire to Get Degrees, Jobs," *ADE*, Feb. 9, 1990; "Prisoners Do the Brunt of the Ice Palace Work," *LPN*, Feb. 12, 1992; "One Step Closer to Freedom," *ADE*, Summer 1996; "Work Crews Involved in Array of Projects," *ADE*, Summer 1996; "Correctional Officers Cite Flexibility of Less-Restrictive Facility," *ADE*, Summer 1996; "Urban Inmates Find Work in the Wild," *ADE*, Feb. 9, 2007.

62. "Camp Gabriels to Close within a Year," *ADE*, Jan. 14, 2008; "Camp Gabriels Employees Speak Out about Prison Closing," *PR*, Jan. 16, 2008; "Town Assesses Impact of Prison Closure," *PR*, Jan. 22, 2008; "Rallying to Stop Prison's Closure," *ADE*, Jan. 25, 2008; "Prison-Closing Plan Gets Public Hearing," *PR*, Feb. 1, 2008; "Chamber: Closing Camp Gabriels Would Cost Local Economy $37M/Year," *ADE*, Feb. 1, 2008; "Inmates Reflect on What May Be Camp Gabriels' Last Ice Palace Effort," *ADE*, Feb. 1, 2008; "Attempt to Save Camp Gabriels Fails," *PR*, Apr. 2, 2009; "Camp Gabriels to Close July 1," *PR*, Apr. 15,

2009; "No Bids for Camp Gabriels," *PR*, Nov. 18, 2010; "Land Use Issues Arise at Camp Gabriels," *PR*, Jan. 11, 2011; "Camp Gabriels Purchase Approved," *PR*, Mar. 23, 2014; "Camp Hamachane Emerges from Camp Gabriels," *PR*, Apr. 3, 2014; "Minimum 2-Year Wait Likely before any Camp Gabriels Sale," *ADE*, Mar. 23, 2018. DOCS, "DOCS Fact Sheet: Prison Closure," (Albany: DOCS, Jan. 2008), 1–2; "New York to Close Correctional Facilities as Part of Continuing Effort to Right-Size State Prison System," (Albany: DOCS, Jan. 11, 2008); Governor Eliot Spitzer, "2007 Report to the People of New York State" (Albany: Office of the Governor, Jan. 9, 2008), 43–46.

Chapter Four: "A Poor Choice"

1. Lawrence Gooley, *Out of the Darkness: In Memory of Lyon Mountain's Iron Men* (Peru, N.Y.: Bloated Toe Publishing, 2005).
2. "Iron Mining Flourished in Area as Early as 1798," *PR*, Jul. 7, 1964; "Republic Steel Closing Lyon Mt. Mine June 1," *PR*, Apr. 25, 1967; "Lyon Mountain . . . Proud Past Recalled," *PR*, Dec. 4, 1971; "Only Massive Tailings Pile Hints of Once Bustling Mine," *PR*, Sept. 18, 1988. Lawrence Gooley, *Lyon Mountain: The Tragedy of a Mining Town* (Peru, N.Y.: Bloated Toe Publishing, 2004), 1–4.
3. "Republic Steel Closing Lyon Mt. Mine June 1," *PR*, Apr. 25, 1967; "Lyon Mountain . . . Proud Past Recalled," *PR*, Dec. 4, 1971; "Only Massive Tailings Pile Hints of Once Bustling Mine," *PR*, Sept. 18, 1988. Gooley, *Lyon Mountain*, 4–7.
4. "Republic Steel Closing Lyon Mt. Mine June 1," *PR*, Apr. 25, 1967; "Lyon Mountain . . . Proud Past Recalled," *PR*, Dec. 4, 1971; "Only Massive Tailings Pile Hints of Once Bustling Mine," *PR*, Sept. 18, 1988. Gooley, *Lyon Mountain*, 7–33.
5. "Republic Steel Closing Lyon Mt. Mine June 1," *PR*, Apr. 25, 1967; "Lyon Mountain . . . Proud Past Recalled," *PR*, Dec. 4, 1971; "Only Massive Tailings Pile Hints of Once Bustling Mine," *PR*, Sept. 18, 1988. Gooley, *Lyon Mountain*, 34–41.
6. "Republic Steel Closing Lyon Mt. Mine June 1," *PR*, Apr. 25, 1967; "Lyon Mountain . . . Proud Past Recalled," *PR*, Dec. 4, 1971; "Only Massive Tailings Pile Hints of Once Bustling Mine," *PR*, Sept. 18, 1988. Gooley, *Lyon Mountain*, 41–75; Joseph R. Linney, *A History of the Chateaugay Ore and Iron Company* (Albany: Delaware and Hudson Railroad, 1934); Joseph R. Linney, *The Touch of Human Hands* (Pittsburgh: Dorrance Publishing, 1947).
7. "Republic Steel Now Operating Lyon Mt. Mines," *The North Countryman* (hereafter *NC*), Aug. 3, 1939; "Republic Steel Leases Mines at Lyon Mountain," *Chateaugay Record* (hereafter *CR*), Aug. 4, 1939; "Lyon Mountain Feeling Effects of New Activities," *CR*, Sept. 1, 1939; "Lyon Mountain Booms as Mines Reopen with 500 Workers; New Plant at Port Henry Will Care for Lyon Mountain Ore," *CR*, Dec. 1, 1939.
8. "H. Dumont Dies from Explosion in Lyon Mt. Mine," *CR*, Oct. 17, 1941; "F.L. Woodward Is Injured in Mine Accident; Lyon Mountain Man Brought to Local Hospital after Mishap on Tuesday," *CR*, Jul. 7, 1944; "Ralph Porter Killed in Mining Mishap at Lyon Mountain," *CR*, Jun. 1, 1951; "Republic Steel Foremen Hurt in Mine," *PR*, Dec. 30, 1955; "Lyon Mountain Miner Killed in 200-Foot Plunge," *PR*, Jan. 23, 1957; "Mine Explosion in Lyon Mountain," *ADE*, Apr. 22, 1960; "Ellenburg Man Killed in Mine Mishap," *NC*, Oct. 20, 1966; "Under Lyon Mountain, Deadly Accidents 'Used to Happen All the Time,'" *ADE*, Jan. 26, 2006. Gooley, *Lyon Mountain*, chap. 5.
9. "650 Lyon Mt. Miners Laid Off Tomorrow," *ADE*, Apr. 3, 1952; "Republic Steel Corp. Mine Lays Off 177 Men," *PR*, Mar. 13, 1954; "New Work Cut Affects 700 Republic Steel Employees," *PR*, Nov. 16, 1957; "Strike Spawns Unemployment in Areas of U.S.; Iron Mines Quiet in Adirondacks," *ADE*, Jul. 16, 1959; "Republic Steel Closes at Lyon Mt.," *ADE,* Nov. 11, 1960; "Mine Activity Still Down," *PR*, Jun. 15, 1961; "Iron Ore Mine to Close Again," *PR*, Aug. 29, 1962; "Lyon Mountain Miners Vote to Take Bonus Pay Cut;

230 to Return to Jobs," *PR*, Jan. 3, 1963; "Republic to Close Lyon Mt. Mines," *ADE*, Aug. 1965.

10. "Republic Steel Plans Expansion," *CR*, May 2, 1947; "Employment at Pre-War Figure, Lyon Mountain Mine Official Says," *PR*, Jun. 15, 1954; "Republic Steel Wage Payments Rise in '55," *PR*, Jan. 31, 1956; "Republic Sinking Shaft at Lyon Mountain," *PR*, Jan. 1960; "$1 Million Investment Doesn't Tell Whole Story," *PR*, Jun. 5, 1962.

11. "Republic Steel Closing Lyon Mt. Mine June 1," *PR*, Apr. 25, 1967; "D&H May Remove Track on Part of Lyon Mt. Line," *PR*, Apr. 26, 1967; "Clinton Eyes Washington for Aid for Lyon Mountain," *PR*, Apr. 28, 1967; "Lyon Mountain Mine Closing Traps Men Too Young to Retire, Too Old to Move," *ADE*, Apr. 28, 1967; "County to Seek Federal Aid for Development at Lyon Mt.," *PR*, May 11, 1967; "New Mineral Resource Survey in 5 County Adirondack Region," *CR*, May 1967; "Steel Company Seeks to Help County Find Use for Mine Land," *PR*, May 1967; "EDA Agent Opening Study of Lyon Mt.," *PR*, May 1967; "Act Quickly on Lyon Mountain Issue, Federal Agent Advises Clinton Leaders," *PR*, May 1967; "King Seeks Solution to Lyon Mt. Closing," *PR*, May 26, 1967; "EDA Official Says: Federal Aid Requires Community Leadership," *PR*, Jun. 5, 1967; "Republic Steel Workers Go on 'Permanent Layoff,'" *PR*, Jul. 1, 1967.

12. Town of Dannemora, Town Board Meeting Minutes, Feb. 17, 1955, 114, Oct. 1, 1955, 117, Nov. 10, 1955, 117–18, Dec. 15, 1955, 118–19, Apr. 10, 1956, 158, in Dannemora, N.Y. (Town) Records, 1869–1995, Microfilm: Roll 3: Town Board Minutes, New York State Archives, Albany, New York (hereafter Dannemora Records).

13. "Lyon Mountain Mine Closing Traps Men Too Young to Retire, Too Old to Move," *ADE*, Apr. 28, 1967; "County to Seek Federal Aid for Development at Lyon Mt.," *PR*, May 11, 1967; "Act Quickly on Lyon Mountain Issue, Federal Agent Advises Clinton Leaders," *PR*, May 1967; "EDA Official Says: Federal Aid Requires Community Leadership," *PR*, Jun. 5, 1967; "Lyon Mountain Committee Organized," *PR*, Jun. 28, 1967; "Lyon Mountain Awaits US Land Plan," *PR*, Jan. 31, 1969. Dannemora Town Board Minutes, Jul. 11, 1985, 390, Dannemora Records.

14. "ETV Ready after 9 Years of Battling Man, Nature," *PR*, Feb. 9, 1977. Dannemora Town Board Minutes, Feb. 5, 1976, 121, May 6, 1976, 4, Dannemora Records.

15. "Leases Dominate Town Meeting," *PR*, May 8, 1978; "Dannemoran Cites Waste, Conflict in Town Project," *PR*, Apr. 25, 1984; "Direction from Voters Seen in Referendum on Town's Future," *PR*, Aug. 13, 1984. Dannemora Town Board Minutes, Feb. 16, 1984, 343, Apr. 5, 1984, 346, May 10, 1984, 350, Aug. 2, 1984, 360, Feb. 20, 1986, 402, Jul. 23, 1987, 436, Jul. 27, 1988, 460, May 23, 1990, 513–14, Jul. 24, 1991, 563, Dannemora Records.

16. DOCS, Draft Environmental Impact Statement (hereafter Lyon Mountain DEIS), Lyon Mountain Correctional Facility, Prepared by McKeown and Franz, Inc., Environmental Consultants (Albany: DOCS, Dec. 1983), 2-1, 2-2, 3-5, 3-8, 5-12, 5-15, 5-16, 5-17, 5-18, in SP 83-13 / W83-25, Lyon Mountain Prison Records, Adirondack Park Agency Records Office, Ray Brook, New York (hereafter Lyon Mountain Records).

17. Ibid., 5–18.

18. "Leases Dominate Town Meeting," *PR*, May 8, 1978; "Lyon Mountain Mines Eyed for Storage; Bonanza Predicted in Oil Scheme," *PR*, May 18, 1978; "Speculative Idea Brings Hope," *PR*, May 22, 1978; "Lyon Mountain Water Panel Quits," *PR*, Nov. 17, 1978.

19. "Dannemora Board Pondering Legality of Certain Water Sales," *PR*, Jul. 13, 1974. Dannemora Town Board Minutes, Jan. 4, 1973, 19, Feb. 7, 1974, 49–50, Jan. 8, 1976, Jan. 17, 1977, Dannemora Records.

20. "Dannemora Board Pondering Legality of Certain Water Sales," *PR*, Jul. 31, 1974; "Dannemora to Sell to Carters," *PR*, Jun. 8, 1976; "Sand, Stone Profits Insufficient for Town," *PR*, Jan. 24, 1977; "Fire Contract Flap Called Hazard," *PR*, Jan. 28, 1978; "Leases Dominate Town Meeting," *PR*, May 8, 1978; "Cycle Traffic Has Dannemora Fretting," *PR*, Apr. 8, 1983. Dannemora Town Board Minutes, Jan. 4, 1973, 7, 19, Feb. 6,

1975, 76, May 1, 1975, 84, May 15, 1975, 87, Jan. 8, 1976, 119, Jan. 17, 1977, n.p., Aug. 7, 1980, 195, Dannemora Records.

21. Lyon Mountain DEIS, 3-1 to 3-5 Lyon Mountain Records. Dannemora Town Board Minutes, Oct. 1, 1981, 245, Feb. 18, 1982, 263, Dannemora Records.

22. "Lyon Mountain School Eyed as Prison," *PR*, Jun. 3, 1983; "NACS Officials Elated with News State Looking at Lyon Mt. School," *PR*, Jun. 4, 1983; "Lyon Mt. School to be State Prison," *PR*, Jun. 25, 1983; "Lyon Mountain Prison to Employ 110 Workers," *PR*, Jul. 21, 1983. Theodore Ruzow to Thomas Coughlin, Jun. 6, 1983; Thomas Coughlin to Theodore Ruzow, Jul. 6, 1983; Lyon Mountain DEIS, 2-1 to 2-6, 3-1 to 3-22, Lyon Mountain Records.

23. "Former Altona School to Be Prison Site," *PR*, Jan. 21, 1983; "Altona Anticipates Prison-Related Boom," *PR*, Jan. 22, 1983; "Planned Prison, Grants Gladden Residents Of Altona," *PR*, Jan. 27, 1983; "School-Turned-Prison to Hire 270 Workers," *PR*, Feb. 10, 1983; "Union Protests Use of Convict Labor at Altona," *PR*, Mar. 29, 1983; "School District Hosts Session on Building to become Prison," *PR*, Apr. 27, 1983; "Voters Lopsidedly OK Sale of Altona School," *PR*, Apr. 28, 1983; "Altona Prison to Provide Local Bonanza," *PR*, May 19, 1983; "Altona Businessman Watches Coming of Prison," *PR*, May 25, 1983; "Lyon Mountain School Eyed as Prison," *PR*, Jun. 3, 1983; "NACS Officials Elated with News State Looking at Lyon Mt. School," *PR*, Jun. 4, 1983; "Local Prison Celebrates 25th Anniversary," *PR*, Aug. 24, 2008. Roger Klingman, "THEN . . . and NOW: 'Not In My Backyard, You Don't,'" *Empire State Report*, Jan. 1984, 25–28, Lyon Mountain Records.

24. "More Funds Targeted for North Country Prisons," *PR*, Feb. 1, 1983; "School District Hosts Session on Building to Become Prison," *PR*, Apr. 27, 1983; "State Will Decide Soon on Purchase for School for Prison," *PR*, Jun. 7, 1983; "Lyon Mt. School to Be State Prison," *PR*, Jun. 25, 1983; "Region Welcomes New Prisons," *PR*, Jan. 26, 1984. Lyon Mountain DEIS, 4-1 to 4-2, 4-5 to 4-7, Appendix A-1 (especially 41–53), Lyon Mountain Records.

25. Executive Advisory Commission on the Administration of Justice, Arthur L. Liman, Chair: Recommendations to Governor Hugh L. Carey Regarding Prison Overcrowding, Jul. 19, 1982, 3, 5–6, 10–13, 47–49, Lyon Mountain Records.

26. State of New York, Court of Appeals, In the Matter of *Board of Visitors—Marcy Psychiatric Center v. Thomas A. Coughlin, III, Commissioner of the Department of Correctional Services,* Jul. 6, 1983, 1–8; Robert Glennon to APA Legal Affairs Committee, Jul. 12, 1983; DOCS, Declaration of Emergency under the Implementing Regulations of the State Environmental Quality Review Act, Lyon Mountain Correctional Facility, Aug. 15, 1983; DOCS, SEQR Positive Declaration: Notice of Intent to Prepare an EIS Determination of Significance, Aug. 26, 1983; Thomas Coughlin to Theodore Ruzow, Sept. 8, 1983; Theodore Ruzow to Thomas Coughlin, Sept. 9, 1983, Lyon Mountain Records.

27. Lyon Mountain DEIS, 2-1, 2-2, 2-5, 2-7, 2-9, 3-5, 3-8, 5-2, 5-3, 5-7, 5-10 to 5-12, 5-15 to 5-18, 5-23, 6-1, 6-2, 6-24 to 6-28, Lyon Mountain Records.

28. Lyon Mountain DEIS, 2-7, 2-8, 3-1, 5-10, 6-1, 6-5, 6-8 to 6-10, 6-12 to 6-15, Lyon Mountain Records. U.S. Bureau of the Census, *U.S. Census of Population: 1960, Vol. I, Characteristics of the Population, Part 34, New York* (Washington, D.C.: U.S. Government Printing Office, 1963), 34-15, 34-22, 34-109, 34-115; U.S. Bureau of the Census, *Census of Population: 1970, Vol. I, Characteristics of the Population, Part 34, New York—Section I* (Washington, D.C.: U.S. Government Printing Office, 1973), 34-12, 34-21, 34-24, 34-68, 34-70, 34-72, 34-186, 34-197; U.S. Bureau of the Census, *Census of Population: 1980, Vol. I, Characteristics of the Population, Chapter B: General Population Characteristics, Part 34, New York, PC80–1–B34* (Washington, D.C.: U.S. Government Printing Office, 1982), 34-10, 34-14, 34-17, 34-21, 34-31, 34-36, 34-38, 34-42.

29. "What's Next a State Dump?" *PR*, Jun. 6, 1983; "Lyon Mountain's Serenity Shortlived," *PR*, Jun. 20, 1983; "Neighbor Doesn't Want Another Prison," *PR*, Jun. 23, 1983. Lyon Mountain DEIS, 2-10, 4-7 to 4-8, Lyon Mountain Records.

30. "Settlement Mulls Prison Plans," *PR*, Jul. 15, 1983; "Lyon Mountain Prison to Employ 110 Workers," *PR*, Jul. 21, 1983; "Hearing on School Sale Planned," *PR*, Aug. 3, 1983; "Sale for Former School on Meeting Agenda Tonight," *PR*, Sept. 13, 1983; "Cash from Sale of Schools to Help Keep Taxes Down," *PR*, Sept. 16, 1983; "Schools Linked in Joining, Folding," *PR*, Sept. 16, 1983.

31. Lyon Mountain DEIS, 2-1 to 2-5, 2-9, 3-1, 3-7, 5-11, 5-17 to 5-20, 6-27; Theodore Ruzow to Thomas Coughlin, Jun. 6, 1983; Thomas Coughlin to Theodore Ruzow, Jul. 6, 1983; DOCS, Declaration of Emergency Under the Implementing Regulations of the State Environmental Quality Review Act, Lyon Mountain Correctional Facility, Aug. 15, 1983; DOCS, SEQR Positive Declaration: Notice of Intent to Prepare an EIS Determination of Significance, Aug. 26, 1983; Thomas Coughlin to Theodore Ruzow, Sept. 8, 1983; Theodore Ruzow to Thomas Coughlin, Sept. 9, 1983; and Thomas Ruzow to Thomas Coughlin, Sept. 28, 1983, Lyon Mountain Records.

32. Lyon Mountain DEIS, 5-17 to 5-20; Thomas Turcotte to Richard McCormick, Sept. 19, 1983; George Glassanos to Robert Glennon, Sept. 20, 1983; Wiley Lavigne and Richard McCormick to Thomas Turcotte, Sept. 22, 1983; Thomas Ruzow to Theodore Coughlin, Sept. 28, 1983; Robert Glennon to George Glassanos, Sept. 28, 1983; George Glassanos to Robert Glennon, Sept. 29, 1983; Robert Glennon to George Glassanos, Oct. 3, 1983, Lyon Mountain Records. Dannemora Town Board Minutes, Aug. 25, 1983, 322; Oct. 27, 1983, 328, Dannemora Records.

33. "Some Effect on Environment from Prison Seen," *PR*, Sept. 8, 1983; "Environmental Impact of Lyon Mt. Prison Slight," *PR*, Dec. 24, 1983. Lyon Mountain DEIS, 2-2 to 2-5, 3-5, 3-11, 5-2, 5-3, 5-9 to 5-12, 5-18, 6-2, 6-3, 6-24 to 6-28; DOCS, Lyon Mountain Correctional Facility, Environmental Assessment Form (EAF), Aug. 5, 1983, Lyon Mountain Records.

34. "Lyon Mountain School Eyed as Prison," *PR*, Jun. 3, 1983; "Lyon Mt. School to Be State Prison," *PR*, Jun. 25, 1983; "School to Become State Prison," *CR*, Jul. 6, 1983; "Lyon Mountain Prison to Employ 110 Workers," *PR*, Jul. 21, 1983; "Some Effect on Environment from Prison Seen," *PR*, Sept. 8, 1983; "Region Welcomes New Prisons," *PR*, Jan. 26, 1984. Lyon Mountain DEIS, 2-6, 2-10, 3-17, 3-21, 5-24, 5-27, 5-28, 6-25, 7-1, Lyon Mountain Records.

35. Thomas Ruzow to Theodore Coughlin, Jun. 6, 1983; Theodore Coughlin to Thomas Ruzow, Jul. 6, 1983; DOCS, Declaration of Emergency Under the Implementing Regulations of the State Environmental Quality Review Act, Lyon Mountain Correctional Facility, Aug. 15, 1983; Frank Sheridan and Donald Wrieden to Edmund Lynch, Aug. 16, 1983; DOCS, SEQR Positive Declaration: Notice of Intent to Prepare an EIS Determination of Significance, Aug. 26, 1983; Theodore Coughlin to Thomas Ruzow, Sept. 8, 1983; Thomas Ruzow to Theodore Coughlin, Sept. 9, 1983; Edmund Lynch to Frank Sheridan and Donald Wrieden, Sept. 12, 1983; George Glassanos to Vincent Moore, Nov. 22, 1983; George Glassanos to Edmund Lynch, Dec. 8, 1983; George Glassanos to Edmund Lynch, Dec. 14, 1983; DOCS, Recommendation for Classification of Lyon Mountain Acquisition, Dec. 15, 1983; DOCS, Notice of Completion of Draft Environmental Impact Statement, Dec. 15, 1983; William Curran and Robert Glennon to George Glassanos, Dec. 23, 1983; Frank Sheridan to William Curran, Dec. 28, 1983; APA, News Release, Jan. 24, 1984; Edmund Lynch to George Glassanos and Frank Sheridan, Jan. 30, 1984; George Glassanos to William Curran, Feb. 21, 1984; Robert Glennon to George Glassanos, Mar. 9, 1984; Vincent Moore to George Glassanos, Mar. 12, 1984; George Glassanos to Robert Glennon, Mar. 16, 1984, Lyon Mountain Records.

36. On phase one: "Transformation Nearly Complete of School into New State Prison," *PR*, Feb. 21, 1984. On sewage plant: Thomas Turcotte to Richard McCormick, Sept. 19, 1983; George Glassanos to Robert Glennon, Sept. 20, 1983; Wiley Lavigne and Richard McCormick to Thomas Turcotte, Sept. 22, 1983; Thomas Ruzow to Theodore Coughlin,

4

Sept. 28, 1983; Robert Glennon to George Glassanos, Sept. 28, 1983; George Glassanos to Robert Glennon, Sept. 29, 1983; Donald Wrieden to Edmund Lynch, Dec. 29, 1983; Vincent Moore to Thomas Monroe, Mar. 26, 1984; Donald Corliss to Vincent Moore, Apr. 9, 1984. On March 1984 hearing: Anonymous to William Curran, Jan. 2, 1984; William Curran, Memo to Agency Members and Designees, Jan. 11, 1984; APA, Notice of Public Hearing on Proposed Lyon Mountain Correctional Facility, Feb. 1984; APA, In the Matter of the Proposal by New York State Department of Correctional Services, to Undertake New Land Use and Development in the Adirondack Park and its Application for Necessary Permits Pursuant to Section 809 of the Adirondack Park Agency Act and 9 NYCRR Part 578, Transcript of Proceedings held at Dannemora, New York, Mar. 20, 1984, 8, 10–13, 18; Testimony of William Curran, 5, 7, 8–11; Testimony of Gary Duprey, 44–47; and, statement of John Kourofsky, 83, 86–87, Lyon Mountain Records.

37. "Bids Received for State Projects," *PR*, May 3, 1984; "Low-Risk Short-Timers Seen for New Prison," *PR*, May 5, 1984; "Prison Doors Opened in Lyon Mountain Sunday," *PR*, Jul. 24, 1984. APA, Notice of Public Hearing on Proposed Amendments to the Master Plan for the Management of State Lands Pursuant to Section 816 of the Adirondack Park Agency Act, Mar. 23, 1984; APA, Staff Draft, In the Matter of the Application of the NYS DOCS for Permits Pursuant to 9 NYCRR Part 5878, Project W83-25, Ray Brook, New York, Apr. 13, 1984; APA, Staff Draft, Agency Determination on State Agency Project after Public Hearing, in the Matter of the Proposal of the NYS DOCS to Undertake New Land Use and Development in the Adirondack Park, State Project No. SP 83-15, Ray Brook, Apr. 14, 1984; William Curran to George Glassanos and Donald Wrieden, Apr. 17, 1984; DOCS, Notice of Completion of Final Environmental Impact Statement, Apr. 25, 1984; James Hill to Richard McCormick, May 18, 1984, Lyon Mountain Records.

38. "Dannemoran Cites Waste, Conflict in Town Project," *PR*, Apr. 25, 1984; "Abandoned Mines May Someday Store Power," *PR*, Sept. 4, 1985; "Townspeople Protest Sale of Lyon Mountain Mine," *PR*, Sept. 23, 1985; "Project Will Make Ecosystem Safer," *PR*, Nov. 4, 1985; "Town Ultimately Responsible for Water District," *PR*, Feb. 24, 1986; "Dannemora OKs Sale of Mines Pending Possible Referendum," *PR*, Apr. 23, 1986; "Sale of Mines Voted Down," *PR*, Jul. 16, 1986. Dannemora Town Board Minutes, Apr. 5, 1984, 346, Apr. 18, 1985, 382, Feb. 20, 1986, 402, Nov. 13, 1986, 421, Dannemora Records.

39. "Program Helps Inmates Prepare for Release," *PR*, Dec. 10, 1984; "Lyon Mountain Prison Brings Jobs to Area," *PR*, Jan. 24, 1985; "Prison Recreation, Classroom Building Going Up," *PR*, Jun. 17, 1985; "Lyon Mountain, Altona Prisons Expanding," *PR*, Jan. 23, 1986; "Rehabilitation Now Means Something, Prison Chief Says," *PR*, Sept. 4, 1986; "Local Economic Impact of Prisons Is Immense," *PR*, Jan. 22, 1987.

40. "A Day of Health Awareness at Lyon Mountain," *CR*, Sept. 26, 1985; "Hundreds Attend Local AIDS Forums," *PR*, Feb. 5, 1986; "Rock Star Speaks Out against Drugs," *PR*, Mar. 12, 1986; "Local Inmates Raise Money for Child Find," *PR*, Apr. 5, 1988; "Inmates' Pride Grows Along with Their Gardens," *PR*, Aug. 25, 1989; "Lions Club Cites Donors," *PR*, Oct. 5, 1989; "Vegetable Gardens Judged," *CR*, Sept. 6, 1990; "Lyon Mountain Prison Plans Health Program," *PR*, Sept. 25, 1990; "Thanking the Prison Leaders," *ADE*, Nov. 25, 1991; "Northern Adirondack to Hold Benefit," *PR*, Mar. 25, 1993; "Prison to Host Child-Identification Program," *PR*, Oct. 21, 1994; "United Way Drive at 47 Percent of Goal," *PR*, Nov. 10, 1994; "State Workers Increase Donations," *PR*, Jan. 6, 1996; "North Country Holiday Helpers Touch Many," *PR*, Jan. 9, 1998; "Correctional Facilities to Kick Off Gardening Season," *ADE*, May 25, 1998. Dannemora Town Board Minutes, May 25, 1988, 456, Jul. 27, 1988, 460, Nov. 28, 1990, 533, Dec. 28, 1990, 536, Apr. 24, 1991, 552, Dannemora Records.

41. On recreational projects: "Bellmont Town Board Meeting Highlights," *CR*, Mar. 26, 1984; "Dannemoran Cites Waste, Conflict in Town Project," *PR*, Apr. 25, 1984; "Direction

from Voters Seen in Referendum on Town's Future," *PR*, Aug. 13, 1984; "Jobs Range from Church Steps to Garage," *PR*, Oct. 2, 1984; "Inmate Work Crews Help with Local Projects," *PR*, Jan. 23, 1986; "Lyon Mountain Inmates Finish Interior of Addition," *PR*, Jan. 22, 1987; "Calling All Santa Clauses," *PR*, Dec. 5, 1987; "Job Well Done," *PR*, Sept. 13, 1988; "Toyland," *PR*, Dec. 8, 1990; "Work Crew," *PR*, Aug. 1, 1993; "North Country Holiday Helpers Touch Many," *PR*, Jan. 9, 1998. Dannemora Town Board Minutes, Jul. 12, 1984, 353, Aug. 22, 1990, 525, Dannemora Records. On public service and environmental projects: "New Addition at Burke Fire Dept.," *CR*, Jul. 1984; "Jobs Range from Church Steps to Garage," *PR*, Oct. 2, 1984; "Paint Job," *PR*, Oct. 25, 1985; "Inmate Work Crews Help with Local Projects," *PR*, Jan. 23, 1986; "Lyon Mountain Inmates Finish Interior of Addition," *PR*, Jan. 22, 1987; "Many Hands Build Wheelchair Ramp," *PR*, Mar. 28, 1987; "Peru Free Library Completes Roomy Addition," *PR*, Jan. 28, 1988; "Mooers Senior Housing Project Modified," *PR*, Sept. 22, 1988; "Many Helped Raise Money," *PR*, May 14, 1989; "Ellenburg School Cleanup Continues, Total Loss Unknown," *PR*, Dec. 6, 1989; "Ice Jams Ready for Blasting," *PR*, Jan. 27, 1990; "Gleaners: Project Has Grown since 1989," *PR*, Sept. 16, 1990; "Reconstruction of NACS Gym Progressing," *PR*, May 12, 1991; "Dodge Memorial Library to Get Repair Funding," *PR*, Aug. 19, 1991; "Malone-Area Gleaners Now Growing Own Produce," *PR*, Aug. 4, 1992; "LCPA Prepares Land for New Animal Shelter," *PR*, Jul. 24, 1993; "Inmates Spiff Up Fire Station," *PR*, May 12, 1996; "New Annex to House CCC Technology Program," *PR*, Aug. 1, 1997; "Storm Cleanup Continues," *PR*, Feb. 4, 1998; "Correctional Facilities to Kick Off Gardening Season," *ADE*, May 25, 1998; "Flooding Tidbits," *PR*, Jun. 30, 1998; Dannemora Town Board Minutes, Apr. 18, 1985, 382, Dannemora Records.

42. "Contract to Sell Mine Sand Could Net Town a Windfall," *PR*, Nov. 16, 1993; "Last of Mining Landmarks Fading Fast," *PR*, Jun. 13, 2010. Dannemora Town Board Minutes, Apr. 19, 1984, 348, May 10, 1984, 350, Jul. 12, 1984, 353, Oct. 25, 1984, 366, Nov. 15, 1984, 368, May 16, 1985, 384, Jul. 11, 1985, 390, May 23, 1990, 514, Jun. 27, 1990, 516, Apr. 28, 1993, 38, Dannemora Records. APA, Memo to Adirondack Mayors, Supervisors, Planning Board Chairpersons, from Barbara Sweet, Sept. 27, 1994, Lyon Mountain Records.

43. "Dannemoran Cites Waste, Conflict in Town Project," *PR*, Apr. 25, 1984; "Direction from Voters Seen in Referendum on Town's Future," *PR*, Aug. 13, 1984. Dannemora Town Board Minutes, Feb. 16, 1984, 343, Apr. 5, 1984, 346, Apr. 19, 1984, 348–49, May 10, 1984, 350, Aug. 2, 1984, 360, Apr. 18, 1985, 382, Feb. 20, 1986, 402, Apr. 17, 1986, 406, Jul. 23, 1987, 436, Jul. 27, 1988, 460, May 23, 1990, 513–14, Jul. 24, 1991, 563, Dannemora Records.

44. "Town Plans to Drain, Clean Pond," *PR*, Jun. 3, 1985; "Lyon Mountain May Get Water Fixup, New Plant," *PR*, Jul. 16, 1985; "County Hike May Overshadow Tax Decrease in Dannemora," *PR*, Nov. 18, 1986; "Water Reservoir Gets Scrubbed by Inmates," *PR*, Jan. 22, 1987; "DEC to Help Lyon Mountain Stop Dumping Raw Sewage," *PR*, Aug. 31, 1988; "Lyon Mt. Sewer-Treatment Cost Is Big Question," *PR*, Sept. 19, 1988; "Town Begins Tackling Lyon Mountain Sewage Woes," *PR*, Mar. 3, 1989; "Councilman Steps Down; New Water Chief Sought," *PR*, Aug. 29, 1989. Dannemora Town Board Minutes, Aug. 25, 1983, 322, Oct. 27, 1983, 328, Dec. 8, 1983, 332, Jan. 26, 1984, 333, Feb. 16, 1984, 343, Mar. 8, 1984, 344, Apr. 5, 1984, 346, Apr. 19, 1984, 348, May 10, 1984, 350, Jul. 12, 1984, 353, Aug. 2, 1984, 361, Oct. 25, 1984, 366, Nov. 15, 1984, 368, Dec. 27, 1984, 370, May 16, 1985, 384, Jul. 11, 1985, 390, May 23, 1990, 513, Jun. 27, 1990, 516, Aug. 22, 1990, 524–25, Nov. 28, 1990, 533, Dec. 28, 1990, 536, Jul. 24, 1991, 562, Apr. 28, 1993, 38, Aug. 24, 1994, 99; Town of Dannemora, Resolution # 95 of the Town of Dannemora Requesting that the NYS Dept. of Environmental Conservation Withdraw the Tentative Freshwater Wetland Maps Noticed in June 1991; DEC, to Town Clerk of Dannemora, Jun. 5, 1991; Town of Dannemora, Town Board Regular Meeting, Resolution Requesting

that the New York State Department of Environmental Conservation Delay Proposed Action on Wetlands, May 27, 1992, Dannemora Records.

45. "Escaped Lyon Mountain Inmate Shot, Captured," *PR*, Aug. 25, 2009; "Authorities Continue to Probe Lyon Mountain Prison Escape," *PR*, Aug. 26, 2009; "Inmate Charged with Escape from Lyon Mountain," *PR*, Jan. 15, 2010; and, "Inmate Sentenced for Lyon Mountain Escape," *PR*, Jun. 3, 2010.
46. "Four Prisons, Including Three in the North Country, Up for Closure," *ADE*, Jan. 20, 2010. "DOCS Planning for Additional Closures, Consolidation in 2010–11 as Inmate Population Continues to Decline," *DOCS Today* (Winter 2010): 1, 5.
47. "Four Prisons, Including Three in the North Country, Up for Closure," *ADE*, Jan. 20, 2010; "Crowd: Save Prison Jobs," *PR*, Feb. 4, 2010; "Future of Lyon Mountain Prison Property Pondered," *PR*, Jan. 29, 2011; "New York Has Some Prisons to Sell You," *NYT*, May 27, 2012.
48. "Lyon Mountain Prison Sold," *PR*, Jul. 11, 2013; "Town May Raise Rates for Ore Sand," *PR*, Jan. 27, 2014; "Sale of Former Lyon Mountain Prison Moving Forward," *PR*, May 19, 2014.

Chapter Five: "This Town Will Die"

1. "Ron Stafford Delivers on His Prison Promise," *Tupper Lake Free Press* (hereafter *TLFP*), Aug. 6, 1997; "Prison in the Forest," *NYT*, Sept. 16, 1997.
2. "New State Prison Urged for Tupper Lake," *ADE*, Jan. 15, 1981; "Tupper Lake Eyed as Prison Site," *PR*, Jan. 16, 1981.
3. "Lefebvre: Don't Waste Tax Dollars on Prison Study," *ADE*, Oct. 1, 1986; "Altamont Seeking Prison for Town," *PR*, Oct. 28, 1986; "Possible Tupper Prison Sites Eyed," *ADE*, Nov. 29, 1986; "Corrections Officials Suggest Tupper Lake Find Better Sites for Possible Prison," *ADE*, Dec. 19, 1986; "Only 1 Tupper Site Deemed Suitable for Prison," *PR*, Dec. 22, 1986.
4. "Lefebvre: Don't Waste Tax Dollars on Prison Study," *ADE*, Oct. 1, 1986; "Altamont Seeking Prison for Town," *PR*, Oct. 28, 1986; "Councilmen Call for Study of Prison Impact," *PR*, Nov. 14, 1986; "Corrections Officials Suggest Tupper Lake Find Better Sites for Possible Prison," *ADE*, Dec. 19, 1986; "Any Local Opposition Seems to Have Faded," *PR*, Dec. 22, 1986; "Writers Express Fear of What Might Happen if Prison Comes to Tupper Lake," *ADE*, Jan. 22, 1987; "Anti-Prison Folks Object to Editorial," *ADE*, Jan. 27, 1987.
5. "Lefebvre: Don't Waste Tax Dollars on Prison Study," *ADE*, Oct. 1, 1986; "Altamont Seeking Prison for Town," *PR*, Oct. 28, 1986; "Prison Plan Forum in Tupper Produces Support and Criticism," *ADE*, Mar. 26, 1987; "Tupper Lake Residents Quiz Officials about Prison," *PR*, Mar. 28, 1987.
6. "Prison Plan Forum in Tupper Produces Support and Criticism," *ADE*, Mar. 26, 1987; "Tupper Lake Residents Quiz Officials about Prison," *PR*, Mar. 28, 1987; "AIDS Victims Called Health Threat," *PR*, Mar. 28, 1987.
7. "Many Uses Seen for Altamont's Evaluation of Prison Impact," *ADE*, Jun. 12, 1987; "Prison Effort Revived in TL," *ADE*, Feb. 22, 1989.
8. "Prison Effort Revived in TL," *ADE*, Feb. 22, 1989; "Tupper, Altamont Finally Agree on Landfill," *PR*, Feb. 23, 1989; "Altamont Renews Effort to Secure a State Prison," *PR*, Mar. 14, 1989; "Altamont Eyes Highway Projects, Weigh Limits," *PR*, Jun. 14, 1989; "4 New Prisons Likely; Other Plans Too," *PR*, Jun. 22, 1989; "One Altamont Prison Site Still in the Running," *PR*, Jun. 23, 1989.
9. "Tupper, Altamont Finally Agree on Landfill," *PR*, Feb. 23, 1989; "Altamont Renews Effort to Secure a State Prison," *PR*, Mar. 14, 1989; "Board Refuses to Support Altamont

Jail," *LPN*, Apr. 19, 1989; "Anti-Prison Group Mobilizes in Tupper," *PR*, Jun. 23, 1989; "Disappointed with Policy," *PR*, Jun. 29, 1989.

10. "Tupper Passed Over in Prison Sitings," *ADE*, Jun. 26, 1989; "Altamont Officials Disappointed at Not Receiving Nod for Prison," *PR*, Jun. 26, 1989; "Altamont Awaits Word on Land for Prison," *PR*, Jul. 14, 1989; "Altamont Supervisor Running on Board's Record," *PR*, Oct. 25, 1989; "Altamont OKs Controversial Amendment to Town Zoning Law," *PR*, Nov. 14, 1989.

11. "Budget Battle to Determine Prison Funds," *ADE*, Jan. 29, 1990; "Prison Reports Have TL Worried," *ADE*, Mar. 30, 1990; "Drug Unit Targeted for Altamont," *PR*, Mar. 31, 1992.

12. "Faction Opposes Tupper Lake Prison Projects," *PR*, Apr. 15, 1992; "Tupper Area Officials Take Tour of Chateaugay Facility," *ADE*, May 13, 1992.

13. "Lefebvre Seeks Support for Prison from H'town Board," *ADE*, May 27, 1996.

14. Daniel Spada to James LaValley, Aug. 8, 1996, SP 97-248, Tupper Lake Records, Adirondack Park Agency Records Office, Ray Brook, New York (hereafter Tupper Lake Records).

15. "Franklin County Eyes State Budget for Prison in Tupper," *ADE*, Jan. 13, 1997; "Pataki Budget Proposes 7000 More Prison Cells," *TLFP*, Jan. 15, 1997; "Community Leaders Buoyed by Prison Plan; Is It Tupper's Year?" *TLFP*, Jan. 22, 1997; "County Backs Prison Idea for TL," *ADE*, Jan. 25, 1997; "Stafford Wins Prison for Tupper," *PR*, Aug. 3, 1997; "Crime-and-Corrections Spending Plan Passed," *PR*, Aug. 4, 1997; "Prison Coming to Tupper Lake!" *TLFP*, Aug. 6, 1997. DOCS, "Budget Agreement OKs Governor's Plan for Largest Cell Expansion in 70 Years," Jul. 30, 1997, Tupper Lake Records.

16. "Prison Coming to Tupper Lake!" *TLFP*, Aug. 6, 1997; "Tupper Prison Plan Minimizes Inmate Contact," *PR*, Aug. 11, 1997. "Adirondack Park Agency Application for Permit, Project No. 40614, 40552, and 40570: Maximum Security Facility: Housing Units, Support Buildings, & Infrastructure: Proposed Franklin County Facility, Tupper Lake, New York," New York State Office of General Services, Sept. 1997, Tupper Lake Records.

17. DOCS, South Franklin CF Draft Environmental Impact Statement (Albany: DOCS, 1997), 9, 10, 19, Tupper Lake Records. U.S. Bureau of the Census, *U.S. Census of Population: 1960, Vol. I, Characteristics of the Population, Part 34, New York* (Washington, D.C.: U.S. Government Printing Office, 1963), 34-15, 34-124, 34-126; *Census of Population: 1970, Vol. I, Characteristics of the Population, Part 34, New York—Section I* (Washington, D.C.: U.S. Government Printing Office, 1973), 34-16, 34-26, 34-71, 34-202; *Census of Population: 1980, Vol. I, Characteristics of the Population, Chapter B: General Population Characteristics, Part 34, New York, PC80-1-B34* (Washington, D.C.: U.S. Government Printing Office, 1982), 34-16, 34-19, 34-37, 34-40.

18. DOCS, South Franklin CF Draft EIS, 5–6, 19–22, Tupper Lake Records.

19. Mr. and Mrs. Rick King to William Curran, Sept. 24, 1997; Russell Randolph to William Curran, Oct. 20, 1997; John Quenell to Glenn Goord, Nov. 22, 1997; seven additional letters, Tupper Lake Records.

20. Christine Randolph to William Curran, Oct. 18, 1997; Betty Howard to Dan Fitts, Oct. 28, 1997; Wendy Pierce to William Curran, Nov. 4, 1997; eleven additional letters, Tupper Lake Records.

21. Richard Purdue, "Statement to APA," Oct. 10, 1997; Joyce Moody to James Frenette, Nov. 3, 1997; Anonymous to William Curran, no date; two additional letters, Tupper Lake Records.

22. Robert Stout to Dick Jarvis, Sept. 25, 1997; Caroline DeClerque to William Curran, Oct. 31, 1997; Lois Rockcastle to William Curran, Nov. 10, 1997; twenty additional letters, Tupper Lake Records.

23. Robert Johnson to George Pataki, Oct. 24, 1997; Glenn Poirier to William Curran,

Nov. 3, 1997; Douglas Ward to Greg Campbell, Nov. 18, 1997; fifteen additional letters, Tupper Lake Records.

24. Charles and Mary Ritchie to Dan Fitts, Oct. 22, 1997; Robert Merrill to William Curran, Oct. 28, 1997; Barbara Cornejo to George Pataki, Nov. 9, 1997; six additional letters, Tupper Lake Records.

25. John Underhill Jr. to William Curran, Oct. 23, 1997; Toni Viertel to William Curran, Nov. 4, 1997; Louis Dwyer to William Curran, Dec. 22, 1997; twenty additional letters, Tupper Lake Records.

26. Bruce and Martha Blanchard to APA, Oct. 29, 1997; Jean Craighead George to William Curran, Nov. 7, 1997; Richard Handler to William Curran, Nov. 24, 1997; twenty-three additional letters, Tupper Lake Records.

27. Sarah and Doug Bencze to William Curran, Oct. 31, 1997; Richard Lockhart to William Curran, Nov. 2, 1997; Elizabeth Moore to William Curran, Nov. 2, 1997; six additional letters, Tupper Lake Records.

28. "Jobs Prompt Malone to Ask for Prison," *PR,* Sept. 21, 1983; "Malone Wins 700-Bed Prison," *PR,* Jun. 27, 1985; "Franklin Prison Opens for Business," *PR,* Aug. 23, 1986; "Franklin County Asks for Second Prison," *PR,* Sept. 17, 1986; "Residents Already Campaigning for Second Prison in Malone," *PR,* Jan. 22, 1987; "Bare Hill Correctional Facility Opens in Malone," *PR,* Nov. 22, 1988.

29. Peter Lourie to William Curran, Oct. 26, 1997; Thomas Small to William Curran, Nov. 6, 1997; Hilary Harp to George Pataki, no date; thirteen additional letters, Tupper Lake Records.

30. Donald Earlin to William Curran, Oct. 22, 1997; Frances Fortune to William Curran, Nov. 20, 1997; Robert Purdy to George Pataki, Dec. 12, 1997; sixteen additional letters, Tupper Lake Records.

31. Ann Seymour to Dan Fitts, Oct. 30, 1997; Donna Lonergan to APA, Nov. 11, 1997; Darlene Willette to APA, no date; six additional letters, Tupper Lake Records.

32. Laurie Drasye to APA, Oct. 23, 1997; Marjorie Gilbert to William Curran, Nov. 10, 1997; Joan Fox to William Curran, Nov. 24, 1997; fourteen additional letters, Tupper Lake Records.

33. Jon Bombard to APA, Nov. 12, 1997; Preston Burl to George Pataki, Nov. 17, 1997; Edith Martin to William Curran, no date; five additional letters, Tupper Lake Records.

34. Paul Maroun to Stephen Dutton, Oct. 17, 1997; Donald Earlin to William Curran, Oct. 22, 1997; Laurie Drasye to APA, Oct. 23, 1997; Marjorie Gilbert to William Curran, Oct. 28, 1997; Gary Levesque to William Curran, Oct. 29, 1997; unsigned form letter to William Curran, Oct. 29, 1997; unsigned form letter to William Curran, Oct. 30, 1997; John Dewyea Jr. to William Curran, Oct. 31, 1997; Dan McClelland to William Curran, Oct. 31, 1997; unsigned form letter to William Curran, Oct. 31, 1997; Briggette Hughes to William Curran, Nov. 4, 1997; Laurie Drasye to William Curran, Nov. 5, 1997; Donna Lonergan to APA, Nov. 11, 1997; Diane Lewandowski to William Curran, Nov. 13, 1997; Preston Burl to George Pataki, Nov. 17, 1997; Frances Fortune to William Curran, Nov. 20, 1997; unsigned form letter to George Pataki, Nov. 1997; Jack Vitvitsky to William Curran, Dec. 6, 1997; Darlene Willette to APA, no date, Tupper Lake Records.

35. "Town May Hold Hearing on Prison Plan," *ADE,* Aug. 12, 1997; "I.P. Still Owns Land to Be Used for Prison," *ADE,* Aug. 1997; "Prison Contracts Coming in January," *PR,* Aug. 21, 1997; "State Crews Taking Samples at Pitchfork Pond Prison Site," *TLFP,* Aug. 27, 1997; "Tupper Plans Utility Upgrade for Prison," *PR,* Sept. 17, 1997; "Prison Site Not Official but Likely Settled," *PR,* Oct. 4, 1997; "DOC Seeks APA Consent Prison," *PR,* Oct. 10, 1997. New York State Office of General Services, "Visual Impact Assessment: 750 Cell Maximum Security Correctional Facility, Town of Altamont, Franklin County, New York," Prepared by Environmental Design & Research, P.C., Syracuse, N.Y., Oct.

1, 1997; Robert Dunn and Francis Sheridan to William Curran, Oct. 6, 1997; DOCS, "Commissioner Seeks Adirondack Park Agency OK for Tupper Lake Prison," Oct. 9, 1997; John Hart to George Glassanos, Oct. 23, 1997, Tupper Lake Records.

36. "APA Promises a Thorough Review of Project," *PR,* Oct. 15, 1997. William Curran to George Glassanos and Robert Dunn, Oct. 2, 1997; Greg Campbell to agency members and designees, Oct. 9, 1997; William Curran to New York State Office of Parks, Recreation, and Historic Preservation, Oct. 20, 1997, Tupper Lake Records.

37. "DOC Seeks APA Consent Prison," *PR,* Oct. 10, 1997; "APA Promises a Thorough Review of Project," *PR,* Oct. 15, 1997. Robert Dunn to William Curran, Oct. 21, 1997; APA, "Notice of Incomplete Application and Request for Additional Information" (Project 97-248, DOCS), Oct. 24, 1997, Tupper Lake Records. "Strict Review Is Sought for Adirondack Prison Plan," *NYT,* Oct. 15, 1997. "Corrections Eyes Additional Prison Sites," *Legislative Gazette,* Oct. 20, 1997.

38. "Town May Hold Hearing on Prison Plan," *ADE,* Aug. 12, 1997; "Environmentalists Debate Tupper Prison," *PR,* Aug. 18, 1997; "Few Oppose Prison Plan," *ADE,* Aug. 1997; "Prison in the Forest," *NYT,* Sept. 16, 1997.

39. Peter and Rhoda Curtiss to William Curran, Oct. 27, 1997; Phyllis Pierce to William Curran, Oct. 31, 1997; Peggy Staats to APA, Nov. 13, 1997; twenty-six additional letters, Nov. 21, 1997, Tupper Lake Records.

40. "DOC Seeks APA Consent Prison," *PR,* Oct. 10, 1997; "APA Promises a Thorough Review of Project," *PR,* Oct. 15, 1997; "Strict Review Is Sought for Adirondack Prison Plan," *NYT,* Oct. 15, 1997; "Corrections Eyes Additional Prison Sites," *Legislative Gazette,* Oct. 20, 1997. Adirondack Council, "Environmental Organizations Call on Park Agency to Reject Tupper Lake Prison Application as Incomplete," Oct. 14, 1997; RCPA, "Position Statement," Oct. 28, 1997; RCPA to George Pataki, Nov. 3, 1997, Tupper Lake Records.

41. Adirondack Council, "Adirondack Council Calls on Park Agency to Investigate Dept. of Corrections for Potential Violations of Park Development Rules," Nov. 5, 1997; Timothy Burke to Dan Fitts, Nov. 5, 1997, Tupper Lake Records.

42. "Tupper Prison Opposed," *PR,* Nov. 19, 1997; "Lawsuit Threat Could Relocate Tupper Prison," *PR,* Nov. 20, 1997; "Malone Would Welcome Tupper Prison," *PR,* Nov. 21, 1997. Sierra Club, "Sierra Club Joins with Tupper Lake Residents to Hire Former APA Chief to Fight Prison," Nov. 19, 1997, Tupper Lake Records.

43. "Tupper Prison Trouble," *PR,* Nov. 1, 1997; "Lawsuit Threat Could Relocate Tupper Prison," *PR,* Nov. 20, 1997; "Malone Would Welcome Tupper Prison," *PR,* Nov. 21, 1997; "Sierra Club Enters Fray; Pledges to Stop Prison," *TLFP,* Nov. 26, 1997; and, "Tupper Reacts to Possibility of Malone Prison," *PR,* Dec. 3, 1997. Robert Glennon to H. Carl McCall, Dec. 1, 1997, Tupper Lake Records.

44. John Dewyea Jr. to William Curran, Oct. 31, 1997; Susan Martin to William Curran, Nov. 22, 1997; Jack Vitvitsky to William Curran, Dec. 6, 1997; eleven additional letters, Tupper Lake Records.

45. "On Purdue, Siy and the Prison Issue," *ADE,* Oct. 3, 1997; "Environmentalists Wrong in Their Call for Halt to APA Prison Review Process," *TLFP,* Oct. 22, 1997; "Tupper Lake Needs a Prison," *TLFP,* Oct. 22, 1997; "It's Time to Take a Stand, Tupper Lake," *TLFP,* Nov. 19, 1997; "Village Board Urges Prison Support," *TLFP,* Nov. 19, 1997; "Conflict of Interest," *PR,* Nov. 20, 1997; "Disturbed by Message," *PR,* Nov. 23, 1997; "Are We Going to Sit By and Let Tree-Huggers Uproot Our Prison?" *TLFP,* Nov. 26, 1997; "Guard Union Backs Tupper Prison Site," *PR,* Nov. 26, 1997; "If Tupper Lake Prison Goes, What's Next?" *PR,* Nov. 26, 1997; "Prison Would Be More Beneficial Than Harmful," *TLFP,* Nov. 26, 1997. Unsigned form letter to William Curran, Oct. 29, 1997; Dan McClelland to William Curran, Oct. 31, 1997; Gary and Rita [last name illegible] to William Curran, Nov. 22, 1997; Joan Fox to William Curran, Nov. 24, 1997; Jack

Vitvitsky to William Curran, Dec. 6, 1997; Darlene Willette to APA, no date, Tupper Lake Records.

46. "Environmentalists Wrong in Their Call for Halt to APA Prison Review Process," *TLFP,* Oct. 22, 1997; "Tupper Lake Needs a Prison," *TLFP,* Oct. 22, 1997; "Prison Is Just What the Economy Ordered," *PR,* Oct. 27, 1997; "Stay Strong, Governor," *TLFP,* Nov. 19, 1997; "Conflict of Interest," *PR,* Nov. 20, 1997; "Support for the Prison," *PR,* Nov. 26, 1997; "Are We Going to Sit By and Let Tree-Huggers Uproot Our Prison?" *TLFP,* Nov. 26, 1997; "Common Sense Goes a Long Way," *TLFP,* Nov. 26, 1997; "Corrects Erroneous Statements," *TLFP,* Nov. 26, 1997; "Prison Would Be More Beneficial than Harmful," *TLFP,* Nov. 26, 1997; "Prison Would Be Our Salvation," *TLFP,* Nov. 26, 1997; "Supporters Mobilize for Prison," *PR,* Nov. 30, 1997; "Residents Say Bring the Jobs," *ADE,* Dec. 1, 1997. Donald Earlin to William Curran, Oct. 22, 1997; Marjorie Gilbert to William Curran, Oct. 28, 1997; Laurie Drasye to William Curran, Oct. 29, 1997; unsigned form letter to William Curran, Oct. 29, 1997; unsigned form letter to William Curran, Oct. 30, 1997; Laurie Drasye to William Curran, Nov. 5, 1997; Jon Bombard to APA, Nov. 12, 1997; Jack Vitvitsky to William Curran, Dec. 6, 1997; E. Martin to William Curran, no date, Tupper Lake Records.

47. Laurie Drasye to William Curran, Nov. 5, 1997; Robert Purdy to George Pataki, Dec. 12, 1997; Darlene Willette to APA, no date, Tupper Lake Records.

48. "Environmentalists Wrong In Their Call for Halt to APA Prison Review Process," *TLFP,* Oct. 22, 1997; "Tupper Lake Needs a Prison," *TLFP,* Oct. 22, 1997; "Prison Is Just What the Economy Ordered," *PR,* Oct. 27, 1997; "Prison Backers Organize Rally in Tupper Lake," *PR,* Nov. 24, 1997; "Are We Going To Sit By and Let Tree-Huggers Uproot Our Prison?" *TLFP,* Nov. 26, 1997; "What Do the Environmentalists Want?" *TLFP,* Nov. 26, 1997.

49. "Supporters Mobilize for Prison," *PR,* Nov. 30, 1997; "Residents Say Bring the Jobs," *ADE,* Dec. 1, 1997; "Tupper Lake Rally: 'We Need This Prison!'" *ADE,* Dec. 1, 1997; "Huge Pro-Prison Rally Draws Nearly 1500," *TLFP,* Dec. 3, 1997; "Rally Coverage Going State-Wide," *TLFP,* Dec. 3, 1997; "Stafford, Ortloff, Maroun Press Supporters to Continue the Push," *TLFP,* Dec. 3, 1997.

50. "Malone Details Prison Needs," *PR,* Dec. 12, 1997; "Tupper Reacts to Possibility of Malone Prison," *PR,* Dec. 13, 1997

51. "Top DEC Official Pans Tupper Prison," *PR,* Dec. 19, 1997; "Pressed by Environmentalists, Pataki Drops Prison Plan," *NYT,* Dec. 20, 1997; "State Caves; Malone Gets Tupper Prison," *PR,* Dec. 20, 1997; "Tupper Loses Prison!!" *TLFP,* Dec. 24, 1997.

52. "Tupper Lake upset, disappointed by loss," *PR,* Dec. 20, 1997; "Altamont looks for options after losing prison," *PR,* Dec. 23, 1997; "Bad sign for park's economy," *PR,* Dec. 23, 1997; Dale French, letter, *TLFP,* Dec. 24, 1997; Marjorie Gilbert, letter, *TLFP,* Dec. 24, 1997; Joy Graton, letter, *TLFP,* Dec. 24, 1997; Jeff Lamere, letter, *TLFP,* Dec. 24, 1997; Bob and Mary Lyle, letter, *TLFP,* Dec. 24, 1997; Frank Morrison, letter, *TLFP,* Dec. 24, 1997; Dennis Pickering, letter, *TLFP,* Dec. 24, 1997; Randall Rolley, letter, *TLFP,* Dec. 24, 1997; "Supervisor calls on community to work together on new goals," *TLFP,* Dec. 24, 1997; "The prison is gone, so let's move on!" *TLFP,* Dec. 24, 1997; "Town leaders angry, frustrated, but also ready to move ahead," *TLFP,* Dec. 24, 1997; "Tupper Loses Prison!!" *TLFP,* Dec. 24, 1997; "Very dismayed, disappointed," *TLFP,* Dec. 24, 1997; "Tupper Lake now needs to tout tourism," *LPN,* Dec. 26, 1997; "Tupper loses $130 million state prison to Malone," *LPN,* Dec. 26, 1997; "Prison idea open for public comment," *PR,* Dec. 30, 1997; "Council deceitful," *PR,* Dec. 31, 1997; "Regarding 'The Grinch' that stole the prison," *LPN,* Jan. 2, 1998; "So what's in the future for this community?" *TLFP,* Jan. 14, 1998; "Tupper supporter speaks out on prison issue," *TLFP,* Jan. 14, 1998; "More thoughts on the prison," *TLFP,* Jan. 28, 1998; "Time cost Tupper Lake prison," *PR,* Feb. 1, 1998; and, "Several factors conspired against prison," *PR,* Feb. 9, 1998.

53. "Harness Altamont's Aquifer," *TLFP,* Dec. 24, 1997; "Even in Wake of Prison Site Switch Supporters Here Continue to Fight," *TLFP,* Jan. 7, 1998; "Prison Backers Pin Hopes on Aquifer," *PR,* Jan. 8, 1998; "Town Supervisor Still Wants Prison in Tupper Lake," *LPN,* Jan. 16, 1998. Emily Tyner to Timothy Burke and Robert Glennon, Jan. 12, 1998, Tupper Lake Records.

54. "Tupper Looks to Restore Its Past," *PR,* Jan. 24, 1998; "New Prison Dubbed Upstate Correctional Facility," *PR,* Aug. 14, 1998; "Museum Seen as Tupper Lake Economy Boost," *PR,* Oct. 7, 1998. DOCS, "New Prison at Malone, Formally Named 'Upstate,' Is 30 Percent Complete," Aug. 13, 1998; DOCS, "Upstate Correctional Facility Opens with First Round of Inmate Transfers," Jul. 7, 1999.

55. "Chateaugay Interested in Prison," *PR,* Dec. 5, 1983; "Chateaugay Again Lobbies for State Prison," *PR,* Jan. 23, 1988; "Chateaugay Seeking Federal Prison," *PR,* Aug. 17, 1988; "Chateaugay Task Force Lobbies for State Prison," *PR,* Nov. 19, 1988; "Chateaugay's Prison Hopes Take Nosedive," *PR,* Jan. 6, 1989; "Chateaugay May Be Next in Line for Prison," *PR,* Feb. 7, 1989; "Chateaugay Drug Annex OK'd," *PR,* Jun. 25, 1989; "Construction Begins on Chateaugay Drug Prison," *PR,* Feb. 13, 1990; "Inmates Arrive at Chateaugay Prison," *PR,* Sept. 5, 1990; "Assembly Targets Chateaugay Prison," *PR,* Mar. 22, 2013; "600 Rally to Save State Prison in Chateaugay, Organizers Say," *ADE,* Oct. 7, 2013; "Clock Is Ticking on Chateaugay Prison Shutdown," *ADE,* Jan. 22, 2014; "Fight Goes On to Keep Local Prison Open," *PR,* Mar. 15, 2014; "State Budget: Ed Funds Up; Chateaugay Prison Left Out," *PR,* Apr. 1, 2014; "New York to Sell Shuttered Prison near Canadian Border," *New York Post,* May 4, 2018; "Former Chateaugay Prison Sells to Company Based in Brooklyn," *North Country Public Radio,* Apr. 19, 2019.

Conclusion

1. "With Power Tools and a Ruse, 2 Killers Escape New York Prison," *NYT,* Jun. 6, 2015.

2. "In Search for Escapees, Voracious Bugs, Poisonous Plants and Muddy Woods," *NYT,* Jun. 13, 2015; "Empty but Also Stocked, Hunting Cabins in Adirondacks Are Ideal Hideout for Escapees," *NYT,* Jun. 25, 2015; "New York Prisoner's Keys to Escape: Lapsed Rules, Tools and Luck," *NYT,* Jul. 20, 2015.

3. "U.S. to Release 6,000 Inmates From Prisons," *NYT,* Oct. 6, 2015; "Senate Passes Bipartisan Criminal Justice Bill," *NYT,* Dec. 18, 2018; "Cuomo Says Close More Prisons, Corrections Officers Push Back," *North Country Public Radio,* Jan. 22, 2020.

4. "Altona Wildfire Covers Hundreds of Acres," *PR,* Jul. 13, 2018.

5. Anastasia Pratt, "Constructing and Preserving History through Community Art Projects," in *Community Built: Art, Construction, Preservation, and Place,* ed. Katherine Melcher, Barry Stiefel, and Kristin Faurest (New York: Routledge, 2017), 122–24.

INDEX

83; Sunmount Veterans Administration
Hospital, 169

Tupper Lake, 166–68; Chateaugay
penitentiary and, 173, 174, 176, 198–99;
Malone prisons and, 168, 171, 183, 185,
192–98; Natural History Museum of the
Adirondacks (Wild Center), 166, 198;
opposition to prison in, 13; prison plan
battles (1981–1992), 168–75; prison plan
battles (1996–1997), 175–85, 181; prison
plan battles (1997–1998), 185–97; prison
plans for, 166–68. *See also* Tupper Lake
Concerned Citizens; Tupper Lake Prison
Task Force

Tupper Lake Concerned Citizens (TLCC),
13; composition of, 167; opposition to
prison by, 13, 167–68, 170–77, 180–86,
181, 188–93, 198

Tupper Lake Free Press, prison opposition
ad in, 181

Tupper Lake Prison Task Force: composition of, 167; pro-prison organizing

effort of, 166–68; South Franklin
Correctional Facility proposals by, 166,
170–80, 183–86, 189, 192–97, 199; study
commissioned by, 172

UNICOR (Federal Prison Industries), 85
United States Council on Environmental
Quality, 65
United States Olympic Committee
(USOC), 70
Upstate Correctional Facility, 197, 198

Vibra Resources International, 142, 144,
156

Wachtler, Solomon, 148
wardens. *See* Cook, Ransom
Wild Center (Natural History Museum of
the Adirondacks), 166, 198
Winter Olympic Games (1980). *See* Lake
Placid Olympic Organizing Committee
Wright, Augustus, 43

CLARENCE JEFFERSON HALL JR. was born in Plattsburgh, New York. He earned BA and MA degrees in history from Binghamton University and a PhD in history from Stony Brook University. His research focuses on the intersection of environmental and carceral histories in the nineteenth- and twentieth-century United States. He is assistant professor in the department of history at Queensborough Community College/CUNY in Bayside, Queens, New York. Hall's work has appeared in *Adirondack Peeks, Environment and History, New York Archives* magazine, and the *History Teacher.* His research has also been featured in a variety of news media outlets including the *Albany Times Union,* CNN, CTV News, MSNBC, National Public Radio, NBC News, and the *New York Times,* among others. Hall lives in New York City.